THE NEW NIETZSCHE

THE NEW NIETZSCHE
Contemporary Styles of Interpretation

edited and introduced by
DAVID B. ALLISON

The MIT Press
Cambridge, Massachusetts
London, England

First MIT Press edition, 1985

This book was printed and bound by The Murray Printing Co. in the United States of America.

Library of Congress Cataloging in Publication Data
Main entry under title:

The New Nietzsche.

Originally published: New York: Dell Pub. Co., 1977.
Bibliography: p.
Includes index.
1. Nietzsche, Friedrich Wilhelm, 1844–1900—Addresses, essays, lectures. I. Allison, David B.
B3317.N44   1985   193   84-26184
ISBN 0-262-51034-0 (paperback)

ACKNOWLEDGMENTS

"Nietzsche and Metaphysical Language" by Michel Haar: translated by Cyril and Liliane Welch. Copyright © 1971 by *Man and World, an International Philosophical Review*. First published in *Man and World*, Vol. 4, No. 4, November 1971. Used by permission of the publisher.

"The Will to Power" by Alphonso Lingis. Copyright © 1977 by Alphonso Lingis. Used by permission of the author.

"Who Is Nietzsche's Zarathustra?" by Martin Heidegger: translated by Bernd Magnus. Copyright © 1967 by Harper & Row, Publishers, Inc. Reprinted by permission of the publisher.

"Active and Reactive" by Gilles Deleuze: translated by Richard Cohen. Reprinted from *Nietzsche et la Philosophie* by permission of the publisher, Presses Universitaires de France, Paris.

"Nietzsche's Experience of the Eternal Return" by Pierre Klossowski: translated by Allen Weiss. © Mercure de France 1969. Reprinted from *Nietzsche et le Cercle Vicieux* by permission of the publisher, Mercure de France, Paris.

"The Limits of Experience: Nihilism" by Maurice Blanchot: translated by John Leavey. © Editions Gallimard 1969. Reprinted from *L'Entretien Infini* by permission of the publisher, Editions Gallimard, Paris.

"Nietzsche's Conception of Chaos" by Jean Granier: translated by David B. Allison. First published as "La Pensée Nietzschéene du chaos" in *Revue de Metaphysique et du Morale,* Vol. 76, No. 2, pp. 132–139. Copyright. Reprinted by permission of the publisher.

"Nomad Thought" by Gilles Deleuze: translated by David B. Allison. First published as "Pensée nomade" in *Nietzsche aujourd'hui,* 1973. Used by permission of the publisher, Union Générale d'Editions, Paris.

"Nietzsche: Life as Metaphor" by Eric Blondel: translated by Mairi Macrae. First published as "Nietzsche: la vie et la métaphore" in *Revue Philosophique,* 1971. Used by permission of the publisher, Presses Universitaires de France, Paris.

"The Question of Style" by Jacques Derrida: translated by Ruben Berezdivin. The present article consists of selections from "La Question du style" first published in *Nietzsche aujourd' hui,* Union Générale d'Editions, 1973. Used by permission of the author. A revised and extended text of the complete article, translated into English, Italian, and German, has been published under the title *The Question of Style* by Corbo e Fiore, Venice, 1976.

"Perspectivism and Interpretation" by Jean Granier: translated by David B. Allison. © 1966 by Editions du Seuil. Reprinted from *Le Problème de la Vérité dans la Philosophie de Nietzsche* by permission of the publisher, Editions du Seuil.

"Metaphor, Symbol, Metamorphosis" by Sarah Kofman: translated by David B. Allison. © 1972 Payot. Reprinted from pages 16–37 of *Nietzsche et la Métaphore* by permission of the publishers, Editions Payot, Paris.

"Beatitude in Nietzsche" by Henri Birault: translated by Alphonso Lingis. First published as "De la beatitude chez Nietzsche" in *Nietzsche: Cahiers de Royaumont,* No. 6, 1966, pp. 13–28. Used by permission of the publisher.

"Eternal Recurrence and Kingdom of God" by Thomas J. J. Altizer. Used by permission of the author.

"Dionysus Versus the Crucified" by Paul Valadier: translated by Kathleen Wallace. Reprinted from *Nietzsche et la critique du christianisme* by permission of the publisher, Les Editions du Cerf, Paris.

CONTENTS

PREFACE

Nietzsche's biography is uninspiring, to say the least. Nonetheless, this subject appears to have been the principal source of inspiration for the tiresome array of books that has followed him. The situation changed, however, with the publication of Heidegger's two-volume study, in which Nietzsche finally emerged as one of the prodigious thinkers of the modern age. Perhaps it is a measure of greatness in a thinker that he demands an equally profound critic to recognize the importance of his thought. In any case, the distinction rests with Heidegger for succeeding in this attempt. Not only was Heidegger the first to seriously take up the principal, and most difficult, themes of Nietzsche—Will to Power, Eternal Return, and Overman—but he demonstrated that, together, they formed an integral conception of the entire development of Western thought: of its very ground and highest expression.

It was the magnitude of this insight that now reveals Nietzsche—posthumously, as he himself correctly foresaw—as one of the underlying figures of our own intellectual epoch, and shows that what remains to be considered within Nietzsche's own thought somehow stands as a model for the tasks and decisions of the present generation. To overstate the case somewhat, the decisions to be taken concern the very validity of our contemporary forms of intelligibility, for we have now effectively seen the finite and axiomatic character of what is meant by the thought of "our age"—all forms of technological control and domination being but one dimension of this problem. In this sense, the prospect of understanding Nietzsche's thought as a confrontation with, or even as an overcoming or a getting-around of, this tradition, is at once the most philosophically critical project since Kant's *and* the one that bears the greatest urgency; for, as Nietzsche suggests, so much rests in the balance. It is an adventure, then, with an urgency that is, strictly speaking, *unheard of*.

If this prospect was opened by Heidegger in Europe, to all appearances it remains a European avenue. With only two exceptions (Heidegger and Haar), none of the essays included here have previously appeared in English; several have been written expressly for the present volume. Each has been selected with two purposes in mind: to address the issues of crucial importance to an understanding of Nietzsche, and to introduce a generation of contemporary thought that is just beginning to find its own inspiration in Nietzsche. While Heidegger, Deleuze, and Klossowski have so far emerged as the most influential figures in this project, their meditation has already been enriched by the thought of post-phenomenological analysis, structural analysis, and modern linguistics, as well as by critical theory and contemporary literary criticism. The unity of the present volume, therefore, should be located in its tasks rather than in any particular orthodoxy, European or otherwise. It certainly does *not* consist in one more pointless series of oversimplifications, biographical anecdotes, or convenient summaries—a tradition to which the English-speaking audience has long ago become accustomed.

Where possible, citations of Nietzsche's texts have been taken from the available English sources, oftentimes with some minor changes of translation. Until the Colli-Montinari edition of Nietzsche's complete works appears in English, the principal translation will continue to be that of Kaufmann. But, while most English citations are from the Kaufmann editions, I have often gone to Reinhardt, Cowan, Hollingdale, Levy, and others when necessary. In all these cases, reference to Nietzsche's texts is made according to chapter and section number of the particular title, rather than to page numbers of any particular translation.

I am deeply grateful for the help and kindness extended to me by each of the contributors to this project, and I am especially grateful to my comrades at Stony Brook, who aided and abetted me at every stage. I would also like to thank Richard Cohen, who prepared the index.

D.B.A.
Stony Brook, New York

INTRODUCTION

Lofty and ennobling: this may well be said to characterize Nietzsche's language, or at least his intent. Yet all too often both are seen as a kind of *rigor mortis* of late romanticism, as the poetic thought of a rekindled belief in transcendence. Understandably, then, most readers of Nietzsche have been quick to place him within the terms of traditional thought. Whether they conceive Nietzsche as a higher-order social Darwinist, as the teacher of a boundless and destructive will, as the nihilist *par excellence,* as the structural complement to Judeao-Christian thought, as the liberator of a culturally repressed sexuality, or as the teacher of a new word or doctrine (Overman, Eternal Return, Will to Power), they not only find his thought to be coherent and continuous with the language of traditional metaphysics, but to be fully circumscribed by it. In short, it is most often claimed that there *is* no new word or doctrine, that Nietzsche is himself fully bounded by the tradition he so strongly attacks—i.e., by what has now come to be called the language and thought of onto-theology, what Nietzsche himself simply called God.

What is at stake in *deciding* these claims is therefore considerable—not merely the nature of one somewhat enigmatic thinker, Friedrich Nietzsche, but the viability of conventional thought itself, its own prospects of limitation, decline, or future. This is perhaps the underlying issue for the present work, even if it is approached from what appear to be divergent standpoints. Thus, each text represented in the present volume constitutes an *interpretation* of Nietzsche's thought in view of this larger issue to be decided. The question of interpretation, then, is no longer marginal. On the one hand, Nietzsche stands to be interpreted, and on the other, his subsequent critics perform the mechanics of interpretation. The value of the interpretations can be judged—at least in part—through the attempts of the present contributors. But as to Nietzsche's writing itself, what kind of access can we claim in the first place? What are the means of interpreting Nietzsche's writing? To what extent is Nietzsche's text something *to be* interpreted?

1. READING NIETZSCHE

Nietzsche himself provides us with several rather specific indications as to how we should approach his work. We know, for example, that he addresses a particular audience. He never tires of invoking the classical distinction between "the few" and "the many," and this results in a two-tiered, if not duplicitous, text: one level, the esoteric, for those few who are capable of understanding it (whom he calls *we* "opposite men," "free thinkers," "attempters," "wanderers," "immoralists"), and another, an exoteric text, for "the others."[1] Indeed, it is on the basis of this distinction of audience that he will construct the whole argumentation for *The Genealogy of Morals,* the distinction between two fundamentally different kinds of humanity—active and reactive—together with their different systems of moral valuation: aristocratic morality, and slave (or "herd") morality. And it is with the latter, he claims, that the *need* arises for postulating every form of transcendence: an otherworldly religion, the metaphysical ideals of unchanging being, permanence, unity, soul, the moral ideals of ascetic virtue, absolute truth, and divine justice. As to the former: "What can it matter to *us* with what kind of tinsel an invalid decks out his weakness?"

Even granting this distinction of audience, Nietzsche knew his contemporary readers were few indeed. To construct a text, much less to have it understood, on some basis other than the reactive tradition of theology, metaphysics, and morality—this requires both a new style of expression and a new audience. Indeed, Nietzsche described himself throughout his life as a posthumous writer, one who writes for the future, one who will live only in the future—as a ghost.

> We, too, associate with "people;" we, too, modestly don the dress in which (*as* which) others know us, respect us, look for us . . . We, too, do what all prudent masks do . . . But there are also other ways and tricks when it comes to associating with or passing among men—for example, as a ghost, which is altogether advisable if one wants to get rid of them quickly and make them afraid. Example: One reaches out for us but gets no hold of us. That is frightening. Or we enter through a closed door. Or after all lights have been extinguished. Or after we have died. The last is the trick of *posthumous* people par excellence. . . . It is only after death that we shall enter *our* life and become alive, oh, very much alive, we posthumous people![2]

Nietzsche's text, therefore, is necessarily ambiguous. There is no simple face or surface value to it. Thus, Nietzsche will call his own works "questions," "hieroglyphs," or "masks," just as he would call any other thing, person, or tradition.

But a tension seems to arise here between the styled ambiguity of Nietzsche's writing and the intensely personal tone of his expression. He repeatedly asserts that his texts are the inscriptions of intense personal experiences, sometimes of elevated moods, feelings, or states, sometimes of the greatest intellectual inspiration.[3] What accounts for this apparent discrepancy, then, this transfer of the text from its "source" in the contracted, individuated personal experience to its "emergence" as an ambiguous text? If the text is a testament to the life of its author, we must be cautious not to judge such a life according to the narrow biographical sense of the term, as if the author's life were itself an open book, an explicit and comprehensive bibliography of sorts.

Rather, Nietzsche asks the reader to consider the general conditions of life—its prognosis for advance and decline, its strength or weakness, its general etiology—as well as that of its sustaining culture and values. Thus, the innermost part of an author—what is most personal—must be understood as having its genesis in conditions outside himself. The texture of the text, therefore, is itself woven from "the hieroglyphic chains" of these universal conditions or forms of existence. Indeed, it is in this sense that Nietzsche will repeatedly criticize the very notion of a personal self or ego as being a "grammatical fiction," or state that the individual consciousness is merely "the surface phenomena" of unconscious forces and drives—and in the same breath claim, "I am every name in history."

The demands imposed on his readers are thus considerable. And if few thinkers have been so maligned and abused as Nietzsche, fewer still have lent themselves to precisely this kind of misinterpretation: "My writings are difficult; I hope this is not considered an objection." Everywhere, Nietzsche's style is to write in excess, in extravagance, or, as he says, "in blood." His thought issues in total profusion, and resists every attempt to make it systematic. Indeed, "It is not easily possible to understand the blood of another."[4]

Nowhere, then, has the *style* of a philosopher's expression so forcefully reflected its content. What he says and how he says it are so much the same. Both style and world, for Nietzsche, emerge as a play of appearances—what he calls the Will to Power, the will to will, to form and create—and the dynamism of this play expresses an overabundance of force, energy, life— teeming and recurrent affirmation.

> How greedily this wave approaches . . . But already another wave is approaching, still more greedily and savagely than the first, and its soul, too, seems to be full of secrets and the lust to dig up treasures. Thus live waves—thus live we who will . . . Carry on as you like, roaring with overweening pleasure and malice—or dive again, pouring your emeralds down into the deepest depths, and throw your infinite white mane of foam and spray over them: Everything suits me, for

everything suits you so well, and I am so well-disposed toward you for
everything; how could I think of betraying you? For—mark my
word!—I know you and your secret, I know your kind! You and I—are
we not of one kind?—You and I—do we not have *one secret*?[5]

It is this kind of fertility or richness that refuses to be systematized,
discretely categorized, and, ultimately, calcified by some ruse or device of
language, some simple definition, or essence, or form. His use of the
aphorism or apothegm, for instance, is fully crucial to this dynamics; in fact,
it is probably his most distinctive stylistic feature:

> *Praise of aphorisms*—A good aphorism is too hard for the tooth of time
> and is not consumed by all millennia, although it serves every time for
> nourishment: thus it is the great paradox of literature, the intransitory
> amid the changing, the food that always remains esteemed, like salt,
> and never loses its savor, as even that does.[6]

The aphorism (i.e., the short, terse, incisive remark that expresses a wider
truth) is itself alive and animate—it responds to the genius and inspiration of
a critical mind, but it resists formalization and catechism. It is a turn of
phrase and thought—a movement of expression that, of itself, directs us
beyond a fixed idea, a fixed place-holder in a static system of rules and
beliefs.[7] Indeed, the aphorism destroys the possibility of such a simple
correspondence because it is essentially incomplete. The aphorism demands
that an operation be performed upon itself for its very intelligibility: that it be
inserted into ever new contexts, that it be related to ever new referential sets.
The aphorism, then, is essentially metaphorical: it gathers, culls, collects,
compares, and assembles—however briefly—this movement of thought.
Like the metaphor, the aphorism brings together scattered elements in a
single move. In this sense, metaphorical thought is continually active.
Like Zarathustra himself, the metaphor is homeless, a wanderer. It gathers
its strength in a continual process of displacement and transference *(meta-
pherein),* in always finding its message from without and above: "I look
down because I am elevated . . . In the mountains the shortest way is
from peak to peak; but for that one must have strong legs. Aphorisms
should be peaks—and those who are addressed, tall and lofty." And, as
Zarathustra will add, "I am *building* a mountain range out of ever more
sacred mountains."[8]

Perpetually active, incomplete, manifold, and alive, the metaphor not
only characterizes a movement of thought, it also stands as an analogue for
what exists. The metaphor is an analogical expression for the dynamic flow
of appearances themselves—what Nietzsche calls the Will to Power.
Moreover, if Will to Power is the most comprehensive of all things, without

itself being *a* thing—or substance, or matter, or form—and if all things are expressions or appearances *of* Will to Power, then Nietzsche can only write about it metaphorically. Thus, when Nietzsche attempts to discuss Will to Power as such, it is always metaphorical: Will to Power as force, as will, as power, as definition, as limitation, as knowledge, as life, etc. Indeed, he describes it as a text that has disappeared underneath its interpretations—in which case there is no unitary being, essence, form, category, or identity that can be applied to the metaphorical "notion" of Will to Power.

If the metaphor is *essentially* relational, so is the Will to Power:

> A quantum of power is designated by the effect it produces and that which it resists. The adiaphorous state is missing . . . It is a question of struggle between two elements of unequal power: a new arrangement of forces is achieved according to the measure of power in each of them.[9]

Essentially relational and not static, what appears to us as existent is only the factored product of other, nonapparent and differential forces. And this factored product stands as a *symptom* or *sign* of the precedent forces, which are themselves only relatively determinate and calculable. Thus, Nietzsche's account of Will to Power provides the basis for two kinds of interpretation—what could be called the differential analysis and the genealogical analysis. Taken together, they are meant to serve as a general theory of signs, of semiotics. Furthermore, the motivation for this general theory of signs is coextensive with the whole question of metaphor.

Even in his earliest work, Nietzsche questioned the veracity of conventional language. Words are only metaphors; indeed, they are doubly metaphorical:

> One designates only the relations of things to man, and to express them, one calls on the boldest metaphors. A nerve stimulus, first transposed into an image—first metaphor. The image, in turn, imitated by a sound—second metaphor.[10]

In which case, Nietzsche denies the fundamental correspondence between the signifier and the signified: the word never expresses an identical meaning, much less an identical object. There is no order of meaning independent of the words or signs used to designate them. Consequently, there is no transcendent meaning, no ideal signification, no privileged reference, no univocal equation between "designations" and "things." The use of words is entirely conventional, and their signification consists in the manipulation of other words—convenient, agreed-upon fictions, that out of habit pass as representatives or rude equivalents for our own perceptual images.[11] If the strict univocal reference between word and object, word and meaning, is thus denied, it follows that the classical concept of propositional truth becomes an impossibility—and this is due precisely to the primacy of metaphor.

> What, then is truth? A mobile army of metaphors, metonyms, and anthropomorphisms—in short, a sum of human relations, which have been enhanced, transposed, and embellished poetically and rhetorically, and which after long use seem firm, canonical, and obligatory to a people: truths are illusions about which one has forgotten that this is what they are; metaphors which are worn out and without sensuous power . . . To be truthful means using the customary metaphors—in moral terms: the obligation to lie according to a fixed convention, to lie herd-like in a style obligatory to all.[12]

Nietzsche is fully willing to embrace the consequences of this position, for what is important is not the pretension to seize upon an unchanging truth, an ideal meaning, or fixed being, but rather to uncover the considerations that incline or impel us to follow such conventions. What is in question, then, is the *deciphering* of the code that assigns a value to certain terms and the rules that govern our use of these terms. What complicates matters is that we are largely unaware of these codes: hence the necessity for grasping these terms as *signs,* and the need for a theory of interpretation understood as a general semiotics.

2. SYSTEM: METAPHOR-METAMORPHOSIS

Let us first state the relation between metaphorical signification and Will to Power that Nietzsche uses to develop this general semiotics (and later elaborate this in terms of differential and genealogical analysis): in brief, it consists in a parallel rejection of transcendence.

a. On the one hand, we have seen that metaphorical signification amounts to a chain of substitutions, of metonyms, that is limited to a field of conventional language. While the number of possible substitutions (or references, transfers, transpositions) is finite—i.e., is bounded by the resources of a given language—the process of substituting one for another is open-ended. The constitution of the metaphor is thus a process that is at least temporally open to infinity. The metaphor, then, enjoys a "finite" but "open" economy.

Finite: Signification is limited to the order of the *signifier* alone (words, references, substitutions, representations, all the grammatical resources of a language—indeed, of all known languages, natural or artificial). Thus, there is no transcendent or transcendental order, nothing beyond language, to guide or subtend linguistic signification from without. Language makes sense because it can draw upon itself; what it has to say can be said. If language seems deficient, this is because its own resources have yet to be fully exploited and expressed. Nietzsche will suggest that such elements as rhythm, style, tempo, music, tone, gesture, image, and metaphor are re-sources *of* language that, as yet, have barely been recognized, much less practiced. In any case, signification comes from within, from the metaphor-ical order of the signifier, and not from without, not from some transcenden-tal signified that would stand *outside* language and pretend to govern it. Consequently, for Nietzsche, there is no divine principle of intelligibility, no first word of grace or truth, no final meaning, no privileged signified—such as God, thing in itself, phallus, pure idea, soul, production, or profit—that would irrevocably determine the sequence and value of the signifiers within language. Within language: that is, within culture, society, politics, and history.

Open: Each element within the signifying order, as well as the relations between these elements, can therefore be continually reinvested, churned, altered, and transformed by virtue of the temporally ''open'' character of the metaphorical economy. It is this infinitely ''open'' aspect of transformation that liberates the whole field of signification from its traditional finitude. It does this by removing the restrictions and prohibitions imposed on it by a particular axiomatic set (e.g., the privilege of one epistemological, logical, or metaphysical set of valuations), by eliminating specific rules of operation and derivation upon this set (which rules, for example, might ultimately result in bureaucratic tyranny, capitalism, psychoanalysis), by extending or dispensing with particular laws (e.g., laws of judgment, classification, action, grammar, decision, behavior, or even laws for codification itself), and, ultimately, by overcoming the conventional hierarchy itself (e.g., slave morality). All such restrictions were previously held to be ''binding'' on a given society and its entire conceptual order; they were thought to have been imposed from without, from beyond, and invariably to enjoy some trans-cendental sanction (God, logos, myth, sacred tradition, or idealized na-ture).[13]

b. If the economy of metaphor is ''finite'' yet ''open,'' this is precisely how Nietzsche describes the metamorphic economy of Will to Power: as the continual expenditure of a finite field of forces.

> Regarded mechanistically, the energy of the totality of becoming remains constant; regarded economically, it rises to a high point and sinks down again in an eternal circle. This ''Will to Power'' expresses itself in the interpretation, in the manner in which force is used up.[14]

Just as any signifier results from the metaphoric play of language, so does every organic or inorganic state result from the metamorphic play of Will to Power. Thus, Will to Power ''expresses'' itself or ''interprets'' itself at every moment. And so far as the finite resources of language "define" every term within the language—with no need to postulate a transcendental source—the same holds for Will to Power. Each state, each "expression" or "interpretation," is produced by the continual metamorphosis of a constant or finite Will to Power and is thus "defined" by it—again, with no need of postulating any transcendental source. Like the economy of language, the economy of Will to Power is also "open": what Nietzsche calls, from his earliest to his latest work, "becoming" (i.e., all movement, metamorphosis, play of appearances, dynamics, mechanics, growth and diminution: in short, all organic and inorganic processes). Only two things remain fixed for the Will to Power: its constant or finite quantity, and its perpetual metamorphosis, its infinite becoming. The Will to Power never attains equilibrium, therefore, even though it accounts for all definition in the natural or cultural world. Here, definition is understood as the temporary limitation of force encountering another force; as the master will controlling and delimiting a subservient will; as the factoring of force vectors that results in their incorporation; as the rivulets of force that coalesce to form a flood, a wave, an impact against a still larger force; as the chemical consolidation of ionic structures; as the legislator imposing direction upon his subjects; as tradition and authority bearing the judgment of the centuries; as the eruption of psychological drives into a concerted effort; as the repression of one impulse by another; as the sublimation of one will by a stronger will; as the submission of the weak to the strong; as the response of the weak to gather together and overcome the strong in turn. In each case Will to Power appears, expresses, or interprets itself as organic or inorganic definition, and it does this through a continual process of differentiation and limitation—of one force by another, whether by fusion, accumulation, or strife. And this is precisely what Nietzsche means by *life*.

Thus, Nietzsche recognizes two kinds of signifier: word and thing. The word, the linguistic sign, stands as the metaphorical product of its linguistic resources, and the thing, the organic or inorganic state of affairs, stands as the metamorphic product of Will to Power. Moreover, both are fully immanent to their respective spheres. While they are both defined *by* their spheres, they also serve as defining elements *within* their respective finite systems—that is, as signifiers, they both point to other signifiers and are pointed to by them; together, they form a finite totality. The function of each signifier within its respective system is thus eternally recurrent or recursive—which is to say that the prospect of transcending either system is denied from the outset. Indeed, the very possibility of transcendence as such—and, most importantly, of one system by the other—is also denied. It is precisely this doctrine of total immanence that will be the "Joyful Wisdom," the "Gay Science." What it teaches us, above all, is that the system Metaphor-Metamorphosis is essentially *one*, that word is no longer opposed to thing, nor thought to nature, *logos* to *physis*, soul to body, speech to writing, presence to absence. In short, Man is no longer opposed to World:

> The whole attitude of "man *versus* the world," man as world-denying principle, man as the standard of the value of things, as judge of the world, who in the end puts existence itself on his scales and finds it too light—the monstrous impertinence of this attitude has dawned upon us as such, and has disgusted us—we now laugh when we find "Man *and* World" placed beside one another, separated by the sublime presumption of the little word "and"![15]

Man and world, word and thing, both belong to the order of the signifier, the *only* order of things—a doctrine that will be variously repeated throughout Nietzsche's works under three titles: Eternal Return, Will to Power, and Overman.[16] For such a doctrine, the whole of this "pure, newly discovered, newly redeemed nature" becomes a text to be interpreted—and so does the reader of the text, he who has become "naturalized" by this doctrine.

3. INTERPRETING NIETZSCHE

Now we can see why the ambiguity of Nietzsche's text extends— pointedly—to the reader. For whether he chooses it or not, the reader is necessarily implicated in the text:

> Ultimately, nobody can get more out of things, including books, than he already knows. For what one lacks access to from experience one will have no ear . . . This is, in the end, my average experience and, if you will, the originality of my experience. Whoever thought he had understood something of me, had made something out of me after his own image—not uncommonly an antithesis to me.[17]

In this sense, the author, too, remains ambiguous: he is "merely mouthpiece, merely the medium of overpowering forces." The text thus stands as a system of exchanges—between the author and his experience, between word and thing, between history and its future. And if, for Nietzsche, consciousness itself seems to be dispossessed of its "subject," its "author," the text is even more so; it no longer seems to be the simple testament of an idiosyncratic will. Strange:

> The involuntariness of image and metaphor is strangest of all; one no longer has any notion of what is an image or a metaphor: everything offers itself as the nearest, most obvious, simplest expression. It actually seems to allude to something Zarathustra says, as if the things

themselves approached and offered themselves as metaphors ("Here all things come caressingly to your discourse and flatter you; for they want to ride on your back. On every metaphor you ride to every truth . . . Here the words and word-shrines of all being open up before you; here all being wishes to become word, all becoming wishes to learn from you how to speak"). This is *my* experience of inspiration.[18]

In a letter to Jacob Burckhardt (22 September 1886), he will describe this kind of inspiration as "uncanny," and claim that "articulating it may well be the most dangerous venture there is, not for the one who dares to express it but for the one to whom it is addressed."

The danger for the reader ultimately lies in the dispossession of his own identity and the loss of his conventional world. And this danger begins once the reader enters into the text, once he interprets it. To understand a text, word, or thing is to interpret it, to decipher it. For Nietzsche, this means to perform a *genealogical* analysis upon it—and in two senses. The first is to perform a historical deconstruction or desedimentation of the terms involved, in order to decipher the conditions of their development. As he says in *The Genealogy of Morals,* this "art of exegesis" must be carried out in the spirit of "rumination"—without guile, meanness, or preconceived intent. The interpretation of morality, for example, begins with the question, "Under what conditions did man devise these value judgments; good and evil? And what value do they themselves possess?" It proceeds by establishing the elements that are included in moral systems generally, the relevant historical facts and their conditions—among which he cites specific ages and epochs, various kinds of peoples, different types of individuals, and their respective social stratification. The analysis then turns to the dynamics of social stratification, where moral value is first fixed according to class distinction. In this way, the claim of any moral value can be understood as precisely that—a claim. What the value signifies, therefore, is far more extensive than its stated surface claim: it can be variously understood as (or in terms of) its consequences, as the symptom of an age, as a mask, as self-righteousness, as the cause of a subsequent state of affairs, as the remedy to a prior state of affairs, as a stimulant, or, even, as a poison.

Furthermore, insofar as the signification of each term derives from its relations to other terms, the relations disclosed by analysis emerge to form a pattern of stress or structural opposition. Thus, the genealogical analysis provides a strictly coherent means of interpreting each term within the context of a more comprehensive set. For Nietzsche, each moral term will find its value and significance with respect to a set of such relational oppositions as body-soul, life-death, strength-weakness, rational-irrational, gain-loss, conscious-unconscious, absolute-relative, pretended-actual, pleasure-pain, public-private, intent-deed, theory-practice, etc. And by viewing one set of oppositions from the perspective of another, one can discern the organic character of a particular system and effectively pursue the questions Nietzsche poses. We can ask, for example, about the stated origin of a given moral term, and follow with its pretended or actual origin—in the conscious intentions of the founder, or in the subconscious habits of its proponents or subjects. We can then ask for its purpose, its organizing principles. We can also ask, "*Who* derives benefits from a particular ethical code?" Only the believers? The public at large? The founders? Its priests? The prince? No one?

Nietzsche performs a genealogical analysis in a second sense, which is both etymological and grammatical. "The signpost to the right road was for me the question: what was the real etymological significance of the designations for 'good' coined in the various languages?"[19] Thus, moral terms themselves stand as the etymological traces of a historical past. In this way they serve as surnames that testify to an origin and a subsequent line of succession. And if etymological analysis locates the origin of moral valuation in the social distinction between the higher and lower classes—where "good" corresponds to "noble" and "bad" to "plebeian"—the analysis of grammatical categories constitutes a genealogy that extends to the whole domain of Western thought. First, it reveals that Western thought is a unified system:

> That individual philosophical concepts are not anything capricious or autonomously evolving, but grow up in connection and with each other; that, however suddenly and arbitrarily they seem to appear in the history of thought, they nevertheless belong just as much to a system as all the members of the fauna of a continent—is betrayed . . . by the fact that the most diverse philosophers keep filling in a definite fundamental scheme of possible philosophies.[20]

Second, the analysis suggests that this system has a single origin that commands its subsequent development, an origin that is itself hidden, nonapparent, or unconscious:

> Under an invisible spell, they always revolve once more in the same orbit; however independent of each other they may feel themselves with their critical or systematic wills, something within them leads them, something impels them in a definite order—to wit, the innate systematic structure and relationship of their concepts. Their thinking is, in fact, far less a discovery than a recognition, a remembering, a return and homecoming to a remote, primordial, and inclusive household of the soul, out of which those concepts grew originally: philosophizing is to this extent a kind of atavism of the highest order.[21]

Finally, this "remote, primordial, and inclusive household of the soul" can be specified. It is the unifying basis of Western intelligibility as such—namely, the very grammar *by which* it thinks:

> The strange family resemblance of all Indian, Greek, and German philosophizing is explained easily enough. Where there is affinity of languages, it cannot fail, owing to the common philosophy of grammar—I mean, owing to the unconscious domination and guidance by similar grammatical functions—that everything is prepared at the outset for a similar development and sequence of philosophical systems; just as the way seems barred against certain other possibilities of world-interpretation. It is highly probable that philosophers within the domain of the Ural-Altaic languages (where the concept of the subject is least developed) look otherwise "into the world," and will be found on paths of thought different from those of the Indo-Germanic peoples and the Muslims . . . So much by way of rejecting Locke's superficiality regarding the origin of ideas.[22]

The grammatical functions determine the terms *of* thought as well as the rules *for* thought: thus, subject, predicate, affirmation, and negation will permit the development of a double axiomatic set (identity and causality) and favor only certain operations to be performed upon this set (e.g., binary opposition). The concepts that derive from this axiomatic system thus circumscribe Western thought as such—i.e., all "possible philosophies." Identity gives rise to the concepts of unity, plurality, specific difference, number, permanence, movement (space and time), subject and substance (self, ego, soul, God, particle). Causality gives rise to the concepts of cause and effect, action and passion, free will, determinism, universal law, mechanism, process and change. Finally, this set is factored according to the operations of binary opposition. This governs the working-out of the system, and the development of subsequent systems of thought, by establishing such regulative limits as true-false, real-apparent, good-evil, worldly-otherworldly, human-divine, body-soul, immanent-transcendent, virtue-sin, and the whole system of conceptual oppositions we inherit today. The very threshold of metaphysics is to be found here, in this genesis of oppositions.[23]

Yet genealogical analysis quickly encounters its own limits: its very form of analysis, the regressive analysis of precedent causes—the quest for a discrete origin that can be evidenced to the inquiring subject—is itself governed by the axioms of identity and causality. Its critical capacity is thus dependent on the system it holds in question. Because of this limitation, Nietzsche will progressively stress the differential form of analysis, an analysis that corresponds to the defining character of Will to Power, in his later work. Now the object of analysis is the apparent product of the differential interaction of force (force taken in its widest sense). Epistemologically, the perceived object is only a sign of the difference between two sets of forces: that of the perceptual and the sense-giving forces on the part of the subject, together with the quantum of natural forces that he initially encounters. Ontologically, the same process occurs: the object is itself the factored product of a multitude of forces, most of which are nonapparent and necessarily obscured by the defining play of forces. Beginning with the object, with the temporary end product of the metaphoric-metamorphic chain, its conditions are *not* necessarily, or even practically, ascertainable. As in vector analysis, one has to *begin* with stated conditions and constants in order to *arrive* at a calculation of the final force vector. And for Nietzsche, this is ultimately not possible, since Will to Power as a finite whole is also chaos, chance, fate. In the process of defining itself—in the process of definition itself—Will to Power necessarily obliterates its origins. Beginning, origin, purpose, etc., are forcibly overcome in the ensuing relational field of Will to Power—i.e., of the system metaphor-metamorphosis. A lacuna arises in the heart of genealogical analysis, therefore—one that testifies to an ultimate *loss* of "meaning" and "purpose" (in the conventional sense of either recovering origins, establishing ends, or deciding the "value" of any text). In the textual *center* of *The Genealogy of Morals* (in the middle section of the middle essay: Part II, §12), Nietzsche concedes this irreparable loss of center:

> All events in the organic world are a subduing, a becoming master, and all subduing and becoming master involves a fresh interpretation, an adaptation through which any previous "meaning" and "purpose" are necessarily obscured or even obliterated.

Thus Nietzsche's conflicting and oftentimes contradictory interpretations of a particular subject matter indeed make sense: that thought, for example, is dictated by the conventions of Indo-European grammar—certainly. But *also,* and just as frequently, he will claim that thought is inexorably dictated by morality, theology, biological utility, the need for communication; by social utility; by psychological, historical, cultural, physiological, occupational, and even nutritional restraints. Where in all this could a discrete origin, meaning, or purpose be found? A discrete genealogy?

A field of signs is thus accessible to analysis, but the analysis itself results in an infinite regress: forms of intelligibility, interpretations, occur for a given culture and obtain for a given epoch (e.g., "two thousand years of Christianized Platonism"), yet the constellations of significance owe their disposition to a continual process of creation and destruction—namely, to the metaphoric-metamorphic field of Will to Power. And, in the end, these generative traces cannot be tracked down, for they precondition all determination, all definition or specificity. Any analysis that relies exclusively on such categories as static and genetic, synchronic and diachronic, etc., must finally confront the fact that they are only relative determinations of chaos itself.

The danger of interpretation, therefore, is the prospect of loss: of a text that no longer makes sense according to the traditional logocentric hierarchy. But the greatest danger, Nietzsche said, belongs to the person *to whom* the text is addressed.

> What did we do when we loosened this earth from its sun? Whither does it now move? Whither do we move? Away from all suns? Do we not dash on unceasingly? Backwards, sideways, forward, in all directions? Is there still an above and below? Do we not stray, as through infinite nothingness? Does not empty space breathe upon us? Has it not become colder? Does not night come on continually, darker and darker?[24]

Such a person will no longer be what he was—i.e., he will no longer be taken up in the rational-moral-theological world of the previous epoch, our epoch. Ultimately, he will attain an entirely new form of thought, of sensibility and affectivity, and find himself in a transformed world. To the extent that present forms of sensibility are themselves evanescent configurations of an epoch, there will emerge ever new forms of humanity, emotions, and aspirations—no longer earth-bound, no longer bound to the past, to the *ressentiment*-laden "it was" or its transcendent surrogates. If this is a danger, it also and at the same time offers the greatest prospect of liberation through its infinitizing economy of Eternal Recurrence.

> If this thought gained possession of you, it would change you as you are or perhaps crush you. The question in each and every thing, "Do you desire this once more and innumerable times more?" would lie upon your actions as the heaviest burden. *Or,* how well disposed would you have to become to yourself and to life to crave nothing more fervently than this ultimate eternal confirmation and seal?[25]

Already this is apparent in the Nietzschean text—let us say that the use of metaphor, aphorism, apothegm, styled ambiguity all stands apart from the very system of Western thought that demands specific unity and identification. The text of Nietzsche no longer is constrained to a foundation of univocal meaning, discrete cause, unifying origin, to the principle of identity and specific difference. It no longer promises a final aim, goal, or purpose. It demands a dangerous explosion on the part of the reader even to follow such a text. Thus, one reads Nietzsche across heretofore unheard-of registers—by way of all the emotions, sensibilities, and dreams that can be brought to bear upon it. The Nietzschean text becomes something to be ingested, digested, transformed, and transfigured, and, together with it, the reader. Such a text becomes inseminated by the reader and disseminated through the reader, just as the reader inevitably undergoes this exchange with the world.

Thus, the invocation of the Eternal Return in the passage cited above is not merely another evangelical rhapsody. Despite its profound psychological appeal, it effectively situates the reader himself as a metaphoric and metamorphic element within the text. First, it asks *us* to be ratified within the eternal cycle. Not only would our lives be repeated to infinity, therefore, but the very cycle of past and future—from antediluvean eons to the final cataclysm—would be ceaselessly, interminably, relived. But second, and more important, if we were to grant the finite and open economics of the system we would also grant the untold, myriad permutations this finite system could endure, and our present dust-speck existence would be taken as one micro-instant of one set of atomic arrangements. This would be a system of crypto-incarnations, of insemination and dissemination of our own sub-particulate matter: like Leibniz' illustrious monads, we would reflect a universe at all times, we would literally inhabit an infinitude of worlds. We would be found on the steppes of Asia, in the forests of the night, under the waves that crash headlong onto Portofino's cliffs—and we would indeed know their secret.

Would not the fear of a vengeful God and the reprobations from a host of priests disappear like a sweet aftertaste in the light of this conception? To be buried—only to rise again and again pass away, metamorphosed by another wrinkle, another fold in the crystalline vaults? Not only would this Eternal Return be a psychological incentive to accept immanence, but it would itself be the highest expression of the will to live. It—the Eternal Return itself—would be the grandest and most complete expression of the Will to Power. Its conception would bring us a superhuman happiness. Its inception would bring us *to* humanity and history:

> In fact, this is one aspect of the new sentiment. He who knows how to regard the history of man in its entirety as *his own history* feels in the immense generalization all the grief of the invalid who thinks of health, of the old man who thinks of the dream of his youth, of the lover who is robbed of his beloved, of the martyr whose ideal is destroyed, of the hero on the evening of the indecisive battle which has brought him wounds and the loss of a friend. But to bear this immense sum of grief of all kinds, to be able to bear it, and yet still be the hero who at the commencement of a second day of battle greets the dawn and his happiness as the one who has a horizon of centuries before and behind him, as the heir of all nobility, of all past intellect, and the obligatory heir (as the noblest) of all the old nobles; while at the same time the first of a new nobility, the equal of which has never been seen nor even dreamt of: to take all this upon his soul, the oldest, the newest, the losses, hopes, conquests, and victories of mankind: to have all this at

last in one soul, and to comprise it in one feeling: —this would necessarily furnish a happiness which man has not hitherto known—a God's happiness, full of power and love, full of tears and laughter, a happiness which, like the sun in the evening, continually gives of its inexhaustible riches and empties into the sea—and like the sun, too, feels itself richest when even the poorest fisherman rows with golden oars! This divine feeling might then be called—humanity.[26]

Here, it is not so much a question of projecting ourselves onto the world from without as if we, too, were neocolonialists surveying an empire; rather, it is the reverse—it would be as if world, history, and humanity became *us*, became transformed and included in our history—it would be as if they constituted precisely what we are. All this unfolds itself through us and across the Nietzschean text. We become the heirs and possessors of this titanic dance: that would be the blood that courses through our veins, the figures and emotions that generate themselves through the faces at Marienbad, that dance "La Ronde."

If text is world, and if style is in some measure capable of expressing content, then Nietzsche has succeeded in overcoming the principle of transcendence. Transcendence in this light now appears fully coextensive with immanence, with the eternalization of metaphor and metamorphosis:

We philosophers and "free spirits" feel ourselves irradiated as by a new dawn by the report that "the old God is dead;" our hearts overflow with gratitude, astonishment, presentiment, and expectation. At last the horizon seems open once more, granting even that it is not bright; our ships can at last put out to sea in the face of every danger; every hazard is again permitted to the discerner; the sea, *our* sea, again lies open before us; perhaps never before did such an "open sea" exist.[27]

NOTES

1. "The long prefaces which I have found necessary for the new edition of my complete works tell with a ruthless honesty some curious things about myself. With these I'll ward off 'the many' once and for all. . . . I've thrown out my hook to 'the few' instead, and even with them I'm prepared to be patient. For my ideas are so indescribably strange and dangerous that only much later (surely not before 1901) will anybody be ready for them." Letter to Malwida von Meysenbug, May, 1887. See also *Beyond Good and Evil,* §30; *The Gay Science,* §381.

2. *GS,* §365. "You see what posthumous thoughts occupy my mind. But a philosophy like mine is like a tomb—it seals one off from the living. *Bene vixit qui bene latuit* (Who has hidden himself well has lived well); that's

what's written on the gravestone of Descartes. An epitaph if there ever was one!'' Letter to Georg Brandes, December, 1887.

3. ''This is also the point for a general remark about my art of style. To communicate a state, an inward tension of pathos, by means of signs, including the tempo of these signs—that is the meaning of every style; and considering that the multiplicity of inward states is exceptionally large in my case, I have many stylistic possibilities—the most multifarious art of style that has ever been at the disposal of one man.'' *Ecce Homo;* ''Why I Write Such Good Books,'' §4.

4. *Thus Spoke Zarathustra;* I, ''On Reading and Writing.''

5. *GS,* §310.

6. *Mixed Opinions and Maxims,* §168.

7. *''Philosopher's error*—The philosopher supposes that the value of his philosophy lies in the whole, in the structure; but posterity finds its value in the stone which he used for building, and which is used many more times after that for building—better. Thus it finds the value in the fact that the structure can be destroyed and *nevertheless* retains value as building material.'' *MOM,* §201.

8. *Zarathustra, loc. cit.* See also III, ''On Old and New Tablets,'' §19.

9. *The Will to Power,* §§634, 633.

10. *On Truth and Lie in an Extra-Moral Sense,* I.

11. ''Every word immediately becomes a concept, inasmuch as it is *not* intended to serve as a reminder of the unique and wholly individualized original experience to which it owes its birth, but must at the same time fit innumerable, more or less similar cases—which means, strictly speaking, *never equal*—in other words, a lot of unequal cases. Every concept originates through our equating what is unequal. No leaf ever wholly equals another, and the concept 'leaf' is formed through an arbitrary abstraction from these individual differences, through forgetting the distinctions.'' *Ibid.*

12. *Ibid.*

13. No less a philologist than St. Thomas Aquinas reminds us that the natural ''law'' derives its authority from divine ''bonds'': that *lex* (law) follows from *ligare* (to bind). In response to this tradition, Nicholas of Cusa and Sade, among others, would stand as Nietzsche's most recognizable precursors.

14. *WP,* §639.

15. *GS,* §346.

16. That the latter is a perplexing doctrine testifies to Zarathustra's own inability to grasp it—an inability, incidentally, which demonstrates that Zarathustra is *not* the Overman. Rather, he has extended a distance between himself and the world, and thus he cannot accept the duality of life itself, of woe and sorrow, joy and happiness, nay and yea, pity and overcoming. Where the Eternal Return is discussed and not merely chanted, Zarathustra is himself *asleep* (and we remember that sleep, for Nietzsche, is the source of

all metaphysics)—this is the case in both ''The Vision and the Riddle'' and the section ''At Noon;'' when he is not asleep he is in a swoon, he is comatose—as in ''The Convalescent.'' In the latter case, it is the *animals* who talk of the Eternal Return. In ''The Great Longing'' he dreams of deliverance and comfort. In question here, it seems, is the final metaphor, Zarathustra's third metamorphosis: to become a child, to embrace the innocence of becoming, and to *forget* that he remains a man, that he is himself all too human.

17. *EH;* ''Why I Write Such Good Books,'' §1.

18. *EH;* ''Thus Spoke Zarathustra,'' §3. ''We cannot change our means of expression at will: it is possible to understand to what extent they are mere signs. The demand for an adequate mode of expression is senseless: it is of the essence of a language, a means of expression, to express a mere relationship.'' *WP,* §625. See also §675, 676.

19. *The Genealogy of Morals;* I, §4.

20. *BGE,* §20.

21. *Ibid.*

22. *Ibid.*

23. ''This way of judging constitutes the typical prejudgment and prejudice which give away the metaphysicians of all ages; this kind of valuation looms in the background of all their logical procedures; it is on account of this 'faith' that they trouble themselves about 'knowledge,' about something that is finally baptized solemnly as 'the truth.' The fundamental faith of the metaphysicians is *the faith in opposite values*. It has not even occurred to the most cautious among them that one might have a doubt right here at the threshold where it was surely most necessary . . . For one may doubt, first whether there are any opposites at all, and secondly, whether these popular valuations and opposite values on which the metaphysicians put their seal are not perhaps merely foreground estimates, only provisional perspectives, perhaps even from some nook, perhaps from below, from some frog perspective.'' *BGE,* §2.

24. *GS,* §125.

25. *GS,* §341.

26. *GS,* §337.

27. *GS,* §333.

PART I
Main Themes

Will to Power, Eternal Return, and Overman: these are surely the most comprehensive of Nietzsche's far-ranging themes, for they condition his reflections on nature, art, religion, morality, psychology, and history. To disengage these themes, to investigate their articulation and coherency at the start, is the principal task of Part I.

In the first essay, Michel Haar sets forth a genealogy of Nietzsche's own volatile terminology and the strategies which motivate it. Beginning his analysis with an assessment of the Will to Power, Haar moves from the conventional forms of nihilism to Nietzsche's own conception of value, and finally to the "transmutation" of humanity into the Overman. Haar finds the "explosions" of language, conceptuality, subjectivity, and nihilism itself all forcefully inscribed in the Nietzschean vision of Eternal Return.

Following with an extensive interpretation of *The Will to Power*, Alphonso Lingis addresses perhaps the most paradoxical element of Nietzsche's thought: in a world devoid of substantial identities and absolute categories of description, explanation, or value, what can the Will to Power itself conceivably mean, and how are we to understand ourselves or anything else by means of such a doctrine? Lingis then proposes a semiotic model of interpretation, one that subverts the traditional logic of identity and substance in order to conceive both the individual and the world across the Dionysian registers of artistic creation, affectivity, and nobility.

In "Who Is Nietzsche's Zarathustra?" Martin Heidegger focuses on the significance of Zarathustra's teaching, specifically, that it unites the doctrine of Eternal Return with that of the Overman—for only through the doctrine of Eternal Return can the spirit of "metaphysical revenge" against the earth and life's transience be overcome. Thus, the Overman is he who identifies his destiny with the Eternal Recurrence of the same, he who will become, as Zarathustra says, "the meaning of the earth." In this sense, Zarathustra's teaching stands as the uncanny "bridge" between humanity and the Overman—a bridge that leads to what is as yet humanly inexpressible, a bridge that is necessarily visionary and enigmatic.

Pierre Klossowski, too, insists on the visionary character of the Eternal Return: it must be conceived first, and most importantly, as an intensely personal mood or feeling, as an ecstatic vision which is at once a dispossession of one's self—of one's own finitude—and an infinitizing feeling of identification with the entire course of past and future possibilities, past and future events. But for Klossowski, the revelation of the Eternal Return means: the *same* self returns. The *enigma* of the Return consists in the fact that while the individual "remembers" this returned self, he must necessarily forget his very remembrance of it. The same self must be forgotten in order for it to become *other* than it is, to make as Klossowski suggests, "a tour of eternity." This vicious circle of "forgetting and anamnesis" underlies the ecstatic experience of personal transformation and is demanded by the economics of the Eternal Return—an economics that Klossowski develops under the headings of will, intensity, fluctuation, and chaos.

For Maurice Blanchot, the vertigo of Eternal Return first appears as the closure of absolute nihilism, as the final step in Nietzsche's "logic of terror." But precisely by willing this "insurpassable" stage, nihilism brings about its own reversal or negation—thereby opening up the infinite cycle of affirmation: at the very limit of experience, the great *no* transforms itself into the universalizing *yes* of existence itself.

Gilles Deleuze's concern is not so much with the affirmation or negation of existence as with locating the affirmative and negative forces within existence. Following Nietzsche, he calls these the "active and reactive" forces of Will to Power. While the initial distinction is qualitative in nature, it is based on the quantitative difference between forces of unequal magnitude. But Deleuze insists that a strictly quantitative (and hence, reductionist or atomist) view of Will to Power is impossible for Nietzsche, precisely because the quantity of any force—force itself—is always a relational consequence of still other forces, which in turn can be neither abstracted nor isolated. On the basis of this differential continuum of forces, Deleuze proposes a model for interpreting the "hierarchy" of expressive forces (i.e., both the qualitative and quantitative aspects of Will to Power) as well as the relative genesis of all forces—the continuous transformation of the "same" forces—in short, the Nietzschean doctrine of Eternal Return.

Michel Haar

NIETZSCHE AND
METAPHYSICAL LANGUAGE

For about a decade now there has been a growing uneasiness with regard to Nietzsche: might he not be more inaccessible, more unapproachable, and more inevitably "betrayed" than any philosopher before or since? Might he not be more veiled and also more thoughtlessly read, and therefore more richly endowed with a future, than any other philosopher?

How did all this come about? No doubt, first of all, the apparent ease with which he can be read—an ease due to his seductive "style" (polemic, poetic, aphoristic) as well as to what can pass superficially for a lack of "technical" vocabulary—gave rise to the illusion that this philosopher lay within easy reach of everybody. Thence, inversely and at the start, came disdain on the part of the "specialists" for a philosophy that is so little concerned with being "coherent" and so manifestly anti-philosophical that it could easily be dismissed as belonging more in the ranks of "literature." The warning indicated by the subtitle of *Thus Spoke Zarathustra* had not been understood: a "book for all" *and* "for none." Then, too, a number of extraneous factors moved in to obliterate Nietzsche's thought: prejudices (e.g., the one propagated by Gide about Nietzsche's supposed "aestheticism"), myths (e.g., the one consisting of the belief that his insanity sold out his work, whereas it merely interrupted it), falsifications and misconceptions (the most odious and most often repeated one being that about his supposed anti-Semitism). But the obstacles do not stop here. Of Nietzsche's unfinished works, more than half are posthumously published fragments, and the editions available to us in translation up to the present time have represented the texts in a partial and mutilated fashion, without due respect for either the manuscripts or the chronology. Finally, if we line up the "literary" versions of Nietzsche (in Thomas Mann, Musil, Jünger, Borges) as well as the strictly philosophical commentaries (by Heidegger, Jaspers, Fink, Klossowski), we are faced with a disconcerting diversity of interpretations testifying all the more to how difficult it is to encompass the vast field opened up by Nietzsche's thought.

However, Nietzsche's inaccessibility might well derive from something more fundamental—namely, his strange and ambiguous language vis-à-vis the traditional language of philosophy. Indeed, Nietzsche develops, in direct opposition to the tradition and its language, a language of his own, a form particularly insinuating, insidious, complex—and designed for the purpose of *subversion*. On the one hand, when making use of current metaphysical oppositions (which, for him, all come down to the Platonic opposition between the "true world" and the "apparent world"), he does so with a view to eradicating and abolishing these very distinctions; there is thus inevitably an ambiguity weighing upon his use of terms having a precise meaning within the tradition, terms such as "true" and "false," "good" and "evil." On the other hand, the key words of his *own* vocabulary (Will to Power, Nihilism, Overman, Eternal Return) elude conceptual logic. Whereas a concept, in the classical sense, comprises and contains, in an identical and total manner, the content that it assumes, most of Nietzsche's key words bring forth, as we shall see, a plurality of meanings undermining any logic based on the principle of identity. Insofar as they include significations that are incompatible with one another, these words could be understood as bursting at the seams: a word such as Nihilism designates at once the most despicable and the most "divine" mode of thought. But they function above all to burst open some traditionally accepted identity (e.g., Will, Ego, Man). The recourse to polysemy and the attempt to destroy the great identities of the tradition base themselves on a theory of language that takes language as a machine fabricating false identities. And for Nietzsche, every identity is "false," in particular any identity born of conceptualization. As he says, "Every concept arises from identifying what is not identical."[1] Every concept results from a series of metaphorical transpositions (so primeval that they are always forgotten), the "truest" concept being simply the one that corresponds to the identification—i.e., image—that is most familiar and most common (most effaced in its character as a mere image). Far from attaining to the "truth," a concept, like language in general, functions as an instrument of "gregarization": *viz.*, it is an identification for the greatest number.

While the dominant words of Nietzsche's discourse (especially Will to Power and Eternal Return) are meant to subvert, fracture, and dismiss concepts, his overall effort is one aiming to set the entire logical, semantic, and grammatical apparatus (in which the philosophical tradition had naïvely taken up its abode) to moving in a direction contrary to its constant tendency: namely, toward the assignment of proper nouns, the reduction to identity, and the passage to the universal. In other words, the specific nature of Nietzsche's discourse might well be defined in the first instance as an attempt to encourage disbelief in the laws of logic and the rules of grammar (the final refuge of a defunct theology): it is necessary, he says, to "know how to dance with words," "dance with the pen."[2] This dancing penmanship wills to rock, to topple, to dissociate, to disperse all conformity. With its various games of irony, parody, interrogation, innuendo—but especially with its ruptures, shifts, displacements and the like (which it would be necessary to delineate in detail)—Nietzsche's style aims finally at destroying, or at least checkmating, all logical and, especially, dialectical "seriousness," the goal of which is always to establish identities or to reveal the one absolute Identity.

Finally, the method of genealogy, that critical method discovered by Nietzsche himself and presenting itself as an art of deciphering symptoms *ad infinitum,* raises a particular difficulty that affects the manner in which we are to render an exposition of Nietzsche's thought. Contrary to Plato's method (consisting in gathering sensuous diversity into a unity of essence), Nietzsche's method aims at unmasking, unearthing, but in an *indefinite* way—i.e., without ever pretending to lift the last veil to reveal any originary identity, any primary foundation. Thus, the method itself manifests a deeply rooted repugnance toward any and all systematization. Hostile to the idea of an ultimate revelation of truth, and rejecting all unique and privileged interpretation ("There is no solely beatifying interpretation"[3]), the method of genealogy is necessarily hostile to all codification of its own results. Moreover, the fragmented, aphoristic, and bursting character of the text corresponds to Nietzsche's own grasp of the world: a world scattered in pieces, covered with explosions; a world freed from the ties of gravity (i.e., from relationship with a foundation); a world made of moving and light surfaces where the incessant shifting of masks is named laughter, dance, game.

Thus, Nietzsche's language and Nietzsche's method both possess an explosive energy: what is volatilized in each case is always identity, on which every system rests.

However, in each instance the destruction is possible only on the basis of a new and more radical affirmation. Thus there arises a most penetrating question: might we not have, in the figure of Nietzsche, a subtle restoration of metaphysics and ethics (to the extent, for example, to which it is difficult *not* to conceive of the Overman in turn as an ideal)? Here we have the supreme perplexity that can remain at the horizon of our own interrogation: in what sense does Nietzsche "overcome" the metaphysics that he combats?

No doubt the strictly Platonic structure of metaphysics (based on the separation of true being and lesser being) is abolished and not just turned around. Every "ulterior world," every foundation, is dissolved, and the final symbol of Dionysus—another word for the Will to Power—summons all the attributes of beings, the "true" as well as the "false," the "real" as well as the "fictitious." These terms become indeed interchangeable insofar as the "true" of which Plato speaks proves to be fictitious and therefore false, and insofar as the real is true if it is taken as false in Plato's sense but as containing *also* within it the fictitious.

If, however, according to another (more Heideggarian) definition, the metaphysical approach consists in "identifying" beings in their totality—i.e., in designating with one name the character of beings as such and in their entirety—is not Nietzsche then still a metaphysician? For if metaphysical thinking is that kind of thought aiming to discover the unique and ultimate word that allots to each present thing the character of presence, then it might well be that Nietzsche, by uttering the term "Will to Power," *did* re-enact the traditional move of metaphysics.

But to what extent is the term Will to Power still an identity? Does it not, like all great themes in Nietzsche, refer back to identities that are broken, disfigured, forever dispersed and unrecoverable? Here is the question that will serve as a constant background for the present inquiry into the Will to Power, Nihilism, Genealogy, the Overman, and the Eternal Return. If this style of approach leaves aside the question of Nietzsche's progressive elaboration of these ultimate themes (and therewith also the problem of distinguishing between the various phases of his work), it is for two reasons: first, such problems pass beyond the limits of the present exposition; second, the exposition is based on the view (not to be established here) that the substance of Nietzsche's effort is already to be found, although in an enveloped, unthought, and veiled way, in *The Birth of Tragedy*—his first work, and one that he never ceased to rethink and to defend, the one that he was finally to complete.

THE WILL TO POWER

Nietzsche explicitly underlines and affirms in various ways that everything that exists is at bottom and in its totality Will to Power: "The essence of the world is Will to Power;"[4] "The essence of life is Will to Power;"[5] "The most intimate essence of being is Will to Power."[6] World, Life, Being—these are not ultimate things, but only formations of the Will to Power: herein we find the "ultimate fact."[7]

We must accordingly discard from the very start, as a gross misconception, any interpretation of the Will to Power that is *solely* psychological or anthropological. So construed, it would simply be synonymous with hunger for power, and it would be a mere matter of each individual desiring to dominate others and to subjugate things. It can easily be shown that such a will would in reality be impotent, constantly suffering from an inadequacy and undergoing a perpetual nostalgia. Alternatively, it might be taken as synonymous with a "superiority complex" (after the fashion of Adler), always wanting to extend itself without seeing any limit to its imperialism. Whatever the psychologizing interpretation might be, power gets understood as a concrete and empirical goal, something exterior to the will (riches, political power, glory), a goal pursued or manipulated with presumption. In any case, there would be a distinction between the power and the will, one being the object desired or possessed by the other.

The Will to Power is something much different from the psychological relationship between a subject *qua* will and an object *qua* power. Will to

Power is indeed "the word of being," but this word is a locution, the two terms being inseparable, and each term losing its habitual meaning. Although it is here a question of an affirmation about the totality of beings (in this sense a "metaphysical" affirmation), the locution is designed first of all to destroy and eliminate the traditional metaphysical concept of the will. As for the term "power," it receives its own meaning only in the course of the attempt to overcome that concept: it comes to designate the very essence of this newly thought will. Thus the Will to Power, a term bursting at the seams, a term that cannot be reduced to an identity, comes to express anything but a variety of volition.

The classical view of the will in effect turns it either into a metaphysical substance or, more commonly, into a faculty of the subject. Moreover, this view sees in the will the cause and source of our actions. Finally, it conceives of the will as a unity, an identity.

In opposition to this classical conception, Nietzsche posits as the guiding theme of his own analyses of the will the astonishing affirmation that "there is no such thing as a will."[8] Why does he do this? First of all because the will as a conscious faculty is neither a unity nor a primary term. It is plurality and complexity itself, and it is derived. What we call will is only the symptom and not the cause. On the one hand, "will" in the psychological sense constitutes in everyday language the simplification of a complex interplay of causes and effects. On the other hand, the will, by being posited as a center or as a foundation, is taken falsely by metaphysics to establish a unique origin within reality as well as within the individual, for there is no center, and there is no foundation. There is no will: this means, as against Schopenhauer, that there exists no unique and universal will constituting what things are in themselves, that behind the phenomena there is no substantiality of the will. No will: the individual does not possess *an* identical and permanent will from which all his actions could flow. What the individual calls his "will" is a plurality of instincts and impulses in constant battle with one another to gain the upper hand. An analysis of the individual's "I will" shows that what we call will is the result of a reduction, according to the dictates of a practical necessity as well as to those of linguistic structure, and that it represents merely an imaginary entity, a pure fiction. Volition is composed of distinct emotions and polarities: there is that which wills and that which *is* willed, and then also, at the very core of the "individual," that which commands and that which obeys, the pleasure of triumphing over a resistance and the different pleasure of perceiving an instrument doing its job. What language designates with the name of will is in reality only a complex and belated sentiment: one accompanying the victory of one impulse over others, or the translation into conscious terms of a temporary state of equilibrium intervening in the interplay of impulses.

The will, like consciousness itself, is indeed for Nietzsche not a beginning but an end, not the first term but the "last link in a chain." The will (like consciousness and thought in general) is the distant echo of a battle that has already been fought out, the aftermath coming to the surface, or the "code language" of a subterranean struggle of impulses. To will is to feel the triumph of a force that has cleared a way for itself quite apart from our knowing anything about it, and the supreme illusion consists in taking this feeling, this sentiment, for a free causality. There is no will: that means there is no fixed and defined center (the center is always shifting and it cannot be grasped), but rather a plurality of elementary "wills"—which is to say unconscious impulses, forever in conflict, alternately imposing themselves and subordinating themselves. "There is no will: there are rather fulgurations of the will which are constantly increasing and diminishing their power."[9] Seen with regard to these impulses, the whole of our conscious motivation comes down to a fiction—or rather a *symptom*. In psychology we never cease to confound effects and causes. Generally speaking, the realm of the intellect and the sphere of consciousness are but symbols to be decoded, symptoms of impulsive movements—i.e., symptoms of bodily movements. That is why it will always be necessary to philosophize—i.e., to interpret the phenomena—by taking the *body* as the "abiding clue.."

Is the Will to Power, then, merely a name designating the realm of the unconscious, the realm of the body? Quite the contrary. On the one hand, the locution applies to every possible kind of force: it does not at all refer uniquely to the forces that underlie psychic phenomena—i.e., the impulses of the body—but rather refers to all the phenomena of the world. On the other hand, the locution applies more precisely to the inner dynamism of these forces, to the orientation that qualifies them. In fact, rather than naming these forces taken in themselves as new metaphysical substances of the sort that Nietzsche rejects as fictitious, the Will to Power names the polarity that orients them, structures them, and defines their *meaning:* not an absolute meaning, nor a univocal direction, nor any finality whatsoever, but a multifaceted meaning that takes its shape from the moving diversity of perspectives. In its widest signification, the Will to Power designates a deployment of forces that is non-finalized but always oriented. Every force, every energy, whatever it may be, is Will to Power—in the organic world (impulses, instincts, needs), in the psychological and moral worlds (desires, motivations, ideas), and in the inorganic world itself—inasmuch as "life is just a special case of the Will to Power."[10] Every force participates in this same essence: "It is one and the same force that one expends in artistic creation and in the sex act; there is but one kind of force."[11] However, the concept of a single force diversifying itself does not suffice to account for the Will to Power: "To the concept of force must be attributed an inner will, what I refer to as 'Will to Power,' i.e., as an insatiable demand for the demonstration of power."[12]

It is this "insatiable demand for the demonstration of power" that expresses the meaning of the complementary phrase "to Power," conveying the sense of the "movement toward" contained in the German *Wille "zur" Macht*. What, then, is this Power? It is precisely the intimate law of the will and of all force, the law that to will is to will its own growth. The will that is Will to Power responds at its origins to its own internal imperative: *to be more*. This imperative brings it before the alternatives: either it is to augment itself, to surpass itself, or it is to decline, to degenerate. According to the direction that the force takes (progression or regression), and according to the response (yes or no) one makes to the conditions imposed upon life or imposed on life by life itself (as Zarathustra says: "I am the one who is ever forced to overcome himself"), there appear *right at the origin,* at the very heart of the Will to Power, two types of force, two types of life: the *active* force and the *reactive* force, the *ascending* life and the *decadent* life. If all volition is a volition to be stronger, if all power is overpower, our volition can also try to escape from itself and from its own demand for growth. There is here a paradox: for, strictly speaking, it is impossible to cease to will, since that would mean to cease to be. However, the decadent will that refuses to "admit the fundamental conditions of life" remains nonetheless a will: "Man would rather will nothingness than not to will at all."[13] Only in this case, the direction of the will is reversed: growth becomes advance in decadence. The "intensification" essential to the Will to Power works itself out backwards. For Nietzsche, in the special case of moral decadence, its most extreme creation is the ascetic ideal.

The Will to Power therefore always has to do with itself. It possesses a fundamental reflexivity—i.e., it is always overcoming itself, be it through action or through reaction. At its origin it presents itself to and for itself as a chaotic and contradictory diversity of elementary impulses; it is primordial affectivity. What Nietzsche calls "chaos" is this primordial indetermination of the Will to Power. Undetermined as it is, it can assume all forms, for it is just so many masks: it is Proteus. Without form because of its excess of possibilities, Chaos signifies, on the one hand, not at all disorder, but rather the multiplicity of impulses, the entire horizon of forces, within which knowledge and art are to delineate their perspectives. On the other hand, Chaos is to represent equally the moment when, all values collapsed, the Will to Power effects a return to itself, a sort of return to point zero.

When thought of in conjunction with Chaos, the Will to Power appears at once as the principle defining a hierarchy for the forces contesting for the upper hand *and* as the tendency to appropriate an ever larger field of action. That will is strong which can harmonize its own forces, forces in themselves divergent, and can dominate their constant development. That man is powerful "who longs to see chaos"—i.e., who agrees to face all impulses (or at least the greatest number possible), and who can master them. This mastery is conveyed in and by such expressions as "grand style," "grand politics," "grand reasoning," "grand educator," "grand hope," in which the adjective "grand" designates a Will to Power attaining, in each case, its fullest affirmation. In contrast, that will is weak which cannot bear this task and seeks out a solution in the elimination or repression of this or that force. When affirmative and strong, the Will to Power takes upon itself variety, difference, and plurality. When negative and weak, it shrinks into reflexes of flight and defense, willing but its own diminution in the shadow of a bloodless ideal, in complete opposition to the grand simplification that perfect mastery can produce.

This initial bipolarity of the Will to Power forms the basis from which the whole enterprise of genealogy receives its definition. The "genealogical" critique of values consists in relating any given value to the originary direction (affirmative or negative) of volition, in unveiling the long lineage issuing from this primordial orientation, and in unraveling the remote thread of encounters that have since frozen into "values."

But what are values? As instruments that the Will to Power grants itself in order to confirm itself in its initial direction, values constitute the conditions of its existence; they are the "points of view" that permit it to maintain itself and to develop itself. Nietzsche defines values as follows: they are "conditions of conservation and increase, namely in regard to complex creatures having a relative duration of life within the realm of becoming."[14] The production as well as the hierarchy of values—i.e., how they are situated with regard to one another (their situation always changing according to their very nature—for example, the rank enjoyed by art relative to knowledge at any given time)—makes sense only in relation to the originary direction of the Will to Power; the "place" of values favors, sustains, and propels movement in this direction.

As the origin of values, and the origin also of every hierarchy of values, the Will to Power fixes the value of all values. But this origin cannot be reduced to a primordial unity, to any kind of identity, because it is nothing but a direction forever to be determined. On the other hand, this origin has and gives meaning only in retrospect—namely in and through the genealogical development that issues from it, and by which it is recognized.

NIHILISM

But what does the genealogical view discover when it turns toward the prevailing—the supposedly "highest"—values? It finds them in the throes of that crisis called Nihilism.

In this word, too, we can read a duality (if not a plurality) of meaning. On the one hand it designates the contemporary situation (probably destined to last for a long time yet) where the "highest"—i.e., the absolute—values are rendered null and void. On the other hand, the word applies to the unfolding as well as to the internal "logic" of all so-called "European" history since Plato. In this second sense, Nihilism has more historical continuity than the "decadence" marking the moments of "weakening" of Will to Power (the Alexandrian civilization as against ancient Greece; Christianity as against imperial Rome; the Reformation as against the Renaissance). Inasmuch as Nihilism presided over the original institution of those values currently tottering, and inasmuch as it directs their evolution and every possible transmutation, Nihilism is in some fashion *always* present, *always* at work—before, during, and after the moment of its violent explosion. Concurring with the very humanity of man, it can rightly be called man's "normal condition" (whereupon the question might be asked whether a race of men who no longer knew nihilism would still be men). But insofar as it is the peculiar disease of contemporary man (one requiring a homeopathic remedy), Nihilism is also a "passing pathological condition."

Indeed, being much more than a *critical thought* that man and his culture might turn against beliefs, values, and ideals, Nihilism assails man and his culture as the experience and sentiment of a *critical condition* that has become brutally actual—for, before crashing down with all its weight, Nihilism approaches as "the most alarming of all guests"[15] and installs itself insidiously as a sentiment that is first of all one of gloom, and then one of terror, at the debacle of all meaning. It is the progressive consumption of everything having signification, the growing predominance of empty significations, sapped to the last drop. It is the moment when we feel ourselves—as in the onrush of a nightmare or as in a complete disorientation in space and time—flowing or drifting toward ill-defined borderlands where every previous meaning, every previous sense, still subsists, but has been converted into non-sense. "The desert is growing," as Zarathustra says. All the old meanings (whether moral, religious, or metaphysical) slip away, steal away, refuse their services: "The goals are missing."[16] All sense totters, vacillates, sputtering like the few last rays of light of a dying sun. Nihilism, the experience of the exhaustion of meaning, amounts to a grand weariness, a "grand disgust," on the part of man, directed toward himself as well. Nothing is worth much anymore, everything comes down to the same thing, everything is equalized. Everything is the same and equivalent: the true and the false, the good and the bad. Everything is outdated, used up, old, dilapidated, dying: an undefined agony of meaning, an unending twilight: not a definite annihilation of significations, but their indefinite collapse.

Precisely because it is *complete* disorientation, this kind of nihilism can abruptly alter its *Stimmung* (its mood, its tone), ceasing to be an anxious inquietude and becoming a complacent quietude. Here we have the experience of a will satisfied with meaninglessness, with non-sense, a will happy that there is no longer any sense or any meaning to look for, a will having found a certain comfort in the total absence of meaning and a certain happiness in the certainty that there is no answer to the question "why?" (or even "what?"). Nietzsche describes this stage as that of the "last man."

A remark made by Zarathustra and taken up again in *The Gay Science* (§125)—namely, that "God is dead"—summarizes the collapse of all values. For disaffection in regard to religious faith is only one sign among many indicating the bankruptcy of every ideal: not only of every ideal, but of every intelligibility, *every idea*. With God there disappears the guarantee for an intelligible world, and therewith the guarantee for all stable identities, including that of the ego. Everything returns to chaos. Nietzsche compares this event to a natural catastrophe: to a deluge, to an earthquake, but most often to an eclipse of the sun. The Sun of intelligibility has grown dark and the Earth has lost its orbit, becoming a roving star that suffers the eclipse by growing dark itself. Here we have "compete nihilism," although it is neither its first nor its last form.

At first, Nihilism is the expression of a decadent will, of impotent Will to Power recoiling from an affirmation of "life" and changing into negation. (That which is negated in and by Nihilism is what Nietzsche calls "life"— i.e., the world as plurality, as becoming, as contradiction, as suffering, as illusion, as evil.) This negation of "life" and of the world proclaims that "this world is worth nothing and nothing in it is worth anything." Taking this proclamation as its point of departure, Nihilism invents a "true world"—i.e., a world that possesses all the attributes that "life" does not have: unity, stability, identity, happiness, truth, goodness. Thus the division of the two worlds, the feat undertaken by Plato, constitutes the nihilistic act *par excellence*. All metaphysical values and all categories of intelligibility contain implicitly a will to negate—i.e., to depreciate and to slander—life. But in its first form (the Socratic and Platonic one), Nihilism remains latent. Negation does not show itself. Only affirmations are in evidence: the affirmation of grand, supersensible values (the True, the Beautiful, the Good), and later on the affirmation of grand principles of logic (identity, causality, sufficient reason, etc.).

Between the larval nihilism of triumphant metaphysics and the "complete" nihilism declaring that none of the earlier constructions, nor any value, has any meaning, we find situated various forms of "incomplete nihilism." In these forms the will for negation comes more and more out into the open. Incomplete nihilism is but the decomposition of the "true world," the recurrent attempt to find replacement values to substitute for the Platonic and Christian ideals (Christianity having only "popularized" the concept of a "true world" with its idea of a "world beyond"). One noteworthy substitute, among others, is the Kantian ethic, which can no longer do more than *postulate* the other world: "At bottom the same old sun, but now obscured by fog and skepticism; the Idea become sublime, pale, northern, Koenigsbergish."[17] And then there are the "secular" ideals: the faith in progress, the religion of happiness-for-everybody (socialism appearing as the successor of Christianity insofar as it promises happiness on earth), the mystique of Culture or of Man. However, after having killed God—i.e., after having recognized the nothingness of the "true world"—and after having placed himself where God once was, Man continues to be haunted by his iconoclastic act: he cannot venerate himself, and soon ends up by turning his impiety against himself and smashing this new idol. Among the forms of incomplete nihilism are to be found the characters that Zarathustra calls the "superior men," the "vestiges of God on earth," those who desperately uphold an ideal the fragility of which they know all too well. They are like that "conscientious soul" who, latching onto the ideal of a perfect science, no matter how limited and ridiculous, studies but one thing, albeit very thoroughly: the brain of the leech! For this study he gives his blood and his life, and he grinds himself into the dust.

Although not yet "consummated," Nihilism is "complete" now that the will to nothingness has become manifest and patent. Up to that point this nothingness—i.e., the condemnation of "life" as non-being—was hidden behind various representations of the ideal and various fictions of the supersensible. It is on these representations and fictions that Nihilism, their proper counterpart, now expatiates. The distrust that had given rise to the "true world" turns against its own creations. The sensible having been depreciated and the supersensible ceasing to be of value, the essential metaphysical difference (Platonic, Christian, and also Kantian) between being-in-itself and appearance, between truth and illusion, ends up rejected. What gets abolished is not only the "true world," whereupon we would have to re-evaluate the "appearance" that would be left over, but also the very distinction between the "simple" appearance and the idea: "With the true world we have also done away with the apparent world."[18]

"Appearances," according to Nietzsche's conception of them, become the "only reality," the All: that is why the whole range of predicates associated with what used to be called appearance, "including contrary predicates," are suited to this reality. This "new" sense of appearance contains both truth and lie, both reality and fiction. It signifies at once "appearance" in the sense of paralogism (a sin against logic) and in the sense of veracious vision of being as Chaos. Gathering within itself all contraries, it deliberately explodes the logic of identity. Appearance, thought of in this new way and transfigured by the abolition of all oppositions, never comes to the point of referring itself back to any ultimate foundation, nor to any central focus of interpretation, nor to anything "in itself": rather, it always refers to a further appearance. Everything is a mask. Any mask once uncovered uncovers another mask. "Becoming" is simply the indefinite play of interpretations, an indefinite shifting of masks.

Thus Nihilism is not overcome simply because the essential metaphysical distinction ceases to be of value. In order to transform "complete" nihilism into "consummated" nihilism (or "ecstatic" nihilism, that which precisely allows us to take leave of—*ek-stasis*, the difference), it is necessary that we pass from a recognition of the dissolution to an active, an affirmative dissolution. The new affirmation includes an act of destruction whereby all the relations issuing from the difference are destroyed. This unity of creation and destruction at the core of a force supremely affirmative (active nihilism) comprises a perspective that Nietzsche also calls "Dionysian": the perspective of the joyous, pure affirmation of the unity of contraries.

It is in this latter sense—namely as an invalidation of all metaphysical differences and as a radical abolishment of the "true world," as a negation of the singular God (Christian representative of the world)—that "nihilism might indeed be a divine manner of thinking":[19] delivered from the paralysis effected by the Singular, the creative instinct of Multiple gods would be re-animated. This "divine" form of Nihilism prefigures an essential transition.

GENEALOGY AND THE FORMER TABLETS

As a kind of symptomology or semiology, the genealogical critique interprets values as so many signs (values being but a "cipher-language" to be decoded), signs of subterranean impulses or, more precisely, signs of the originary direction, whether ascendent or decadent, of these impulses. Genealogy shows at once a birth and an affiliation: it allows us to see how the initial direction prevailing in such-and-such evaluation persists through each and every derivation and transformation, no matter how distant from the origin. Like all values, the True and the Good serve as instruments, as conditions for the possibility of a Will to Power maintaining and developing itself thanks to them. Just where and how the line is to be drawn between the true and the false, the good and the bad, depends upon the kind of life that these values uphold. They have no intrinsic value at all; their entire "truth" lies in their adequation to a particular Will to Power. "You will always have only that ethic which is becoming to your own force,"[20]—i.e., which will harmonize with the orientation of this force. Values that advise being prudent—or taking risks—are dictated by a particular type of force. In exactly the same way, the supposedly immutable principles of logic, as well as the discoveries of science, serve as a support, as a base of operations for a determinate type of humanity. "The force of the various modes of knowledge does not lie in their degrees of truth, but . . . in their character as conditions of life."[21]

Thus Nietzsche strives to demonstrate, by the genealogical method, that science (and knowledge in general), contrary to its own pretentions, is not at all disinterested, but rather is supremely "interested."

There is no "immaculate knowledge," says a chapter of *Thus Spoke Zarathustra* (II, "On Immaculate Perception"). And Nietzsche attacks the myth of a "pure" objective knowledge that could cruise over reality without being implicated in it, that could, without prejudice or point of view, be the faithful mirror of reality. The illusion peculiar to knowledge—namely, the illusion of objectivity—consists in imagining that it is possible to penetrate, right down to its innermost recesses, the essence of things, while at the same time simply reflecting it. However, knowledge is essentially active even when it believes itself to be passive, essentially solar even though it takes itself to be lunar (i.e., revolving around reality and borrowing from it what little cold light it possesses for itself). All knowledge thus comes down to *belief* and *conquest*.

It is *belief* inasmuch as truths (including the principles and categories of logic) do not correspond to any "in themselves" of things, are not adequations to "objects" but rather to the Will to Power. We are forced to believe in a logic in order to bring things under our control. To "deduce" logic from the Will to Power means to relate it to needs and desires: the desire for stability introducing simplicity, order, identity; the need for prediction inventing the categories of causality and finality, which in turn make possible various systems of repetition and the consequent foreseeability of phenomena. Logic rests upon a useful and necessary falsification, being born of the vital need to lean upon identities despite the fact that nothing real is reducible either to unity or to identity. Therefore, "truth is that kind of error without which a certain kind of living being cannot live."[22] But truth is, in addition, falsification of the False, for the "in itself," namely "pure becoming," presents itself to us as Chaos—i.e., as non-(logical)-truth, eternal and infinite.

Then, too, knowledge is *conquest* inasmuch as it is by nature imperative, inasmuch as it imposes laws upon Chaos, inasmuch as it is an assimilating activity. Knowledge behaves despotically because it never ceases to suppress, to simplify, to equalize. Like ethics, logic springs from a will to reduce all phenomena to "identical cases." While feigning objectivity, the enterprise of knowing schematizes and creates fictitious coherences, meanwhile appropriating with an inexhaustible voracity everything strange to or other than it, with the sole view of mastering it. But that is not all: the schematizing and assimilating activity of knowledge is not even the work of consciousness. This activity emerges already at the level of the body, and from there enters onto the conscious level. Knowing and judging are simply matters of recognizing a particular schema of assimilation that happens to be available because it is already traced out by the body—i.e., by the Will to Power.

The destruction of logic by means of its genealogy brings with it as well the ruin of the psychological categories founded upon this logic. All psychological categories (the ego, the individual, the person) derive from the illusion of substantial identity. But this illusion goes back basically to a superstition that deceives not only common sense but also philosophers—namely, the belief in language and, more precisely, in the truth of grammatical categories. It was grammar (the structure of subject and predicate) that inspired Descartes' certainty that "I" is the subject of "think," whereas it is rather the thoughts that come to "me": at bottom, faith in grammar simply conveys the will to be the "cause" of one's thoughts. The subject, the self, the individual are just so many false concepts, since they transform into substances fictitious unities having at the start only a linguistic reality. Moreover, the "self," once brought into relation with the Will to Power, proves to be a simple illusion of perspective insofar as it is posited as an underlying unity, permanent center, source of decision. Rather, the "self" and the individual are fictions concealing a complexity, a plurality of forces in conflict. Conscious and personal identity, aside from being but a "grammatical habit," hides the original and fundamental plurality constituting the Will to Power in bodily form. "We are a plurality that has imagined itself a unity":[24] a multiplicity of impulses that have provided themselves with an arbitrarily coherent and substantial center. The actual "functioning" of the Will to Power comes into clearest view with regard to the body understood as a multiplicity originally unintegrated but ascribing to itself a unity. To philosophize by taking the body as the "abiding clue" amounts to revealing the "self" as an instrument, an expression, an interpreter of the body. It also amounts to revealing the body (in opposition to our petty faculty of reasoning, where only surface "causes" make their appearance) as the "grand reason"—i.e., as the totality of deeply buried causes in their mobile and contradictory diversity. Philosophy has never ceased to show disdain for the body; it has not wished to recognize that it is the body that whispers thoughts to the "soul," and that consciousness is only a superficial and terminal phenomenon. Psychology has always idolized superficial unities for fear of facing the unsettling multiplicity at the depths of being.

Our logical and psychological categories derive their falsehood precisely from this "will to find out the truth"—i.e., from that which is fixed, stable, identical, and noncontradictory. But by devaluing contradiction, we bring into evidence a moral prejudice at the very basis of knowledge. This prejudice can be summed up as follows: that which is always stable, always identical, is not only True, but also *Good,* and in a twofold way: knowledge claims to bring salvation and is itself haunted by an ideal of ethical honesty. It is as shameful to deceive as it is to be deceived, and the true has more *ethical* value than the false. If the will to know the true is the will to be good and to be saved, this will is, then, for Nietzsche, a way of negating "life."

Indeed, if the logically true takes shape in the course of searching out identity at all costs and rejecting the contradictory character of life, the will to truth is associated with a nihilistic Will to Power—or, more bluntly, with a covert will to die, a covert death-wish. All knowledge is motivated by this ascetic will, this will to self-destruction that turns out to be the supreme form of ethics. There is in all knowledge an aspiration to situate oneself definitively beyond all contradiction, and this, for Nietzsche, lies in situating oneself within nothingness.

Thus, any genealogy, whether it be of logic, science, psychology, or anything else, comes down to a genealogy of morals, since the ethical ideal is the archetype and source of every ideal, and especially of truth. Things are true or false only inasmuch as they are good or evil. The ideal of knowledge turns out to be but a special and derived case of the general ideal: "The need to know what *should be* gave rise to the need to know what is."[24] The genealogy of morals, being more radical, poses the question about the *meaning* of the Ideal—i.e., about the originary direction of that Will to Power to which such an invention corresponds and renders service. While at the same time detailing and unveiling the process by which the Ideal is fabricated, a genealogy reveals moral consciousness as a formation issuing from a long development and assuming varying degrees.

From a genealogical point of view, it appears that ethical systems can only be defined univocally, in purely negative and pejorative terms: moral consciousness, as well as its ideal, are analyzed and unmasked as inventions of "resentment." But what does resentment mean if not a hatred, a condemnation, a depreciation of "life"? In other words, ethical systems derive from a weak and impotent Will to Power reacting against the most affirmative impulses and favoring negation and destruction. Resentment is, as Nietzsche most generally defines it, the negating instinct of life, "the instinct of decadence." Since every value expresses the point of view necessary for the maintenance and growth of certain beings and for a certain period of time, and since every value also serves as a condition of existence, an ethical system, itself a sign of sickness, constitutes at the same time a remedy, or rather an attempted recovery. It serves the purpose of a defensive wall, of a systematic protection against the unrelenting impulses of sex, egoism (every ethic being a disdain for the self, an ousting of the self, an *Entselbstung*), aggression, cruelty, etc. Since these impulses cannot be taken up and expressed as such, they are kept at a distance—or, if at all possible, extirpated (morality playing, for Nietzsche, the role of an instrument of castration) by assigning to them their specific nature: the embodiment of Evil and of immorality. Their "immoral" nature amounts to a projection of the fear they arouse.

But why can't these impulses be expressed? Two obstacles, one internal and the other external, stand in the way. On the one hand, these impulses are already weakened, degenerate, and sickly, in such a way that they could not in any case find a satisfactory outlet (witness the case of Socrates, who distrusts instincts simply because his own are decadent). Furthermore, of the two this internal obstacle is by far the more complex, for it arises from an ambivalence: although the decadent type is characterized by an unprecedented decay as far as his instincts go (Socrates: the "amystical" creature *par excellence,* monstrously insensitive to art and to music) and by a hypertrophy of his reasoning and conscious faculties, he is also one who feels that he is "capable of every evil"—i.e., one who is incessantly at the brink of brutally expressing his desires and erupting into all sorts of bestiality. The decadent man feels within himself the terrifying proximity of animality, and animality that is poorly constrained by a frail film of civilization, of civility and good manners, and which is on the verge of breaking out. "Instincts want to play the tyrant: it is necessary to invent a counter-tyrant that is stronger yet."[25] The Socratic ethic (virtue is knowledge, the only sin is ignorance, a virtuous man is a happy man) represents this counter-tyranny; it is the ultimate and obligatory recourse in the face of instincts that are at once weakened and yet also threatening at any moment to boil over into anarchy. On the other hand, the *external* obstacle consists of the repressive external organization (society, in essence) that *forbids* these impulses to express themselves.

The development of man's "interiorization" and the birth of his ethical consciousness takes its foothold and beginning from the impotence of the instincts, their powerlessness to find a way of expressing themselves outwardly, and the resultant turn inward. However, precisely in the figure of his adversary Plato—Plato the man rather than Plato the philosopher—Nietzsche envisages still a third possibility to account for the origin of the reactive (ascetic) ethic: there are indeed people in whom the overabundance of life and sensuality is such that asceticism, for them, redoubles their strength by giving them a victory in the face of an obstacle that they set to themselves solely for the pleasure they take in proving themselves triumphant over it. In this sense we might say that Plato was an extremely sensuous man who happened to be "enamoured with his own contrary." But this explanation holds neither for Platonism nor for Christianity.

Whatever the case may be, the illusion peculiar to any ethic lies in its erecting into a universal rule, into an *imperative,* that which is only a *constraint*—i.e., a need, a domineering condition of existence.

Meanwhile, and at the same time, the genealogical method reveals the ambivalence and the duplicity of the concept of "morality." For even if it is ordinarily a function of a weak and reactive Will to Power, it can also arise from the values willed by a strong and active will. Still, though, the *highest* point of view of the affirmative Will to Power necessarily situates itself beyond good and evil, since even the distinction is the work of weakness. To the affirmative Will to Power, the strong and the weak appear equally moral and equally immoral. Immorality finds itself assessed from two different angles. Unilateral morality is thereby dissolved. As Nietzsche says in *The Genealogy of Morals,* the concept "good" has no one meaning. There are neither "virtues" nor "vices" that could not be taken in at least two diametrically opposed ways. Just as there is a lowly and vile prudence of the weak, so is there a noble and proud prudence of the strong; a cowardly and weak cruelty as well as courageous and strong cruelty; a pessimism that is a symptom of exhaustion and decomposition as well as a pessimism that manifests a superabundance of energy, that constitutes a kind of luxury of strength. The need for destruction and change can be the expression just as much of an exuberant and overflowing strength as of a hatred and malcontent in the face of what is. In the same way, the need for stabilizing, fixing, and "externalizing" can come as much from generosity and happiness as from rancor and a morbid desire to perpetuate suffering and unhappiness. In the same culture, the "good" man can mean "he who is courteous and nice," but also "he who longs for battle and victory." Thus, the genealogical point of view brings to light a typology of antithetical morals: the initial fundamental opposition between "strong" and "weak" crops up again in the gregarious type (passive, defensive, vulgar) and the solitary type (active, aggressive, noble). The profound insight of Nietzsche is that this antagonism is necessary and not to be overcome: "The moral instinct consists in constructing types; for that it needs antinomical values."

Of course, Nietzsche's analysis does not preclude a multiplicity of degrees and intermediary stages, even mixed types. However, the antagonism of the two types must be thought of not as a conflict that brings them into mutual relations and attaches them to each other, but as a mutual separation that detaches and *distinguishes* them from each other. A caesura, a fault, keeps the two apart. The Hegelian opposition of master and slave is a dialectic, a reciprocity of relations. Nietzsche's opposition is based upon a rupture, a cleavage within humanity. Nietzsche does not want the moat between them to be filled in. He rather wants to underscore what he calls the "pathos of distance." The antagonism must be further aggravated, pushed as far as possible, to bring out the two irreversible propensities leading, on the one hand, toward gregarization, leveling, uniformity, and, on the other hand, toward the formation of higher men, exceptional men, "great solitary figures."

At first, the antithesis was present not only in the opposition between the "noble" as self-affirmation and the "vile" as self-negation, but also in the opposition between Dionysian tragedy (affirmation, even one of suffering) and Christian theory (negation, even one of happiness). It then repeated itself in the modern opposition between the classical type (capable of mastering all contradictions) and the romantic type (expressing the weakness of instinct). Finally, it is bound to recoil in the future to the other extreme—i.e., for Nietzsche, it is bound to result in the ultimate opposition between the "last man," the complete nihilist, and the Overman.

But, to come right to the point, why and how did the weak man, the man of resentment, come to be exclusively identified with the moral man? From whence derives this prolonged immobilization of the Good exclusively on one side—this "hemiplegia of virtue," as Nietzsche calls it?

By inventing moral inwardness, from which stem the ideas of doing wrong and being justified, of being in debt and having responsibilities, the weak man has "triumphed" over the strong, happy man who affirms himself in his individuality apart from obligations and without having need of ratification. Once moral inwardness was discovered, the strong man was driven to doubting the legitimacy of his actions. Ever since Socrates, the Good has not taken care of itself; instinctive action has become suspect; only that action is good which can answer up before the inner court. The logical and disinterested appearance of Socratic dialectic is now unmasked: it is the "weapon" of the weak man who seeks to unsettle whatever is affirmative without daring or being able to engage in mortal combat with it—for the man of resentment, the "slave," never enters into a truly reciprocal relationship with the man of strength, the "master": the weak man rather receives his only definition as the one who rejects the ethic of the "master." It is clear enough that, for Nietzsche, the "master" (and such will be the Overmen, the future "Masters of the Earth") is not the master of the slave, but the master of himself, his acts, and, above all, his "inward chaos." The master is the individual who gives himself his own law, and whose ethic is built on pure self-affirmation. The master is the one who is *different:* "My ethic would be to deprive man more and more of his universal character and to specialize him, to make him to a certain extent unintelligible to others."[26] Here we have the ethical principle of the master: "That which is good for me is good in itself." In contrast, the man of resentment rejects every form of affirmation, of joy, of happiness. He bears a grudge against life. Nothing is good enough for him. He posits as evil that which is Other, different or affirmative. He suffers incessantly. He is incapable of either forgetting or assimilating events. He is also plagued by memories, by the past. "He cannot shake anything off, he cannot get rid of it. Everything is an injury. Man and things clutter in about him with no discretion. Every event leaves its mark. Memory is a purulent wound."[27] Furthermore, the underlying meaning of resentment, what Nietzsche also calls the "spirit of revenge," becomes in the course of time a certain version of the Will to Power: it is a rebel will taking revenge on a temporality dominated by the dimension of the past and understood Platonically as disappearance and non-being. Meanwhile, this "insane" will does not see that it is its own prisoner.

The impotence of the weak man is so great that he cannot bring his resentment to an external expression. He can only turn it against himself, in this way suppressing it. This repressed hatred and cruelty, this grudge and accusation (not only against the strong and against affirmation, but also against time itself and the entire world), by turning into self-accusation produces that mutation of resentment called *bad conscience.* Whereas at first it is everything external that was accused and found guilty, it is now the ego, the self. Just as the master was the master of himself, so the slave is enslaved to himself. The inwardness, the "interiorization" of man, thereby results in a "regression" of strength as it takes a retrograde effect upon itself: aggressiveness and cruelty, whose own impotence as well as the repressive social structure forbid them to manifest themselves in any external fashion, direct themselves inwardly, and find on the inside a vast field of "new and subterranean satisfactions." Suffering thereby assumes, for the first time, an internal signification ("it's my fault") that the Christian religion, the religion of the weak, is well able to nourish, refine, and exploit: "You suffer, therefore you have sinned: suffering is punishment for having done wrong," says the priest, securing for himself infinite powers over those who accept this article of faith. However, we should bear in mind that, if there is a religion of the weak, there is also a religion of the strong, or rather two such religions: the primitive Greek religion of Dionysus, and the future religion of the Eternal Return.

But resentment necessarily evolves into its third stage, where the ultimate realization of its peculiar goal is embodied (a goal already present from the beginning): *the suppression of the self.* One's conscience, being its own executioner, ends up not being able to stand itself. It wills its own death—i.e., it becomes necessary to live and experience one's own death. The ascetic ideal, with its fiction of an afterlife, of a "true world" possessing all the characteristics contrary to the world of "life," represents the means of achieving this death at the heart of life. The will can live out its own impossible self-destruction, continuing to exercise itself as a will, just by willing nothingness (the nothingness of itself and of the world). Self-accusation changes into self-destruction. At first, man immolates himself to the "beyond" prescribed by religion, undergoing the privations of an ascetic existence. When the religious ideal has gone bankrupt and finds itself replaced by the scientific ideal, the sacrifice is still determined by the ascetic ideal. Whether life is sacrificed to God or to truth makes no difference with regard to the principle of the ideal. Finally, then, even the suppression of the ideal—not just the ideal of God, but of each and every ideal—appears as the simple prolongation and work of the very principle of negation already present in the ascetic ideal. Atheism and nihilism result from the application, from the unconditional practice, of the ideal "truth at all costs!"—the ideal born of the ascetic ethic. Indeed, as Nietzsche shows, atheism has as its source none other than the ideal of scrupulous sincerity, the ideal of rigorous intellectual honesty as it developed under the influence of that notion created by Christianity itself: the refinement of conscience. Thus atheism is, in the genealogical sense, "the awe-inspiring catastrophe of a two-thousand-year training in truth, a training which in the end forbids itself that lie which is faith in God."[28] Atheists, and above all the scientists, are the most pious of men. Religion and morality thus die from their own exigencies: they commit suicide. "God has killed God." Everything great can only perish by "an act of self-suppression": thus wills the Will to Power.

Nihilism proves that until now only pain, sacrifice, destruction of the self have given meaning to life, that there has never been any other ideal. But this Ideal *is* no longer: "The goals are missing." The Will to Power demands of

humanity that it surpass itself. But how are we to define this *new goal,* the
More-than-human, with regard to all those who are of the strictly human
type?

THE OVERMAN AND THE TRANSMUTATION

As the ultimate ''goal,'' the Overman obviously cannot be identified with
any type or level of humanity actually existing. In this sense, the philosophy
of the Overman unfolds as a philosophy of the Future while yet presenting
something quite different from a philosophy of Progress.

Insofar as the strong type of man has disappeared at the present time of
nihilism (complete or incomplete, but not yet ecstatic), and insofar as there
are no longer any ''masters,'' it might seem that the Overman could
incontestably be taken to mean some strong type of the future—i.e., the man
who has vanquished nihilism. But this is not at all the case.

To be sure, we do have already under our eyes the absolute ''opposite'' of
the Overman—namely, the ''last man,'' the extreme representative of
weakness, a man frozen at the level of passive nihilism, totally reduced to a
''herd animal,'' rendered uniform, equal, and level—the man who has
found happiness. But, as an ultimate horizon, isn't the Overman radically
different from any *human* type we might be able to describe? One thing is
sure: he is not incarnated by the ''higher man'' *(der höhere Mensch),* who is
still the prisoner of an ideal (e.g., the scientific ideal held up by the
scrupulous specialist on the leech) and thereby of Nihilism. Even
Zarathustra himself is not the Overman, but rather his ''messenger,'' his
prophet. Might not the Overman, then, be the ''total'' man become once
again affirmative, the ''highest man'' *(der höchste Mensch)* undertaking and
completing the task of transmuting all values? This, again, does not seem to
be the case, since it is the More-than-human, the Overhuman, that stands
already as the goal toward which the ''strong men of the future'' surge; these
men have to prepare the way for, have to make possible, the appearance of
the Overman. What Zarathustra does is to announce the coming of a new
type of man: he calls himself ''the herald who summons numerous legislators.'' But it is in the midst of these highest men, beyond and above them,
that there will flash, in sparse solitude, the ''lightning'' of the More-than-
human.

The image of lightning underscores the absoluteness of the emergence.
The idea of the Overman seems to correspond to the possibility of an ecstatic
break away from humanity. Isn't the appearance of the More-than-human
foreseen precisely as a break with humanity, as a series of explosive faults
destroying the very concept of humanity considered as an identity, a unity, a
totality universally embracing all thinking beings? The Overman will thus

bring it about that the identity of humanity will, by itself, "burst at the seams" insofar as it is the highest form of life and a universal.

One question is of utmost importance: are we to interpret the Overman to be some sort of highest type of man, the perfect embodiment of the essence of man (who actualizes what was, in the past, only a potentiality)—or are we to interpret the Overman in a much different way—as a species higher than man (perhaps a god) and, in any case, as some living being other than man? The question is of decisive importance because the point is not simply to quarrel over a difference of degree or of nature. The point is to determine whether Nihilism is so coextensive with the essence of man that it will prove possible to overcome it only by overcoming humanity itself. Meanwhile, though, Nietzsche's answer to the question is clear enough. To the humanism of progress (implying an accumulation of gains for the entire species—i.e., the distribution to each and every man of the "attributes" they have picked up together) Nietzsche opposes a non-egalitarian and anti-universalist vision of the future where hierarchy and selection will come more and more into power and evidence. On the one hand, to be sure, there will be "gregarized" humanity subsisting and prospering precisely by stabilizing itself at the nihilistic level of the search for happiness: in this quarter the nihilism of the last man will install itself and spread itself out. On the other hand, though, the new "masters," turning toward the ultimate goal, will create the primer for the counter-movement that will make it possible for the More-than-human to thunder forth at some undetermined time in the future: this they will achieve by destroying the old values with a "blow of the hammer"—a blow that must both smash and liberate—and by instituting new tablets. It is this operation in which certain men are separated off and isolated from the others that will constitute the condition for the possibility of the production of beings surpassing man. The total man, the synthetic man, therefore represents only a stage of transition (a type no doubt allowing of various degrees) on the way toward the Overman. The "highest" man, the "legislator of the future" (i.e., the man who lays down the law, submitting himself to it as well), amounts to only an effort on the part of the Will to Power to attain the Overman—a bold and dangerous experiment.

In any event, the Overman is "an attempt at something which is no longer man."[29] Once again the logic of identity breaks down, not because the Overman contains an ambiguity (he is not, after all, at the same time both the fulfillment of man and the surpassing of man), but because he stands in opposition to the identification of man with himself as the highest living being. Man can no longer idolize himself. The "will for justice" ("justice" meaning, for Nietzsche, at once a respect for distance and separation as well as an adequation to the Will to Power) commands Zarathustra to "smash, according to the image of the Overman, *all your images of man.*"[30] Having irrevocably sold itself into slavery, humanity ceases to be the goal: "The

Overman is now the goal." The Overman stands out as that type of living being who finally cuts himself loose from all the ties that even an affirmative humanity keeps on having with Nihilism. For Nietzsche, this "detachment" constitutes the future of the future, its promise. It presupposes as already accomplished the immense task of the transmutation, a task itself belonging to the future.

The Overman, as different from man as man is from the animals, is not a myth, but rather an "economical" exigence of the Will to Power. In fact, he represents the necessary compensation for the degradation, the loss of energy, evidenced by the present species that has been leveled down. The Will to Power must be able to retrieve itself wholly in the figure of the Overman, since it has degenerated wholly in the figure of man. Thus, the Overman does not fulfill humanity but rather that which, in humanity, is more originary than humanity—namely, the Will to Power: the Overman is the fulfillment not of the essence of man, but of the essence of life.

It might seem utopian that two such different species of thinking beings, which Nietzsche envisages "separated as much as could possibly be," could ever subsist "side by side" far in the future. But that is only because we find it so difficult to think of the opposition master/slave in terms *other* than those of domination or dialectical reciprocity. Meanwhile, though, the opposition Overman/man first of all simply continues to push to the very limit the fundamental antinomy governing any type of moral construction: the opposition between gregarious/passive/vulgar and solitary/affirmative/ noble. These two fundamental determinations of the Will to Power end up by existing in absolute separation. Secondly, though, for Nietzsche it is possible to conceive of a *reign* that is not at all a *domination:* "Beyond those who dominate, freed from all ties, is where the highest men live: and these make use of the dominators as of instruments."[31] The future "Masters of the Earth" will possess neither political power, nor wealth, nor any effective governing force. Those who actually govern and dominate will themselves be of the slave class. The Overman will not govern or dominate leveled-down humanity. Nietzsche describes him as soft, austere, isolated, sober, powerful, resembling a "god of Epicurus," not concerning himself with men. His reign will therefore be a secret reign. But how will he reign if he places himself beyond all political action and finds himself the butt of disdain for the slaves? He will reign in the sense that he will exercise over humanity an indirect influence, what Nietzsche calls by the name of "grand politics": having been the only one to preserve the power of creating, he will steer the world toward a goal that necessarily remains unknown to men. He will reign inasmuch as he will incarnate precisely the possibility of a future. The Caesarism of the Overman—nonviolent Caesarism ("Caesar with the soul of Christ")—must be understood as a *tyranny of an artist.* The "Masters of the Earth" will, as artists do, mold and fashion the masses of humanity to the extent to which, unknown to these masses, they can serve the "masters" as an instrument. Indeed, only these latter will be conscious of any higher goal. Moreover, this "artistic" side of the Overman does not only signify that he shall gather into himself all the characteristics of various creators of the past (scholars, heroes, poets); it really points to something quite different from artistic talents or gifts, even prodigious ones. It points out that art is henceforth to be acknowledged as the highest value, that the principle of evaluation has been fundamentally turned about.

The Overman is only possible once the transmutation of values is accomplished. By its very nature, this transmutation presupposes a radical transformation at the core of the Will to Power, a transformation in which weakness and negation are once and for all eliminated. Everything will be transfigured, because all creation will find itself liberated at long last from every fetter. In its final form, the transmutation will no longer retain anything but affirmation: it will place at the summit of the hierarchy the value of pure affirmation—that value which, throughout all its infinite differences, will procure the highest differentiation of the Will to Power— namely, *Art*. Thus the Platonic domination of science over art gets abolished or, rather, turned about. It is no longer the artist, but rather the scholar, who will be placed at several removes from the truth (thought of here in terms of adequation to the Will to Power). Why, though, does art have "more value" than truth? In Nietzsche there is not to be found any sort of aestheticism. Art is not a refuge, although there are certain statements that might suggest a withdrawal in the face of truth (considered, however, as knowledge): "We have art so that we will not perish from truth."[32] But the (future) primacy of art rests on a twofold necessity governing the very relation between art and knowledge, once these are envisaged in genealogical fashion. *First,* knowledge is always derived: it comes from a primordial and forgotten artistic creation that is none other than the very creation of language as "an artistic formation of metaphors" (these being later mummified into concepts). Science retrieves, in the form of icy, bloodless, and discolored concepts, the images and the schemas that language had primordially superimposed on the world. But it is art that first of all made the Chaos over into anthropomorphic form. The man of knowledge, the conquering and faithful one, is an artist who does not know himself. To know means simply to rediscover schemas that the artistic instinct has already cast over things. *Second,* if art has to become the highest value, it is because art corresponds best to, is most adequate to, the essence of the Will to Power as permanent growth of the self, as unfathomable depth of beneficent and exalting illusion, and as reinforced affirmation. If ever since *The Birth of Tragedy* Nietzsche has called art "the highest task and the authentically metaphysical activity" (see the end of the preface of that work), it is because art is the "great stimulus of life": art drives the creator on to overcome himself, art enlarges the world by returning it to its originally explosive and chaotic character. Art is drunkenness, celebration, orgy, break with identity—whereas science contents itself with ordering that which is basically already acquired. If art intensifies the feeling of power, it is because art reaffirms all reality in and through its power of establishing as real any "appearance" simply by confirming it *as* an appearance. The appearance is selected, corrected, and magnified; but this procedure entails an adherence to what has always been regarded merely as illusory: it entails a glorification of illusion as illusion.

Finally, the transmutation gives birth to the ideal of a species of knowledge that need no longer be the enemy of art but that, in submitting itself to art, would be submitting itself directly to the Will to Power. Such is the ideal of the "Gay Science," a science that is also *tragic* (for what is in Nietzsche's sense "tragic" is not at all sad or pessimistic: it is the state in which, thanks to an affirmation of the highest degree, we are able to include within ourselves, and to vindicate, even the deepest suffering). In *The Birth of Tragedy* Dionysian tragedy found its most original representation in the phenomenon of musical dissonance—i.e., in the pleasure felt in pain itself. Suffering thereby ceases to be an argument against life. Now, the enterprise of knowing has always up to the present time been seriousness, pain, and labor (all previous judgments of value have been dominated by the idea of work). Knowing has been funereal, deathly, a desire to finish up with life, a will to die, individual and moralizing asceticism. In contrast, an artistic manner of knowing tends toward breaking down the narrow limits of individual identity, something that the Dionysian wisdom of the first Greeks, the Greeks before Plato, had been able to do. What *The Gay Science* teaches is the loftiest teaching of Nietzsche (we can just as well say "of Dionysus," since this teaching ultimately destroys even the identity of the proper name of him who proffers it), "innocence of becoming," which is the same as the "Eternal Return of the Same."

THE ETERNAL RETURN

The doctrine of the Eternal Return makes itself felt first and foremost as an experience: a *multifaceted experience,* since it presents itself to us at the same time as a pure effort of thought, as a test, as a particular moment of lived experience, and, finally, as an attempt at having an ethical character.

In *Thus Spoke Zarathustra,* in the chapter "On Redemption," the doctrine is introduced in the form of a question: how can the Will to Power liberate itself from resentment, specifically that resentment which is turned into hatred of time? How can it apprehend time differently than as a passage, a disappearance, a non-being, wherein it recognizes its own passage, its own disappearance, its own nothingness? How can it liberate itself from the entire weight of the negative, from that which at the bottom of its heart is but its own will to disappear, its will to nothingness?

How can the condemnation, the "vengeance" that is brought to bear upon Becoming, be erased? How are we to escape the idea that everything that passes deserves to pass, is therefore without value and is therefore, by disappearing, simply undergoing its just punishment for the sin of having ever existed? Nietzsche sees this idea as very old: he finds it even at the origin of Greek philosophy—namely in the thought of Anaximander, according to which Becoming is guilty, the death of beings representing castigation for their mistake of having been born. In the face of this long tradition, how are we to recover "the innocence of Becoming"?

For the Will, "redemption" must be something quite different from "reconciliation," for thus would still remain, by its dialectical operation, the negative at the core of the positive. The redeemed Will must cut itself off, absolutely and radically, from the Will's saying "No!" in order to refashion itself into the pure Will saying "Yes!" But what is it that this "Yes!" affirms? It affirms that against which the malignant will revolted, namely, time itself: time as the past that has already passed by, as the action of passing away, as the passage itself. The Will to Power must learn to "will backwards" *(zurückwollen)*—i.e., so deeply to will the past and the passage itself that the passage vanishes of its own accord as *mere* passage, changing itself thereby into incessant passage, into a passage that is always present, into Eternal Return. In this way, not only will human time be "saved" from death, but the Becoming of the entire world will find its redemption. However, this enigmatic metamorphosis of Becoming into Re-coming, into coming back, is only announced as a possibility: it depends on the will's being able to "will backwards"—i.e., being able, on the one hand, to affirm in all truth both the past and the passage itself, and, on the other hand, to turn back into itself in order to affirm itself as willing the passage. What we have here, then, is the possibility of a conversion of the will. In the chapter entitled "On the Vision and the Riddle," this possibility, still *purely hypothetical,* reappears, this time no longer as one of a new relationship of volition with the past, but as a possibility of a new relation between the present taken in itself and the past taken in *itself.* Nietzsche does not at all set out to prove that the Return is actually inscribed in the course of things; he rather introduces a simple fiction or a hypothesis, like a free play of the imagination, that comes out in the form of a question: "And if everything that *is* has already *been?*" Now, this fiction assumes an intrinsic value to the extent that it immediately proves itself capable of conferring a value by making one thing appear as a double necessity correlative to, or following upon, the fiction: if the present is a repetition of the past, then every instant must find itself multiplied to infinity, both forward and backward, and be swollen by its own repetition until it is equal to eternity. Then, too, every future must already be past and what is possible must be defined in terms of what is already accomplished. Finally, if everything comes back, no cause exterior to Becoming is thinkable, and Becoming determines itself simply because it is *already* determined the moment it is past. Everything is equally necessary.

The idea of this consequence appears first off as rather sinister and dismal. But then the idea of the Eternal Return is itself a *test:* it represents "the heaviest burden" weighing down on us.[33] In fact, it comes uncomfortably close to complete nihilism. If everything has already been, if everything is bound to come back, not just in a similar but in identical fashion, isn't everything indifferent? What goal could such a repetition have? Thus it is the ghastly gnome (in the chapter "On the Vision and the Riddle," §2), that "spirit of heaviness," who enunciates for the first time an affirmation fit to inspire disgust at one's own existence as well as to drive one into despair, namely: "Time itself is a circle." In his mouth the formula "everything returns" resonates as an eternal "in vain!" If everything comes back, everything is eternal: but if one thing is worth as much as the next, everything is equally useful and useless, and the best and the worst are worth the same. Thus, although it is the very reverse, the idea of the Eternal Return resembles at first, and in caricature, the most extreme form of Nihilism: as Nietzsche says, "Let us think this thought in its most terrifying form: present existence, just as it is, without either meaning or goal, but unavoidably returning, without even a finale in nothingness: 'the Eternal Return.' "[34] He places quotation marks around the expression because this thought is a test—i.e., an instrument of discrimination: who would want to start his life all over again under absolutely identical conditions? Only those who are strong, only those who consider their existence as worth being infinitely repeated, will be able to bear such a thought. If this doctrine ever takes hold, it will accentuate the cleavage between the strong and the weak, it will reinforce the strong by driving them to affirm themselves even more, while in contrast it will crush the weak by driving them to want to negate themselves even more still. It will thereby contribute to the great task of selection. But how will this doctrine come to take hold? In the same way a religion does, the elect here being those who have faith in their own lives as lives worthy of being repeated innumerable times. A religion diametrically opposed to all religions that only promise a better life, happiness in a world beyond, this doctrine offers happiness *on earth* to all those who are capable of this faith. It is a religion that, Nietzsche says, will be "easy" on unbelievers, for although it has a paradise, it has no hell: "He who does not believe will be conscious of life as fugitive."[35] It is a religion without sin and without error, for everything that repeats itself infinitely is neither good nor bad, it is innocent; it simply *is*. As the only religion devoid of nostalgia, eliminating all desire to flee the world and every devaluation of the "here and now" for the sake of some transcendence or other, this doctrine establishes, as any religion does, a tie with the divine understood as a totality and a unity of self and world. But, as we shall see, Nietzsche's sense of "divinity" is not synonymous with that of perfection; it is rather synonymous with absolute affirmation embracing imperfection itself. Finally, the Eternal Return must be understood as a religion of pure possibility: just as the simple thought of eternal damnation was able to modify the actions of men, so the faith in each instant of life as being worthy of returning should raise humanity far beyond itself. Just as the religion of the Return represents a test as the level of the individual, the Return of everything constitutes a test for the Will to Power in general, inasmuch as it implies the return of all forms of Nihilism, the return of weakness and the return of decadence. For the Return signifies that even if the Will to Power liberates itself and attains to the Overman, the nihilistic and reactionary man will nonetheless eternally return. Here lies the greatest obstacle that the Will to Power will have to face. It can only triumph over this obstacle by adhering to a new kind of "necessity," one that also includes, but does not itself resuscitate, the negative.

As an experience, in the sense of a possibility and a test, the Return also appears as an apparently very simple experience of a privileged moment: that of having said "yes" to the instant. An affirmation that is truly full and complete is also contagious: it bursts into a chain of affirmations that knows no limits. "If we say *yes* to a single instant we say *yes* to all existence." However, this instant is a privileged one: only an instant of joy can be affirmed in this way. Only joy possesses the power to will itself and thereby to will the totality of things, including pain: "Have you ever said *yes* to a joy? Oh, my friends, then you have also said *yes* to all pain. All things are enchained with one another, wrapped up in one another, bound together by love."[36] In a single instant felt as necessary—necessary right through to its most extreme contingency—a necessity reveals itself to us that ties this instant to all others. Such an instant cannot exist without implying all the others. Once its own contingency is eliminated, all contingencies are eliminated. Any experience of joy that is supremely affirmative is also, by being an experience that proliferates and multiplies the instant, the experience of the necessity of eternal and universal ties: "If you have ever, just once, willed that one time come a second time, . . . then you have willed the return of everything!" This experience represents the exact *reverse* of the fundamental experience of Nihilism that had conferred value and meaning on everything from the standpoint of pain, from the standpoint of the experience of a will that could not will itself, that willed only to be rid of itself. The experience of joy is so strong that it can will, as being part of the eternal ties, pain itself, death and the "grave." "All joy wills the eternity of all things."[38] The idea of the Return is begotten and sustained by joy.

Finally, considered as applicable to action, the doctrine of the Return constitutes an ethical claim. We are to act at every instant as though each of our acts were destined to be repeated an infinite number of times in exactly the same way: in my own life I am to try to modify my relationship with the instant, to will each act just as intensely as though it were *not* destined to pass, but rather to remain eternally. I should will the idea that what I now do involves my eternal being. However, this ethic opposes in reality every categorical imperative ("I should") and proposes in contrast an imperative of necessity ("I am constrained to"). As Nietzsche says: "My doctrine teaches to live in such a way that you are *forced* to wish to relive everything all over again." The law of the Eternal Return cannot be formulated in the indicative mood, but its imperative is at the same time a necessity. "Let us impress upon our life the image of eternity."[39] This life is your eternal life: *Non alia, sed haec vita sempiterna.* I am to act in such a way as to be forced to will the repetition of my acts, and, inversely, I am to will whatever it is I am constrained to do. This ethic—namely, being forced to will a necessity that is the necessity of volition itself—is circular. The significance of this circle is: the Will which wills the Eternal Return is that will which wills itself, which finds *in itself* the necessity to will itself.

But just what is the "necessity" of which we speak here? Nietzsche declares that he has set himself the task of "liquidating the concept of necessity," and as a matter of fact the formula that sums up the wisdom of the Eternal Return, *Amor fati,* is meant to shatter the traditional concept of necessity. For fate, in Nietzsche's sense of *fatum,* revolves around a necessity that is neither the causal necessity of the laws of nature (mechanism), nor that of a blind fatalism "in the Turkish sense" (as Nietzsche says), nor that of a liberty determining itself. In his sense of the term, "necessity" is no longer a category; rather, it encompasses those logical contraries that are Chaos and Form, chance and law. "I want to learn more and more to see what is necessary in things and what is beautiful in them: in this way I will be one of those who make things beautiful. *Amor fati:* may that be my love from now on!"[40] Inasmuch as everything is necessary, *Amor fati* is, for conceptual logic, a contradiction. But what has been eliminated is precisely the opposition between love as an activity of the will, and destiny as a purely passive determination of that which is already settled. Volition that has been transfigured by the Return is no longer qualified by desire, aspiration, or want: it is no longer a will in search of what is not yet. Rather, what here presents itself is the fullness and perfection of a will that bears down on what is. This volition is love, where to love is to will that what is (as such and not otherwise) be what it is an infinite number of times over. In the Volition that loves necessity, the apparent difference is narrowed down between the Will to Power as "being more" and the Eternal Return as "being settled." Here, "necessity" embraces all at once the *fatum,* the will, and the tie uniting the two—a tie that is also the "ring" uniting all things. For a volition that loves necessity to the point of being *its own* necessity (*ego fatum*), there is no longer any contradiction between determinism, freedom, and contingency. That is why "the most extreme fatalism is identical with chance and creativity."[41] There is no longer really any chance for a Will that affirms itself indissolubly as its own destiny and that of the world. This will is absolute freedom within absolute necessity, since it wills so strongly, and affirms so invariably, whatever happens to itself or to the world, no matter whether it has chosen it or not. "Every 'it was' is a fragment, an enigma, terrifying chance until such time as the creative will says in addition: but that is just what I wanted!"[42] Meanwhile, though, does not the *ego,* by unifying itself in this way with the fatalism of the Return, lose its own unity and identity?

Indeed, the idea of the Return, once it is *experienced* in all its varying forms, leads to time-honored distinctions being shattered—distinctions that, according to the principles of identity and contradiction, traditionally defined the modalities of existence. Just as individuality cannot be the same as totality of the world, in the same way things cannot belong at the same to the categories of possibility, contingency, and necessity, any more than they can refer back at the same moment to time and to eternity. Traditional logic prohibits us from confounding the order of freedom, the order of chance, the order of destiny. Even the speculative logic of Hegel places these conflicting categories as "moments" within the reconciled totality of Absolute Knowledge. But Nietzsche attacks the very idea of metaphysical contradiction and antimony. If the thought of the Eternal Return is the "most easy-going" thought, it is so because it melts the glaze of metaphysical antitheses and volatizes logical contraries. Indeed, the Eternal Return is neither real nor ideal, but something like a fatal possibility. As a way in which a Will to Power can be supremely affirmative, it gives birth to a new tie, to a new necessity, out of the dissolution of the old oppositions. This new "necessity" harmonizes itself with its old "contrary," namely chance, disorder, and dispersion—just as did the word "appearance" (which, in the end, contained as well the sense of the "true world"). In other words, the complete circle of the Return (the coherence of everything) includes Chaos (the incoherence of everything). The divine ring of eternity is a broken ring. However, the theory of the Eternal Return, just like the theory of the "vicious circle," consists precisely in according the most positive value, in attributing perfection, to the break in the circle. The break signifies here that the circle is a form without goal, a form that contains in itself chaos. "Universal chaos of the sort excluding all activity having a final purpose does not contradict the idea of circular movement: it's just that this movement is an arational necessity. . . ." Thus the inclusion of Chaos in the necessity of the circle does not constitute a synthesis or a reconciliation in the manner of Hegel: chance and disorder are not "surpassed" by, but rather gathered up into, the perfect circle, such a circle being in its very essence defective. The totality of the Return is bursted totality, a shattered totality. As a symbol, its necessity is expressed in the coherence that unites the scattered starts of a single constellation: "Supreme constellation of being! . . . Emblem of necessity." Produced by a pure affirmation "which no

wish attains, which no negation sullies'' (being emancipated from all desire
and want), this necessity within and of disorder surpasses every antithesis
thinkable: it is ''the celestial necessity that forces even chance events to
dance in stellar formation.''[43]

It is clear why Nietzsche was never able to offer a scientific demonstration
of his doctrine as a theory of nature, or arrive at the point of defending the
Eternal Return in realistic terms: he would have had to submit his argumentation to the logical principles that science obeys but that his own doctrine
repudiates.

Thus though all the while annulling the major metaphysical opposition,
namely being/becoming, the thought of the Eternal Return still preserves the
one as well as the other of these two terms as possible ''points of view.''
That which is still permanent within Becoming is the circle itself. Being the
law of Becoming, the circle is not itself something that has become. Even
though Becoming is in itself what is unstable, namely Chaos, the circle is the
highest stabilization possible for this instability. As a consequence, the
Eternal Return appears to be just one more interpretation, an interpretation
of Becoming *according to the perspective of Being;* but it is at the same time
the *highest* to which the Will to Power can raise itself, for this interpretation
secures for the Will to Power the greatest of triumphs, the eternal triumph.
By willing the circle, the Will secures itself for itself and secures for itself
constant mastery over Chaos—i.e., the certainty of always being able to
overcome even the Return of the negative. Here we have what Nietzsche
calls the ''summit of contemplation'' as well as a ''recapitulation,'' the
summation of his abyssal thought: ''To impress upon Becoming the character of Being—*this* is the highest form of the Will to Power . . . That
everything returns—here a world of Becoming comes closest to the world of
Being.''[44] Thus the Eternal Return appears as that perspective of the Will to
Power that confers upon a world fundamentally interpreted as a world of
Becoming the highest value it can have. This perspective eternalizes the
world of Becoming from the very same point of view that, throughout all of
history, has devalued it—namely, the fictitious point of view of a world of
Being. Thus values are reversed in a twofold way.

In the end, by effacing all the differences on which language and history
are built (especially the opposition between remembering and forgetting),
the thought of the Return leaves us face to face with a most exacting aporia.
Paradoxically, the affirmation of the Return of the Identical and the Same
destroys all partial identities, especially the firm identity of the self as
opposed to the identity of the world, since the ''total'' identity of self and
world does away with the particular identity of the individual self. What is,
then, the ''new history'' that Nietzsche proclaims shall now begin once the
idea of the Return has taken hold? The ''logic'' that eliminates personal
identity from the *ego fatum* makes Nietzsche say: ''At bottom I am all the

names of history."[45] Every identity, including that of the self and that of proper names, comes down to an interchangeable mask bound up with the universal Game, which is itself only an indefinite shifting of masks. What is the significance of this loss of "proper" names? Is this ultimate explosion merely the leap into madness of Nietzsche the man, the lived moment when the abolition of the antitheses nourishing metaphysical language reduces the philosopher to science? The language that the self uses to provide itself with a fictitious center, the language of fixed and arbitrary identities, appears to be so much bound up with this system of contradistinctions that *denying* this system casts one back into the dissociated and inexpressible clutches of Chaos. From the moment when the self of Nietzsche coincides with the totality of history, he deprives himself of both speech and writing. Like Dionysus, his last "identity," Nietzsche's self is torn to pieces and scattered about, all in accordance with the perspective of the dispersed totality that he will henceforth incarnate. The final silence of madness shall be, as he put it shortly before ceasing to write, "the mask that hides a knowledge which is fatal and *too sure.*" But what kind of knowledge is this? Perhaps it is knowledge that language cannot smash the principle of identity without smashing itself, and yet cannot submit itself to this principle without renouncing the effort to bring the depth of Being to words. Thus the destruction of metaphysical language can, in the case of Nietzsche, be looked at as an experiment pushed so far as to destroy the destroyer *qua* speaker. This attempt at subversion—one that both succeeded and misfired, since it forced to the forefront the essential impasse of Western metaphysical discourse— makes Nietzsche the greatest "tempter" for we who have no other language.

If, as Nietzsche says, "every word is a prejudice,"[46] and if grammar will always be re-establishing an indefinite multitude of substitutes for the God who is dead, what more precious does he bequeath to us than that which, throughout the derailed syntax of these destroyed words and the astonishing distribution of the terms (i.e., the limits) of this discredited language, will never cease to awaken in us the infinite carefulness of a "great distrust" that can return language to its proper course?

NOTES

1. *On Truth and Lie in an Extra-Moral Sense,* §1.
2. *Twilight of the Idols,* "What the Germans Have Lost," §7.
3. "Letter to Fuchs, 26 August 1888."
4. *Beyond Good and Evil,* §186.
5. *The Genealogy of Morals;* II, §12.
6. *The Will to Power,* §693.
7. *The Innocence of Becoming;* II, §874.
8. *WP,* §46 *et al.*

9. *WP*, §715.

10. *WP*, §692.

11. *WP*, §815.

12. *WP*, §619.

13. *GM*, very last sentence.

14. *WP*, §715.

15. *WP*, §1.

16. *WP*, §269.

17. *TI*, "How the 'True World' Finally Became a Fable."

18. *Ibid*.

19. *WP*, §15.

20. *IB;* II, §496.

21. *The Gay Science*, §110.

22. *WP*, §493.

23. *IB;* II, §116.

24. *WP*, §333.

25. *TI;* "The Problem of Socrates," §9.

26. *IB;* II, §362.

27. *Ecce Homo;* I, §6.

28. *GM;* III, §27.

29. *IB;* II, §1270.

30. *IB;* II, §1274.

31. *WP*, §998.

32. *WP*, §822.

33. *GS*, §341.

34. *WP*, §55.

35. *IB;* II, §1347.

36. *Thus Spoke Zarathustra;* "The Drunken Song," §10.

37. *Ibid*.

38. *Ibid*.

39. *IB;* II, §1343.

40. *GS*, §276.

41. *IB;* II, §1369.

42. *Zarathustra;* "On Redemption."

43. *Zarathustra;* "The Seven Seals."

44. *WP*, §617.

45. "Letter to Burckhardt, 6 January 1889."

46. *Human, All Too Human;* II, §355.

Alphonso Lingis

THE WILL TO POWER

We would like to ask of Nietzsche: what is meant by the will to power? What is meant by saying that life is will to power? What are the powers of life? What does it mean to say that the will to power is the basis of all that is?

Thus we would put to Nietzsche the familiar form of the philosophical question. It asks after the essence of the Will to Power. The philosophical question "what is . . . ?" is answered by supplying the quiddity, the essence. Philosophical thought is a questioning of appearances, an investigation of their essence, their organizing structure, their telos, their meaning.

This questioning assumes that the sequences of appearances mean something, indicate, refer to an underlying something, a *hypokeimenon*. It is metaphysical; it takes the appearances to be signs. Philosophical interrogation of the world is a reading of the world, an assumption of the succession of sensorial images as signs of intelligible essences.

Nietzsche refuses this reading of the world; he declares that the essences that the philosophical intelligence arrives at are in fact only the senses of the things—their meanings. The metaphysical reading of the world is a world-hermeneutics—an interpretation, an estimation, a valuation. "Insofar as the word 'knowledge' has any meaning, the world is knowable; but it is interpretable otherwise, it has no meaning behind it, but countless meanings.—'Perspectivism.' "[1]

It is possible to interpret this as Nietzsche's virulent and extremist statement of the central thesis of modern idealism: the essences found through philosophical interrogation do not reveal the things themselves productive of their appearances, issuing signs of themselves, but reveal the acts and laws of the subject that interprets. In this sense Heidegger has called Nietzsche the most coherent subjectivist and the last Cartesian.

But there are Nietzschean reasons behind his statement, not Kantian ones. First, if the philosophical reading finds behind the flow of appearances an order of essences that accounts for them, Nietzsche finds behind those very essences, those senses, those interpretations, the Will to Power that accounts for them. But the Will to Power is not an essence, a quiddity behind the essences. It is, Nietzsche says, just "the last instance which we could go back to. . . ." It is an instance rather than a substance or a substrate; it is the force behind all the forms. Heidegger says that it is the Being in all the beings—that is, the productivity that pro-duces, that brings forth to their stance and their constancy, and brings out into the open, into the light, the forms of being that scintillate in the theater of the world.

The will to power is not just power or force, but Will to Power: always will for more power.[2] It is not an essence; it is neither structure, telos, nor meaning, but continual sublation of all telos, transgression of all ends, production of all concordant and contradictory meanings, interpretations, valuations. It is the chaos, the primal fund of the unformed—not matter, but force beneath the cosmos, which precedes the forms and makes them possible as well as transitory.

Will to Power can function neither as the reason that accounts for the order of essences, nor as the foundation that sustains them in being. What could function as ground—as ratio and as foundation—for the order of essences is the stability of ultimate unity, is God or the transcendental ego, both of which Nietzsche declares to be dead. The Will to Power is an abyss *(Abgrund),* the groundless chaos beneath all the grounds, all the foundations, and it leaves the whole order of essences groundless. "Indeed, he will doubt whether a philosopher could *possibly* have 'ultimate and real' opinions, whether behind every one of his caves there is not, must not be, another, deeper cave—a more comprehensive, stranger, richer world beyond the surface, an abysmally deep ground behind every ground, under every attempt to furnish 'grounds.' "[3]

If Being, then, is not a ground, but an abyss, chaos, there is consequently in Nietzsche a quite new, nonmetaphysical or transmetaphysical understanding of beings, of things.

We noted a moment ago that Nietzsche attacks metaphysical thought for its character of being a reading of the world: an assumption that the appearances that emerge in the theater of the world are signs. But, no doubt even more radically, especially in the *Nachlass* notes, he offers a determined and coherent attack on the metaphysical concept of things—not only on the metaphysical quest for essences, telos, or meanings behind the sensorial configurations, but even on the also metaphysical quest for *things* in the appearances. The metaphysical concept of a being, of one thing appearing diversely, appeals to the notion of unity, of the one in the many. But Nietzsche declares, "Whatever is real, whatever is true, is neither one nor even reducible to one."[4]

Beings are appearances staggered across space in retardation systems. Each appearance diverges from the preceding one; no two snowflakes that fall are identical, and no two scintillations of one snowflake are identical. Hegel jeered at Leibniz for having invited the court ladies to do experimental metaphysics strolling in the gardens, and seeing that two tree leaves do not have the same aspect. But scientific detectives also find that there are no two grains of sand absolutely identical, no two hands with the same fingerprints, no two typewriters with the same type, no two revolvers that scratch their bullets with the same striations.

To see difference is not to see absolute opposition, contradition; it is to see gradations of divergence. But if we see greater and lesser difference, that means we also see lesser and greater similarity. If in a succession of appearances each differs from the preceding one, each is also similar to it; otherwise one would not say even that this one diverges from that one.

Thus Being, *physis,* incessant unfolding of a show of ever new, ever divergent appearances—continual differentiation—is also continual *logos,* continual assembling, assimilation, of all that appears.

Now, philosophical thought is com-prehensive thought, a taking of many in one grasp, a taking of many *as* one. It is grounded in the inaugural metaphysical thesis that if two entities appear as similar, that, whereas in some respects they are not the same, in other respects they *are* the same. It is this identification of the identical that is constitutive of the consciousness of things in the flux of appearances. The philosophical consciousness of things is essentially hermeneutical; taking the ever divergent appearances of a sequence to refer to, to have one and the same significance, it constitutes them as signs.

The identical, the ideal being, whose presence is not removed by the extensivity of space and is not deferred by the passage of time, functions as the condition for the possibility of things. It is the ground of things: the reason for their recognizability and the foundation, the basis, of their presence in ever dispersing time and ever separating space.

It is the *reiteration* of the same ideal terms—the essences, the self-identical unities—that make it possible for there to be a display of ever different and ever similar appearances across time and space.

To comprehend is to see the identical—what space does not dissociate and what time does not defer—in the different. This does not mean that one sees beyond space and time, that a metaphysical vision opens upon horizons of eternity—nonspatial horizons that do not separate what they exhibit. Philosophical thought determines the seen being as *ousia:* the present. To see is to become present to something; it is to see what is present in the present.

The ideal, then, is not an existent utterly indeterminate as to time; rather, the ideal is the ever present. That is always what the metaphysical insights and arguments establish: not that there is a sublime mind that sees eternal beings subsisting in eternal horizons, but rather that there is, in the sequences of ever divergent appearances, a recurrence of the same: a recurrence of the same meaning in different expressions, a recurrence of the same genus in different though similar individuals. The real metaphysical distinction is not between one realm of realities all of which are temporal in their existence and another realm of idealities, utterly impervious to and independent of time in every sense; it is between one order of realities whose existence is transient, and another order of idealities whose existence is reiterated as time itself advances by the reiteration of the present.

The ground, then, the reason and the foundation for a sequence of ever divergent appearances, is unity, the self-identical that recurs. Unity is the origin of being: the different is the derived. A thing, metaphysically understood, is a unity that recurs across time, that reiterates itself across time and space and, in doing so, generates a sequence of differing appearances of itself.

If at the basis of foundation of things is an order of unities, at the ground of the order of self-identical idealities there is the One itself, identity itself. Identity is not only the condition for us to know the species and to know real individual things in the flux; it is also the metaphysical condition for the very reality of realities, and for the very ideality of essences.

The One, identity, exists in repetition, reiterating itself, recurring. It is thus the source of the world. The world is the show, the exhibition, of ever different and ever similar beings generated by a ground, a force of unique Being.

In the Christian epoch the One, source of the world, ground of all existence and of all intelligibility, was equated with the God of Jewish monotheism. In the modern epoch it is identified with the ego. The transcendental ego is the self-identical existence, the pole of unity that recurs across time, that identifies itself in all its experiences; as such, it is the source and foundation, the ground, of the reality that unfolds about it.

To affirm that the ground is Will to Power means, it is said, that Nietzsche conceives of Being as force, as dynamism; to exist is to make one's presence felt. And it is to affirm that the ground is not only the support of constancy, but is also productivity, parturition, creativity. No doubt. But more radically, to affirm that the ground is will to power means that the ground is *not* identity, the One, but original difference. We have in Nietzsche a thought that is not persuaded by the immemorial metaphysical thesis that similitude presupposes identity, that to see a sequence of appearances as different, and therefore as similar, is to see something that, from one to the next, recurs.

God is dead—specifically the God of monotheism, the monotonotheistic God. The gods have died, Nietzsche writes, but they have died of laughter upon hearing the Jewish god claim to be the sole god.[5] And in Nietzsche the ego—sometimes called a grammatical fiction, sometimes called a mask— has lost its self-identity. (Nietzsche carries out this repudiation of the identical consistently, carries it into a rejection of atomism as ultimate understanding in physics; his critique of science is essentially a polemic against logical identity, mathematical equality, and physical equilibrium.) For Nietzsche the identical is always the derived, the *become*.

The Will to Power is originally plural.[6] It is not an origin that generates the differing and the differed by reiterating itself. Difference is constitutive of the original being of force: force is in its quantitative difference from another force. Force cannot exist in the singular. And force from its origin is different from itself: power is of itself always will unto more power.[7] Force does not exist in self-identity, but only in the discharge—that is, in the surpassing of itself. There cannot have been an ideal moment of origin when force existed in self-identity, was one with itself.

> A quantum of force is equivalent to a quantum of drive, will, effect—more, it is nothing other than precisely this very driving, willing, effecting, and only owing to the seduction of language (and of the fundamental errors of reason that are petrified in it) which conceives and misconceives all effects as conditioned by something that causes effects, by a "subject," can it appear otherwise. . . . The popular mind separates the lightning from its flash and takes the latter for an action, for the operation of a subject called lightning. . . . But there is . . . no "being" behind doing, effecting, becoming; "the doer" is merely a fiction added to the deed—the deed is everything. . . . Scientists do no better when they say "force moves," "force causes," and the like . . . our entire science still lies under the misleading influence of language and has not disposed of that little changeling, the "subject" (the atom, for example, is such a changeling, as is the Kantian "thing-in-itself") . . .[8]

Will is force that commands. Will exists originally in relationship, but not in relationship with the involuntary; it is not, for example, exercised mysteriously on muscles and nerves, still less on matter in general. It is not a force that is simply transmitted to passive matter; it is exercised on another will.[9] Will to power orders, ordains, but not with a demiurgic or hylomorphic action, which presupposes a primal passivity. To Nietzsche what is unformed is not matter, but force, is not passive, but chaotic. Power, then—domination, ordering—cannot be conceived except in original contention, in *polemos*. Will exists in the relationship between a commanding will and an obeying will—one that obeys always, more or less—for in order to be able to obey, it is necessary to be able to command oneself.[10]

The will, in Will to Power, is not of the order of representation; will and power are not to be conceived in terms of psychic and physical. The will, in Will to Power, is the differential element of force. Difference is enacted not in a reiteration of the same, but in the self-affirmation of a force exercised against another force. A will commands; it affirms itself. For Nietzsche, profoundly anti-Hegelian, that does not mean that it comprehends the other, assimilates, appropriates the non-self. For a will to affirm itself is rather for it to affirm its difference. For Nietzsche, the feeling of distinction—the pathos of distance—is the fundamental affect of power.

Power affirms its difference; difference occurs as power, as the *force* of Being. Nietzsche's thought still has the form of an understanding, of a movement beneath the appearance to their ground. But this thought is no longer a comprehension in the specific sense of a thought dependent on the idea of identity. It is a thought in which the exhibition of Being is no longer conceived as a process by which an origin existing as unity, as self-identity, differentiates itself without dissipating itself, differentiating itself in the reiteration of itself.

There are consequences, then, for the way persons and things are to be conceived. Properly speaking, there are no longer any things or any persons. There are no facts, there are only interpretations and interpretations of interpretations.[11] There are no persons, selves, egos; there are only masks and masks of masks. For, to be a mask, the mask must mask its very nature as mask, and thus it continually generates a sequence of masks and masks of masks, without there being any person, any self, any self-identical ego, behind.

Is it possible to think of the beings that unfold in sequences of appearances, and to conceive of the faces, the personas, that make their appearance in the theater of the world, in such a way that they do not require God and do not require a transcendental ego in order to be beings and in order to be personas? Is it possible to think that similarity need not presuppose identity?

To find such beings intelligible we would have to learn an entirely new apprehension—not an essential comprehension, but a differential and genealogical apprehension of appearances (which are autogenerative differential powers).

In the metaphysical conception of a thing, the force of its being consists, on the one hand, in an internal factor of ideal unity, ground of its constancy, by which it can differentiate itself without dispersing itself; and, on the other hand, in the telos, the internal finality by which it coheres with itself, commanding its own limits, its own ends. For Nietzsche, a being is a power surpassing itself in time and space, maintaining its own force, its difference, in contention with forces in affinity with it and forces in opposition to it. Time and space completely measure the Being of the beings; Being is transience. A being maintains itself by dissociating in space and by deferring its Being through time, thereby generating forms of itself by divergence. Its own force is thus *not* the foundation for the inert stability of its form, but for a plurality of new forms of itself.[12]

A being has not one form, but different forms; it has not one telos, but as many as there are powers orienting it; it has not one essence, but multiple essences, not one meaning behind it, but multiple meanings in its appearances, multiple apparent meanings. There is no essence to be sought behind the appearances, no telos behind the differentiation of the appearances. Nietzsche declares that to understand a being we must keep quite separate the question of its origin and the question of its telos, essence, meaning, morphological structure.[13] A being, a sequence of appearances, is not founded on the reiteration of unity, of identity; difference is original—unity, identity, is something *become*. Thus, Nietzsche teaches that for all things existence precedes essence; the surface is the ground of the depth, the ever divergent appearances are the ground of unity, form, telos, essence, sense. Perspectivism, then, in Nietzsche means something quite different from what it has come to mean in phenomenology: it does not mean that the appearances are profiles of an essential invariant; it means that there are only perspectives. Each appearance is not an appearance of a thing, but the apparition of a power. It is itself a power, it is itself generative. The generating power is not a unity ever present, reiterating itself; each appearance generates the next appearance, divergent from itself. Each *is* by generating difference from itself. The force of its being is not just force, but has the form of Will to Power: that is, always, the will to more power.

The formulation of the eternal return as a cosmological doctrine, in Book IV of *The Will to Power,* is directed against the idea of unity in things— against a teleology in things, against essential unity in things. Nietzsche argues that if the world had a goal, it must have been reached;[14] that if a state of equilibrium is never reached it is not possible.[15] The ideal order of metaphysical essences exists by eternal recurrence. But the Nietzschean doctrine of the Eternal Return states the fate of the Dionysian theater of sensible appearances, of a world without being, without unity, without identity. Metaphysical reiteration of the ideal is founded on God and on the ego; recurrence in the Dionysian world is founded on the death of God and on the dissolution of the ego. Recurrence in the Dionysian world must not be understood as the return of *something* that is, that is one, or that is the same. What recurs is not being, but becoming; not identity, ideality, but difference.

> To impose upon becoming the character of being—that is the supreme will to power. Twofold falsification, on the part of the senses and of the spirit, to preserve a world of that which is, which abides, which is equivalent, etc. That *everything recurs* is the closest *approximation of a world of becoming to a world of being:* the high point of the meditation.[16]

Recurrence is affirmed of the appearances themselves; the appearance itself, as apparition of a force, has the reiterative power to affirm itself. But for an appearance to recur is for it to distend its being in space, to defer in time. There is recurrence *not* of the same essence in different appearances, but of ever divergent appearances.

Such a Dionysian universe is not impervious to understanding, for a sequence of appearances that has different forms, different telos, different essences in a continual but perhaps systematic differentiation can be delivered over to a *new* kind of differential and genealogical understanding. Indeed, it is always delivered over to an artistic understanding, a legislating and commanding power of interpretation.[17] The essence of the thing is but the sense of the thing: it is not an internal morphological power that commands the progression of the unfolding appearances; it is a sense forced upon the appearances in an interpretation.

> The question "what is that?" is an imposition of meaning from some other viewpoint. "Essence," the "essential nature," is something perspective and already presupposes a multiplicity. At the bottom of it there always lies "what is that for *me?*" (for us, for all that lives, etc.). A thing would be defined once all creatures had asked "what is that?" and had answered their question. Supposing one single creature, with its own relationships and perspectives for all things, were missing, then the thing would not yet be "defined." In short: the essence of a thing is only an *opinion* about the "thing." Or rather: "it passes for" is the real "it is," the sole "this is."[18]

The essence—the sequence of essences, of senses—is determined in an interpretation. But that does not mean that for Nietzsche a being is reducible to a pure medley of inconsistent material that the will, the interpreting will, can endow with meaning as it chooses, or in accordance with its own subjective laws for the constitution of objectivity. What interprets is not a contemplative spirit both impotent to act on the things and omnipotent to charge them with its meanings; what interprets is power, is Will to Power, and there can be no such thing as absolute power, solitary power. And if it takes power to interpret, to give sense to, to orient, it is because the being interpreted is itself a force, affirming itself, generating divergent perspectives.[19]

> The "evolution" of a thing, a custom, an organ is thus by no means its *progressus* toward a goal, even less a logical *progressus* by the shortest route and with the least expenditure of force, but a succession of more or less profound, more or less mutually independent processes of subduing, plus the resistances they encounter, the attempts at transformation for the purpose of defence and reaction, and the results of successful counteractions. The form is fluid, but the "meaning" is even more so.[20]

Interpretation then is not merely projecting over the inert stupor of matter the immaterial glow of meaning visible only to the mind that projects it; to assign meaning to a being is not to exercise absolute sovereignty over it. To give sense to it is to orient it; it is to positively struggle with it, it is to concretely overcome the form it has by force.

> Whatever exists, having somehow come into being, is again and again reinterpreted to new ends, taken over, transformed, and redirected by

some power superior to it; all events in the organic world are a subduing, a *becoming master,* and all subduing and becoming master involves a fresh interpretation, an adaptation through which any previous "meaning" and "purpose" are necessarily obscured or even obliterated.[21]

Interpretation proceeds not by some idealist sovereignty of the mind, nor does it proceed by frontal assault, which could only result in a physical equilibrium of forces; it proceeds by the ruse and dissimulation that are laws of life. Life, nascent, must mask itself under the guise of matter in order to be possible at all; a force would not survive did it not first don the masks of the antecedent forces against which it struggles.[22] What is sovereign is always masked.

Thus things are meaningful for Nietzsche in an entirely different way from metaphysical thought. For metaphysical thought the meaning—structure—constitutive of things lies in the sign-character of the appearances by which they refer to and reveal the ideal essences at the ground of reality. For Nietzsche the appearances *are themselves* powers; they generate one another by continual differentiation, and the essences, the meanings interpretation places on them, are symptoms of a Will to Power that orients them. Interpretation of this interpretation can then determine the quality of the forces with which the being is in affinity, and which command it. To interpret its meaning is to determine the quality of the force that gives it meaning. And to determine that quality is to determine whether the Will to Power is affirmative or reactive—noble, sublime, sovereign, or base, vile, servile; it is to determine the order of rank of the interpreting power.

THE WILL TO POWER AS LIFE

What do we mean when we say that life is Will to Power? What do we mean by a powerful life? Just what are the powers of life? Let us take these questions not in the sense of the metaphysical question "what is . . . ?," but rather as the genealogical question "who is . . . ?" Who, then, are powers? This properly Nietzschean question leads us into the Nietzschean kind of genealogical interpretation of that interpretation of all beings that is the Will to Power; this question aims not at a metaphysical essence, but at determining the quality of the Will to Power.

Here, I shall discuss only the forces by which life is affirmation, upsurge, action. The reactive forces, expressed in the functions of conservation, adaptation, utility, mechanical accommodations, regulations involved in life, are comprehensible only in terms of an essentially active conception of life, the revolutionary Nietzschean premise. It is in the figures of the artist, the noble, and the sovereign individual that the powers of life become visible.

The Artist

What is strong in the artist, what makes life in him artistic, is the compulsion to dream and the compulsion to intoxication. The compulsion to dream, the visionary power, is the origin of sculpture, Apollonian art *par excellence,* and then the plastic arts and epic poetry.

It is striking, first, that the artistic power is not to be conceived as a formative power, hylomorphic power, power to form or inform matter, which is passivity and resistance. Sculpture is not to be seen as a development from craft and artisanry, from "making" in the sense of *technè;* it is rather to be conceived as a development from dreams. Apollo, god of the Greek art of sculpture, is "the ruler over the beautiful illusion of the inner world of fantasy."[23] Thus the artistry, the power productive of the art, is not a demiurgic production, an imposition of form by force, but rather imagination—that is, the power to make the invisible visible, the power to make the void radiant. It is an illuminating power: Apollo's name etymologically means, Nietzsche explains, " 'the shining one,' the deity of light."[24] Life is light: vital power means here the power to make phosphoresce what does not make its presence felt of itself, the power to make appear what does not appear of itself.

Secondly, Nietzsche's conception is separated from that of classicism by "the raving discord between art and truth." The work of truth is to set forth, to bring the essence out into the open. Classicism destined art for the work of truth by assigning to the sensorial datum a signifying function; its being is signifying. Thus a form cut in marble, a quick sketch, a few lines on paper, a color, condenses an inexhaustible transphenomenal power. But for Nietzsche, the light, radiant Apollo, is the very element of illusion; the plastic arts are essentially hallucinatory. There are appearances without anything appearing; there is no truth in the luminous visions the artist dreams. It is their inconsistency that is their radiance; they do not reveal a transphenomenal power of the essences of reality. They are rather symptoms of the protean power of life, of the play of light, ever differentiating itself. Here "the will to appearance, to illusion, to deception, to becoming and change (to objectified deception) counts as more profound, primeval, 'metaphysical' than the will to truth, to reality."[25]

The Apollonian art of sculpture is a vision of a world of forms immobilized in stillness, tranquility, time arrested—the suffering, the striving of time suspended. For Nietzsche the serenity of the Olympian friezes is not the stupor of the matter in which they are embedded, but precisely the serenity of illusions that do not have any generating essence, any inexhaustible transphenomenal power, behind them, that are fixed in their own individuality, in the absoluteness of their presence, without a future, in fatality.

And illusion heals. What is healing in dreams, and what is redemptive in the elaboration of those public waking dreams that are the works of plastic art, is their manifest illusoriness. The recognition of the falsity and error of dreams, the not taking them to be real, is constitutive of their importance; they leave the dreamer free, they give him free space for the upsurge of his power. "Perhaps many will, like myself, recall how amid the dangers and terrors of dreams they have occasionally said to themselves in self-encouragement, and not without success: 'It is a dream! I will dream on!' "[26]

The artistic vision exalts power, heals the will, and gives strength to look upon the horrible and the absurd, transfigured by the light, redeemed. Before a world whose absurdity defeats its will to know, whose cruelty destroys its action, the sick, suffering will introjects its active force, becomes reactive inwardly against itself, produces pain. The healing artistic vision does not consist in the formation of an intelligible and benevolent ersatz spectacle that would be the simple denial of the horrible and absurd reality, for the artistic power is not a formative power, but an illuminating power. The light, element of illusion, in illuminating individuates; it fixates the luminous appearance in itself. "Apollo . . . appears to us as the apotheosis of the *principium individuationis*."[27] This individuation, effected by the light, is of itself deification, is sublime; before the individuality of the individual neither the monotony proper to the cognitive life,[28] which proceeds by generalization, nor the chewed staleness, the devaluation of reality characteristic of appropriation, are possible; the perception of the individuality of the individual is awe. The Apollonian light does not clarify reality for the understanding, but transfigures the tone of the will. The light individuates, exalts, deifies, and thus produces a change in the tonality, the affectivity, of the will; horror and defeatism, which issue in the reactive, introjective production of pain, change into awe and hilarity. The horrible and the absurd are neither negated nor dissimulated in art—which ultimately is tragic art: the horrible is sublimated, rendered sublime; the absurd is rendered comic.

Thirdly, art is ascribed not to a faculty, but to a compulsion. Classically, a faculty is a formative power, and all the faculties are powers that form, demiurgic powers. But what dreams? Dreaming is not a power of a self; it is indeed not an activity executed by an agent; we attribute it to an ego by grammatical fiction. We say "I dream" as we say "I think," but we should rather say "It dreams" and "It thinks"—in the sense that we say "It rains."[29] What there is is the compulsion, which *is* in exercise, which does not first exist condensed in itself and contained in itself by the ego; on the contrary, the latter is released when the containment of the ego is dissipated.

Insofar as the subject is the artist . . . he has already been released from his individual will, and has become, as it were, the medium through which one truly existent subject celebrates his release in appearance. For to our humiliation *and* exaltation, one thing above all must be clear to us. The entire comedy of art is neither performed for our betterment or education nor are we the true authors of this art world [the will to power]. On the contrary, we may assume that we are merely images and artistic projections for the true author, and that we have our highest dignity in our significance as works of art . . . while of course our consciousness of our own significance hardly differs from that which the soldiers painted on canvas have of the battle represented on it. Thus all our *knowledge* of art is basically quite illusory, because *as knowing beings* we are not one and identical with that being which, as the sole author and spectator of this comedy of art, prepares a perpetual entertainment for itself. Only insofar as the genius in the art of artistic creation coalesces with this primordial artist of the world does he know anything of the eternal essence of art; for in this state he is, in a marvelous manner, like the weird image of the fairy tale which can turn its eyes at will and behold itself; he is at once subject and object, at once poet, actor, and spectator.[30]

The second dimension of artistic power is the compulsion to an orgiastic state. Here is the origin of the Dionysian art of music—melody, song, dance, play, mime, and lyric poetry. Here the artwork is not, as in the plastic arts, set up, deified, in its individuality; the musical arts exist only in the performance, only when vivified by the life of the performer, itself become a work of art—here "the noblest clay, the most precious marble, man, is kneaded and hewn."[31] The Dionysian compulsion remains within the living body, activating it into the perpetual movement of the dance. It does not produce a form fixed in its individuality, but issues in an orgiastic state in which forms are continually created and dissolved in an apotheosis of force. In the body it is an inspired movement, not a linear movement deployed by an initiative of the individual, but the emergence of rhythmic movement deploying itself in the individual. In this movement, out of this compulsion, life sings.

Nietzsche speaks of a compulsion to intoxication *in* life; the orgiastic state, then, is not simply the result of an increase of external stimulation projected upon the living being, it is not simply reactive in nature. There is in life itself a compulsion to frenzy that is an action of life upon itself, auto-intoxication. Intoxication is a phenomenon of intensification; the Dionysian consciousness is a conscious state envisaged not as an intentional state, with a transcendent, centripetal movement, but as an intensive state, with an essentially periodic movement. Phases of intensification alternate with phases of reflux independently of the attractions of the world and of the intentions of the ego.

The Dionysian states are states of intensified power, affirmative and creative of themselves. Dionysian frenzy is "above all the frenzy of sexual excitement, this most ancient and original form of frenzy."[32] Sexual frenzy is "art as an organic function."[33] It is a state of surging, overflowing animal vigor, and it arises as a sovereign will to lies.

> Love, and even the love of God, the saintly love of "redeemed souls," remains the same in its roots: a fever that has good reason to transfigure itself, an intoxication that does well to lie about itself. And in any case, one lies well when one loves, about oneself and to oneself: one seems to oneself transfigured, stronger, richer, more perfect, one *is* more perfect.[34]

Sexual intoxication is essentially, intrinsically, ambivalent, polyvalent, polysignifying; an organic theme transposed on the register of religious ecstasy; Platonically disguised in the love of the Ideas; a handsome young man, animal beauty, somehow divine;[35] voluptuous provocativeness in the guise of a communication of souls; a seeking of insight, cosmic nostalgia for union in the epileptic spasms of wet organs, in the spasmodic madness touched off when the penis penetrates the vagina and the wolf, the crab, the praying mantis that are in man and in woman are confronted. Sexual frenzy, proceeding by double meanings and insinuation, expressed in an undergrowth of innuendo, fluctuating meanings, snickerings and nonsense, is a *transpositional, metaphorizing power,* continual and essential equivocation, as Levinas has said.[36]

The world becomes perfect through love, Nietzsche says; making perfect, seeing as perfect characterizes the cerebral system bursting with sexual energy.[37]

> In this state one enriches everything out of one's own fullness: whatever one sees, whatever one wills, is seen swelled, taut, strong, overloaded with strength.[38]

> Out of this feeling one lends to things, one *forces them to accept from us,* one violates them—this process is called *idealizing.*[39]

> The sensations of space and time are altered: tremendous distances are surveyed and, as it were, for the first time apprehended; the extension of vision over greater masses and expanses; the refinement of the organs for the apprehension of much that is extremely small and fleeting; *divination,* the power of understanding with only the least

assistance, at the slightest suggestion: "intelligent" *sensuality;* strength as a feeling of domination in the muscles, as suppleness and pleasure in movement, as dance, as levity and *presto;* strength as pleasure in the proof of strength, as bravado, adventure, fearlessness, indifference to life or death—all these climactic moments of life mutually stimulate one another.[40]

Sexual frenzy—"art as an organic function"—issues in Dionysian art, in music. In the body its first emanation is the rhythmics, dynamics, and harmony of the dancing body,[41] where the polyvalence of sexual intensity, its equivocal play, is expressed in the harmonics of a movement playing across the lips, throat, trunk, arms, legs, gestures—each member answering, symbolizing, the others.

Frenzy issues in rhythmic, and not intentional, movement. The movement of the dance is nonutilitarian locomotion, a movement without teleology, not a progression toward a terminus. The nonteleological movement of the dance is the divine movement, archetype of all vital movement; Zarathustra could only believe in a god who could dance. Thus life, frenzied life, is governed not by a law of meaning, but by rhythm. Rhythm is the emergence of closed ensembles whose elements call for one another like the syllables of a verse, but answer to one another only by activating us. Rhythm is not properly assumed, subsumed, in the sense that the Kantian subject subsumes the medley of sensations under its own law; one does not assume a rhythm, makes it one's own by understanding—one participates in it without consent, assumption, initiative, without freedom. And yet the power and presence of rhythm is in no way unconscious: on the contrary, it intensifies into consciousness, fills and obsesses consciousness. The feeling of intensifying, augmenting power, is joy. Rhythm interests life in spite of itself, but not by offering it utility or meaning; it effects a deconceptualization of reality. And, indeed, it interests, involves, captivates life not even "in spite of itself," for it effects a depersonalization of the subject, a passage from the self to anonymity. "Through the spirit of music we can understand the joy involved in the annihilation of the individual."[42]

From the beginning, Nietzsche presents the Dionysian compulsion as deliverance and joy because it is the intensification of will dissolving the ego, metamorphosing the ego into multiple affirmations, multiple personas, multiple masks. Frenzy dissolves the ego not in alienation but in voluptuousness. For the classical philosophy, a will belongs properly to an ego, because an ego is a moment of self-consciousness, and a being that is conscious of itself is sovereign over itself; and, being a moment of sovereignty, it is an origin, a point of origin, from which force comes. Will, which means sovereignty, force, propulsion, must originate from a node of sovereignty in being. But for Nietzsche the force, the power of the will, does not come out of the sovereignty of an ego, the sovereignty of self-consciousness; rather, it comes out of the fact that the Will to Power is fundamentally receptive and continually draws force from the universe, from the dispersed, the distance, the different, and the beyond. It owes its force not to the sovereignty of the self-conscious ego-formation, but to its essentially receptive, affective nature.

This is sometimes not clearly understood. One assumes that when Nietzsche says that life is Will to Power, upsurge of force, that this should be interpreted in the classical sense, by which *a* life is a unity which of itself is expansive, forceful, propulsive, energy, *conatus essendi,* spontaneity, activity. But when Nietzsche says that a life is Will to Power, he is conceiving of that life not in and for itself, but rather in contention with other lives, other powers; it is an essentially dramatic concept. What makes this life, then, my life, *a* life in its own right, something individual and identifiable, is not the fact that it has an inner principle of unity, issuing from the identity-pole of a self-sovereign ego; it is rather that this life, this force, marks a difference in the field of forces. It is only conceivable in a field of force, and it is itself *something* by marking a difference in that field, by forcefully maintaining a line of tension in that field. But that means, then, that it is affected by the forces of that field, and exists due to them as much as due to itself. Its sensitivity yields its activity, its power, and its Will to Power makes it sensitive.

Thus, affectivity is contained in the Nietzschean concept of will, and power is measured by feeling rather than by the sovereignty of self-consciousness. Before Nietzsche had yet introduced his concept of Will to Power, he spoke of feeling of power; power was taken to be a matter of feeling rather than of will. But the final Nietzschean term "will" does not merely replace, it incorporates that dimension of feeling; for Nietzsche, power—being not a solitary upsurge in being, but a differential element in a field of force—is essentially affective. And we find this affective dimension of will in all of Nietzsche's own concepts of power—in his idea that the upsurge of life, of power, is also the reverberation of happiness, of joy; in his idea that the ideal represents the maturation, or, quite literally, the coming to light, of an impulse, a pulsation of feeling (and that therefore values—which do not come out of the world, since they represent what is not present, what does not exist—come forth out of happiness); and in the general intention of the Nietzschean philosophy of the will, which is not to teach a new way of acting but a new way of feeling.

For Nietzsche, then, the force of life does not come out of an ego, a zone where life, becoming self-conscious, becomes master and sovereign over itself; it rather comes out of the sensitivity of life to life external to it, life essentially *different* from it. The ego, as a factor of unity, is *become,* and is not an origin. For classical philosophy, a will issues from an ego; for Nietzsche, an ego issues from a will, and *multiple* egos issue from the essentially rhythmic Dionysian compulsion.

The compulsions arising from the depths of the night to produce dreams, and the compulsions to frenzy, to an orgiastic state, are moments by which life, out of its own plenitude, out of its own fullness of power, valuates being, augments being, radiates upon being its own light and its own musicality. The moments of heightened, intensified life, of exalted vitality, evolve upsurging force into affirmative judgment and affirmative imagination, evaluation; they justify existence, they reconcile us to our lives and to a world that is striving, eternally powerful, and pleasurable in its unending creation and dissolution of forms. Dreaming and intoxication, the visionary life and the dancing life, the Apollonian and Dionysian compulsions, are the very justification of life; they "make life possible and worth living."[43] A life without dreams and without intoxication is a life sick, rancorous, and without value. One lives for dreams and for festive intoxication.

The Noble

The noble life is *not* the life that is domineering, oppressive, ambitious, tyrannical—as though, Nietzsche says, what were essential and powerful in such "higher men" were their capacity for setting masses in motion: in short their effect,[44] not power itself, but the amortization of power. The power of the noble life should not be confused with social, political, or military power, where power does not lie in the life itself, but in the role occupied by an individual in an institutional apparatus. "But the 'higher nature' of the great man lies in being different, in incommunicability, in distance of rank, not in an effect of any kind—even if he made the whole globe tremble."[45] Thus, what measures the nobility of a man is not a power over other men, over organizations, or over history that he owes to institutional structures; what measures the nobility of a man is rather the power by which he molds and fashions a human type, the power of his own dignity, his own distinction, his own difference, the power to make of his own life something distinguished. The strength of nobility creates a strong type of life in itself.

The servile life is conformist and routine, "cowardly, anxious, petty, intent on narrow utility,"[46] dominated by the past; it is life too weak to create new forms of response, new forms of feeling. It lives in one sentiment: rancor; the sickness of the will is rancorous in tone; rancor is the very form of the sickness of the impotent will.[47]

The rancorous life is a particular form of life become reactive. It begins in an inner dissociation of the will, a retardation between the affective and the active dimensions of the will. The active force of the will is retarded; the external force has passed before it has been able to act. But it does not thereby evaporate; turning back upon the affect left in itself, it produces pain. Life reacts no longer to the force outside, but the affect of that force inside; its force is interiorized, introverted; its reaction is no longer enacted, but felt. Turned back upon the affect impressed upon itself, the active force of life comes to be turned back upon its past. This form of introversion is sadness and regret, is pain, because it is life turned to its dissipating being. It is concern with the hurt and weakness and humiliation of the past; it wills that that impotency be compensated for, be revenged. Vengefully, then, it seeks to hold onto the past, refuses to let the past die.

It is, according to Nietzsche, the origin of our meanness, our malice. It is because we are rancorous and resentful that we are cruel.

> The *sick* are man's greatest danger; *not* the evil, *not* the "beasts of prey." Those who are failures from the start, downtrodden, crushed— it is they, the *weakest,* who must undermine life among men, who call into question and poison most dangerously our trust in life, in man, and in ourselves. Where does one not encounter that veiled glance which burdens one with a profound sadness, that inward-turned glance of the born failure which betrays how such a one speaks to himself—that glance which is a sigh! "If only I were someone else," sighs this glance: "but there is no hope of that. I am who I am: how could I ever get free of myself? And yet—*I am sick of myself!*"[48]

Life fixated on its own impotency, on its past phase, turns to every kind of foreign power with the venomous and deceitful will to devalue and depreciate and diminish. We are cruel to others with the force of our own rancor. Turned rancidly back upon our own past, twisted in rancor and vengefulness against a past that we cannot forget and cannot let die, we are closed to the force of the other, to what comes in the present, to what presents itself.

The noble life has the power to make of the present its own law; that is the source of its distinction, of the difference that marks each thought, each glance, each gesture, each feeling of that life. The source of the great power of the noble life, its welcoming openness to what comes, to what presents itself, lies in that it has the power to forget, to forget the past, to forget what is irrevocable, to let what dies die.

> Forgetting is no mere force of inertia as the superficial imagine; it is rather an active and in the strictest sense positive faculty of repression that is responsible for the fact that what we experience and absorb enters our consciousness as little while we are digesting it (one might call the process "impsychation") as does the thousandfold process involved in physical nourishment—so-called incorporation. To close the doors and windows of consciousness for a time; to remain undisturbed by the noise and struggle of our underworld of utility organs working with and against one another; a little quietness, a little *tabula rasa* of the consciousness, to make room for new things, above all for the nobler functions and functionaries, for regulation, foresight, premeditation (for our organism is an oligarchy)—that is the purpose of

active forgetfulness, which is like a doorkeeper, a preserver of psychic order, repose, and etiquette: so that it will be immediately obvious how there could be no happiness, nor cheerfulness, no hope, no pride, no *present,* without forgetfulness.[49]

What, then, is characteristically noble is the ability to forget: not merely to *forgive* one's hurts and humiliations, one's impotencies, but what is more to *forget* them, to be able to pass over the past to welcome the rushes of what comes in the present. That is the secret of the power of the noble life: the life that arises innocent before each moment, each event, each person, as though the past had no claim and no law, as though all the ghosts and phantoms of the past had dissipated before the light of the present.

Each one of us began by being weak, impotent, infantile. According to psychoanalysis, fate is not the name for a higher cosmic power to which we are subjected; it is but the name for our infancy; every impotency of life is but the force of infancy. For each one our past is a succession of impotencies, humiliations, mortifications, ignorance, baseness. We cannot be strong sexually now, we cannot love strongly now, unless we forget the narcissism, the sordid groping infantile sexuality, the homosexuality, the incestuous cravings each has indulged in. No one would be capable of a moment of pride now if he remembered all the humiliations, the abjections, the degenerate cravings, the wretched pettinesses of which the twenty years of his life until now consisted in. No one could be capable of real abandon, of innocent happiness, of pure pleasure, unless he could liberate himself from remorse and regret over stupidities and vicious desires he basked in in the past.

The weak, morbid life, remembering twenty years of stupidities, degenerate and hopeless sexual indulgence, disgraces, shames, cowardices, asks: however could human life be noble?

The condition for the possibility of nobility in a man is the strong power to forget, to let the past pass, let the weakness of one's being dissipate, let one's dying self die, to break the chains of memory, of remorse, of regret, to face the man or the woman you have wronged as though you are meeting him or her for the first time, to look upon the man or the woman you have defiled as though you are gazing upon virgin territory, denuded now for the first time, to enter into each day as though a new response will have to be invented for each event, to enter into each landscape as though everything is unexpected, full of promises, dreams, surprises.

> To be incapable of taking one's enemies, one's accidents, even one's misdeeds seriously for very long—that is the sign of strong, full natures, in whom there is an excess of the power to form, to mold, to recuperate, and to forget (a good example of this in modern times is Mirabeau, who had no memory for insults and vile actions done him and was unable to forgive simply because he—forgot). Such a man

shakes off with a *single* shrug much vermin that eats deep into others; here alone genuine "love of one's enemies" is possible.[50]

Indeed the noble life has the power even to forget its own good deeds, for

> . . . there are occurrences of such a delicate nature that one does well to cover them up with some rudeness to conceal them; there are actions of love and extravagant generosity after which nothing is more advisable than to take a stick and give any eyewitness a sound thrashing: that would muddle his memory. Some know how to muddle an abuse in their own memory in order to have their revenge at least against this only witness: shame is inventive.[51]

The Sovereign Individual

The third figure of powerful life is the sovereign individual. He is sovereign to himself; he is his own legislator, autonomous and supramoral. What is powerful in the sovereign individual is his memory. It is not a memory of his sensibility, but a memory of his will; not a memory of impressions, but a memory of words. It is not his remembering of what happened to him, what affected him, a remembering of affects and sensations, but his remembering of what he himself said, his remembering of his own word. He is a man of his word; he has the right to make promises because he has the power to keep them. The power to remember one's word, to make and keep promises, is the power to dominate and command one's own future.

The sovereign individual does not remember what the noble life forgets. (As we have seen, what the noble life forgets are the hurts, the humiliations, the mortifications received, the impotencies undergone.) The memory of the sovereign individual is a veritable memory of the future: to remember one's word is not to recall that a promise was made at a given past moment, but rather that it is to be kept at a given future moment.

> This involves no mere passive inability to rid oneself of an impression, no mere indigestion through a once-pledged word with which one cannot "have done," but an active *desire* not to rid oneself, a desire for the continuance of something desired once, a real *memory of the will:* so that between the original "I will," "I shall do this" and the actual discharge of the will, its *act,* a world of strange new things, circumstances, even acts of the will may be interposed without breaking this long chain of will. But how many things this presupposes! To ordain the future in this way, man must first have learned to distinguish necessary events from chance ones, to think causally, to see and anticipate distant eventualities as if they belonged to the present, to

decide with certainty what is the goal and what the means to it, and in general to be able to calculate and compute. Man himself must first of all have become *calculable, regular, necessary,* even in his own image of himself, if he is to be able to stand security *for his own future,* which is what one who promises does![52]

This power, the power to remember one's word, belongs intrinsically to the very concept of Will to Power as conceived by Nietzsche. For Nietzsche, Will to Power does not mean tension or potential energy in being that can set masses in motion; to will is always to order, to command.

> "Willing" is not "desiring," striving, demanding: it is distinguished from these by the affect of commanding. . . . It is part of willing that something is commanded (which naturally does not mean that the will is "effected"). That state of tension by virtue of which a force seeks to discharge itself is not an example of "willing."[53]

But to order, for Nietzsche, is not to impose order hylomorphically upon a passive materiality; it is to command another will.

To command, for Nietzsche, is not to give signs to another person conveying the communicable content of one's will. First, to will at all is already to command; to form a will in oneself is already to command something within oneself that renders obedience. But when we say that to will is to command oneself, we already introduce a duality within the self. What is the nature of this duality? If we were to take it hylomorphically, understanding that what happens is that there occurs a contraction of a form in the materiality of the will, in the substance of the soul, then we would find ourselves back in the classical conception by which this duality is but the presupposition of a higher unity, the unity of the ego that exists reflecting itself in immanence, existing for itself and existing as one, as unity, because it exists for itself. But that is not Nietzsche's conception. For Nietzsche, the self as a unitary concept is a metaphysical fiction; what there is is the body as a multitude *not* of atoms, but of forces, "subwills"—a chaos in the midst of which there arises a dominating force that comes to command, to impose perspective—and not necessarily one perspective ("for one must bear a great deal of chaos within oneself in order to be able to give birth to a dancing star."[54]). "In all willing it is absolutely a question of commanding and obeying, on the basis . . . of a social structure composed of many 'souls.' "[55]

> But now let us notice what is strangest about the will—this *manifold* thing for which people have only one word: inasmuch as in the given circumstances we are at the same time the commanding *and* the obey-

ing parties, and as the obeying party we know the sensations of constraint, impulsion, pressure, resistance, and motion, which usually begin immediately after the act of will; inasmuch as, on the other hand, we are accustomed to disregard this duality, and to deceive ourselves about it by means of the synthetic concept "I," a whole series of erroneous conclusions, consequently of false evaluations of the will itself, has become attached to the act of willing—to such a degree that he who wills believes sincerely that willing *suffices* for action. Since in the great majority of cases there has been exercise of will only when the effect of the command—that is, obedience; that is, the action—was to be *expected,* the *appearance* has translated itself into the feeling, as if there were *a necessity of effect.* In short, he who wills believes with a fair amount of certainty that will and action are somehow one; he ascribes the success, the carrying out of the willing, to the will itself, and thereby enjoys an increase of the sensation of power which accompanies all success. "Freedom of the will"—that is the expression for the complex state of delight of the person exercising volition, who commands and at the same time identifies himself with the executor of the order—who, as such, enjoys also the triumph over obstacles, but thinks within himself that it was really his will itself that overcame them. In this way the person exercising volition adds the feeling of delight of his successful executive instruments, the useful "under-wills" or under-souls—indeed, our body is but a social structure composed of many souls—to his feelings of delight as commander.[56]

Thus the power to command oneself belongs to the will as such, and it is because the will that commands first orders and ordains itself that it can then command others. Sovereignty depends on the measure to which the will has the power to determine and fix its own future, to give its word and keep it, to stand security for its own future. A man who has this power Nietzsche calls an

... emancipated individual, with the actual *right* to make promises, this master of a *free* will, this sovereign man. [He has] his own independent, protracted will and *the right to make promises.* In him a proud consciousness, quivering in every muscle, of *what* has at length been achieved and become flesh in him, a consciousness of his own power and freedom, a sensation of mankind come to completion. Such a man is sovereign, like only to himself, liberated from the morality of custom, autonomous and supramoral. . . . The proud awareness of the extraordinary privilege of *responsibility,* the consciousness of this rare freedom, this power over oneself and over fate, has in his case penetrated to the profoundest depths and become instinct, the dominating instinct. What will he call this dominating instinct, supposing he feels the need to give it a name? The answer is beyond doubt: this sovereign man calls it his *conscience*.[57]

THE PHANTASM OF ETERNAL RECURRENCE

We have seen that the artist is a first figure of powerful life. What is powerful in the artist is the compulsion to dream and the compulsion to an orgiastic state. The noble is a second figure of powerful life. What is powerful in the noble is the power to forget. The third figure of powerful life is the sovereign individual; what is powerful in the sovereign individual is the memory of his will, his power to keep his word. The power to dream and the power to intensify itself to intoxication, to frenzy, are powers that command the present. The power to dream, illuminating power, is life's power to present to itself what does not make itself present *of* itself. The power to intensify itself of itself, the compulsion to an orgiastic state, is life's power to intensify exorbitantly its own presence in the world. The power to forget is a power life has over the past, a liberating power, the power to move out from under the crushing weight of the past. The power to remember one's word, to promise, is the power to dominate and command one's own future.

The conjugation of the artistic, noble, and sovereign will yields the image of a life that effects an utterly powerful, positive, affirmative relationship with transience. This would be a life in which the spirit of rancor, of vengefulness, with regard to the passing, the dissipating being, of the past, would have been overcome. For Nietzsche, pain over the passing of life, the spirit of resentment, vengefulness, has characterized the whole of Western metaphysical history, with its devaluation of transience, of time and of all transitory beings—and therefore of this world and this life. The Nietzschean image of a life in which the figures of artist, noble, and sovereign individual would be conjoined yields the image of a life fully delivered from the spirit of revenge, from nihilism, from the Western decadence.

Such a will is not at all a kind of desiring, striving, demanding appetite, aspiration, longing; it is not, for example, a will that longs for power. The Nietzschean image of the will is not suffering—it is not a longing for an end, which would be the terminus of its aspiration, the cure for its indigence, and its own termination. It commands, it gives; it proceeds out of plenitude and not out of indigence. As compulsion to dream and compulsion to frenzy, it radiates its light and its musicality over the world; it values, it augments, it heightens, it exalts. As power to forget, it liberates itself continually from its own dissipating being; as power to remember its word, it orders and ordains its own future.

And as a means to contract such an utterly affirmative will, Nietzsche offers the phantasm of the Eternal Return of all things. Salvation through illusion! This thought, which came upon Nietzsche like a hallucination at Sils Maria, "6,000 feet beyond man and time," is presented, in *The Gay Science,* both as a phantasm contracted in a moment of ecstasy, and as a selective (and not cosmological) principle:

> What if a demon crept after you into your loneliest loneliness some day or night, and said to you: "This life, as you are living it at present, and have lived it, you must live it once more, and again innumerable times; and there will be nothing new in it, but every pain and every joy and every thought and every sigh, and all the unspeakably small and great in your life must come to you again, and all in the same series and sequence—and likewise this spider and this moonlight among the trees, and likewise this moment, and I myself. The eternal sand-glass of existence will ever be turned once more, and you with it, you speck of sand!" Would you not throw yourself down and gnash your teeth, and curse the demon that so spoke? Or have you once experienced a tremendous moment in which you would answer him: "You are a god, and never did I hear anything so divine!" If that thought acquired power over you as you are, it would transform you, and perhaps crush you; the question with regard to all and everything: "Do I want this once more—and for innumerable times?" would lie as the heaviest burden upon your activity! Or, how you would have to become favorably inclined to yourself and to life, so as to long for nothing more ardently than for this last eternal sanctioning and sealing?[58]

The Eternal Return is also a cosmological doctrine for Nietzsche, as we have indicated in the first part of this paper. Here I want to indicate how it is, first, an essentially Dionysian phantasm, the phantasmal structure of the ecstasy of the will; and, second, a selective principle—one of those *powerful* thoughts that do something to the one who thinks them, that cannot be thought with impunity, that transfigure the thinker, that are situated not only in the register of the true and the false, but also in that of the base and the noble, the sick and the powerful, the nihilistic and the affirmative.

The Eternal Return is here not so much a theory—a mental vision—as an experience of high intensity. To have been able, to have had the power, to answer to the demon: "You are a god, and never did I hear anything so divine!" one would have to be "favorably inclined to oneself and to life" so as to will oneself to affirm one's difference without reservation, and to will anew, and now, all that one has ever been, all that one has ever willed, without any remorse, regret, or rancor. The will of the Eternal Return is thus the contraction of a certain structure of the will, an ecstasy of the will—a contraction of utter and unreserved reconciliation with itself and with the universe. The circle of the Eternal Return is thus the sign, the emblem of a will intensified to the extreme, a moment of extreme Dionysian fever, willing without remorse and without regret all forms of itself, the whole succession of forms of itself passing, dissolving, and forming anew.

The Dionysian structure of this phantasmal image can be recognized if we reflect on two dimensions involved in its eruption into a life: first, the transformation of the will that the hallucination of the Eternal Return effects; secondly, the forgetfulness, the anamnesis it presupposes.

Nietzsche presents it as a selective principle.[59] It operates to eliminate certain forms of will, and to intensify to the extreme other forms of will, those that are of themselves affirmative, innocent, generous, valuing. But a laziness that would will its eternal return—a foolishness, a baseness, a servility, a cowardice, a meanness, a spitefulness that would will its eternal return—would no longer be the laziness, foolishness, baseness we know. All these forms of negative will we know are accompanied with the inner ceremonial of the obsessive: they are forms of will we permit ourselves only by including in them a resolve not to repeat them tomorrow. For us a laziness that would *cease* to say "Tomorrow I will do something," a cowardice or an abjection that would will its eternal return, are as yet unknown, unexplored forms of will.

"If that thought acquired power over you as you are, it would transform you. . . ." The vision of eternal recurrence is not just the cognitive, theoretical vision of a recurrence of the same ego that I am now; it dissolves, transforms the ego that I am now in the measure that it "acquires power" over me; it is for this reason that I call it a hallucinatory vision and not a theoretical vision.

It is the power, the extreme intensity of this moment that transforms. The condition for the possibility of this power, of this extreme intensity, is the forgetting that it has occurred before. This transformation could occur on condition that the revelation of the Eternal Return—which has already occurred innumerable times—has been forgotten innumerable times. The I is really transformed, the ego to which this has occurred before has become past and has been forgotten; the new, transfigured will resolves itself, promises itself to ask with regard to all and everything the question: "Do I want this once more—and for innumerable times?"

This kind of remembering and this kind of forgetting intensify to extreme the presence of the will in the present, affirming itself and affirming its affirmation of itself, like a light reiterating itself infinitely from the start on mirror surfaces facing one another. Such is the Nietzschean experience of eternity—not an eternity in extension, the endurance of a stagnant moment without past and without future, stretched out linearly without end, but an infinity in the present moment, an eternity in intensity—the "deep, deep eternity."

And how many new ideals are, at bottom, still possible! Here is a little ideal I stumble upon once every five weeks on a wild and lonely walk, in an azure moment of sinful happiness. To spend one's life amid delicate and absurd things; a stranger to reality; half an artist, half a bird and metaphysician; with no care for reality, except now and then to acknowledge it in the manner of a good dancer with the tips of one's toes; always tickled by some sunray of happiness; exuberant and encouraged even by misery—for misery *preserves* the happy man; fixing a little humorous tail even to the holiest things.[60]

And how many new gods are still possible! As for myself, in whom the religious, that is to say god-forming, instinct occasionally becomes active at impossible times—how differently, how variously the divine has revealed itself to me each time! So many strange things have passed before me in those timeless moments that fall into one's life as if from the moon, when one no longer has any idea how old one is or how young one will yet be . . .[61]

NOTES

1. *The Will to Power*, §481.
2. *WP*, §688.
3. *Beyond Good and Evil*, §289.
4. *WP*, §536.
5. *Thus Spoke Zarathustra;* III, "On Apostates."
6. "Willing seems to me to be above all something *complicated*, something that is a unity only as a word. . . ." *BGE*, §19.
7. *WP*, §702.
8. *The Genealogy of Morals;* I, §13. Cf. *WP*, §481: "Against positivism, which halts at phenomena—'There are only *facts*'—I would say: No, facts are precisely what there are not, only interpretations. . . . 'Everything is subjective,' you say; but even this is interpretation. The 'subject' is not something given, it is something added and invented and projected beyond what there is. Finally, is it necessary to posit an interpreter behind the interpretation? Even this is invention, hypothesis."
9. *BGE*, §36; *WP*, §490.
10. *BGE*, §19.
11. *WP*, §481.
12. "However often 'the same form is attained,' it does not mean that it *is* the same form—what appears is always something new, and it is only we, who are always comparing, who include the new, to the extent that it is similar to the old, in the unity of the 'form.' As if a *type* should be attained and, as it were, was intended by and inherent in the process of formation."

WP, §521. Thus there is not a form-unity—a type—that would function as the teleological source of the appearances.

13. *GM;* II, §12.
14. *WP,* §1062.
15. *WP,* §1064.
16. *WP,* §617.
17. *BGE,* §211.
18. *WP,* §556.
19. " 'True': from the standpoint of feeling is that which excites the feeling most strongly . . . from the standpoint of thought is that which gives thought the greatest feeling of strength; from the standpoint of touch, seeing, hearing, is that which calls for the greatest resistance. Thus it is the highest degrees of performance that awaken belief in the 'truth,' that is to say, reality, of the object. The feeling of strength, of struggle, of resistance convinces us that there is something that is here being resisted." *WP,* §533.
20. *GM;* II, §12.
21. *GM;* II, §12.
22. "The philosophical spirit always had to use as a mask and cocoon the *Previously established* types of the contemplative man—priest, sorcerer, soothsayer, and in any case a religious type—in order to be able to *exist at all:* the *ascetic ideal* for a long time served the philosopher as a form in which to appear, as a precondition of existence—he had to *represent* it so as to be able to be a philosopher; he had to *believe* in it in order to be able to represent it. The peculiar, withdrawn attitude of the philosopher, world-denying, hostile to life, suspicious of the senses, freed from sensuality, which has been maintained down to the most modern times and has become virtually the *philosopher's pose par excellence*—it is above all a result of the emergency conditions under which philosophy arose and survived at all; for the longest time philosophy would not have been *possible at all* on earth without ascetic wraps and cloak, without an ascetic self-misunderstanding. The *ascetic priest* provided until the most modern times the repulsive and gloomy caterpillar form in which alone the philosopher could live and creep about." *GM;* III, §10.
23. *The Birth of Tragedy,* §1.
24. *BT,* §1.
25. *WP,* §853.
26. *BT,* §1; cf. *BGE,* §193.
27. *BT,* §4.
28. On the tone of the cognitive life: "Physiologically, too, science rests on the same foundation as the ascetic ideal: a certain *improverishment of life* is a presupposition of both of them—the affects grown cool, the tempo of life slowed down, dialectics in place of instinct, seriousness imprinted on faces and gestures (seriousness, the most unmistakable sign of a labored metabolism, of struggling laborious life)." *GM;* III, §25.

29. *BGE*, §17.
30. *BT*, §5.
31. *BT*, §1.
32. *Twilight of the Idols;* "Skirmishes . . . ," §8.
33. *WP*, §808.
34. *WP*, §808.
35. *WP*, §806.
36. Emmanuel Levinas, *Totality and Infinity*, trans. Alphonso Lingis (Pittsburgh: Duquesne University Press, 1969), p. 255.
37. *WP*, §805.
38. *TI;* "Skirmishes . . . ," §9.
39. *TI;* "Skirmishes . . . ," §8.
40. *WP*, §800.
41. "To make music possible as a separate art, a number of senses, especially the muscle sense, have been immobilized (at least relatively, for to a certain degree all rhythm still appeals to our muscles); so that man no longer bodily imitates and represents everything he feels. Nevertheless, that is really the normal Dionysian state, at least the original state. Music is the specialization of this state attained slowly at the expense of those faculties which are most closely related to it." *TI;* "Skirmishes . . . ," §10.
42. *BT*, §16.
43. *BT*, §1.
44. *WP*, §876.
45. *WP*, §876.
46. *BGE*, §260.
47. *Ecce Homo;* I, §6.
48. *GM;* III, §14.
49. *GM;* II, §1; cf. *BGE*, §230.
50. *GM;* I, §10.
51. *BGE*, §40.
52. *GM;* II, §1.
53. *WP*, §668.
54. *Zarathustra;* "Prologue," §5.
55. *BGE*, §19.
56. *BGE*, §19.
57. *GM;* II, §2.
58. *GS*, §341.
59. *WP*, §1058.
60. *WP*, §1039.
61. *WP*, §1038.

Martin Heidegger

WHO IS NIETZSCHE'S ZARATHUSTRA?

Who is Nietzsche's Zarathustra?

It would seem that the question is easy to answer, for we find Nietzsche's own answer stated in clear sentences that are even italicized. They occur in his book devoted specifically to the figure of Zarathustra. The book has four parts, was written from 1883 to 1885, and bears the title *Thus Spoke Zarathustra*.

Nietzsche gave it a subtitle: *A Book for Everyone and No One. For Everyone* does not, of course, mean for just anybody. *For Everyone* means for each man as man, insofar as his essential nature becomes at any given time an object worthy of his thought. *And No One* means for none of the idle curious who come drifting in from everywhere, who merely intoxicate themselves with isolated fragments and particular aphorisms from this work; who won't proceed along the path of thought that here seeks its expression, but blindly stumble about in its half-lyrical, half-shrill, now deliberate, now stormy, often lofty and sometimes trite language.

Thus Spoke Zarathustra: A Book for Everyone and No One. In what uncanny fashion the subtitle has come true in the seventy years since its first appearance—though precisely in the reverse sense! It became a book for every man, and to this day no thinker has appeared who is equal to its fundamental thought and able to assess the full significance of its origin. Who is Zarathustra? If we read the title of the work attentively, we will find a hint. *Thus Spoke Zarathustra*. Zarathustra speaks. He is a speaker. What sort of speaker? Is he an orator, even a preacher? No. The speaker Zarathustra is an "advocate"—a *Fürsprecher*. Here we meet a very old German word, with several meanings. *"Für"* (for) actually means *"vor"* (fore). (*"Fürtuch"* is still in use today in the Alemannic dialect for "pinafore.") The "advocate" *(Fürsprecher)* advocates and is the spokesman. But "für" also means "for the benefit, or in behalf, of" and "in justification of." An advocate is ultimately the man who interprets and explains that of and for which he speaks.

Zarathustra is an advocate in this threefold sense. But what does he advocate? In whose behalf does he speak? What does he endeavor to interpret? Is Zarathustra just any advocate for just anything, or is he *the* advocate for the one thing that always and first of all addresses man?

Toward the end of Part Three of *Thus Spoke Zarathustra,* there is a section called "The Convalescent." He is Zarathustra. But what does "the convalescent" mean? "To convalesce" *(genesen)* is the same as the Greek *néomai, nóstos.* This means "to return home;" nostalgia is the aching for home, homesickness. The convalescent is the man who collects himself to return home—that is, to turn in, into his own destiny. The convalescent is on the road to himself, so that he can say of himself who he is. In the passage referred to, the convalescent says: "I, Zarathustra, the advocate of life, the advocate of suffering, the advocate of the circle. . . ."

Zarathustra speaks on behalf of life, suffering, the circle, and this is what he advocates. These three things, "life, suffering, circle," belong together, are the same. If we were able to think this threefoldness correctly, as one and the same thing, we could surmise whose advocate Zarathustra is, and who he himself would be *as* that advocate. Of course, we could now break in with a crude explanation, and assert with undeniable correctness that in Nietzsche's language, "life" means the will to power as the fundamental characteristic of all beings, not only of man. What "suffering" means Nietzsche states in the following words: "All that suffers, wills to live;"[1] i.e., everything whose way is the Will to Power. This means: "The formative powers collide."[2] "Circle" is the sign of the ring, which flows back into itself and so always achieves the recurring selfsameness.

Accordingly, Zarathustra presents himself as the advocate of the fact that all being is Will to Power, which suffers as creative, colliding will and thus wills itself in the eternal recurrence of the same.

With that statement we have reduced the essence of Zarathustra to a definition, as one says in the classroom. We can write this definition down, memorize it, and produce it as needed. We can even substantiate the matter by referring to those sentences, italicized in Nietzsche's work, that state who Zarathustra is.

In the section already mentioned, "The Convalescent," we read: "*You* [Zarathustra] *are the teacher of the eternal recurrence . . . !*" And in the preface to the whole work we read: "*I* [Zarathustra] *teach you the superman.*"

According to these passages the advocate Zarathustra is a "teacher." He seems to teach two things: the Eternal Recurrence of the same, and the Superman. But it is not immediately apparent whether what he teaches belongs together, and, if so, in what manner. Yet even if the connection became clear it would remain uncertain whether we are hearing the advocate, whether we are learning from the teacher. Without such hearing and learning we never quite know who Zarathustra is. Hence, it is not enough merely to compile sentences showing what the advocate and teacher says about himself. We must heed *how* he says it, on what occasions, and with what intent. The decisive words, "You are the teacher of the Eternal Recurrence," Zarathustra does not utter to himself. It is what his animals tell

him. They are identified immediately at the beginning and more clearly at
the conclusion of the work's prologue. Here it says: ". . . when the sun
stood high at noon, then he [Zarathustra] looked into the air inquiringly, for
overhead he heard the shrill call of a bird. And behold! An eagle soared
through the air in wide circles and on him there hung a snake, not like prey
but like a friend: for she kept herself wound around his neck." In this
mysterious embrace we already have a presentiment of how circle and ring
are implicitly entwined in the circling of the eagle and the winding of the
snake. So this ring, called *anulus aeternitatis,* sparkles: seal ring and year of
eternity. The sight of the two animals, circling and forming circles, shows
where they belong. For the eagle and the snake never first compose a circle;
rather, they conform to it, thus to obtain their own nature. At their sight,
there emerges what concerns Zarathustra, gazing into the air inquiringly.
Therefore, the text continues:

> "They are my animals!" said Zarathustra and rejoiced.
> "The proudest animal under the sun and the wisest animal under the
> sun—they have gone out on a search."
> "They want to ascertain whether Zarathustra still lives. Indeed, do I
> still live?"

Zarathustra's question retains its importance only if we understand the
indeterminate word "life" in the sense of "Will to Power." Zarathustra
asks: does my will accord with the will that, as will to power, prevails in all
beings?

Zarathustra's animals ascertain his nature. He asks himself whether he
still is—i.e., whether he already is who he really is. In a note to *Thus Spoke
Zarathustra* from the literary remains we read: " 'Do I have time to *wait* for
my animals? If they are *my* animals, they will know how to find me.'
Zarathustra's silence."[3]

So Zarathustra's animals, in the passage from "The Convalescent" cited
before, tell him the following, which the italicized sentence must not cause
us to overlook. They say: "For your animals know well, Zarathustra, who
you are and must become: behold, *you are the teacher of the eternal
recurrence*—that is now *your* destiny!"

And so it comes out. Zarathustra must first of all *become* who he is.
Zarathustra recoils in horror from this becoming. That horror pervades the
entire work presenting his character. That horror determines the style, the
hesitant and constantly arrested course, of the entire book. That horror stifles
all Zarathustra's self-assurance and arrogance from the very outset. One
who has not previously and does not constantly perceive the horror in all the
discourses—seemingly arrogant and often ecstatically conducted as they
are—will never know who Zarathustra is.

If Zarathustra is still to become the teacher of the Eternal Recurrence, he obviously cannot begin with this doctrine. That is why that other phrase stands at the beginning of his path: *"I teach you the superman."*

But when we use the word "superman" we must from the start ward off all the false and confusing overtones the word has to the common understanding. Nietzsche does not give the name "superman" to man such as exists until now, only super-dimensional. Nor does he mean a type of man who tosses humanity aside and makes sheer caprice the law, titanic rage the rule. Rather, taking the word quite literally, the Superman is the individual who *surpasses* man as he is up to now, for the sole purpose of bringing man-till-now into his still unattained nature, and there to secure him. A posthumous note to *Zarathustra* says: "Zarathustra wants to *lose* no past of mankind, to throw everything into the melting pot."[4]

But where does the call of distress for the Superman come from? Why does prevailing man no longer suffice? Because Nietzsche recognizes the historical moment in which man prepares to assume dominion over the whole earth. Nietzsche is the first thinker who, in view of a world history emerging for the first time, asks the decisive question and thinks through its metaphysical implications. The question is: Is man, as man in his nature till now, prepared to assume dominion over the whole earth? If not, what must happen to man as he is so that he may be *able* to "subject" the earth and thereby fulfill the word of an old testament? Must man as he is, then, not be brought *beyond* himself if he is to fulfill this task? If so, then the "superman" rightly understood cannot be the product of an unbridled and degenerate imagination rushing headlong into the void. Nor, however, can the Superman species be discovered historically through an analysis of the modern age. Hence, we may never seek the Superman's essential structure in those personages who, as the chief functionaries of a shallow and misconstrued Will to Power, are pushed to the top of that will's various organizational forms. One thing, however, we ought soon to notice: this thinking that aims at the figure of a teacher who will teach the Superman concerns us, concerns Europe, concerns the whole earth—not just today, but tomorrow even more. It does so whether we accept it or oppose it, ignore it or imitate it in false accents. All essential thinking passes inviolably through all partisanship and opposition.

What is at stake, then, is that we must first learn how to learn from the teacher, even if it is only to raise questions that go beyond him. Only then will we one day discover who Zarathustra is—or we will never discover it.

Still, it remains to be considered whether the inquiry beyond Nietzsche's thinking can be a continuation of his thought, or must be a step backward. And it remains first to be considered whether this "step backward" signifies only a retreat to an historically ascertainable past that one may wish to revive (for instance, Goethe's world), or whether the "step backward" points to a past whose origin still awaits remembrance in order to become a beginning that breaks upon the dawn.

But let us here confine ourselves to learning a few preliminaries about
Zarathustra. The best way to accomplish this is to try to accompany the
teacher's first steps. He teaches by showing. He looks ahead into the nature
of the Superman and gives it visible shape. Zarathustra is only the teacher,
not yet the Superman himself. And again, Nietzsche is not Zarathustra, but
the questioner who attempts in thought to grasp Zarathustra's nature.

The Superman surpasses previous and contemporary man, and is therefore a passage, a bridge. If we, the learners, are to follow the teacher who
teaches the Superman, we must, to stay with the metaphor, get onto the
bridge. The passage will be understood fairly completely if we observe three
things:

1. That from which the person passing over departs.
2. The bridge itself.
3. The destination of the person crossing over.

The destination must be kept in view—by us, first of all; by him who
crosses over; and, above all, by the teacher who is to reveal it. If foresight
into the destination is lacking, then the crossing over remains without
direction, and that from which the one who crosses must free himself
remains undetermined. On the other hand, what summons the person crossing over shows itself in full clarity only when he has crossed. To the person
crossing over, and indeed to the teacher who is to show the bridge, to
Zarathustra himself, the destination remains always at a distance. The
distant abides. By abiding it remains near, in that nearness that preserves
what is distant as distant, in recalling it and thinking toward it. This
proximity in recollection to what is distant is called *"Sehnsucht"* (longing)
in German. The word *"Sucht"* (sick) is a variant of "seek," and is
mistakenly associated with "search." The ancient word *"Sucht"* means
sickness, suffering, pain.

Longing is the agony of the nearness of the distant.

The longing of the person crossing over is directed toward that to which he
crosses. The person crossing over, and even the teacher who shows him the
way, is, as we said before, on the way to his authentic nature. He is the
convalescent. In Part Three of *Thus Spoke Zarathustra*, "The Convalescent" is followed immediately by "On the Great Longing." With this
section, the third from the end of part III, the entire work *Thus Spoke
Zarathustra* reaches its climax. Nietzsche writes in a posthumous note: "A
divine suffering is the content of Part Three of *Zarathustra*."[5]

In "On the Great Longing," Zarathustra is conversing with his soul.
According to Plato's doctrine, which became decisive for Western
metaphysics, the essence of thought resides in the soul's conversation with
itself. It is the *logos hon aute pros auten he psyche diexerchetai peri on an*

skope: the self-gathering in conversation, which the soul undergoes on its way to itself in the surroundings of whatever it perceives.[6]

Zarathustra, in conversation with his soul, thinks his "most abysmal thought."[7] He opens the section "On the Great Longing" with the words: "O my soul, I taught you to say 'Today' and 'One Day' and 'Formerly' and to dance away over all Here and There and Yonder."

The three terms, "Today," "One Day," and "Formerly" are capitalized and set in quotation marks. They name the fundamental features of time. The manner in which Zarathustra pronounces them points toward what he must henceforth tell himself in the foundation of his being. And what is that? That "One Day" and "Formerly," future and past, *are like* "Today." And the present is like the past and like the future. All three phases of time merge as one, as the selfsame, into a single present, an eternal Now. Metaphysics calls the permanent Now "eternity." Nietzsche, too, conceives the three phases of time from the standpoint of eternity as a permanent Now. But for Nietzsche, the permanence does not consist in something static, but in a recurrence of the same. When Zarathustra teaches his soul to say those words, he is the teacher of the Eternal Recurrence of the same. Eternal Recurrence is the inexhaustible fullness of joyful-painful life. That is the point of the "great longing" of the teacher of the Eternal Recurrence of the same. And that is why the "great longing" is, in the same section, also called "the longing of overfullness."

"The great longing" lives mostly by virtue of that from which it draws its sole solace—that is, confidence. The older German word *"Trost"* (*solace,* compare: *betroth, trust*) has been replaced by the word "hope." "The great longing" that inspires Zarathustra attunes and determines him to his "greatest hope."

But what entitles and leads him to it?

What bridge allows him to cross over to the Superman, and in that crossing allows him to take leave of man as he is until now, so that he frees himself from him?

It is in the peculiar structure of *Thus Spoke Zarathustra,* which is to show the crossing, that the answer to this question is presented in the preparatory part II. Here, in the section "On the Tarantulas," Nietzsche has Zarathustra say: "For *that man be delivered from revenge,* that is the bridge to the highest hope for me, and a rainbow after long storms."

How strange and puzzling these words must seem to the prevailing view of Nietzsche's philosophy that has been fabricated. Isn't Nietzsche considered the promoter of the Will to Power, of power politics and war, of the frenzy of the "blond beast"?

The words "that man be delivered from revenge" are in fact italicized. Nietzsche's thinking meditates on deliverance from the spirit of revenge. It intends to serve a spirit that, as freedom from vengefulness, precedes all mere brotherhood, but also precedes every desire merely to punish; a spirit prior to all quests for peace and war-mongering, and also outside of that spirit that would establish and secure *pax,* peace, by pacts. In the same way, the sphere of this freedom from revenge lies outside of pacifism, power politics, and calculating neutrality. It also lies outside of limp indifference and the shirking of sacrifice, and outside of blind acquisitiveness and action at all costs.

Nietzsche's alleged free thinking is a part of the spirit of freedom from revenge.

"That man be delivered from revenge." Even if we do no more than vaguely grasp this spirit of freedom as the foundation of Nietzsche's thinking, then the still-prevailing image of Nietzsche must crumble.

"For *that man be delivered from revenge:* that is the bridge to the highest hope for me," says Nietzsche. He thereby clearly states, in the language of preparatory concealment, where his "great longing" aims.

But what does Nietzsche mean here by revenge? What does deliverance from revenge consist of, according to him?

We shall be content to shed a little light on these two questions. Perhaps the light will allow us to see more clearly the bridge that is to lead such thinking from man-to-date across to the Superman. That to which man crosses over becomes visible in the crossing. We will then see more clearly how Zarathustra, as the advocate of life, of suffering, of the circle, is at the same time the teacher of the Eternal Recurrence of the same *and* of the Superman.

But why does something so decisive depend upon deliverance from revenge? Where does its spirit hold sway? Nietzsche gives the answer in the third section from the end of part II of *Thus Spoke Zarathustra*. It is called "On Deliverance." There it says: *"The spirit of revenge,* my friends, has so far been the subject of man's best reflection; and wherever there was suffering, there punishment was also wanted."

This sentence relates revenge at the outset to all of mankind's reflection to this date. Here reflection means not just any pondering, but that thinking in which man's relation to what is, to all beings, is grounded and attuned. Insofar as man relates to beings, he represents being with reference to the fact that it *is,* what and how it is, how it might be and ought to be; in short, he represents being with reference to its Being. This representation is thinking.

According to Nietzsche's statement, that representation has so far been determined by the spirit of revenge. People assume that their relationship to that which is is best if it is so determined.

In whatever manner man may represent beings as such to himself, he represents them in view of their Being. Because of this, man always goes beyond beings and crosses over to Being. In Greek, "beyond" is *meta*. Hence, man's every relationship to beings as such is in itself metaphysical. In understanding revenge as the spirit that attunes and determines man's relation to beings, Nietzsche conceives revenge metaphysically from the start.

Revenge is here not a mere theme of morality, nor is deliverance from revenge the task of moral education. Nor are revenge and vengefulness objects of psychology. Nietzsche sees the nature and significance of revenge metaphysically. But what does revenge really mean?

If for the moment we stay close to the literal meaning of the word, though with the necessary circumspection, we shall find a hint. *"Rache,"* "to *wreak* vengeance," (ME) *"wreken,"* (L) *"urgere,"* all signify "to press close or hard," "drive," "drive out," "banish," "pursue." In what sense is revenge a persecution? Revenge does not, after all, simply intend to chase something, capture and take possession of it. Nor does it intend merely to destroy what it pursues. Avenging persecution opposes in advance that upon which it takes revenge. It opposes its object by degrading it so that, by contrasting the degraded object with its own superiority, it may restore its own validity, the only validity it considers decisive. For revenge is driven by the feeling of being vanquished and injured. During the years when Nietzsche created *Thus Spoke Zarathustra,* he wrote down the remark: "I advise all martyrs to consider whether it was not revenge that drove them to extremes."[8]

What is revenge? We may now say tentatively: Revenge is opposing, degrading persecution. Is this persecution supposed to have sustained and pervaded all reflection so far, all representation to this day of beings with regard to their Being? If the spirit of revenge deserves such metaphysical significance, it must be discernible in the structure of metaphysics. In order to succeed in discerning that to some degree, let us observe the essential character in which the Being of beings appears within modern metaphysics. That essential character of Being finds its classic expression in a few sentences written by Schelling in 1809, in his *Philosophical Investigation Concerning the Nature of Human Freedom and Its Object.* They declare: "In the final and highest instance there is no being other than willing. Willing is primal being and to it [willing] alone belong all [primal being's] predicates: being unconditioned, eternity, independence of time, self-affirmation. All philosophy strives only to find this highest expression."[9]

The predicates that thought has since antiquity attributed to Being Schelling finds in their final, highest, and hence most perfected form in willing. But the will in this willing does not here denote a capacity of the human soul. The word "willing" here signifies the Being of beings as a whole. It is will. That sounds strange to us, and indeed is strange as long as we remain strangers to the sustaining thoughts of Western metaphysics. And we will remain strangers as long as we do not think these thoughts but merely go on forever reporting them. We can, for instance, ascertain Leibniz' statements about the Being of beings with historical precision, and yet never think a jot of what he thought when he defined the Being of beings from the perspective of the monad, as the unity of *perceptio* and *appetitus,* the unity of representation and striving—that is, as will. The object of Leibniz' thought finds expression through Kant and Fichte as the rational will, which Hegel and Schelling, each in his own way, then reflect upon. Schopenhauer has the same thing in mind when he titles his major work *The World* (not Man) *as Will and Representation.* And Nietzsche thinks the same thing when he recognizes the primal Being of beings as the Will to Power.

That the Being of beings here emerges throughout as will does not depend upon opinions a few philosophers have formed about beings. What this appearance of Being as will signifies no learned analysis will ever disclose; it can only be searched for in thought when it is deemed worthy of questioning as that which is pursued in thought, and thus can be secured in recollection.

For modern metaphysics, and within its particular expression, the Being of beings appears as will. Man is man, however, in that he thoughtfully relates to beings and is thereby sustained in Being. Thought must correspond in its own nature to that to which it is related, to the Being of beings as will.

Now, according to Nietzsche, thought so far has been determined by the spirit of revenge. How does Nietzsche conceive the nature of revenge, assuming he thinks of it metaphysically?

In part II of *Thus Spoke Zarathustra,* in the section "On Deliverance," Nietzsche has his Zarathustra say: "This, yet this alone, is *revenge* itself: the will's aversion to time and its 'It was.' "

That a determination of the essence of revenge stresses what is repugnant and resistant in vengeance, and thus stresses an aversion, corresponds to the peculiar persecution that we have characterized as revenge. But Nietzsche does not merely say: "Revenge is aversion." That is true also of hatred. Nietzsche says: "Revenge is *the will's* aversion." But "will" signifies the Being of beings as a whole, not only human willing. By characterizing revenge as "the will's aversion," it retains its resistant persecution from the outset within the region of the Being of beings. That this is the case becomes clear when we observe what the will's aversion is directed against. Revenge is "the will's aversion to time and its 'It was.' "

At a first, a second, and even a third reading of this determination of the essence of revenge, the emphasized relationship of revenge to "time" will seem surprising, incomprehensible, and finally arbitrary. This must be so—if we no further reflected upon what the term "time" here means.

Nietzsche says revenge is "the will's aversion to time . . . ." This does not say "aversion to something temporal." Nor does it say "aversion to a specific characteristic of time." It simply says "aversion to time."

To be sure, the words "aversion to time" are immediately followed by "and its 'It was.' " But this says that revenge is aversion to the "it was" within time. It will rightly be pointed out that time includes not only the "it was" but, just as essentially, the "it will be" and the "it is now," for time is determined not only by the past, but also by the future and the present. Therefore, when Nietzsche places great stress on time's "it was," he obviously does not intend his characterization of the nature of revenge to refer to "the" time as such, but to a particular aspect of time. Yet what is the situation with regard to "the" time? Time is situated in passing. Time passes by ceasing to be. That which arrives in time arrives not to abide, but to pass on. Where to? Into transience. When a person has died, we say that he has passed on. The temporal signifies what must pass, the transient.

Nietzsche defines revenge as "the will's aversion to time and its 'It was.'" That appended definition does not single out one characteristic of time by neglecting the other two. Rather, it identifies the foundation of time in its entire and intrinsic time essence. Nietzsche's "and" in "time and its 'It was,'" is not simply a transition to an additional specific feature of time. "And" here is the same thing as "and that means." Revenge is the will's aversion to time, and that means the ceasing to be, its transience. The will no longer has any influence over it, and its willing constantly runs up against it. Time and its "it was" is the stumbling block that the will cannot budge. Time, as transience, is the adversity that the will suffers. As a suffering will, it suffers transience, wills its own cessation as suffering, and, thereby, wills the disappearance of all things. The aversion to time degrades the transient. The earthly, the earth and all that is part of it, really should not be, and, at bottom, is devoid of true Being. Plato had already called it *me on,* nonbeing.

According to Schelling's statements, which only express the principal idea of all metaphysics, "independence of time, eternity" are primal predicates of Being.

But the deepest aversion to time does not consist of the mere degradation of the earthly. For Nietzsche, the most profound revenge consists of that reflection which posits eternal Ideals as the absolute, compared with which the temporal must degrade itself to actual non-being.

How is man to assume dominion over the earth, how is he to take the earth, as earth, into his guardianship, if and as long as he degrades the earthly in that the spirit of revenge determines his reflection? If saving the earth as earth is at stake, then the spirit of revenge must first vanish. That is why deliverance from the spirit of revenge is the bridge to the highest hope for Zarathustra.

Yet, of what does this deliverance from aversion to transience consist? In a liberation from the will itself? In Schopenhauer's sense, and that of Buddhism? To the extent that the Being of beings is will in modern metaphysical theory, deliverance from the will would, simultaneously, be deliverance from Being, a fall into empty nothingness. To Nietzsche, deliverance from revenge is indeed deliverance from what is repugnant, resistant, and degrading in the will, but not a release from all willing.

Deliverance liberates aversion from its *no,* and frees it for a *yes.* What does this *yes* affirm? Precisely what the aversion of the spirit of revenge negates: time, transience.

This *yes* to time is the will that would have transience abide, would not have it degraded to nihility. But how can transience abide? Only in such a way that, as transience, it does not just constantly pass, but always comes to be. It would abide only in such a way that transience and what ceases to be return as the selfsame in its coming. But this recurrence itself is abiding only if it is eternal. According to metaphysical theory, the predicate "eternal" belongs to the Being of beings.

Deliverance from revenge is the bridge from contempt for time, to the will that represents beings in the Eternal Recurrence of the same, in which the will becomes the advocate of the circle.

In other words: only when the Being of beings is represented to man as the Eternal Recurrence of the same, only then can man cross the bridge and, crossing over, be delivered from the spirit of revenge, be the Superman.

Zarathustra is the teacher who teaches the Superman. But he teaches his doctrine solely because he is the teacher of the Eternal Recurrence of the same. This thought of the Eternal Recurrence of the same is of primary importance; it is the "most abysmal" thought. That is why the teacher expresses it last of all, and then always reluctantly.

Who is Nietzsche's Zarathustra? He is the teacher whose doctrine would liberate previous reflection from the spirit of revenge unto a *yes* to the Eternal Recurrence of the same.

As the teacher of the Eternal Recurrence, Zarathustra teaches the Superman. A posthumous note expresses the refrain of this doctrine thus: "Refrain: *Love alone shall have jurisdiction* (creative love which *forgets* itself in its works)."

Zarathustra does not teach two different things as the teacher of the Eternal Recurrence and the Superman. What he teaches belongs internally together, because each demands the other in response. This response, its mode of being and the manner in which it withholds itself, conceals within itself and yet also reveals the figure of Zarathustra, and, thus, lets it become worthy of thought.

But the teacher knows that what he teaches remains a vision and an enigma. In this reflective knowledge he abides.

Because of the peculiar ascendency of modern science, we modern men are ensnared in the singular error that holds that knowledge can be obtained from science, and that thought is subject to the jurisdiction of science. But that which is unique in what a thinker is able to express can neither be demonstrated nor refuted logically or empirically. Nor is it a matter of faith. It can only be made visible in questioning-thinking. What is then seen always appears as that which is always *worthy* of questioning.

So that we may see and retain the vision of the enigma that Zarathustra's figure reveals, let us again observe the view of his animals that appears to him at the beginning of his journey: ". . . then he looked into the air inquiringly, for overhead he heard the shrill call of a bird. And behold! An eagle soared through the air in wide circles and on him there hung a snake, not like prey but like a friend: for she kept herself wound around his neck. 'They are my animals,' said Zarathustra and rejoiced.''

And the passage from ''The Convalescent,'' §1, which was purposely quoted only in part earlier, runs: ''I, Zarathustra, the advocate of life, the advocate of suffering, the advocate of the circle—I summon you, my most abysmal thought!''

Zarathustra identifies the thought of the Eternal Recurrence of the same with the same words—''my most abysmal thought''—in the section ''On the Vision and the Enigma'' (§2) in part III. There, in the altercation with the dwarf, Zarathustra tries for the first time to think of the enigmatic character of what he sees as corresponding to his longing. The Eternal Recurrence of the same remains a vision for him, but also an enigma. It can be neither verified nor refuted logically or empirically. At bottom, that is true of every thinker's essential thought: envisioned, but enigma—worthy of questioning.

Who is Nietzsche's Zarathustra? We can now answer in a formula: Zarathustra is the teacher of the Eternal Recurrence of the same and the teacher of the Superman. But now we see, perhaps we see even more clearly, beyond the bare formula: Zarathustra is *not* a teacher who teaches two different things. Zarathustra teaches the Superman *because* he is the teacher of the Eternal Recurrence. But conversely as well, Zarathustra teaches the Eternal Recurrence because he is the teacher of the Superman. Both doctrines belong together in a circle. By its circling, the doctrine accords with what is, with the circle that constitutes the Being of beings—that is, the permanent within Becoming.

The doctrine and its thought reach this circle when they cross the bridge that is called deliverance from the spirit of revenge. Through it, all previous thought is to be overcome.

There is a note from the period immediately after the completion of *Thus Spoke Zarathustra* in 1885, marked entry §617 in the material patched together from Nietzsche's literary remains and published under the title *The Will to Power,* that bears the underlined heading ''Recapitulation.'' Nietzsche here gathers together the main point of his thinking, in a few sentences, with extraordinary lucidity. A parenthetical commentary on the text specifically mentions Zarathustra. The ''Recapitulation'' begins with the sentence: ''To *impress* the character of Being upon Becoming—that is *the highest will to power.*''

The highest will to power—that is, the life force in all life—is to represent transience as a fixed Becoming within the Eternal Recurrence of the same, and so to render it secure and stable. This representation is a thinking that, as

Nietzsche notes emphatically, ''impresses'' upon being the character of its Being. This thinking takes becoming under its care and protection— becoming of which constant collision, suffering, is a part.

Is reflection-to-date, is the spirit of revenge overcome by this thinking? Or is it that in this ''impressing,'' which takes all becoming under the protection of the Eternal Recurrence of the same, there is nonetheless concealed an aversion to mere transience and, therefore, a supremely spiritualized spirit of revenge?

As soon as we ask that question, the impression arises that we are trying to impute to Nietzsche as his very own precisely what he seeks to overcome, that we are of the opinion that by such an imputation this thinker's thought is refuted.

But zealous attempts at refutation never get us on a thinker's path. They are part of the pettiness that must vent itself for the entertainment of the public. Moreover, Nietzsche himself had long ago anticipated the answer to our question. The work immediately preceding *Thus Spoke Zarathustra* appeared in 1882 under the title *The Gay Science (Die Fröhliche Wissenschaft)*. In its next-to-last section (§341), Nietzsche's ''most abysmal thought'' is presented for the first time under the heading ''The Greatest Stress.'' The concluding section (§342) which follows ''The Greatest Stress,'' is incorporated verbatim into *Thus Spoke Zarathustra,* as the beginning of the prologue.

Rough drafts for the preface to *The Gay Science* can be found in the literary remains.[10] There we read:

> A spirit strengthened by wars and victories, to whom conquest, adventure, danger, even pain have become a necessity; the habituation to sharp mountain air, to wintry walks, to ice and mountains in every sense; a sort of sublime malice and extreme exuberance of revenge— for there is *revenge* in it, revenge against life itself, when one who suffers greatly *takes life under his protection.*

What else remains for us to say but that Zarathustra's doctrine does not bring deliverance from revenge? We will say it. But we say it in no way as an alleged refutation of Nietzsche's philosophy. We do not even say it as an objection to his thinking. But we do say it in order to bring into focus how much and in what way even Nietzsche's thinking moves within the spirit of reflection-to-date. Whether the spirit of thought till now has been encountered at all in its decisive nature when characterized as the spirit of revenge we leave undecided. In any case, thought up to now is metaphysics, and Nietzsche's thinking presumably brings it to an end.

That is why something comes to the fore in Nietzsche's thought that that thinking itself can no longer think. Such a falling behind what has been thought is typical of creative thinking. And when a way of thinking brings metaphysics to completion, it points in an exceptional sense toward something unthought, something clear and confused at the same time. But where are the eyes to see it?

Metaphysical thinking rests on the distinction between that which truly is and that which by comparison does not constitute true being. But what is decisive for the *essence* of metaphysics does not lie by any means in the fact that this distinction appears as an opposition between the super-sensible and the sensible. Instead, this distinction, in the sense of cleavage, remains the first and sustaining one. It persists even when the Platonic hierarchy of the super-sensible and sensible is reversed and the sensible is experienced in a more essential and broader sense, which Nietzsche called by the name Dionysus. For the overfullness that is the object of Zarathustra's "great longing" is the inexhaustible permanence of becoming, as which the Will to Power wills itself in the Eternal Recurrence of the same.

Nietzsche raised what is essentially metaphysical in his thinking to the extreme form of aversion in the last lines of his last book, *Ecce Homo: How You Become What You Are.* He wrote it in October, 1888; it was not published until twenty years later, in a limited edition, and in 1911 it was included in Volume XV of the Grossoktav edition. The last lines of *Ecce Homo* run: "Have I been understood?—*Dionysus versus the Crucified. . . .*"

Who is Nietzsche's Zarathustra? He is the advocate of Dionysus. That is to say: Zarathustra is the teacher who teaches the Eternal Recurrence of the same in, and for the sake of, his doctrine of the Superman.

Does that last sentence answer our question? No, it does not, even if we follow the references that explained it in order to trace Zarathustra's path, to follow his first step across the bridge. But the sentence, which looks like an answer, makes us attentive, and brings us back more attentively to the title question.

Who is Nietzsche's Zarathustra? The question now is: Who is this teacher? Who is this being who appears within metaphysics at its stage of completion? Nowhere else in the history of Western metaphysics is the essential form of its respective thinkers actually expressed in this way, or more precisely and literally thought out; nowhere else, except at the beginning of Western thought in Parmenides, and there only in veiled contours.

It remains essential in the figure of Zarathustra that the teacher teaches something twofold that belongs together—Eternal Recurrence and Superman. In a sense, Zarathustra himself is this belonging-together. From that perspective he, too, remains an enigma that we have still hardly caught sight of.

"Eternal Recurrence of the same" is the name of the Being of beings. "Superman" is the name of the human being who corresponds to this Being.

In what respect do Being and human being belong together? How do they belong together, if Being is not of man's making, in man's power, nor man only a special case within being?

Can the belonging-together of Being and human being be discussed at all, as long as thought remains dependent upon the traditional concept of man? According to that concept, man is the *animal rationale*. Is it a coincidence or merely a poetic adornment that the two animals, eagle and snake, are with Zarathustra, that *they* tell him what he must become in order to be who he is? In the figure of the two animals, the union of pride and wisdom is to become apparent to the thoughtful reader. Yet we must know what Nietzsche thinks about the two. In notes from the time when *Thus Spoke Zarathustra* was composed, we read: "It seems to me that *modesty* and *pride* are intimately connected. . . . Common to them is the cold, steady gaze of appraisal in both cases."[11]

Elsewhere we read:

> We speak so stupidly about *pride*—and Christianity has even made us feel that it is *sinful*! The point is: he who *demands and obtains great things from himself* must feel very remote from those who do not—this *remoteness* is interpreted by those others as "a high opinion of himself;" but he knows it (the remoteness) only as ceaseless labor, war, victory, by day and night: of all this, the others know nothing![12]

The eagle—the proudest animal; the snake—the wisest animal. And both joined in the circle in which they soar, in the ring that encircles their being; and circle and ring once more intertwined.

The enigma—who Zarathustra is as the teacher of Eternal Recurrence *and* the Superman—becomes a vision to us at the sight of the two animals. At that sight, we can immediately and more easily grasp what the exposition endeavored to show as worthy of questioning: the relation of Being to the human being.

> And behold! An eagle soared through the air in wide circles, and on him there hung a snake, not like prey but like a friend: for she kept herself wound around his neck.
>
> "They are my animals!" said Zarathustra and rejoiced.

NOTE ON
THE ETERNAL RECURRENCE OF THE SAME

Nietzsche himself knew that his "most abysmal thought" remains an enigma. We are all the less free to think that we can solve the enigma. The obscurity of this final thought of Western metaphysics should not seduce us into avoiding that thought by subterfuge.

There are, fundamentally, only two subterfuges.

Either we say that this thought of Nietzsche is a kind of "mysticism" and has no place before thought, or we say: this thought is already ancient. It amounts to the familiar cyclical view of the course of the world. In Western philosophy it can first be found in Heraclitus.

This second account, like all others of this variety, says absolutely nothing, for what is gained by establishing that a thought is, for example, "already" to be found in Leibniz, or even "already" in Plato? What use is this information, if it leaves Leibniz' and Plato's thought in the same obscurity as the thought that such historical references are supposed to have cleared up?

As to the first evasion, however, according to which Nietzsche's thought of the Eternal Recurrence of the same is a fantastic mysticism, it would seem that the present age should teach us to know better; assuming, of course, that thought is destined to bring the essence of modern technology to light.

What is the essence of the modern dynamo other than *one* expression of the Eternal Recurrence of the same? But the essence of that machine is not anything machinelike or even mechanical. Just as little may Nietzsche's thought of the Eternal Recurrence of the same be interpreted in a mechanical sense.

That Nietzsche experienced and expounded his most abysmal thought from the Dionysian standpoint only suggests that he was still compelled to think it metaphysically, and only metaphysically. But it does not preclude that this most abysmal thought conceals something unthought, which also is impenetrable to metaphysical thinking.

NOTES

1. Kröner; VI, §469.
2. K; XVI, §151.
3. K; XVI, §279.
4. K; XIV, §271.
5. K; XIV, §285.
6. Cornford translates: "A discourse that the mind carries on with itself about any subject it is considering" (*Theaetetus*, 189e). "Thinking is, precisely, the inward dialogue carried on by the mind with itself without spoken sound" (*Sophist,* 263e).
7. "The Convalescent," §1; c.f. III, "On the Vision and the Enigma," §2.
8. K; XIII, §298.
9. F.W.J. Schelling, *Philosophische Schriften* (Landshut, 1809), Vol. I, p. 419.
10. K; XIV, §404.
11. K; XIV, §99.
12. K; XIV, §101.

Gilles Deleuze

ACTIVE AND REACTIVE

THE BODY

Spinoza opened up a new way for philosophy and the sciences. He said that we do not even know what a body *can do,* that we speak and chatter on about consciousness and spirit, but we neither know what a body is capable of, which forces are its own, nor what these forces hold in store for us.[1] Nietzsche knows that the hour has arrived: "We are in the phase of the modesty of consciousness."[2] To recall consciousness to its necessary modesty is to take it for what it is: a symptom, and nothing but a symptom, of a deeper transformation, a symptom of the activity of forces wholly other than spiritual. "Perhaps it is uniquely a question of the body in all spiritual development." What is consciousness? Like Freud, Nietzsche thinks that consciousness is the region of the ego affected by the external world.[3] Nevertheless, consciousness is defined less in relation to exteriority, in terms of the real, than in relation to *superiority,* in terms of values. This distinction is essential to a general conception of the conscious and unconscious. In Nietzsche, consciousness is always the consciousness of an inferior in relation to the superior to which it is subordinated or "incorporated." Consciousness is never *self*-consciousness, but the consciousness of an ego in relation to the self that is not conscious. It is not the master's consciousness, but the slave's consciousness in relation to a master who does not have to be conscious himself. "Consciousness ordinarily only appears when a whole wishes to subordinate itself to a superior whole . . . Consciousness is born in relation to a being of which we could be the function."[4] Such is the servility of consciousness; it testifies merely to "the formation of a superior body."

What is the body? We do not define it by saying that it is a field of forces or a nutritive medium in which a plurality of forces quarrel. For in fact there is no "medium," no field of forces or battle. And there is no quantity of reality, for all reality is already a quantity of force. There are nothing but quantities of force "in a relation of tension" between one another.[5] Every force is related to other forces, and it either obeys or commands. What defines a body is this relation between dominating and dominated forces. Whether chemical, biological, social, or political, every relation of forces constitutes a body. Any two forces, being unequal, constitute a body as soon as they enter into relation, which is why the body is always the fruit of chance, in the Nietzschean sense, and why it appears as the most "wonderful" thing, much more wonderful in truth than consciousness and spirit.[6] But chance, the relation of force with force, is also the essence of force. Thus, one does not ask how a living body is born, since every body lives as the "arbitrary" product of the forces that compose it. Composed of a plurality of irreducible forces, the body is a multiple phenomenon; its unity is that of a multiple phenomenon, the "unity of domination." In a body, the superior or dominating forces are called *active,* and the inferior or dominated forces are called *reactive.* Active and reactive are precisely the basic qualities that express the relation of force with force. The forces that enter into relation with one another have no quality *per se,* unless (at the same time) they bear a quality that corresponds to their difference in quantity. This difference of qualified forces, active and reactive, in accordance with their quantity, will be called their *hierarchy.*

THE DISTINCTION OF FORCES

Inferior forces (as distinct from those that command) do not cease being forces even though they obey. To obey is a quality of force as such, and it is just as much tied to power as commanding is:

> Individual power is by no means surrendered. In the same way, there is in commanding an admission that the absolute power of the opponent has not been vanquished, incorporated, disintegrated. "Obedience" and "commanding" are forms of struggle.[7]

Inferior forces are defined as reactive; they lose nothing of their force, or their quantity of force; they exercise it in securing means and ends, in serving the conditions of life and the functions and tasks of conservation, adaptation, and utility. And here is the point of departure for Nietzsche's important concept of reaction: the mechanical and utilitarian accommodations, the *regulations* that express all the power of inferior and dominated forces. We should also note the immoderate taste of modern thought for this reactive aspect of forces. We always think we have done enough when we understand the organism on the basis of its reactive forces. The nature, the quivering character of reactive forces, fascinates us. This is why mechanism and purpose are opposed for any theory of life; but these two interpretations only hold for reactive forces themselves. Indeed, it is true that we do understand the organism from the standpoint of its forces. But is it also true that we can grasp reactive forces for what they are, as forces and not as mechanical means or final ends? Only if we relate them to what dominates them and is not itself reactive:

> One overlooks the essential priority of the spontaneous, aggressive, expansive, form-giving forces that give new interpretations and directions, although "adaptation" follows only after this; the dominant role of the highest functions within the organism itself in which the will to life appears active and form-giving is denied.[8]

No doubt it is more difficult to characterize these active forces, for by nature they escape consciousness: "The great principal activity is unconscious." Consciousness merely expresses the relation of certain reactive forces to the active forces that dominate them. Consciousness is essentially reactive, and this is why we do not know what a body can do, or what activity it is capable of. And what we say of consciousness we must also say of memory and habit. Furthermore, we must again say it of nutrition, reproduction, conservation, and adaptation. These are all reactive forces, reactive specializations, expressions of one or another reactive forces.[9] It is inevitable that consciousness sees the organism from its own viewpoint and understands it in its own way—that is to say, in a reactive manner. What happens is that science follows the paths of consciousness and relies entirely on *other* reactive forces, the results being that the organism is always seen from the petty side, from the side of its reactions. According to Nietzsche, the problem of the organism is not the issue between mechanism and vitalism. Why should vitalism have a better claim to discovering the specifics of life within the reactive forces when mechanism interprets the same forces differently? The real problem is the discovery of active forces, without which the reactions themselves would not be forces.[10] What makes the body something superior to all reactions, and, in particular, superior to the ego's reaction of consciousness, is the activity of necessarily unconscious forces:

> From the intellectual viewpoint, the entire phenomenon of the body is as superior to our consciousness, our spirit, our conscious ways of thinking, sensing, and willing, as algebra is superior to the multiplication table.[11]

The active forces of the body make it a self and define the self as superior and wonderful: "A mighty ruler, an unknown sage—whose name is self. He inhabits your body, he is your body."[12] The real science is that of activity, but the science of activity is also the science that is necessarily unconscious. The idea that science should go at the same pace and in the same directions as consciousness is absurd. One feels the savor of morality in this idea. In fact, science can only occur where there is no consciousness, where there can be no consciousness.

"What is 'active'? Reaching out for power." Appropriating, possessing, subjugating, and dominating are the characteristics of active force. Appropriating means to impose forms, to create forms by exploiting circumstances.[13] Nietzsche criticizes Darwin because Darwin interprets evolution, and even chance within evolution, in an entirely reactive manner. He admires Lamarck because Lamarck foretold the existence of a truly active *plastic force,* prior in relation to adaptation: a force of metamorphosis. For Nietzsche, as for energetics, transformative energy is held to be "noble." The power of transformation, Dionysian power, is the foremost definition of activity. But each time that we thus note the nobility of action and its superiority over reaction, we must not forget that reaction, just as much as action, designates a type of force. Reactions simply cannot be apprehended or scientifically understood as forces if we do not relate them to the superior forces that are precisely of another type. The reactive is a basic quality of force, but can only be interpreted as such in relation to and starting from the active.

QUANTITY AND QUALITY

Forces have a quantity, but they also have the quality that corresponds to their difference in quantity: the qualities of forces are active and reactive. We have the presentiment that the problem of measuring forces will be delicate because it calls into play the art of qualitative interpretation. The problem is posed as the following: (1) Nietzsche always believed that forces were quantitative and ought to be defined quantitatively.

> Our knowledge has become scientific to the extent that it is able to employ number and measurement. The attempt should be made to see whether a scientific order of values could be constructed simply on a numerical and quantitative scale of force. All other "values" are prejudices, naïvetés, and misunderstandings. They are everywhere *reducible* to this numerical and quantitative scale.[14]

(2) However, Nietzsche no less believed that a purely quantitative determination of forces remained at once abstract, incomplete, and ambiguous. The art of measuring forces brings in the whole question of interpreting and evaluating qualities: "Mechanistic interpretation desires nothing but quantities; but force is to be found in quality. Mechanistic theory can therefore only describe processes, not explain them." Also, "Might all quantities not be signs of quality? . . . The reduction of all qualities to quantities is nonsense."[15]

Is there a contradiction between these two kinds of texts? If a force is inseparable from its quantity, it is no less inseparable from the other forces it relates to. *Quantity itself is thus inseparable from the difference in quantity.* The difference in quantity is the essence of force, and the relation of force to force. To dream of two equal forces, even if one grants them an opposition of meaning, is an approximate and coarse dream, a statistical dream in which the living is submerged, but which chemistry dispels. Each time Nietzsche criticizes the concept of quantity we must take it to mean that quantity, as an abstract concept, always and essentially tends toward an identification, an equalization of the unity that composes it, an annulment of difference within this unity. What Nietzsche reproaches in every purely quantitative determination of forces is that it annuls, equalizes, or compensates for all differences in quantity. On the other hand, each time he criticizes the concept of quality, we should take it to mean that qualities correspond to the difference in quantity between the two forces that are alleged to be in relation. In short, what interests Nietzsche is never the irreducibility of quantity to quality; or, rather, this interests him only secondarily and as a symptom. From the standpoint of quantity itself, Nietzsche is primarily interested in the irreducible difference between quantity and equality. Quality is distinguished from quantity, but only because it is a remainder: it is what cannot be equalized in quantity, what cannot be annulled in the difference between quantities. Thus, in one sense the (difference in) quantity is the irreducible element *of* quantity; and in another sense, this element is irreducible *to* quantity itself. Quality is nothing other than quantitative difference; the two correspond in every force relation. "We cannot help feeling that mere quantitative differences are something fundamentally distinct from quantity, namely, that they are *qualities* which can no longer be reduced to one another."[16] And what is still anthropomorphic in this text should be corrected by the Nietzschean principle that there is a subjectivity to the universe—which, precisely, is no longer anthropomorphic but cosmic. "The reduction of all qualities to quantities is nonsense . . . ."

Along with chance we affirm the relation of *all* forces. And, doubtless, we affirm the whole of chance at one stroke in the thought of the Eternal Return. But all the forces do not enter into relation at once. Their respective power, in fact, is occupied in relation to a small number of forces. Chance is the contrary of a *continuum*. The encounters of various quantities of force are thus concrete parts of chance, affirmative parts of chance, and, as such, foreigners to every law, as are the followers of Dionysus. Now, in this encounter, each force receives the quality that corresponds to its quantity; i.e., the state that effectively expresses its power. Nietzsche can thus say, in an obscure text, that the universe supposes "an absolute genesis of arbitrary qualities," but that the genesis of qualities itself supposes a (relative) genesis of quantities. That the two geneses are inseparable means that we cannot calculate forces abstractly; in each case we must concretely evaluate their respective quality and the nuance of this quality.

FIRST ASPECT OF THE ETERNAL RETURN:
AS COSMOLOGICAL AND PHYSICAL DOCTRINE

Nietzsche's account of the Eternal Return supposes a critique of the terminal state, or the state of equilibrium. If the universe were to have a state of equilibrium, if becoming had an end or a final state, it would have already attained it. But the present moment, the passing instant, proves that it is not attained, and therefore that an equilibrium of forces is not possible. Yet why would equilibrium, the final state, have to have been attained if it were possible?—by virtue of what Nietzsche calls the infinity of past time. The infinity of past time only means that becoming cannot have started to become, that it is not something that *has* become. Now, not being something that has become, it is no more the becoming of something. Not having become, it would already be what it becomes if it were to become something. All of which is to say that if past time were infinite, becoming would have attained its final state—if it had one. Indeed, it amounts to the same thing to say that becoming would have attained its final state if it had one, and that it would not have left its initial state if it had one. If becoming becomes something, why has it not long ago finished becoming? If it is something that has become, how could it have started to become?

> If the universe were capable of permanence and fixity, and if it had in its entire course a single moment of being, in the strict sense, it could no longer have anything to do with becoming, and thus one could neither conceive nor observe any becoming whatever.[17]

This is the thought that Nietzsche claims to have found "in earlier thinkers." If becoming as a whole (as Plato said in the *Parmenides*) can never escape the present, then as soon as it is there it ceases to become—and is thus what it was about to become. "But each time that I have encountered this thought from antiquity," Nietzsche comments, "it has been determined by other, and generally theological, ulterior motives." In persisting to demand how becoming could have started and why it has not yet finished, the philosophers of antiquity are false tragics, invoking hubris, crime, and punishment.[18] Excepting Heraclitus, they face neither the thought of a pure becoming nor the occasion for this thought. That the present moment is not an instant of being, or of the present "in the strict sense," that it is rather the passing moment, *forces* us to think about becoming, but to think of it precisely as what could not have started, and what cannot finish, becoming.

How does the thought of pure becoming found the Eternal Return? It suffices merely to stop believing in being, as distinct from and opposed to becoming; but it is also enough to believe in the being of becoming itself. What is the being of what becomes—of what neither starts nor finishes becoming? *Recurring is the being of what becomes.* "That everything recurs is the closest approximation of a world of becoming to a world of being: high point of the meditation."[19]

This problem for meditation must be formulated in yet another way: how can the past be constituted within time? How can the present pass? The passing moment could never pass if it were not already past and yet to come—as well as being present at the same time. If the present did not pass in and of itself, if it had to await a new present in order to become past, the past in general would never be constituted within time, and neither would this present pass. But we cannot wait: the moment must be at once present and past, as well as present and yet to come, in order for it to pass (and to pass for the sake of other moments). The present would have to coexist with itself as past and future; it is the synthetic self-relation of present, past, and future that in turn grounds the relation between this moment and other moments.

The Eternal Return is thus the answer to the problem of *passage*.[20] And in this sense it must not be interpreted as the return of something that is, something that is one or that is the same. We misconstrue the expression "eternal return" when we take it as the return of the same. It is not being that recurs, but, rather, that recurrence itself constitutes being insofar as it affirms becoming and passing. It is not some one thing that recurs, but that recurrence is itself affirmed by the passage of diversity or multiplicity. In other words, identity in the Eternal Return does not designate the nature of what recurs, but, to the contrary, the fact of recurring difference. This is why the Eternal Return must be conceived as a synthesis: a synthesis of time and its dimensions, a synthesis of diversity and its reproduction, a synthesis of being and becoming that affirms becoming—a synthesis of double affirmation. The Eternal Return, then, itself depends *not* on a principle of identity, but on one that must in all respects fulfill the demands of a truly sufficient reason.

Why is mechanism so wrong an interpretation of the Eternal Return? Because it neither necessarily nor directly implies the eternal return, and because it does entail the false consequence of a final state. This final state is held to be identical with the initial state, and, to that extent, one concludes that the mechanical process would once again run through the same set of differences. This is the basis for the cyclical hypothesis so often criticized by Nietzsche. For we do not understand how this process can possibly emerge from its initial state, or re-emerge from its final state, or run through the same differences once again, and yet not even have the power to run through whatever differences there are once. The cyclical hypothesis is incapable of accounting for either the diversity of coexisting cycles or (above all) the existence of diversity within the cycle.[21] This is why we can only understand the Eternal Return as the expression of a principle that serves to explain diversity and the reproduction of diversity, or difference and its repetition. Nietzsche presents such a principle as one of his most important philosophical discoveries. He names it *Will to Power*. "I call it 'will to power,' because it expresses the characteristic that cannot be thought out of the mechanistic order without thinking away this order itself."[22]

WHAT IS THE WILL TO POWER?

One of the most important texts Nietzsche wrote to explain what he meant by Will to Power is the following:

> The *victorious* concept of "force," by which means our physicists have created God and the world, still needs to be *completed:* an *inner* will must be *ascribed* to it, which I designate as "will to power."[23]

Will to Power is thus attributed to force, but in a very special way, for it is at once a complement to force *and* something internal. It is not attributed in the manner of a predicate. Indeed, if we ask the question "what?," we cannot say that force is *what* wills. The Will to Power alone is what wills; it is neither relegated nor removed to another subject, even by force. But how then can it be "attributed"? Let us remember that the essence of force is its quantitative difference with respect to other forces, and that this difference is expressed as the force's quality. The difference in quantity, thus understood, necessarily refers to a differential element of related forces, which is also the genetic basis for the qualities of these forces. So what the Will to Power is is the genealogical element of force, at once differential and genetic. *The Will to Power is the element out of which issue both the quantitative difference of related forces and the quality that, due to this relation, devolves to each force.* Here the Will to Power reveals its nature; it is the principle for bringing forces into a synthesis. In this synthesis—which is related to time—the forces either run through the same differences once again, or diversity is reproduced. The synthesis is one of forces, of their difference and reproduction. The Eternal Return, then, is the synthesis that has the Will to Power as its principle. We should not be surprised at the word "will," for *what*, if not the will, is capable of serving as a principle to synthesize forces, in determining a relation of force with force? But in what sense should we take the term "principle"? Nietzsche always reproaches "principles" for being too general in relation to their application, for always having too loose a mesh to pretend to capture or regulate what they set out after. He likes to oppose the Will to Power to Schopenhauer's will to live, if only because of the latter's extreme generality. If the Will to Power is a good principle, if it reconciles empiricism with strict principles, if it constitutes a superior empiricism, this is because it is an essentially *plastic* principle that is no wider than its field of application; it metamorphoses itself within this field and determines itself, in each case, along with what it determines. The Will to Power, in fact, is always inseparable from any such set of determined forces, from their quantities, qualities, and directions. It is never superior to the determinations it brings about in a relation between forces; it is always plastic and metamorphic.[24]

Inseparable does not mean identical. The Will to Power cannot be separated from force without falling into a metaphysical abstraction. But to confuse force and will is to risk still more: one no longer understands force as force, one falls back into mechanism, forgetting the difference between forces that constitutes their being and ignoring the element from whence their reciprocal genesis is derived. Force is what can exercise power; Will to Power is what wills that it be exercised.

What does this distinction mean? The previously cited text invites us to comment on each word. The concept of force is by nature *victorious* because the relation of force with force, as it is taken in this concept, is one of domination; of the two relating forces, one is dominating and the other dominated (even God and the universe are held in a relation of domination, however arguable the interpretation of such a relation may be in this case). Nevertheless, this victorious concept of force needs a *complement,* and this complement is something *internal,* an internal willing. It would not be victorious without such an addition. The force relations remain indeterminate as long as one does not add some element to force itself so that it would be capable of determining these relations. This determination, moreover, would be from two perspectives. Relating forces point back to a twofold yet simultaneous genesis: the reciprocal genesis of their difference in quantity, and the absolute genesis of their respective quality. The Will to Power is thus added to force, but as the differential and genetic element, as the element that is internal to its production. There is nothing anthropomorphic about its nature. More precisely, it is added to force as the internal principle of its qualitative determination in a relation $(x + dx)$, and, as the internal principle of the quantitative determination of the relation itself $\left(\frac{dy}{dx}\right)$. Will to Power must be said to be the genealogical element both of force *and* of forces. Thus, it is always through Will to Power that one force prevails over others and dominates or commands them. Furthermore, it is still Will to Power *(dy)* that makes one force obey within the relation, and it is by Will to Power that it obeys.[25]

We have, in a certain way, come upon the relation between the Eternal Return and Will to Power, but we have neither elucidated nor analyzed it. Will to Power is both the genetic element of force and the synthetic principle of forces. However, we do not yet have the means to understand how is it that this synthesis forms the Eternal Return, and how the forces within this synthesis necessarily reproduce themselves in conformity with its own principle. On the other hand, the existence of this problem reveals an historically important aspect of Nietzsche's philosophy: its complex situation with regard to Kantianism. The concept of synthesis is at the center of Kantianism, it is its very discovery. And we know that the post-Kantians reproached Kant from two viewpoints for having compromised this discovery: they reproached him from the perspective of the principle that governs the synthesis, and from the perspective of the objects reproduced within the synthesis itself. They called for a principle that would not only condition objects but would also be truly genetic and productive (a principle of internal difference or determination). They also pointed out the survival of miraculous harmonies between terms that were entirely external to one another. So far as a principle of internal difference or determination goes, they asked for reasons: not only for the synthesis, but for the reproduction of the manifold within the synthesis as such.[26] Now, if Nietzsche is inserted into the history of Kantianism, it is by the original way he takes up these post-Kantian demands. He made synthesis into a synthesis of forces—and by not seeing it in this way one fails to recognize the meaning, nature, and content of synthesis. Nietzsche understood the synthesis of forces as the Eternal Return, and thus found, at the heart of synthesis, the reproduction of the manifold—i.e., of diversity. He claimed the Will to Power as the synthetic principle, and determined this as the differential and genetic element of forces that were present to one another. Leaving this supposition to better verify it later, perhaps, we not only believe that there is a Kantian heritage in Nietzsche, but a half-avowed and half-hidden rivalry. Nietzsche does not take the same position as Schopenhauer with respect to Kant, for he does not, like Schopenhauer, attempt an interpretation that would uproot Kantianism from its dialectical misadventures and open up new channels for it. For Nietzsche, these dialectical misadventures did not come from without; they have all the deficiencies of the Kantian critique as their first cause. Nietzsche seems to have sought (and to have found, in the "eternal return" and "will to power") a radical transformation of Kantianism, a re-invention of the *Critique* that Kant betrayed at its very conception, and a resumption of the critical project on new foundations and with new concepts.

NIETZSCHE'S TERMINOLOGY

Even while anticipating the analyses that remain to be done, it is time to fix certain points in Nietzsche's terminology. Not only does all the rigor of this philosophy depend upon it, but it would be wrong to question its systematic precision. Wrong, in any case, whether this be cause for rejoicing or regret. In truth, Nietzsche employs very precise new terms for very precise new concepts.

  1. Nietzsche calls Will to Power the genealogical element of force.

Genealogical means differential and genetic. Will to Power is the differential element of forces—i.e., the element that produces the difference in quantity between two or several supposedly relating forces. Will to Power is the genetic element of force—i.e., the element that produces the quality of each force in this relation. As a principle, Will to Power does not suppress chance; on the contrary, it *implies* chance, because without chance it would neither be plastic nor metamorphic. Chance is the bringing of forces into relation, while Will to Power is the determining principle of this relation. Will to Power is necessarily added to force, but it can only be added to those forces that are brought into relation by chance. Will to Power embraces chance in its heart, for it alone is capable of affirming all chance.

2. The difference in quantity and respective quality of relating forces both stem from Will to Power, understood as a genealogical element. Forces are said to be dominating or dominated according to their difference in quantity. They are said to be active or reactive according to their quality. Will to Power belongs to the reactive or dominated force just as well as to the active or dominating force. Now, since the difference in quantity is irreducible in each case, it would be a vain attempt to want to measure it without interpreting the qualities of the respective forces that are presented to one another. Forces are essentially differentiated and qualified. They express their difference in quantity by the quality that devolves to each. An event or phenomenon being given, to estimate the quality of the force that gives it meaning, and, from that, to measure the relation of forces present to one another—this is the problem of interpretation. We must not forget that, in each case, interpretation comes up against all kinds of delicate problems and difficulties. For this, we need an "extremely fine" perception, the kind one finds in a chemist.

3. The qualities of force have their principle in the Will to Power. And if we ask: "Who interprets?," we answer: *the Will to Power,* for it is the Will to Power that interprets.[27] But to be at the source of the qualities of force, Will to Power would itself require qualities, particularly fluid qualities, subtler still than those of force. "What rules is the entirely momentary quality of will to power." These qualities of Will to Power that are thus immediately related to the genetic or genealogical element, these fluid, primordial, and seminal qualitative elements, must not be confused with the qualities of force. It is also essential to insist on the terms employed by Nietzsche: *active* and *reactive* designate the basic qualities of force, but *affirmative* and *negative* designate the primordial qualities of Will to Power. To affirm and deny, to value and devalue, express Will to Power, just as acting and reacting express force. And just as reactive forces are no less forces, the will to deny, Nihilism, is no less Will to Power: ". . . a will to nothingness, an aversion to life, a rebellion against the most fundamental presuppositions of life; but it is and remains a *will*."[28]

If we must now attach the greatest importance to this distinction between two kinds of qualities, it is because we always find it at the center of Nietzsche's philosophy. There is a profound affinity, a complicity, but never a confusion between action and affirmation, or between reaction and negation. Furthermore, the determination of these qualities puts the whole of philosophy into play. On the one hand, it is evident that there is affirmation in every action and negation in every reaction. But on the other hand, action and reaction are rather the means or instruments of a Will to Power that affirms and denies, just as reactive forces are instruments of Nihilism. Then again still, action and reaction need affirmation and negation as something that exceeds them but is necessary for them to realize their own ends. Finally, and more profoundly, affirmation and negation extend beyond action and reaction, because the former are the immediate qualities of becoming itself. Affirmation is not simply action, but the power of becoming active, the *becoming active* in person; and negation is not simply reaction, but a *becoming reactive*. It all happens as if affirmation and negation were both immanent and transcendent with respect to action and reaction; along with the framework of forces, they constitute the chain of becoming. Affirmation makes us enter into the glorious world of Dionysus, the being of becoming, and negation hurls us down to the disturbing ground from which reactive forces emerge.

4. For all these reasons, Nietzsche can say that Will to Power is not merely what interprets, but what evaluates. To interpret is to determine the force that gives meaning to a thing. To evaluate is to determine the Will to Power that gives a thing value. Thus, from the perspective of origin, from the source from which they draw their value, values are left no more abstract than meaning—i.e., from the perspective from which it draws its signification as a genealogical element, Will to Power is that from which meaning derives signification, and values their value. The signification of a meaning consists in the quality of force expressed in a thing. One asks if this force is active or reactive, and by what nuance. The value of a value consists in the quality of Will to Power expressed in the corresponding thing. One asks here whether the Will to Power is affirmative or negative, and by what nuance. The art of philosophy is found to be even more complicated to the extent that these problems of interpretation and evaluation refer back to and extend one another. What Nietzsche calls "noble," "high," and "master" is sometimes active force and sometimes affirmative will. What he calls "base," "vile," and "slave" is sometimes reactive force and sometimes negative will. We will understand later why these terms are used. But a value always has a genealogy upon which depends the nobility or baseness of what it invites us to believe, feel, and think.

The genealogist alone is fit to discover how a certain baseness can find its expression in one value and a certain nobility in another, for he knows how to deal with the differential element: he is a master at the critique of values.[29] We remove all meaning from the notion of values so long as we do not see in them so many receptacles to be pierced, so many statues to be broken open, to find what they contain of the most noble, the most base. Only out of such things as the scattered limbs of Dionysus can the statues of nobility be once again formed. To talk about the nobility of values generally testifies to a thought that has too much at stake to hide its own baseness. It is as if a whole domain of values did not find its meaning, and precisely its value, in serving as the refuge and manifestation of all that is base, vile, and slavish. Nietzsche—the creator of the philosophy of values—would have seen, if he had lived longer, his most critical notion serve and turn into the basest and most insipid ideological conformism; the hammer strokes of his philosophy of values becoming strokes of flattery, polemic and aggressivity replaced by *ressentiment*—captious guardian of the established order and watchdog of current values—and genealogy taken up in hand by slaves. All of which testifies to the forgetting of qualities, the forgetting of origins.[30]

ORIGIN AND INVERTED IMAGE

Originally, there is the difference between active and reactive forces; and from the start, action and reaction are not related in terms of succession, but in terms of coexistence. We also find that the complicity between active forces and affirmation, as well as that between reactive forces and negation, is revealed in the principle that the negative is already entirely on the side of reaction. Conversely, only active force asserts itself; it affirms its difference, and makes its difference an object of delight and affirmation. Reactive force, even when it obeys, limits active force; it imposes limitations and partial restrictions on it, and is already possessed by the spirit or negation.[31] This is why the origin itself in some sense bears an inverted self-image: seen from the side of reactive force, the genealogical and differential element appears backwards, difference having become negation and affirmation having become contradiction. A reversed image of the origin accompanies the origin—what is "yes" from the viewpoint of active forces becomes "no" from the viewpoint of reactive forces, and what is affirmation of the self becomes negation of the other. This is what Nietzsche calls "the inversion of the value-positing eye."[32] Active forces are noble, but they find themselves before a plebeian image, reflected by reactive forces.

Genealogy is the art of difference or distinction, the art of nobility, but it sees itself backwards in the mirror of reactive forces. Its image then appears as that of an "evolution." Sometimes this evolution is understood in the German way, as a dialectical and Hegelian evolution, as the development of contradiction; sometimes in the English way, as a utilitarian derivation, as the development of profit and interest. But genuine genealogy is always caricatured in the image given it by an essentially reactive evolutionism; and whether it be German or English, evolutionism is the reactive image of genealogy.[33] Thus, at the start, it is characteristic of reactive forces to deny the difference that originally constitutes them, to reverse the differential element from which they are derived, and to give it a deformed image. "Difference breeds hatred." It is for this reason that they do not understand themselves as forces, that they prefer to turn against themselves rather than understand themselves as such and accept the difference. The kind of "mediocre" thought that Nietzsche denounces always amounts to the mania for interpreting or evaluating phenomena on the basis of some reactive force—each species of national thought choosing its own sort. But this mania itself originates in the reversed images, the reversed origin. Conscience and consciousness are simply swellings of this reactive image.

Going one step further, suppose that with the help of favorable external or internal circumstances the reactive forces sweep over and neutralize the active forces. Here, we have left the origin; it is no longer a question of the reversed image, but of a development of this image, an inversion of values themselves so that the low has been placed on high and the reactive forces have triumphed. If they triumph, this is due to the negative will, the will to nothingness that develops the image. Nonetheless, their triumph is not imaginary. The question is, how do reactive forces triumph? Which is to say, when they sweep over active forces, do reactive forces become dominating, aggressive, and subjugating in turn? Do they all form, together, a greater force that would be active in turn? Nietzsche answers that, even when joining together, the reactive forces do not compose a greater force, one that would be active. They proceed entirely otherwise: *they decompose, they separate active force from what it can do,* they take away a part—or nearly all—of its power. In doing so, the reactive forces do not themselves become active; on the contrary, they make the active force rejoin them so that it becomes reactive in a new sense. On the basis of its origin and development, we suspect that the concept of reaction changes in its signification; that an active force *becomes reactive* (in a new sense) when reactive forces (in the first sense) separate it from what it can do. Nietzsche will analyze in detail how such a separation is possible. But it must be said already that Nietzsche is careful never to present the triumph of reactive forces as a compound force, superior to active force, but as a subtraction or division. Nietzsche devotes a whole book (*The Genealogy of Morals*) to analyzing the figures of reactive triumph in the human world—*ressentiment,* bad conscience, and the ascetic ideal—and in each case he shows that the reactive forces do not triumph by composing a superior force, but by "separating" or dividing the active force. And in each case this separation rests on a fiction, a mystification, or a falsification. It is the will to nothingness that develops the negative and reversed image and makes the subtraction.

In the operation of subtraction there is always something imaginary, which is testified to by the negative use of number. Thus, if we want to give a numerical transcription to the victory of reactive forces, we must appeal not to addition, by which the reactive forces would together become stronger than the active forces, but rather to subtraction; this would separate active force from its own power and would deny any difference, thus making it a reactive force. It is not enough, consequently, that reaction prevail over action for it to cease being reaction. On the contrary. While active force is separated from the exercise of its power by a fiction, it is not, for that reason, any less reactive; indeed, it is by this means that it really does become reactive. Thus, when Nietzsche employs the words "vile," "ignoble," and "slave," these words designate the state of reactive forces that place themselves on high and lure the active forces into a trap, replacing masters with slaves—who nonetheless remain slaves. As one of the great remarks from *The Will to Power* expresses it, "One has always had to defend the strong against the weak."

WILL TO POWER AND THE FEELING OF POWER

We know that Will to Power is the differential and genealogical element that determines the relation of force with force and produces the quality of force. We know also that Will to Power must *manifest itself* as force. Because the dynamism of force depends entirely on Will to Power, the study of its manifestations must be made with the greatest care. But what does it mean for Will to Power to manifest itself? The relation between forces in each case is determined insofar as one force is *affected* by other inferior or superior forces. It follows that Will to Power is manifested as a capacity for being affected. This capacity is not an abstract possibility, but is necessarily fulfilled and actualized at each instant by the other forces with which it relates. We should not be surprised by the double aspect of Will to Power: it determines the relation between forces from the standpoint of their genesis or reproduction, but it is determined by the relating forces from the standpoint of its own manifestation. This is why the Will to Power is always and at the same time determined and determining, qualified as well as qualifying.

In the first place, then, Will to Power manifests itself as the capacity for being affected, and as the determined capacity of force to be itself affected. It is difficult to deny here a Spinozistic inspiration in Nietzsche. Spinoza, in an extremely profound theory, wanted every quantity of force to correspond to a capacity for being affected. A body would have all the more force so far as it could be affected in a greater number of ways. It is this capacity that either measures the force of a body or expresses its power. In addition, and on the one hand, this capacity was not simply a logical possibility, for at every moment it was actualized by relations between this and other bodies. On the other hand, this capacity was not a physical passivity; the only passive elements were the affect not adequately caused by the body in question.[34]

It is the same for Nietzsche; the capacity for being affected does not necessarily mean passivity, but *affectivity*, sensibility, and sensation. It is in this sense that Nietzsche—even before elaborating the concept of Will to Power and giving it its full significance—already spoke of a *feeling of power*. Nietzsche treated power as an affair of feeling and sensibility before he treated it as a question of the will. But when he did elaborate the complete concept of Will to Power, this first characteristic did not altogether disappear; it became the manifestation of Will to Power. This is why Nietzsche ceaselessly tells us that Will to Power is "the primitive form of affect;" it is that from which all other feelings are derived. Or better still, "Will to power is neither a being nor a becoming, it is a pathos." This means that Will to Power manifests itself as the sensibility of force, that the differential element of forces manifests itself as their differential sensibility.

> The fact is that will to power rules even in the inorganic world, or, rather, that there is no inorganic world. One cannot eliminate action at a distance, for one thing attracts another and one thing feels attracted. Here is the fundamental fact . . . *So that will to power can manifest itself it needs to perceive the things it sees and feel the approach of what is assimilable to it.*[35]

A force's affects are active insofar as the force appropriates what resists it or compels the obedience of inferior forces. Conversely, they are submissive—or, rather, acted upon—when the force is affected by superior forces that it obeys. Here again, obeying is a manifestation of Will to Power. But an inferior force can bring about the disintegration, the scission of superior forces; it can explode the energy they have accumulated. In this sense Nietzsche likes to bring together the phenomena of atomic disintegration, protoplasmic division, and the reproduction of organic life.[36] And not only do disintegration, splitting, and separation always express Will to Power, but also *being* disintegrated, *being* split, and *being* separated: "Duality appears as the consequence of will to power." Two forces being given, one superior and the other inferior, one sees how the capacity to be affected is necessarily fulfilled in each. But this power of being affected is not fulfilled unless the corresponding force itself enters into a history, into a process of sensible becoming. Thus, (1) active force is the power of acting or commanding; (2) reactive force is the power of obeying or being acted upon; (3) developed reactive force is the power of splitting, dividing, and separating; (4) active force become reactive is the power of being separated and of turning against itself.[37]

All sensibility is only a becoming of forces; there is a cycle to force, in the course of which force "becomes" (e.g., active force becomes reactive). There are even several becomings of force that can struggle against one another. Thus, it is not enough either to parallel or to oppose the respective characters of active and reactive force. The active and reactive are qualities of force that issue from Will to Power. But Will to Power itself has qualities, *sensibilia,* that exist as the becomings of force. Will to Power manifests itself first as the sensibility of forces, and second as the becoming sensible of forces. Becoming results, therefore, from the most elementary fact of pathos.[38] The becoming of forces, in general, must not be confused with the qualities of force, for the quality of the Will to Power is precisely the becoming of these qualities themselves. Indeed, one can no more abstract the qualities of force from their becoming than force from Will to Power; the concrete study of force necessarily implies a dynamics.

THE BECOMING-REACTIVE OF FORCES

The dynamics of forces leads us to a distressing conclusion. When reactive force separates active force from its own power, this latter force becomes reactive in turn. *The active forces become reactive.* Here, the word becoming must be taken in the strongest sense; the becoming of forces appears as a becoming-reactive. Are there no other becomings? It remains that we do not feel, experience, or know any other form of becoming than becoming-reactive. We are not merely noting the existence of reactive forces; we ascertain their triumph everywhere. But how do they triumph? Through the will to nothingness—owing to the affinity between reaction and negation. What is negation? It is a quality of Will to Power, and it qualifies it as Nihilism, or will to nothingness. This is what constitutes the becoming-reactive of forces. We must not say that active force becomes reactive because reactive forces triumph; on the contrary, they triumph because, by separating active force from its power, they give it over to the will to nothingness in the form of a becoming-reactive even more deep-seated than themselves. This is why the figures for the triumph of reactive forces (*ressentiment,* bad conscience, and the ascetic ideal) are forms of Nihilism in the first place. Force becoming-reactive, becoming nihilistic, seems essentially included in the relation of force with force. Is there another becoming? Everything tempts us into thinking that perhaps there is. But, as Nietzsche frequently says, this would require another sensibility, another way of feeling. Barely envisioning this question, we cannot yet reply to it. But we can ask why it is that we only feel and know a becoming-reactive of force. *Ressentiment,* bad conscience, and nihilism are not psychological traits, but the foundation of humanity in man. They are the principles of human being as such. Man is the "diseased skin" of the earth, the reaction of the earth. It is in this sense that Zarathustra speaks of his "great contempt'' and ''great disgust'' for man. Would another sensibility and becoming still be man's?

This condition of man is of the greatest importance for the Eternal Return. It seems to compromise or contaminate it so gravely that it becomes itself an object of anguish, repulsion, and disgust. Even if the active forces recur, they would again become reactive, eternally reactive. The eternal return of reactive forces, moreover, is the return of the becoming-reactive of forces. Zarathustra not only presents the thought of the Eternal Return as mysterious and secret, but as nauseating, as difficult to bear. The first exposition of the Eternal Return is followed by a strange vision of a young shepherd, ''writhing, gagging, in spasms, his face distorted,'' with a heavy black snake hanging out of his mouth. Later, Zarathustra himself explains the vision: ''The great disgust with man—*this* choked me and had crawled into my throat . . . Eternally recurs, the man of whom you are weary, the small man . . . Alas, man recurs eternally! . . . And the eternal recurrence even of the smallest—that was my disgust with all existence! Alas! Nausea! Nausea! Nausea!''[39] The eternal return of the small, petty, reactive man not only makes the *thought* of the Eternal Return something unbearable, it also makes the Eternal Return something unbearable, it makes the Eternal Return itself something impossible; it puts contradiction into the Eternal Return. The snake is an animal of the Eternal Return, but the snake uncoils; it becomes a ''heavy black snake'' and hangs out of the mouth that prepared to speak— i.e., so far as the Eternal Return is one of the reactive forces. For how could the Eternal Return, being of becoming, affirm a nihilistic becoming? To affirm the Eternal Return one must bite off and spit out the snake's head. Then the shepherd is no longer man or shepherd: he ''was transformed radiant, *laughing!* Never on earth has a human being laughed as he laughed.'' Another becoming, another sensibility: the Overman.

AMBIVALENCE OF MEANING AND VALUES

A becoming-active of forces, a becoming-active of reactive forces, would be another becoming than that which we now know. The evaluation of such a becoming raises several questions and should serve us one last time to test the systematic coherence of Nietzsche's concepts in his theory of force. A first hypothesis arises. Nietzsche calls that force active which goes right to the end of its consequences. The active force, separated from its power by reactive force, thus becomes reactive in turn. But doesn't the reactive force go right to the end of its power, too, in its own way? If active force, being separated, becomes reactive, doesn't reactive force, which separates, conversely become active? Isn't this its way of being active? Concretely, is there not a kind of baseness, villainy, stupidity, etc., that becomes active by dint of following out its power to the end? "Rigorous and grandiose stupidity," Nietzsche writes.

This hypothesis brings the Socratic objection to mind, but is in fact distinguished from it. One no longer means, as Socrates, that inferior forces triumph only when forming a greater force, but, rather, that reactive forces triumph only when pursuing their consequences to the end, thus forming an active force.

It is certain that a reactive force can be considered from different viewpoints. Sickness, for example, prevents me from exercising my powers; as a reactive force it renders me reactive, it narrows my possibilities and condemns me to a diminished milieu which I can do no more than adapt myself to. But in another way it reveals a new power to me and endows me with a new will that I can make my own, pursuing this strange new capacity to its end (this intense capacity sets up a variety of things—e.g., the possibility of "looking from the perspective of the sick toward healthier concepts and values"). Here we see an ambivalence dear to Nietzsche: all the forces that were denounced for their reactive character, are, a few lines or pages later, avowed to fascinate him—they are held to be sublime because of the perspective they open up for us, and because they testify to a disturbing Will to Power. They separate us from our own power, but at the same time they give us another power, so "dangerous" and "interesting." They bring us new feelings and teach us new ways of being affected. There is something admirable in the becoming-reactive of forces, something admirable and dangerous. Not only the sick man but also the religious man presents this double aspect: reactive on the one hand, and possessing a new power on the other.[40] "Human history would be altogether too stupid a thing without the spirit that the impotent have introduced into it."[41] Each time Nietzsche speaks of Socrates, Christ, Judeaism, and Christianity, or of some other form of decadence and degeneration, he discovers this same ambivalence of things, beings, and forces.

Nevertheless, is it precisely the same force that separates me from my exercise of power and endows me with a new power? Is it the same sick man with the same sickness who is slave to his sickness and yet uses it as a means of exploring, dominating, and being powerful? Is it the same religion that is claimed by the faithful, who are like bleating sheep, as well as by certain priests who are like new "birds of prey"? Indeed, reactive forces are not the same, and they change their nuance accordingly as they more or less develop their degree of affinity with the will to nothingness. One reactive force both obeys and resists; another separates active force from the exercise of its power; another contaminates active force and carries it off to the point of becoming-reactive in a will to nothingness; and yet another reactive force was at first active but became reactive, cut off from its power, drawn down into the abyss, and turned against itself: these are all different nuances, affects, and types that the genealogist must interpret, and that no one else knows how to interpret.

> Need I say after all this that in questions of decadence I am *experienced?* I have spelled them forward and backward. Even that filigree art of grasping and comprehending in general, those fingers for *nuances,* that psychology of "looking around the corner," and whatever else is characteristic of me.[42]

The problem of interpretation is in each case to interpret the state of the reactive forces—i.e., the degree of development they have attained in relation to negation and the will to nothingness. The same problem of interpretation could be posed from the side of active forces: in each case, to interpret their nuance or state—i.e., the degree of development in the relation between action and affirmation. There are reactive forces that become grandiose and fascinating by dint of following the will to nothingness, and there are active forces that collapse because they cannot follow out their affirmative powers. (This is the problem of what Nietzsche calls "culture" or "the superior man.") Finally, evaluation presents ambivalences profounder still than those of interpretation. To judge affirmation itself from the viewpoint of negation itself, and negation from the viewpoint of affirmation; to judge affirmative will from the viewpoint of nihilistic will, and nihilistic will from the viewpoint of affirmative will—such is the genealogist's art, and the genealogist is the doctor.

> Looking from the perspective of the sick toward *healthier* concepts and values and, conversely, looking again from the fullness and self-assurance of a *rich* life down into the secret work of the instinct of decadence . . .[43]

But whatever the ambivalence of meaning and values, we can not conclude that a reactive force becomes active by following out its own power to the end. For "to go right to the end," right to "the ultimate consequences," has two meanings, depending on whether one affirms or denies, whether one affirms his own difference or denies what is different. When a reactive force works out its final consequences, this is in relation to negation; the will to nothingness serves as its motive. Becoming-active, on the contrary, supposes the affinity of action and affirmation; and in order to become active it is not enough that a force follow out its own power to the end; it must make its own power an object of affirmation. Becoming-active is affirming and affirmative, just as becoming-reactive is negating and nihilistic.

SECOND ASPECT OF THE ETERNAL RETURN: AS AN ETHICAL AND SELECTIVE THOUGHT

Being neither felt nor known, becoming-active can only be thought of as the product of *selection:* a double and simultaneous selection by the activity of force and the affirmation of will. But what brings about the selection? What serves as the principle of selection? Nietzsche's answer is: the Eternal Return. Formerly the object of disgust, the Eternal Return overcomes disgust and turns Zarathustra into a "convalescent"—it "consoles" him. But in what sense is the Eternal Return selective? First of all, as a thought, it gives the will a practical rule.[44] The Eternal Return gives the will a rule as rigorous as the Kantian imperative. We have pointed out that the Eternal Return, as a physical doctrine, was the new formulation of the speculative synthesis. As an ethical thought, the Eternal Return is a new formulation of the practical synthesis: *Whatever you will, will it in such a way that you also will its Eternal Return.*

> If in all you will to do, you begin by asking yourself: Is it certain that I will to do it an infinite number of times?—this would be your most solid center of gravity.[45]

Only one thing in the world disheartened Nietzsche: the little compensations, the little pleasures, the little joys, and everything one agrees to, once—and only once. Everything one can do again the next day *only* on the condition that it be said the eve before: tomorrow I will no longer do it—the whole ceremonial of the obsessed. We are like those old women who permit themselves an excess only once—and we act and think like them.

> Oh, that you would reject all *halfhearted* willing and would become resolute in sloth and deed. Alas, that you would understand my word: Do whatever you will, but first be such as are *able to will*.[46]

A laziness, stupidity, baseness, cowardliness, or spitefulness that would will its own eternal return would no longer be the same laziness, the same stupidity, etc. Let us see more clearly, then, how the Eternal Return brings about selection. It is the *thought* of Eternal Return that selects. It makes the will into something whole. All that falls outside the Eternal Return is eliminated from the will by the thought of Eternal Return; it makes willing a creation, and brings about the equation willing = creating.

Clearly, such a selection remains inferior to Zarathustra's ambitions. It is content to eliminate certain reactive states, certain states of reactive forces among the less developed. But the reactive forces that pursue their power to the end in their own way, and find a powerful motive in the nihilistic will—these resist the first selection. Far from falling outside of the Eternal Return, they enter into it and seem to recur with it. So we must expect a second selection, very different from the first. But this second selection puts the most obscure parts of Nietzsche's philosophy into question, and forms an almost esoteric element in his doctrine of eternal return. We should, therefore, merely register these Nietzschean themes with the hope of giving a more detailed conceptual explanation later.

1. Why is the Eternal Return called "the most extreme form of nihilism"?[47] And if the Eternal Return is the extremest form of Nihilism, Nihilism itself, separated or abstracted from the Eternal Return, is always an "incomplete nihilism"—however far it goes, and as powerful as it is.[48] The Eternal Return alone makes the nihilistic will a full and complete will.

2. The will to nothingness as we have examined it up to now, has always appeared allied with reactive forces. Its essence was to deny active force and to lead active force into denying, and turning back against, itself. But at the same time it thus founded the conservation, triumph, and contagion of reactive forces. Will to nothingness means universal becoming-reactive, the becoming-reactive of force. This is the sense, then, in which Nihilism is always incomplete by itself. Even the ascetic ideal is contrary to what one might expect, it is "an expedient of the art of conserving life." Nihilism is the principle of conservation for a weak, diminished, reactive life; the depreciation and negation of life form the principle in the shadow of which reactive life conserves itself, survives, triumphs, and becomes contagious.

3. What happens when the will to nothingness is related to the Eternal Return? This is the only place where it breaks its alliance with reactive forces. Only the Eternal Return can make Nihilism into a *complete* nihilism, *because it turns negation into a negation of the reactive forces themselves*. In the Eternal Return, Nihilism no longer expresses itself as the conservation and victory of the weak, but as their destruction, their *auto-destruction*.

> This perishing takes the form of a self-destruction—the instinctive selection of that which must destroy . . . The will to destruction as the will of a still deeper instinct, the instinct of self-destruction, the will for nothingness.[49]

This is why Zarathustra, as early as the Prologue, sings to him "who wants to go under," "for he wants to perish," "he does not want to preserve himself," "for he goes gladly over the bridge." The prologue of *Zarathustra* contains the Eternal Return as though it were a premature secret.

4. The turning against oneself should not be confused with this self-destruction, this auto-destruction. In the reactive process of turning against oneself, the active force becomes reactive. In auto-destruction the reactive forces are themselves denied and led to nothingness. This is why auto-

destruction is said to be an active operation, an *"active destruction."* [50] It and it alone expresses the becoming-active of forces; and forces become active to the extent that the reactive forces deny and suppress themselves in the name of a principle that, scarcely a moment ago, assured their conservation and triumph. Active negation or active destruction is the state of the strong-minded who destroy the reactive element within themselves, submitting it to the test of Eternal Return and submitting themselves to this test, even if it entails willing their own decline; ''it is the condition of strong spirits and wills, and these do not find it possible to stop with the negative of 'judgment;' their nature demands *active negation.*''[51] Such is the only way that reactive forces *become active*. Furthermore, this is why negation—as the negation of reactive forces themselves—is not only active, but is indeed *transmuted*. It expresses affirmation, and it expresses becoming-active as the power of affirming. Nietzsche thus speaks about ''the eternal joy of becoming—that joy which includes even joy in destroying . . . the affirmation of annihilation and destruction, which is the decisive feature of a Dionysian philosophy.''[52]

5. The second selection in the Eternal Return therefore consists in this: Eternal Return produces the becoming-active of force. It suffices to relate the will to nothingness to the Eternal Return in order to realize that reactive forces *do not* return. However far they go, however deep the becoming-reactive of forces is, reactive forces *will not* recur. The small, petty, reactive man will not recur. In and through the Eternal Return, negation as a quality of Will to Power transmutes itself into affirmation; it becomes an affirmation of negation itself, and becomes a power of affirming, an affirmative power. This is what Nietzsche presents as Zarathustra's cure and as Dionysus' secret: ''Nihilism vanquished by itself,'' thanks to the Eternal Return.

Now, this second selection is very different from the first. It is no longer a question of using the simple thought of Eternal Return in order to eliminate from the will everything that falls outside this thought; rather, by invoking the Eternal Return, it is now a matter of making what cannot enter into being—without changing its nature—enter into it. Thus, it is no longer a question of a selective thought but of selective being; for Eternal Return is being, and being is selection (selection=hierarchy).

THE PROBLEM OF THE ETERNAL RETURN

All this should be taken as a simple registering of texts to be clarified in terms of the following points: the relation of the two qualities of Will to Power, negation and affirmation; the relation of Will to Power itself with Eternal Return; the possibility of transmutation as a new way of feeling, thinking, and, above all, as a new way of being (the Overman). In Nietzsche's terminology the *reversal* of values signifies the active in place of the reactive (properly speaking, it is the reversal of a reversal, since reaction had begun by taking the place of action). But the *transmutation* of values, or *transvaluation,* signifies that affirmation takes the place of negation. More precisely, perhaps, it means that negation is transformed into a power of affirmation—the supreme Dionysian metamorphosis. All these points, which still must be analyzed, form the summit of the doctrine of Eternal Return.

From afar, we scarcely see where the summit is. The Eternal Return is the being of becoming. But becoming is double: becoming-active and becoming-reactive, as well as the becoming-active of reactive forces and the becoming-reactive of active forces. Only becoming-active has any being; it would be contradictory for the being of becoming to be affirmed by a becoming-reactive—that is, by a becoming that is itself nihilistic. The Eternal Return would itself become contradictory if it were the return of reactive forces. The Eternal Return teaches us that becoming-reactive has no being. In fact, it also teaches us the existence of a becoming-active of force. It necessarily produces the becoming-active of force in that it reproduces becoming. This is why affirmation is paired; for one cannot fully affirm the being of becoming without also affirming the existence of becoming-active. The Eternal Return thus has a double aspect, for it is the universal being of becoming. But the universal being of becoming calls for a single becoming. Only becoming-active has any being, which is the being of becoming as a whole. To return is everything, but everything is affirmed in a single moment. However much one affirms Eternal Return as the universal being of becoming—however much, in addition, one affirms becoming-active as the symptom and product of the universal Eternal Return—affirmation alters its nuance and becomes deeper and deeper. As a physical doctrine, the Eternal Return affirms the being of becoming. But as a selective ontology, it affirms this being of becoming as the "self-affirmation" of becoming-active. One sees that at the core of Zarathustra's collusion with his animals a misunderstanding arises as a problem the animals neither understand nor recognize, but which is the problem of Zarathustra's own disgust and recovery: " 'O you buffoons and barrel organs!' Zarathustra replied and smiled again. . . . 'Have you already made a hurdy-gurdy song of this?' "[53] The old song, this old refrain, is the cycle and the all, universal being. But the complete formula for affirmation is the all, yes, universal being, yes; but universal being calls for a single becoming, the all calls for a single moment.

NOTES

1. Spinoza, *Ethics,* Part III, proposition 2: "I have just pointed out that the objectors cannot fix the limits of the body's power, or say what can be

concluded from a consideration of its sole nature, whereas they have experience of many things being accomplished solely by the laws of nature, which they would never have believed possible, except under the direction of mind." See *The Chief Works of Benedict de Spinoza* (New York: Dover Publications, 1951), vol. II, p. 133.

2. *The Will to Power,* §676.

3. *WP,* §524; *The Gay Science,* §357.

4. Kröner, XII; part I, §306.

5. *WP,* §635.

6. "The human body is a more wonderful idea than the soul of a short time ago." *WP,* §659. "What is much more wonderful, is rather the body; one never ceases to be amazed at the idea that the human body has become possible." K, XII; part I, §306.

7. *WP,* §642.

8. *The Genealogy of Morals;* II, §12.

9. *GS,* §354; *WP* §§167, 473, 657, 660.

10. Here we see the originality of Nietzsche's pluralism. What interests him in his conception of the organism is not the plurality of constituting forces, but the diversity of active and reactive forces, and the investigation of the active forces themselves.

11. K, XIII; §599.

12. *Thus Spoke Zarathustra;* I, "On the Despisers of the Body."

13. *WP,* §§647, 657; *Beyond Good and Evil,* §259.

14. *WP,* §710.

15. *WP,* §§564, 660.

16. *WP,* §565.

17. K, XII; part I, §104. See analogous text: *WP,* §1062; also §§1064, 1066.

18. *Philosophy in the Tragic Age of the Greeks,* §4: "But then Anaximander sees another question: Why hasn't all that came-to-be passed away long since, since a whole eternity of time has passed? Whence the ever renewed stream of coming-to-be? And from this question he can save himself only by a mystic possibility."

19. *WP,* §617.

20. The account of the Eternal Return in terms of the passing moment is to be found in *Thus Spoke Zarathustra;* III, "On the Vision and the Riddle."

21. "From whence comes the diversity within a cycle? . . . by admitting that an equal concentration of energy exists for each force center in the universe, we would have to ask how the least bit of diversity could arise." K, XII; part I, §106.

22. *WP,* §634.

23. *WP,* §619.

24. "My proposition is: that the will of psychology hitherto is an unjustified generalization, that this will *does not exist at all,* that instead of

grasping the idea of the development of one definite will into many forms, one has eliminated the character of the will by subtracting from it its content, its 'direction'—this is in the highest degree the case with Schopenhauer: what he calls 'will' is a mere empty word.'' *WP*, §692.

25. ''How does this happen? I asked myself. What persuades the living to obey and command, and to practice obedience even when it commands? Hear, then, my word, you who are wisest. Test in all seriousness whether I have crawled into the very heart of life and into the very roots of its heart. Where I found the living, there I found will to power; and even in the will of those who serve I found the will to be master.'' *Zarathustra;* II, ''On Self-Overcoming.''

26. On these problems, posed after Kant, cf. M. Gueroult, *La Philosophie transcendentale de Salomon Maïmon, La Doctrine de la science chez Fichte;* and M. Vuillemin, *L'Héritage Kantien et la révolution copernicienne.*

27. *WP*, §§556, 643.

28. *GM;* III, §28.

29. ''We need a *critique* of moral values, *the value of these values themselves must first be called in question.*'' *GM;* Preface, §6.

30. The theory of values is ever farther removed from its origins inasmuch as it loses sight of the principle that to evaluate means to create. In any case, from Nietzsche's point of view, the correlate to creating values can in no way be the contemplation of them; rather, it must be the radical critique of all ''current values.''

31. See especially *GM;* II, §11.

32. *GM;* I, §10. Instead of affirming itself, and having denial come as a simple consequence, the reactive forces begin by denying what is different from themselves; from the start, they are opposed to whatever is not part of themselves.

33. On the English conception of genealogy as evolution, see *GM;* Preface, §7, and *GM;* I, §§1–4. On the mediocrity of this kind of English thought, see *BGE,* §253. On the German conception of genealogy as evolution, and on its mediocrity, see *GS,* §357, and *BGE,* §244.

34. If our interpretation is correct, Spinoza saw—before Nietzsche—that force was inseparable from its capacity for being affected, and that this capacity expressed its power. Nonetheless, Nietzsche criticizes Spinoza, but on another point: Spinoza was never able to bring himself to the conception of a *will* to power. He confused power with simple force, and he conceived force in a reactive way (e.g., *conatus* and conservation).

35. K, XIII; §204.

36. *WP*, §§348–49, 654, 660.

37. ''This highest force, which, turning against itself when it no longer has anything left to organize, expends its force on disorganization.'' *WP,* §712.

38. *WP*, §638.

39. *Zarathustra;* III, "On the Vision and the Riddle," §2, and "The Convalescent," §2.

40. "It was on the soil of this *essentially dangerous* form of human existence, the priestly form, that man first became an *interesting animal,* that only here did the human soul in a higher sense acquire *depth* and become *evil.*" *GM;* I, §6. And on the ambivalence of the priest: "He must be sick himself, he must be profoundly related to the sick—how else would they understand each other?—but he must also be strong, master of himself even more than of others, with his will to power intact, so as to be both trusted and feared by the sick." *GM;* III, §15.

41. *GM;* §7.

42. *Ecce Homo;* I, §1.

43. *Ibid.*

44. *WP*, §§1053, 1056: "The great selective Thought."

45. K, XII; part I, §117 (1881–82).

46. *Zarathustra;* III, "On Virtue That Makes Small," §3. Also, *Zarathustra;* II, "On the Pitying": "Worst of all, however, are petty thoughts. Verily, even evil deeds are better than petty thoughts. To be sure, you say: 'The pleasure in a lot of petty nastiness saves us from many a big evil deed.' But here one should not wish to save."

47. *WP*, §55.

48. *WP*, §28.

49. *WP*, §55.

50. *Ibid.;* also, *EH;* III, §1.

51. *WP*, §24.

52. *EH;* III, "The Birth of Tragedy," §3.

53. *Zarathustra;* III, "The Convalescent."

Pierre Klossowski

NIETZSCHE'S EXPERIENCE OF THE ETERNAL RETURN

To Peter Gast

Sils-Maria, 14 August 1881

. . . The August sun is overhead, the year is slipping away, the mountains and forests are becoming more hushed and more peaceful. Thoughts have emerged on my horizon the likes of which I've never seen—I won't even hint at what they are, but shall maintain my own unshakable calm. I suppose now I'll have to live a few years longer! Ah, my friend, I sometimes think that I lead a highly dangerous life, since I'm *one of those machines that can burst apart!* The intensity of my feelings makes me shudder and laugh. Several times I have been unable to leave my room, for the ridiculous reason that my eyes were inflamed. Why? Because I'd cried too much on my wanderings the day before. Not sentimental tears, mind you, but tears of joy, to the accompaniment of which I sang and talked nonsense, filled with a *new vision* far superior to that of other men.

If I couldn't derive my strength from myself, if I had to depend on the outside world for encouragement, comfort, and good cheer, where would I be! What would I be! There really were moments and even whole periods in my life (e.g., the year 1878) when a word of encouragement, a friendly squeeze of the hand would have been the ideal medicine—and precisely then I was left in the lurch by all those I'd supposed I could rely on, and who could have done me such kindness. Now I no longer expect it, and feel only a certain dim and dreary astonishment when, for example, I think of the letters I get: it's all so meaningless. Nothing's happened to anyone because of me; no one's given me any thought. It's all very decent and well-intended, what they write me, but distant, distant, distant. Even our dear Jacob Burckhardt wrote such a meek and timorous little letter. . . .

FORGETTING AND ANAMNESIS IN THE EXPERIENCE OF THE ETERNAL RETURN OF THE SAME

The idea of the Eternal Return came to Nietzsche as a sudden *awakening,* thanks to a *feeling,* a certain state or tonality of mind. Initially confused with this feeling, the idea itself emerges as a specific doctrine; nonetheless, it preserves the character of a revelation—a sudden unveiling. Here the ecstatic character of this experience must be distinguished from the notion of the universal ring, a notion that obsessed Nietzsche in his youth, in his Hellenistic period.

But how does forgetting function in this revelation? More specifically, isn't forgetting the source and indispensable condition not only for the appearance of the Eternal Return but *for tranforming the very identity* of the person to whom it appears? Forgetting thus raises eternal becoming and the absorption of all identity to the level of being.

Isn't there a tension implicit in Nietzsche's own experience between the revealed content and didactic message of this content—at least (as an ethical doctrine) when it is formulated in the following way: act as though you had to relive your life innumerable times and wish to relive it innumerable times—for, in one way or another, you must recommence and relive it.

The imperative proposition serves to supplement (the necessary) forgetting by invoking the will (to power); the second proposition foresees the necessity that was undiscerned in the act of forgetting.

Anamnesis coincides with the revelation of the return. But how can the return fail to bring back forgetfulness? Not only do I learn that I (Nietzsche) am brought back to the crucial moment in which the eternity of the circle culminates—at the very point when the truth of its necessary return is revealed to me—but, by the same token, I learn that I was *other* than I am *now* for having forgotten this truth, and thus I have become another by learning it. Will I change and forget once more that I will necessarily change throughout eternity, until I relearn this revelation anew?

The accent must be placed on the loss of a given identity. The "death of God" (of the God who guarantees the identity of the accountable self) opens the soul to all its possible identities, already apprehended through the diverse feelings of the Nietzschean soul. The revelation of the Eternal Return necessarily brings on the successive realizations of all possible identities: "All the names of history, finally, are me"—in the end, "Dionysus and the Crucified." The "death of God," then, corresponds to a feeling in Nietzsche in the same way as the ecstatic moment of the Eternal Return does.

DIGRESSION

The Eternal Return is a necessity that must be willed: only he who I am now can will the necessity of my return and all the events that have resulted in what I am—i.e., inasmuch as the will here supposes a subject. Now this subject can no longer will itself as it has been up to now, but must will all its previous possibilities; for, in adopting the necessity of the return as universal law at the outset, I de-actualize my present self to will myself in *all the other selves,* whose entire series must be gone through so that, following the circular movement, I can again become *what I am at the moment in which I discover* the law of the Eternal Return.

The moment the Eternal Return is revealed to me, I cease being my own self, *here and now*. I am capable of becoming innumerable others, and I know that I shall forget this revelation once I am outside my own memory. This forgetting forms the object of my own limits. Likewise, my present consciousness will be established only in the forgetting of my other possible identities.

What is this memory? It is the necessary circular movement to which I yield myself, to which I deliver myself over from myself. Now, if I proclaim the will—and, willing it necessarily, I shall have re-willed it—I shall forcibly have extended my consciousness to this circular movement. And, in the meantime, even though I were to identify myself with the circle, I would never re-emerge from this image as myself. In fact, at the moment when I am struck by the sudden revelation of the Eternal Return, *I no longer am*. In order for this revelation to have any meaning, it is necessary that I lose consciousness of myself, and that the circular movement of the return be merged with my unconsciousness until such time as it leads me back to the point where the necessity of living through the entire series of my possibilities is revealed to me. All that remains, then, is for me to re-will myself, no longer as the outcome of these previous possibilities, no longer as one realization among thousands, but as a fortuitous moment the very fortuity of which entails the necessary and integral return of the whole series.

But to re-will myself as a fortuitous moment is to renounce being myself *once and for all;* it is not the other way around—i.e., it is not once and for all that I have renounced being myself. Also, the renunciation must in any case be willed. Moreover, I am not even this fortuitous moment *once and for all* if, indeed, I must re-will this very moment; *one more time!* For nothing? For myself. And here, nothing serves as the circle *once and for all.* It is a valid sign for all that has happened, for all that happens, for all that will *ever* happen in the world.

HOW CAN THE WILL INTERVENE WITHOUT FORGETTING WHAT MUST BE WILLED AGAIN?

Indeed, at the very moment when the circular movement was revealed to me as necessary, this experience appeared to my life as never having taken place before! The high feeling, the elevated state of soul, was required in order for me to know and feel the necessity that all things return. If I meditate upon the elevated state in which the circle is suddenly revealed to me, I conclude that it is not possible that it has not already appeared to me innumerable times, perhaps in other forms. But this conclusion is possible *only* if I admit that this heightened state is not my own obsession; that on the contrary it is the only valid apprehension of being, of reality itself. But I had

forgotten all about this, because it is inscribed in the very essence of the
circular movement that the movement itself be forgotten from one state to
the next (in order that one move on to another state and thus be cast outside of
oneself; the alternative being that everything would come to a halt). And
even if I didn't forget what I had been in this life, I would still have forgotten
that I was cast outside myself into another life in no way differing from the
present one!

At the risk of everything coming to a halt? Is this to say that at the time of
this sudden revelation the movement was arrested? Far from it. For I myself,
Nietzsche, was not able to escape it. This revelation did not occur to me as a
reminiscence, nor as an experience of *déjà vu*. All would stop *for me* if I
remembered a previous identical revelation that—even though I were to
continually proclaim this necessary return—would serve to keep me within
myself and, thus, outside the truth that I teach. It was therefore necessary
that I forget this revelation in order for it to be *true!* For the series that I
suddenly glimpse, the series that I must live through in order to be brought
back to the same point, this revelation of the Eternal Return of the same
implies that *the same revelation* could just as well have occurred *at any
other moment* of the circular movement. It must be thus: in order to receive
this revelation, I am *nothing* other than the capacity to receive this revelation
at all other moments of the circular movement: nowhere in particular for me
alone, but always in the movement as a whole.

Nietzsche speaks of the Eternal Return of the same as the supreme thought
and also as the supreme feeling, as the loftiest feeling. Thus, in unpublished
material written at the same time as *The Gay Science,* he states:

> My doctrine teaches: live in such a way that you must desire to live
> again, this is your duty—you will live again in any case. He to whom
> effort procures the loftiest feeling, let him make the effort; he to whom
> repose brings the loftiest feeling, let him rest; he to whom the act of
> joining, of following and of obeying procures the loftiest feeling, let
> him obey. Providing that he becomes aware of what procures the
> loftiest feeling and that he draws back before nothing. Eternity depends
> upon it.

And he had noted earlier that, unlike natures endowed with an eternal soul fit
for an eternal becoming and a future amelioration, present human nature no
longer knows how to *wait*. The accent here is less on the will than on desire
and necessity, and this desire and this necessity are themselves tied to
eternity: whence the reference to the loftiest feeling, or, in Nietzschean
terms, to the high feeling—to the elevated state of the soul.

It is such a high state of the soul, in such a feeling, that Nietzsche lived in
the moment during which the Eternal Return appeared. But how can a state

of soul, a feeling, become a thought, and how can the loftiest feeling—the highest feeling, the Eternal Return—become supreme thought?

1. The state of the soul is a fluctuation of intensity.

2. In order that it be communicable, the intensity must take itself as an object and thus return upon itself.

3. In returning upon itself, the intensity interprets itself. But how can it interpret itself? By becoming a counterweight to itself. For this the intensity must divide, separate, and rejoin: now, this is what happens to it in what could be called moments of rise and fall. However, this is always a matter of the same fluctuation, of the wave in the concrete sense (and let us simply note, in passing, the important place that the spectacle of sea waves holds for Nietzsche's reflection).

4. But does an interpretation presuppose the search for signification? Rise and fall: these are designations, nothing else. Is there any signification beyond this ascertainment of a rise and fall? The intensity never has any sense other than that of being an intensity. It seems that of itself the intensity has no meaning. What is a meaning, and how can it be constituted? Also, what is the agent of meaning?

5. It seems that the agent of meaning, and therefore of signification, is once again the intensity, and this according to its diverse fluctuations. If by itself the intensity has no meaning (other than that of being an intensity), how can it be the agent of signification, or be signified as this or that state of the soul? A little earlier we asked how it could interpret itself, and we answered that it must act as a counterweight to itself in its rise and fall, but this did not go beyond a simple assertion. How, then, can it acquire a meaning, and how can meaning be constituted within the intensity? Precisely in returning upon itself—indeed, through a new fluctuation in which, by repeating itself and imitating itself, it would become a sign.

6. But first of all, a sign traces the fluctuation of an intensity. If a sign keeps its meaning, it is because the degree of intensity coincides with it. It signifies only by a new afflux of intensity, as it were, which rejoins its first trace.

7. But a sign is not only the trace of a fluctuation. It can just as well mark an *absence* of intensity. Here, too, what is peculiar is that a new afflux is necessary, if only to signify this absence.

Whether we name this afflux attention, will, memory, or whether we call this reflux indifference, relaxation, or forgetfulness, it is always a question of the same intensity, in no way differing from the movement of the waves of the same swell: "You and I," Nietzsche used to say, "we are of the same origin! of the same race!"

This flux and this reflux become intermingled, fluctuation within fluctuation, and, just like the shapes that float at the crest of the waves only to leave froth, are the designations left by intensity. And this is what we call thought.

But nonetheless, there is something sufficiently open in us—we other, apparently limited and closed natures—for Nietzsche to invoke the movement of waves. This is because signification exists by afflux; notwithstanding the sign in which the fluctuation of intensity culminates, signification is *never absolutely disengaged* from the moving chasms that it masks. Every signification, then, remains a function of the chaos out of which meaning is generated.

INTENSITY AS SUBJECT TO A MOVING CHAOS WITHOUT BEGINNING OR END

An intensity is at work in everyone, its flux and reflux forming the significant or insignificant fluctuations of thought. And while each appears to be in possession of this, in point of fact it belongs to no one, and has neither beginning nor end.

But, contrary to this undulating element, if each of us forms a closed and apparently limited whole, it is precisely by virtue of these traces of signifying fluctuations; i.e., by a system of signs that I will here name the everyday code of signs. So far as the beginning or end of our own fluctuations is concerned—on which basis these signs permit us to signify, to speak to ourselves as well as to others—we know nothing, except that for this code *a* sign always corresponds to the degree of intensity, sometimes the highest, sometimes to the lowest: even if this sign be the *me,* the *I,* the *subject of all our propositions.* It is thanks to this sign, however, which is nothing but an ever variable trace of fluctuation, that we constitute ourselves as *thinking,* that a thought as such occurs to us, even though we are never quite sure that it is not others who think and continue to think in us. But what is this other who forms the *outside* in relation to the *inside* that we hold ourselves to be? Everything leads back to a single discourse, to fluctuations of intensity that correspond to the thought of everyone and no one.

The sign "me" in the everyday code of communication, so far as it verifies our various internal and external degrees of presence and absence, thus assures a variable state of coherence in ourselves and with our surroundings. Thus the thought of no one, this intensity in itself, without determinable beginning or end, finds a necessity in him who appropriates it, and comes to know a destiny in the very vicissitudes of memory and forgetfulness; and this for the subject or the world at large. For a designation to occur, for a meaning to be constituted, *my will* must intervene—but, again, it is no more than this appropriated intensity.

Now, in a feeling, in a state that I will term the loftiest feeling and that I will aspire *to maintain* as the highest thought—what has happened? Have I not exceeded my limits, and by the same token depreciated the everyday code of signs, either because thought abandons me or because I no longer discern the difference between the fluctuations from without and from within?

Up to now, in the everyday sense, thought could always rely on the use of the term "myself." But what becomes of my own coherence at such a degree of intensity where thought ceases to include me in the term "myself" and invents a sign by which it would designate its own self coherency? If this is no longer my own thought, doesn't it signify my exclusion from all possible coherence? If it is still mine, how is it conceivable that it should designate an absense of intensity at the highest degree of intensity?

Let us suppose that the image of the circle is formed when the soul attains the highest state: something happens to my thought so that, by this sign, it dies—so that my thought is no longer really my own. Or, perhaps, my thought is so closely identified with this sign that even to invent this sign, this circle, signifies the power of all thought. Does this mean that the thinking subject would lose his own identity because a coherent thought would itself exclude that identity? Nothing here distinguishes the designating intensity from the designated intensity—i.e., nothing serves to re-establish the ordinary coherency between self and world as constituted by ordinary usage. The same circuit brings me back to the everyday code of signs, and leaves me once again at the mercy of signs as soon as I try to explain the events they represent.

If, in this ineffable moment, I hear it said: "You will return to this moment—you have already returned to it—you will return to it innumerable times," as coherent as this proposition seems according to the sign of the circle from which it flows, all the while remaining this selfsame proposition, so far as this is really me in the context of everyday signs, I fall into incoherency. Incoherency here assumes two forms: in relation to the very coherence of this thought itself, as well as in relation to the everyday code of signs. According to the latter, I can only will *myself once and for all;* it is on this basis that all my designations together with their sense are communicable. But *to will myself again, once more,* implies that nothing ever gets constituted in a *single sense, once and for all.* The circle opens me to inanity and encloses me within the following alternative: *either* all returns because nothing has ever made any sense whatever, *or else* things never make any sense except by the return of all things, without beginning or end.

Here is a sign in which I myself am nothing, that I always return to—for nothing. What is my part in this circular movement in relation to which I am incoherent, or in relation to this thought so perfectly coherent that it excludes me *at the very moment* I think it? What is this emblem of the circle that empties all designation of its content for the sake of this emblem? The soul's elevated state became the *highest thought* only by yielding to its own intensity. In yielding to this state, chaos is restored to the emblem of the circle—i.e., the source of intensity is joined to the product of intensity.

By itself, the circle says nothing, except that existence has sense only in being existence, or that signification is nothing but an intensity. This is why it is revealed in a heightened state of the soul. But how can intensity attain to the actuality of the self that, nevertheless, is exalted by this high state? By freeing the fluctuations that signified it as *me* so that what is willed again once more re-echoes its present. What fascinates Nietzsche about this moment is not the fact of *being there,* but the fact of *returning* in what becomes: this necessity to be experienced and relived defies the will for and the creation of sense.

Within the circle, the will exhausts itself by contemplating this return within becoming, and it is revived only in the discordance outside the circle—whence the constraint exercised by *the highest feeling.*

The lofty Nietzschean states found their immediate expression in the aphoristic form: even there, recourse to the everyday code of signs is presented as an exercise in continually maintaining oneself discontinuous with respect to everyday continuity. When these states of feeling blossom forth into fabulous configurations, it seems as if the flux and reflux of contemplative intensity seeks to create points of reference for its own discontinuity. So many elevated states, so many gods, until the universe appears as a dance of the gods: *the universe being only a perpetual flight from and rediscovery of itself through a multitude of gods. . . .*

This dance of the gods pursuing themselves is still only a clarification, in Zarathustra's mythic vision, of this movement of flux and reflux, of the intensity of Nietzschean states, the loftiest of which occurred to him under the sign of the *divine vicious circle.*

The divine vicious circle is only a name for the sign that here takes on a divine countenance, under the aspect of Dionysus: Nietzschean thought breathes more freely in relation to a divine and fabulous countenance than when it struggles against itself, as in the trap of its own thought. Doesn't he say, in fact, that *the true essence of things is an illusion*—an affabulation— by which being represents things, an illusion *without* which being could not be represented at all?

The exalted state of mind in which Nietzsche experienced the vertigo of Eternal Return gave rise to the emblem of the vicious circle; there, the highest intensity of thought (self-enclosed, coherent thought) was instantaneously realized together with a parallel lack of intensity in everyday expression. By the same token, even the term "me" was emptied of all content—the term to which, heretofore, all else had led back.

In effect, so far as the emblem of the *vicious circle* serves to define the *Eternal Return of the same,* a sign occurs to Nietzschean thought *as an event, one that stands for all that can ever happen,* for all that will ever happen, for all that could ever happen in the world, or to thought itself.

THE EXPERIENCE OF ETERNAL RETURN AS COMMUNICABLE THOUGHT

The very first version Nietzsche gives (in *The Gay Science,* §341) of his Sils-Maria experience—and later, in *Zarathustra*—is expressed essentially as a hallucination: at once, it appears that the moment itself is reflected in a burst of mirrors. Here it is I, the same "I" who awakens to an infinite multiplication of *itself* and of its own life, while a sort of demon (like a genie of the *Thousand and One Nights*) says: You will have to live this life once more and innumerable times more. Subsequent reflection declares: If this thought gained control over you, it would make of you an other.

There is no doubt here that Nietzsche speaks of a *return* of the *identical self*. This is the obscure point that was the stumbling block of his contemporaries and of posterity. Thus, from the outset, this thought of Eternal Return was generally considered to be an absurd fantasy.

Zarathustra considers the will as being bound to the irreversibility of time: this is the first reflective reaction to the obsessional *evidence*. Nietzsche seeks to grasp the hallucination once more at the level of conscious will by means of an "analytical" cure of the will. What is its relation to three-dimensional time (past-present-future)? The will projects its powerlessness on time and thus gives time its irreversible character. The will cannot stem the *flow of time*—the non-willed that time establishes as the order of accomplished fact. The result is the spirit of *vengeance* in the will with respect to what is immovable or unshakable, as well as its belief in the *punitive* aspect of existence.

Zarathustra's remedy is to re-will the *non-willed* insofar as he desires to take the order of accomplished fact upon himself and thus render it *unaccomplished*—i.e., by re-willing it *innumerable times*. This ruse removes the "once and for all" character from all events. Such is the subterfuge that the (in itself unintelligible) Sils-Maria experience first offers to reflection, to the kind of reflection that hinges on the *will*.

Such a ruse, however, is only one way of eluding the temptation inherent in the very reflection upon the Eternal Return: *non-action,* which Zarathustra rejects as a fallacious remedy, is no less subject to the same inversion of time. If all things return according to the law of the vicious circle, then *all voluntary action is equivalent to a real non-action, or all conscious non-action is equivalent to an illusory action*. On the level of conscious decision, not to act corresponds to the *inanity* of the individual will. It would express the soul's intensely elevated state just as much as it would the decision to pursue an action. So how would re-willing the re-willed be creative? To adhere to the return is also to admit that *forgetfulness alone* enabled us to undertake old creations as new creations *ad infinitum*. Formulated at the level of the *conscious, identical self,* the imperative to re-will would remain a tautology: it seems that this imperative (although it demands a decision for eternity) would only concern the behavior of the will for the interval of an individual life—yet what we live through every day is exactly the re-willed, the non-willed, and the enigma of horrifying chance. This tautology is both in the emblem of the circle and in Nietzsche's own thought; and it represents the *return* of all things as well as itself.

The parabola of the two opposite paths, rejoining under the arch of a doorway on whose pediment is inscribed "The Moment" (in *Zarathustra*), only serves to recall the image of the aphorism in *The Gay Science:* the same moonlight, the same spider, will return. The two opposite paths, then, are *one.* An eternity separates them: individuals, things, events, ascending by one, redescending by the other, return alike to the *doorway* of the *moment,* having made *a tour of eternity.* Whoever halts in this "doorway" is *alone* capable of seizing the circular structure of eternal time. But there, as in the aphorism, it is still the individual self who leaves and returns *identical to himself.* Between this parabola and the will's *cure,* by re-willing the re-willed, the connection is certain. Except that it does not carry conviction.

Yet the aphorism claims that in re-willing, the self *changes,* becomes other. Here is precisely where the solution of the enigma resides.

Zarathustra seeks a change not of the *individual,* but of his will: to re-will the re-willed non-willed, this is what the "will to power" would consist in.

But Nietzsche himself dreams of an entirely different sort of change through the change in individual behavior. Re-willing the re-willed, if it is only the will's *assumption of the non-willed* as creative recuperation (in the sense that the enigmatic, the fragmentary, together with a horrifying chance, are all reconstituted into a meaningful unity), nonetheless remains at the level of a "voluntarist" fatalism.

The change of the individual's moral behavior is not determined by the conscious will, but by the economy of the Eternal Return itself. Under the emblem of the *vicious circle,* the very nature of existence (independent of the human will) and, therefore, also of individual acts, is intrinsically modified. Nietzsche says in a note as revealing as it is brief: "*My overcoming of fatalism:* 1. By the Eternal Return and by pre-existence. 2. By the liquidation of the concept of 'will.' "

A fragment from Sils-Maria, dated August, 1881, states: "The incessant metamorphosis: in a brief interval of time you must pass through several individual states. Incessant combat is the means."

What is this brief interval? Not just any moment of our existence, but the eternity that separates one existence from another.

This indicates that the object of re-willing is a *multiple alterity* inscribed within the individual. If this is an *incessant* metamorphosis, we can understand why Nietzsche claims that "pre-existence" is a necessary condition for an individual's *being-as-he-is*. Incessant combat would indicate that from now on the follower of the vicious circle must practice this multiple alterity. But this theme will be taken up later on when he envisages a *theory of the fortuitous case*.

These fragments bear so many new elements for developing the thought of the vicious circle: no longer is it only a matter of the will being faced with irreversible time—a will that, when cured of its belief in a punitive existence, would break the chains of its captivity by re-willing the non-willed, thence to recognize itself (within a reversible time) as Will to Power, as creative will.

On the other hand, these fragments give an account of a transfigured existence that—because it is always the circle—wills its own reversibility, to the extent that it relieves the individual of the weight of his own acts *once and for all*. What is at first sight the most crushing pronouncement—namely, *the endless recommencement of the same acts, the same sufferings*—henceforth appears as redemption itself, as soon as the soul knows that it has already lived through other selves and experiences and thus is destined to live through even more. Those other selves and experiences will henceforth deepen and enrich the only life that it knows *here and now*. What has prepared the present life and what now prepares it in turn for still others remains itself totally unsuspected by consciousness.

Re-willing, then, is pure adherence to the vicious circle; to re-will *the entire series one more time*—to re-will every experience, all one's acts, but this time, not as *mine:* it is precisely this *possessiveness* that no longer has any meaning, nor does it represent a goal. Meaning and goal are liquidated by the circle—whence the silence of Zarathustra, the interruption of his message. Unless, of course, a burst of laughter can bear all its own bitterness.

At this point Nietzsche becomes divided in his own interpretation of the Eternal Return. The "overman" becomes the name for the subject of Will to Power, as well as the *meaning* and the *goal* for the Eternal Return. The Will to Power is only a *humanized* term for the soul of the vicious circle, while the circle itself is pure intensity *without intention*. On the other hand, as Eternal Return the vicious circle is presented as a chain of existence that forms the very individuality of the doctrine's adherents—those who know that they have *already existed* otherwise than they now exist, and that they will yet exist differently, from one "eternity to another."

In this way Nietzsche introduces a renewed version of metempsychosis.

The necessity of a purification, and therefore of a culpability, to be expiated across successive existences before the initiate's soul recovers a pure state of innocence—all this already admits of an immutable eternity (precisely the kind of ancient schema that has been transmitted to gnostic Christianity by the esoteric religions of India and Asia).

But there is nothing of the kind in Nietzsche—neither "expiation" nor "purification" nor "immutable purity." Pre-existence and post-existence are always the surplus of the same present existence, according to the economy of the vicious circle. It supposes that an individual's capacity could never exhaust the full differentiated richness of a single existence, much less its affective potential. Metempsychosis represents the *avatars* of an immortal soul. Nietzsche himself says: "If only we could bear our immortality— that would be the supreme thing." Now, this immortality is not, for Nietzsche, properly individual. The Eternal Return suppresses abiding identities. Nietzsche urges the follower (of the vicious circle) to accept the *dissolution* of his fortuitous soul in order to receive another, equally fortuitous. Having traversed the entire series, this dissolved soul must in turn come back—namely, to the degree of spiritual excitation where the law of the circle appears.

If the law of the vicious circle dictates the individual's metamorphosis, how can it be willed? Suddenly we become aware of the circle's revelation: to remain in this awareness it suffices to live in conformity with the necessity of the circle: to re-will this same experience (the moment when one becomes *him who* is initiated into the secret of the vicious circle) supposes that *all the livable experiences* have been lived through. Therefore, all existence previous to this moment—which privileges one existence among thousands—no less than all that follows, is necessary. To re-will all experiences, all possible acts, all possible happiness and suffering, means that if such an act were accomplished now, if such an experience were now lived, it would have been necessary both for a series to have preceded it and for others to follow; not within the same individual, but in all that belongs to the individual's very potential, so that one day he could find himself *one more time*.

THE DIFFERENCE BETWEEN THE ETERNAL RETURN AND TRADITIONAL FATALISM

Nietzsche completes his thought of fatalism within the image of the circle. Fatalism in itself (the *fatum*) posits a chain of events that is pre-established according to a certain disposition and whose development is realized in an irreversible way. Whatever I do and whatever I decide to do, my decision, contrary to what I think, obeys a *project* that escapes me and of which I am ignorant.

The vicious circle reintegrates the experience of the *fatum* (in the form of a movement without beginning or end) with the play of chance and its thousandfold combinations as so many series forming a chain. As an image of destiny, the circle can only be *re-willed,* for, in any case, it must *recommence*.

Chance is but *one thing* for each of the moments (i.e., for each individual, singular, and therefore fortuitous existence) that compose it. It is by "chance" that the figure of the circle appears to an individual. Henceforth, he will know how to re-will the entire series in order to re-will himself; or, in other words, by virtue of his very existence, he cannot *fail* to re-will the entire series that both leads up to and surpasses his own existence.

The feeling of eternity and the eternalization of desire are merged in a single moment; the representation of an anterior life and of an ulterior life no longer concerns a beyond, or an individual self that would attain this beyond, but, rather, it concerns living the *same life,* experienced across its individual differences. The Eternal Return is only the way it unfolds. The feeling of vertigo results from the *once-and-for-all* when the subject is surprised by the whirl of *innumerable times*. The once-and-for-all disappears: intensity itself issues forth as the vibrations of being—an unending series of vibrations that projects the individual self *outside of itself* as so many dissonances. All resounds until the consonance of the moment is restored—the moment itself in which these dissonances are once again reabsorbed.

At the level of consciousness, meaning and goal are lost. They are *everywhere* and *nowhere* in the vicious circle, since no point of the circle can be both beginning and end at once.

Finally, and from its very inception, the Eternal Return is not a representation, nor is it exactly a postulate. Rather, it is a *lived fact*—as a thought, it is a *sudden* thought. Fantasy or not, the Sils-Maria experience exercises its constraint as an ineluctable necessity. Alternating between dread and delight, the interpretations of Nietzsche will be inspired by this moment, by this felt necessity.

HOW NIETZSCHEAN FATALISM IS CONCLUDED BY ELIMINATING THE CONCEPT OF WILL

Nietzsche does not say that the thought of the Eternal Return and the pre-existence it presupposes can itself bring fatalism to a close, for, in the second place, he *does* say that his fatalism is necessary in order to eliminate the concept of will. If the thought of the Eternal Return in its various extensions already abolishes the identity of the self along with the traditional concept of the will, then Nietzsche seems, under the second aspect of his fatalism, to make an allusion to his own physiology. According to this, there is no will but one of *power,* and in this context the will is nothing other than a primordial *impulse.* No moral interpretation grounded on the intellect could ever suspend the innumerable metamorphoses it lives through, the shapes it adopts, or the pretexts that provoke them—whether this be an invoked *goal* or a meaning that is supposedly given within these metamorphoses, within this impulse, or even at the level of consciousness. In this way, fatalism becomes merged with the impulsive force that, precisely, exceeds the initiate's "will" and *already modifies it,* therefore threatening its very continuous identity.

Maurice Blanchot

THE LIMITS OF EXPERIENCE: NIHILISM

Nietzsche's thought remains associated with Nihilism, a word he no doubt borrowed, ironically, from Paul Bourget.[1] Nonetheless, he examined it enthusiastically and fearfully; sometimes by simple and radical statements, at other times by an uncertain, hesitating approach, in an impossible kind of thought. In short, it stands like an extreme that cannot be gotten beyond, and yet it is the only true path of going beyond; it is the principle of a new beginning. These oscillations are not to be attributed to Nietzsche's unstable genius or character, to his own ''shortcomings.'' They are the very sense of his thought. Certainly the question: ''What is Nihilism?'' can be answered without difficulty, and Nietzsche has given many clear responses, such as the following: ''That the highest values are devalued.'' He no less clearly indicates the origin of this degradation: ''God is dead.'' But while Nietzsche has given a sort of tiresome celebrity to this dramatic event, he does not have the personal phenomenon of unbelief in mind. Kierkegaard's Christianity and, more specifically, Dostoevsky's, like Nietzsche's atheism or the young Marx's (''I hate all gods''), belong to that turning point in the history of the world from which the divine light has withdrawn. God is dead. God: this means God, but also everything that, in rapid succession, has tried to take its place—e.g., the ideal, consciousness, reason, the certainty of progress, the happiness of the masses, culture, etc. Everything not without value nevertheless has no *absolute* value of its own—there is nothing man can rely on, nothing of any value other than the meaning given to it in an endless process.

That analysis can no longer move us, so familiar has it become. What would Nihilism be? A mere humanism! Or the recognition of the fact that (deprived or freed of the ideal of some absolute meaning conceived on the model of God) from now on, man must create the world and give it meaning—and from the start, this is an immense, intoxicating task. Nietzsche, with a joy only he felt so purely and expressed so fully, has seen in this movement of infinite negation, which withdraws every solid foundation from us, the opening onto a suddenly boundless space of knowledge: ''At last the horizon seems open once more . . . every hazard is again permitted to the discerner; and the sea, *our* sea, again lies open before us . . . There is yet another world to be discovered—and more than one!

Embark, philosophers!''[2] We could fill pages with citations. Nietzsche is inexhaustible in expressing this happiness to know and to search freely, infinitely, and at all risks, without having the sky as boundary, or even truth, the all-too-human truth, as measure. We cannot read him without being taken up with him by the pure movement of this search. What disparages him is the fact that he became insensitive to this movement, a movement that is in no way a call to some vague, irrational awareness, but the affirmation of a rigorous knowledge—''clear, transparent, manly''—the kind that is manifest in the natural sciences. ''And that is why: long live physics! And even more, what compels us to arrive at that: our probity!''

Here, then, is a first approach to Nihilism: it is not an individual experience or a philosophical doctrine, nor is it a fatal light cast over human nature, eternally vowed to nothingness. Rather, Nihilism is an event achieved in history, and yet it is like a shedding off of history, a moulting period, when history changes its direction and is indicated by a negative trait: that values no longer have value by themselves. There is also a positive trait: for the first time, the horizon is infinitely opened to knowledge—''All is permitted.'' When the authority of old values has collapsed, this new authorization means that it is permitted to know all, that there is no longer a limit to man's activity. ''We have a still undiscovered country before us, the boundaries of which no one has seen, a beyond to all countries and corners of the ideal known hitherto, a world so over-rich in the beautiful, the strange, the questionable, the frightful . . .''[3]

Nietzsche, we are told, had only a mediocre acquaintance with the sciences. That is possible. But, in addition to the fact that he had been professionally trained in a scientific method, he knew enough of it to have a presentiment of what science would become, to take it seriously and even to foresee—not to deplore—that from now on all the modern world's seriousness would be confined to science, to the scientist, and to the prodigious power of technology. On one hand, he saw with striking force that since nihilism is the possibility of all going beyond, it is the horizon for every particular science as well as for the maintenance of scientific development as such. On the other hand, he saw no less clearly that, when the world no longer has any meaning, when it only bears the pseudo-meaning of some nonsensical scheme or another, what can alone overcome the disorder of this void is the cautious movement of science, its power to give itself precise rules and to create meaning (but of a limited and, so to speak, operational kind)—a power, therefore, to extend its field of application to the furthest limits or to restrict it immediately.

Agreed. And that, once more, is reassuring. The moment Nihilism outlines the world for us, its counterpart, science, creates the tools to dominate it. The era of universal mastery is opened. But there are some consequences: first, science can only be nihilistic; it is the meaning of a world deprived of meaning, a knowledge that ultimately has ignorance as its foundation. To which the response will be that this reservation is only theoretical; but we must not hasten to disregard this objection, for science is essentially productive. Knowing it need not interpret the world, science transforms it, and by this transformation science conveys its own nihilistic demands—the negative power that science has made into the most useful of tools, but with which it dangerously plays. Knowledge is fundamentally dangerous. Nietzsche has given the bluntest formulation of this danger: "We experiment on truth! Perhaps humanity will be destroyed by it! Well, so be it!" That is what the scientist is liable to say and *must* say, if he renounces the hypocrisy of deploring the catastrophe that is one of science's results—for a universe cannot be constructed without having the possibility of its being destroyed. Destruction and creation, when they bear on the essential, are hardly distinguishable, Nietzsche says. The risk, then, is great. Moreover, in its temperance and integrity, science bears this very contradiction within itself: it can produce a world in which scientists no longer would continue to exist as such, and in which work would no longer be permitted pursuant to the objectivity of knowledge, but in accordance with the arbitrary sense of some new world. In other words, by making science possible, Nihilism becomes the possibility of science—which means that the human world can be destroyed by it.

Another consequence is the following: to the void of Nihilism, there corresponds the movement of science; to the achievement of science, the domination of the earth. The greatest force of overcoming is set in motion. Now, what happens to man when this transformation is realized and history turns? Does he become transformed? Is he set to go beyond himself? Is he ready to become what he is, a clear-headed man who can depend on nothing and who is going to make himself master of all? No. Man, such as he is, the bourgeois at the end of the nineteenth century that Nietzsche knew, is a man of small aims, of small certainties, evil and inadequate; he still knows nothing of the event that is in the process of being achieved by his intervention, an event beyond him, so to speak, an event that is going to give to him infinite powers and impose on him as extreme an obligation as he has ever had, since he must freely create the meaning of the world and himself in proportion to this world without measure.

I pass over the succession of overthrows, "the formidable logic of terror," and the immense wars that Nietzsche foresaw to be the prerogative of the twentieth century, all of which stem immediately from the following imbalance: present-day man believes himself to be definitive, stable in his nature, happy in the small circle closed around himself, resigned to the spirit of revenge; yet, pushed by the impersonal force of science and by the force of that event which liberates him from values, he possesses a power in excess of himself—even without his trying to surpass himself in that power. Present-day man is man of the lowest rank, but his power is that of a being who is already beyond man: how would this contradiction not harbor the greatest danger? Now, instead of resting content with the conservative attitude and condemning knowledge, in order to safeguard the eternal in man (i.e., the man of his time), Nietzsche sides with science and the whole question of overcoming, which shall be humanity's future evolution.

In several commentaries, Heidegger has indicated that such was the meaning of the Overman: the Overman is not the man of today raised even to disproportion, nor a species of man who would reject the human only to make the arbitrary his law and titanic madness his rule. He is not the eminent functionary of some Will to Power; no more is he the enchanter, destined to introduce paradisical bliss on earth. The Overman is he alone who leads man to be what he is: the being who surpasses himself, who affirms the necessity to pass beyond himself and to perish in this crossing.

If such is the case (but is it?), we see why the Overman could be considered as the first decisive affirmation to follow the extreme negation of Nihilism—without himself, however, being anything other than this consequent negation: the Overman is the being who has overcome the void (created by the death of God and the degradation of values) because he could find the power of overcoming in this void, a power that for him has become not only power, but will—the will to overcome himself. Freed of all that thrusts or turns aside, of all that pulls down the will in its capacity to will, free of all reactive will, there is no longer anything negative in what he wills: by a free act, he dictates and decides the extent of his destiny.

However, the figure of the Overman, even interpreted in this way, remains ambiguous. As the end of human evolution, self-surpassing is thereby denied in this figure. And if this figure is *not* the end, it is because there is still something to overcome. Its will, therefore, is not free of all external meaning: its will is still Will to Power. With the Overman, Nietzsche had a fine presentiment of a man who is indistinguishable from present-day man except by negative characteristics, and because of this, he is qualitatively different—poorer, simpler, more moderate, more capable of sacrificing himself, slower in his resolution, quieter in his speech. Nonetheless, it is his essential trait, the will, that would make the Overman the very form of Nihilism, rigorous and austere—for, according to Nietzsche's clear statement, "The will loves even more to will nothingness than not to will." The Overman is the one in whom nothingness makes itself be willed and who, free for death, maintains this pure essence of will in willing nothingness. That would be Nihilism itself.

Enthusiastically and with categorical clarity, Zarathustra announces the Overman; then, he anxiously, hesitatingly, fearfully announces the thought of Eternal Return. Why this difference of tone? Why is the thought of the Eternal Return, thought of the abyss, in the very person who pronounces it unceasingly deferred and put off, as if it were the detour of all thought? There is its enigma and, no doubt, its truth. I should also like to point out that, for a long time, nearly all the commentators, whether they were on the right or left (Bäumler, the official Nazi interpreter of Nietzsche, eliminated the theory of the Eternal Return), have been hindered by this "doctrine," which seemed arbitrary, useless, mystical, and, furthermore, very antiquated, since it already lay about in Heraclitus. That a modern man could come to such an idea is, strictly speaking, conceivable. But even if he were seized by such a terror in his approach, even if he were to see this idea as the heaviest, most anguishing, and most proper thought to overturn the world, even then there was an absurdity everyone hastened to avoid by thinking that the idea derived all its force precisely from the ecstatic vision in which Nietzsche had grasped it. One of the changes in Nietzschean interpretation is that this idea is taken seriously. Karl Löwith, to whom we do owe some important books, has contributed a great deal to making us more attentive to this idea. Also, no doubt, the very spirit of our age has led us to reflect on time, on the circularity of meaning, and on the end of history: to reflect on the absence of being as a recommencement.

Thought of the Eternal Return remains strange in its antiquated absurdity. It represents a logical vertigo. Nietzsche himself could not escape this. It is nihilistic thought *par excellence;* it is how Nihilism surpasses itself absolutely by making itself definitively insurpassable. Thus, such a thought is more capable of enlightening us as to the kind of trap that Nihilism is when the mind decides to approach it head-on. Nietzsche (or Zarathustra) has said with perfect clarity that when the will becomes liberator, it lashes out against the past. The rock of accomplished fact, which the will (however powerful and willful it is) cannot displace, that is what transforms all sentiment into *ressentiment.* The spirit of revenge consists in the movement that turns the will back into a counter-will, a willing-against: this occurs when the former, the will, stumbles on the "it was." Now, so long as man is characterized by *ressentiment,* he will remain on the level of his present sufficiency, seeking only to lower all earthly things, himself, and time in the name of some absolute ideal—far from the highest hope. He must no longer be limited, then, in his temporal dimension, by the necessity of a nonrecoverable past and an irreversible time; he needs time as total achievement.

But the return behind time is what escapes the possible; it is an impossibility that here takes on the highest meaning: it signifies the check, the defeat of the Overman as Will to Power. The Overman will never be able to do the extreme. Eternal Return is not on the order of power. The experience of the Eternal Return involves a reversal of all these perspectives. The will that wills nothingness becomes the will that wills eternity—and in that process, eternity, with neither will nor end, would turn back on itself. Personal and subjective omnipotence is transformed into the impersonal necessity of "being." Transvaluation does not give us a new scale of values on the basis of negating every absolute value; it makes us attain an order for which the notion of value ceases to apply.

Having thus recovered the idea of eternity and the idea of "being"—and love of the eternal and knowledge of the depths of "being"—does it not seem that we are definitively sheltered from Nihilism? In fact, we are at the heart of Nihilism. With his own incisive simplicity (which, according to Lukacs, leads him to discuss what is inhuman), Nietzsche has expressed it well: "Let us think this thought in its most terrible form: existence as it is, without meaning or aim, yet recurring inevitably without any finale of nothingness: 'the eternal recurrence.' This is the most extreme form of nihilism."[4] What does this remark tell us? Until now we thought Nihilism was tied to nothingness. How rash that was: Nihilism is tied to being. Nihilism is the impossibility of coming to an end and finding an outcome in this end. It tells of the impotence of nothingness, the false renown of its victories; it tells us that when we think nothingness, we are still thinking being. Nothing ends; all begins again, the other is still the same, midnight is only a covered-over noon, and the highest noon is the abyss of light from which we can never escape—even through death and that glorious suicide Nietzsche recommends. Nihilism here tells us its final and rather grim truth: it tells of the impossibility of Nihilism.

This has the air of a joke. But if, indeed, we want to admit that all modern humanism, the work of science, and planetary development have as their object a dissatisfaction with what is, and hence the desire to transform being itself, to deny it in order to derive its power, and to use this power to deny the infinite movement of human mastery—then it will appear that this kind of negative weakness, and the way that nothingness is undeniably unmasked as being, lay waste at one stroke to our attempts to dominate the earth and to free ourselves from nature by giving it a meaning—i.e., by denaturalizing or perverting it. But this is only a first way of translating the strange account of the abyss, one that partly explains Zarathustra's distress in understanding that he will never definitively go beyond man's inadequacies, or that he will only be able to do this, paradoxically, by willing his return. But what does this return mean? It affirms that the extreme point of Nihilism is precisely where it is reversed, that Nihilism is reversal itself: it is the affirmation that, in passing from the *no* to the *yes,* refutes Nihilism—even though it does nothing other than affirm it, at which point Nihilism is extended to all possible affirmations. From this we conclude that Nihilism would be identical with the will to overcome Nihilism *absolutely.*

NOTES

1. Jean Granier (*Le Problème de la vérité dans la philosophie de Nietzsche,* Éd. du Seuil) cites diverse sources for this term: Jacobi, Jean-

Paul, Turgenev, Dostoevsky, and Paul Bourget. We should add others, but it does not matter. Not only is the word flat, but it is self-contradictory as well, in that it pretends to be systematic. Yet the contradiction only causes an accusation of dryness or aridity, the semantic play between nothingness and nothing shows that it is apparently difficult to deny what has not first been affirmed. In any case, the term's lack of depth does not simply render it inactive. Descartes, Kant, Hegel, and Bergson, for example, not only refused to think of nothingness apart from being, but were irritated with it for several reasons. (Hegel, perhaps, is the exception. In a supreme act of mischievousness, Hegel identifies it with the immediate, and thus turns immediacy into nothingness.) For one, it is the sign of the will's fullness (thus, a mark of perfection); for another, it is either the absence of a concept or an empty concept with no object; and for another, it is a void without object or concept—i.e., it is merely a word or the illusion of a word. At best, it is little more than a vestige—which, perhaps, is something. All these reductions (founded on the hidden demands of continuity and plenitude) have served for nothing, therefore, not even for deciding whether a language that holds onto this nothing has something to say, or, on the contrary, has nothing to say. It hasn't even been decided whether or not *no thing* might not precede language itself.

2. *The Gay Science,* §§343, 289.
3. *GS,* §382.
4. *The Will to Power,* §55.

PART II
Oblique Entry

Access to Nietzsche's thought is invariably a matter of difficulty and dispute. The usual strategy for interpreting Nietzsche is to stress some particular incident in his life, to focus selectively on one or two issues such as ethics, morality, or religion, etc., or to try to impose a system on his work *en bloc*. Taken severally or together, these approaches are rarely satisfying. At best they seriously distort—though perhaps entertain—and at worst they are futile. The problem of orientation and interpretation is compounded by Nietzsche's repeated assertions that his own thought is *essentially* "perspectival"—that what he writes is a function of his own idiosyncratic viewpoint, disposition, culture, and person. Furthermore, Nietzsche instructs the reader that "the important thing is style"—that the conceptual content of his thought is bound to the means of its expression. In a section of *Ecce Homo*, rather modestly entitled "Why I Write Such Good Books," he declares: "I have many stylistic possibilities—the most multifarious art of style that has ever been at the disposition of one man."

What is *introduced* into the Nietzschean text, then, at the level of style or perspective? Something that is not immediately visible, that appears perhaps as an aftereffect, but nonetheless governs the coherency or consistency of the text: it may be a "fabric" or "texture"; a principle of stress and displacement; the silent advancement of a plea. This kind of writing may evoke the exchange of gifts or a kind of sexuality; perhaps it suggests a certain tempo or the hyperborean flight of death, the sense of woman, the secrets of fetishism, or the force of ecstasy.

In "Nietzsche's Conception of Chaos," Jean Granier sets forth the Nietzschean dynamics of interpretation. What Nietzsche calls "appearance" is a relational complex of three terms: phenomena, manifestation, and dissimulation. For Nietzsche, appearances themselves conceal nothing; there is no substratum, no reality *behind* them. Rather, they are what Granier calls the "significant manifestations of chaos," and chaos must in turn be understood from the start as "interpreted" being, as both nature *and* mask. Granier then shows how this concept of chaos opens up an additional "epistemological space," thus making the observer or reader a necessary participant within a new kind of "text." Finally, he describes how the various dimensions of the world as text (or, text as world) can be deciphered according to the double or circular register of art and life.

Granier continues these themes in his second essay. He not only explains why certain "interpretive" and "perspectivist" considerations dictate Nietzsche's own conception of "reality" and "truth," but shows how all this operates on the level of the Nietzschean text. His analysis thus demonstrates how Nietzsche—and Nietzsche's readers—can successfully overcome the apparently insoluble conflict between relativism and dogmatism.

Gilles Deleuze sees Nietzsche's work as engaged in the task of "decodification." If Nietzsche is a unique figure in modern thought, it is because (unlike Freud or Marx) he is the first to conceive of the individual in the *absence* of all forms of codification—whether these be the "fundamental bureaucracies" of state, family, law, contracts, institutions, conventional values, or even sanity itself. Deleuze pursues this confounding strategy of "decodification" or "deterritorialization" on the levels of style, method, text, language, and action. Furthermore, he goes on to argue that the kind of pulsional drift, transmission, and externalization that Nietzsche has in mind is not a form of representational thinking, nor is it merely concerned with transgression. Rather, it all belongs to an entirely new order, to what Deleuze characterizes as "Nomad Thought."

By examining Nietzsche's account of cultural "origins," Eric Blondel locates what he calls Nietzsche's "primordial" metaphor, one that systematically governs both the rhetorical and philosophic dimensions of the Nietzschean discourse—the metaphor of *vita femina:* "life is a woman." If Nietzsche finds the origin of culture in the *displacement* between body and thought, in the *conversion* of instinct into expression, Blondel sees these two forms of transfer as essentially meta-phoric. He then goes on to show how the *vita femina* metaphor is the generating principle of metaphor itself: eternally fertile, productive, and self-overcoming.

Jacques Derrida explores the operation of what he calls Nietzsche's "pointed" or "spurred" style—a style that intrudes, defends, and withdraws in a series of feints. Derrida sees this as a kind of "feminine voice" within the text, a beguiling and dreamlike voice that speaks at a distance (of art, dissimulation, and death—among other things). It is the "distance" opened up by this voice, this feminine operation of style, that interests Derrida: separation, removal, destruction, opening, spread, abyss, deviation, etc. All these constitute a certain *negative* aspect of truth, a truth that defies possession. Furthermore, these various kinds of "distancing" are textual tools or weapons, and they make for a congruent skepticism within the text, a skepticism which is at once modest, fearful, and indecisive. All this leads to Derrida's analysis of the "heterogeneity" of Nietzsche's text. As woman, Nietzsche is neither simply for nor against "the system of truth" (which Derrida describes as a "system of castration"). Rather, he both dwells within and works upon the delusions of truth, always in a state of skepticism, attraction, ruse, naïveté, parody, divergence, and ambiguity—i.e., as woman. This feminine style assumes different values: Nietzsche condemns it both as a figure of lying and as a figure of truth; he affirms it as an artistic and as a dissimulating power. Together, these values are unassimilable; they are irreducible to any logic of truth. The feminine style retains these values, and in doing so, remains essentially *undecidable*.

Sarah Kofman analyzes the extremely important role of music in Nietzsche's thought, and particularly, how it functions in his conception of language. She shows that in Nietzsche's early writing, music emerges as "the most suitable symbolic sphere"—especially its highest form, Dionysian music. Conventional language only becomes what Nietzsche calls a "universal language" when it is supplemented by the musical elements of tone, accent, melody, rhythm, etc. Together, these elements naturally symbolize what for the early Nietzsche are the two basic categories of existence: pleasure and pain, together with will. Music alone, therefore, can successfully express the infinite diversity and multiplicity of life, for it is the mother of all the arts as well as the foundation for all subsequent forms of metaphorical expression—such as the language of words. But Kofman points out that Nietzsche's concept of music is essentially metaphysical, since it is founded upon the most traditional and conventionally philosophic account of nature. Only with the loss of this term (i.e., "nature") can the metaphysical closure of language and interpretation be circumvented. She maintains that Nietzsche *did* succeed in doing this, the moment he asserted the "propriety" or "priority" of musicality, poetry, myth, and metaphor itself—a model Nietzsche found, incidentally, in the "personality" of Presocratic thought.

Jean Granier

NIETZSCHE'S CONCEPTION OF CHAOS

One of the principal themes in Nietzschean thought is "the *interpretive* character of all that happens. No event exists in itself. Everything that happens consists of a group of phenomena that are gathered and *selected* by an interpretive being."[1] For Nietzsche, these phenomena are not masks attached to a thing in itself, some lesser beings, or nothingness, or facts; their being belongs to an interpretive process, which consists only in the difference between an interpreting activity and a text. Being *is* text. It appears and makes sense; and the sense is multiple, manifested not in the way that an object is for a subject, but as an interpretation that is itself construed in terms of a multiplicity of perspectives. Interpretation, here, comprises the act of interpretation and the text interpreted, the reading and the book, the deciphering and the enigma. "One may not ask: 'Who then interprets?' for it is the interpretation, a form of the Will to Power, that exists."[2] We are, Nietzsche claims, "ingenious interpreters and fortune-tellers whom destiny has placed as spectators on the European stage, faced with an enigmatic and *undeciphered* text whose meaning is gradually revealed."[3]

Being is manifest, and this manifestation is a great rumbling and agitation of sense. But the sense is not directly decipherable. It receives nothing from beyond, and one would look in vain for an intelligible ground beneath the shimmer of appearance. No intuition or mental inspection can grasp it, still less synthesize it into a logical system. The very concept of totality—a logical system—is itself the product of an interpretation, and would not serve as immediate evidence. Because the phenomenon of being is a "text" and not a painting (which would display its contents to naïve perception or to the philosopher's intelligence), it is essentially ambiguous: it withholds as much as it shows, it is an opaque revelation, a blurred sense—in short, *an enigma*. Because of this quality of ambiguity, Nietzsche will call the phenomenon a *mask* or *veil*.

Once again, this mask conceals no transcendent reality. Perplexed by this peculiar state of affairs, the philosopher gives in to the temptation to break up the continuity of phenomena (a continuity whose dissonances agree and whose contraries blend) by separating out the clear and the obscure, being and its appearance. Thinking he can be clever in dealing with phenomena, the metaphysician becomes entrapped by them—*because phenomena cheat:*

they *seem* to be masks that we can easily penetrate or remove as soon as we perform an intelligent critique upon them, guided by contradictions in the real world. But this is precisely not the case! The phenomenon masks what it manifests, *without enabling us to dissociate dissimulation from manifestation*. The phenomenon *is* a mask; it turns its own appearing into an appearance—i.e., it appears as pretense. Beyond it, one would find *nothing*—a nothing, moreover, that would still be qualified as a metaphysical negative of phenomenal being: the *nihil* of nihilism.

We must admit that there is something deceptive and frustrating to the human mind in this ambiguity of phenomena. But, instead of becoming indignant with this "travesty" of the sensible order, Nietzsche advises that we ask instead: what is it in man that becomes indignant and protests? The answer is that reason desires to recognize its own logical categories within phenomena. But, after all, why should the real world be compelled to please reason and logic? And what if the phenomena themselves directed this poem of the world to our aesthetic taste, to our will to art?

To try to imitate Parmenides by rejecting perceptible appearances for an absolute being (which would wholly conform to the principle of identity) would mean exchanging a convenient appearance—an authentic yet irrational manifestation of reality—for a fiction, for an inadequate appearance, an imaginary appearance:

> *Appearance,* as I understand it, is the true and unique reality of things; it is what all existing predicates belong to, and what to some extent could best be designated by the sum of these predicates, and this would even include contrary predicates. But this word plainly signifies a reality that is *inaccessible* to the operations and distinctions of logic, an "appearance," therefore, in relation to "logical truth," which—it must be added—is only possible in an *imaginary* world. I am not claiming that appearance is opposed to "reality;" on the contrary, I maintain that appearance is reality, that it is opposed to whatever transforms the actual into an imaginary "real world." If one were to give a precise name to this reality, it could be called "will to power." Such a designation, then, would be in accordance with its internal reality and not with its proteiform, ungraspable, and fluid nature.[4]

If the wish to circumvent phenomena is idle, it is nonetheless legitimate *to describe them as they are,* in order to understand their organization and to disengage their subtle articulations. By describing them, we should be able to discern the texture of the text.

This texture corresponds to what Nietzsche calls a "scrawl." The phenomenon masks because it manifests a sense that is not only mutiple but subjected to a multitude of shiftings, transfers, superimpositions, overlappings, and sedimentations that produce the disconcerting impression of a rebus. The lines are broken, the contours blurred, the language anomalous, and the syntax incoherent. To all of this we must add the principal characteristic: the text is not static; it is not a monument, a museum; it is not really even a book, because everything in it changes, is transformed, *becomes*. The text itself is a becoming, and the interpreter, too, is a becoming. Interpretation, therefore, is the peculiar state of affairs that occurs, so to speak, at the intersection of these two sequences of becoming, where the one is determined as "sense" and the other as "the activity of deciphering."

Through concern for method, philosophers usually invoke a limiting principle that presupposes a primitive text, a base of sense that would serve as the real ground of the phenomenon—not, indeed, a substantial ground, but one that would prevent the phenomenon from dissolving into nothingness, one to guarantee precisely that it *exists*. What serves as this base, and is given within the phenomenon, is *nature*.

> To translate man back into nature; to become master over the many vain and overly enthusiastic interpretations and connotations that have so far been scrawled and painted over that eternal basic text of *homo natura;* to see to it that man henceforth stands before man as even today, hardened in the discipline of science, he stands before the *rest* of nature.[5]

But be careful! The danger is to fall back into metaphysical illusion by turning the hypothesis of "nature" into an abstraction that would surreptitiously lead back to an intelligible *substratum* of being in itself. Let us resist the seduction of such a reading and say: if the phenomenon clearly warrants our distinguishing several levels within its interpretation and allows us to decipher the more or less archaic strata of sense by going back to a text that is said to be primitive—then this primitive text of nature has absolutely nothing in common with a "thing in itself," with an intelligible "being," or with a "cosmos." It is not a book written by a superior intelligence, it is what Nietzsche calls *chaos*.

The primitive text of nature is thus the *chaotic being that manifests itself as a significant process*. Its figures delineate not a system or a cosmos, but, precisely, a *mask*. *Nature and mask determine phenomenal being, the phenomenon in its being, as chaos*. In their very being, therefore, nature and mask are the same, and the worst possible mistake would be to oppose these two terms. In reality, they are strictly bound up with one another, and it is this interdependence that the sameness of their being expresses: the Same, and not a logical or ontological identity. *The Same*—the being that comes back in eternal recurrence, that renders nature and mask copresent in the equivocal unity of the *text*.

The Same—which denotes the being of the phenomenon—joins nature and the scrawl of interpretations together in such a way that the text is enigmatic for every interpreter. Performed and preserved by the Same, this conjunction is also a differentiation between terms. Thus, Nietzsche himself can distinguish a text from its interpretations, nature (the primitive text) from the inscriptions that cover it up. This difference has two dimensions, then: one, *epistemological* (the difference between an interpreted text and an interpretive operation); the other, *temporal* (the difference between the archaic and the recent, between the primitive and the modern). Since—as we have just pointed out—the sameness of chaos joins nature and mask, engendering the unique phenomenon of the text, and this sameness is the work of Eternal Recurrence, Nietzsche's thought here reveals its radicality: we see, in effect, that the theory of interpreted being, the theory of the text, involves an essential relation among *being, appearance,* and *time.* Because nature is subject to time, chaotic being constitutes itself as a text out of the confusion of appearance—i.e., across the perpetual "scrawl" of interpretations. Nonetheless, it is always the Same that is manifested; whether or not one attempts to restore its primordial truth, its "natural" truth, it is the Same that reappears across the flow of interpretations. There *really are* a text and its interpretations; moreover, the two are united (because the sameness is real) as Will to Power.

One essential element is still missing in our reconstruction of this Nietzschean problem of the mask: the *antagonism* that is played out between nature (chaotic being) and phenomena, whereby nature manifests itself while concealing itself. According to Nietzsche, this antagonism is what accounts for the difference, within the Same, between nature and interpretation: thus, nature is necessarily a mask, and the text is an enigma.

In an early fragment that prefigures the rest of his philosophical work, Nietzsche discusses the solution of the enigma: "For the Greek Gods, the world was an ever changing veil that hid the most terrible reality." For the Greeks, phenomena dissimulated what they showed, because what they showed was the most terrible. The name of this most terrible is chaos. In no other way can chaos appear than as masked: to look at it is intolerable—mortal. Every interpretation is thus in principle a concealment, since it cannot permit chaos to appear without masking it in a veil of appearance. "It would be possible that the true constitution of things was so hostile to the presuppositions of life, so opposed to them, that we needed appearance in order to be able to live."[6]

Nietzsche calls this masking *art.* Art is the veil of beautiful appearance thrown over the horrors of chaos: "Greek art has taught us that there is no beautiful surface without a terrible depth." Beauty is the illusion that makes us forget that appearing is the manifestation of an unfathomable depth; it is the interpretation of its antagonist, the real.

To hold resolutely to appearances, to better accept an illusory mask, to interpret the text in such a way that its absurdity is concealed under the play of aesthetic significations and becomes a spectacle of beauty—this is the naïveté of the Greeks, those masters of interpretation. Naïveté characterizes the intentional superficiality of the profound man, the wisdom of the philosopher radical enough to become the poet of appearance.

In the Greek sense, the text phenomenon (or interpreted being) would stand as "the terrible in the mask of beauty."

What is most terrible, then, is also *the truth*. The truth designates the chaotic being of a groundless depth. If the mask is beauty, then truth is the ugliness of chaos: "because the truth is ugly." The phenomenon conceals its being in the appearance of beauty; thus, the beauty of the world hides the horror of nature. No more could one oppose being and phenomenon, nature and interpretation, text and "scrawl," revealed and concealed, than one could apprehend truth itself without its masks:

> We no longer believe that truth remains truth when the veils are withdrawn; we have lived too much to believe this. Today we consider it a matter of decency not to wish to see everything naked, or to be present at everything, or to understand and "know" everything. [7]

As for the "grounds" of truth, we only imagine them. Chaotic being has no grounds, no reasons; it is *groundless*—an abyss. Mask, therefore, becomes one with life. "We should," Nietzsche emphasizes, "understand the fundamentally *aesthetic* phenomenon called 'life.' " Life is a beautiful appearance, then, one with no regard for truth, one that allows us to continue to exist despite the truth: "Is it to avoid chance that we take refuge in life? In its brilliance, its *falseness*, its *superficiality*, its shimmering falsehood? If we seem joyous, is it because we are profoundly sad? We are grave, we know the abyss." [8] The most alive love what is most superficial—out of depth!

This conception of life, of course, is not the principal concern of the biological sciences. Rather, for Nietzsche, life determines the essence of interpreted being insofar as the latter involves a protective mask of lies. Lies, then, designate precisely the order of appearance—i.e., the texture of the text, the chaotic conglomeration of meanings. Lies indeed, since this phenomenon *masks* its own nature: it makes the illusion *of* truth surface from the terrible abyss—and because this is an illusion, truth is not so much divulged as denied, even when it seems to occur.

If the mask (life) characterizes interpreted being, then being in its interpretive aspect is an authoritarian insertion of sense, a sense-giving: Thus, when compared with the text, interpretation is a "creation." Life and art are two words that characterize a single creative act: namely, the act of ordering chaos, stabilizing becoming, and inventing categories by which the abyss of truth can be organized into various forms and constellations.

Identity of nature between the conqueror, the legislator, and the artist—the same way of material expression. . . . Metaphysics, religion, morality, science—all of them only products of his will to art, to lie, to flight from "truth," to *negation* of "truth." This ability itself, thanks to which he violates reality by means of lies, this artistic ability of man *par excellence*—he has it in common with everything that is.[9]

At this level of reflection, for Nietzsche, interpretation constantly takes the value of a creative imposition of form upon matter; here, the image of the relation between the artist and his material, the sculptor and his block of stone, replaces the textual metaphor and, thereby, enriches our understanding of phenomena. For Nietzsche, interpretation is synonymous with imposing sense, with molding chaos, with drawing a world of luminous figures out of what is hidden by the night of ignorance, impotence, and death. "The highest relation remains that between the creator and his material: that is the ultimate form of jubilation and mastery." To this, Nietzsche adds:

This has given me the greatest trouble and still does: to realize that what things *are called* is incomparably more important than what they are. The reputation, name, and appearance, the usual measure and weight of a thing, what it counts for—originally almost always wrong and arbitrary, thrown over things like a dress and altogether foreign to their nature and even to their skin—all this grows from generation unto generation, merely because people believe in it, until it gradually grows to be part of the thing and turns into its very body. What at first was appearance becomes in the end, almost invariably, the essence, and is effective as such. How foolish it would be to suppose that one only needs to point out this origin and this misty shroud of delusion in order to *destroy* the world that counts for real, so-called "reality." We can destroy only as creators. —But let us not forget this either: it is enough to create new names and estimations and probabilities in order to create in the long run new "things."[10]

Each individual, then, as an interpreter, is still creative.[11]

Interpreted being, consequently, is itself the masking of chaos. The difference is still maintained here, since the mask both conceals the abyss and appears "alien" to the nature of things. Alien not because it would transcend, or be dialectically opposed, or be arbitrarily added on to this nature, but alien in that it would be the self-interpretation of chaos, its own self-informing, its cosmological structuring, its very life—something that could only be thought of as a proximity within the separation of its "difference," as simultaneously being *and* interpretation, as sense *and* nonsense, truth *and* lie. "It should be explained that the 'falsity' of things results from our own creative force." In other words, it is the act of interpretation and the interpreter that hide nature! And since the interpreter and the act of interpretation are already the life of being, it is being that interprets itself within its own self-dissimulation. We conclude the great cycle of being by returning to our starting point: being *is* mask, it *is* phenomenon.

NOTES

1. Kröner, XIII; §158.
2. *The Will to Power*, §556.
3. K, XIII; §77.
4. K, XIII; §121.
5. *Beyond Good and Evil*, §230.
6. *WP*, §583.
7. *The Gay Science;* Preface, §4.
8. K, XIII; §692.
9. *WP*, §853.
10. *GS*, §58.
11. See *WP*, §767.

Gilles Deleuze

NOMAD THOUGHT

Probably most of us fix the dawn of our modern culture in the trinity Nietzsche-Freud-Marx. And it is of little consequence that the world was unprepared for them in advance. Now, Marx and Freud, perhaps, do represent the dawn of our culture, but Nietzsche is something entirely different: the dawn of counterculture.

Modern society clearly does not function on the basis of codes. Yet if we consider the evolution of Marxism or Freudianism (rather than taking Marx and Freud literally), we see that they are paradoxically launched in an attempt at recodification: recodification by the state, in the case of Marxism ("You have been made ill by the state, and you will be cured by the state"—but not the same state), and recodification by the family, in the case of Freudianism ("You have been made ill by the family, and you will be cured by the family"—but not the same family). Marxism and psychoanalysis in a real sense constitute the fundamental bureaucracies—one public, the other private—whose aim is somehow or other to recodify everything that ceaselessly becomes decodified at the horizon of our culture. Nietzsche's concern, on the contrary, is not this at all. His task lies elsewhere: beyond all the codes of past, present, and future, to transmit something that does not and will not allow itself to be codified. To transmit it o a new body, to invent a body that can receive it and spill it forth; a body .hat would be our own, the earth's, or even something written . . .

We are all familiar with the great instruments of codification. Societies do not vary much, after all, and they do not have so very many means of codification. The three principal ones are law, contracts, and institutions, and they are easily to be found, for example, in the relations we have, or have had, with books. With certain books of law, specifically called codes, or even sacred texts, the reader's relation is itself governed by law. Another sort of book reflects the bourgeois contractual relationship, which is at the basis of secular literature in its commercial aspects: "I buy from you, you give me something to read." This contractual relationship involves everyone: author, publisher, reader. There is also the political book (revolutionary in inclination) presented as a book of extant or future institutions. All sorts of mixtures among these types take place (contractual or institutional books may be treated as sacred texts, for example), for the various kinds of codification are so pervasive, so frequently overlapping, that one is found embedded in the other.

Let us take another very different kind of example: the codification of madness. First of all, there were the legal forms: the hospital, the asylum. This is repressive codification, incarceration, the old-fashioned committal that will be invoked in the future as the final hope of health (when the insane will say, "Those were the good times, when they locked us up; even worse things happen today"). And then came the incredible event, psychoanalysis. It had been understood that there were people who escaped the bourgeois contractual relation, as it appeared in medicine; these people were judged insane because they could not be contracting parties; they were held legally "incapable." Freud's stroke of genius was to bring one sort of insanity (neurosis in the broadest sense of the term) under the contractual relationship, explaining that in this case one could make a special contract—one that permitted hypnotic "abandon." The novelty of Freudian psychoanalysis consisted, then, in the introduction of the bourgeois contractual relationship into psychiatry, an element that had until then been excluded. More recent solutions, solutions often with political implications and revolutionary ambitions, we may call institutional. Here, again, is the triple means of codification: if not the legal, the contractual relation; if not the contractual, then the institutional. Upon these codes all our forms of bureaucratic organization thrive.

Confronted with the ways in which our societies become progressively decodified and unregulated, in which our codes break down at every point, Nietzsche is the only thinker who makes no attempt at recodification. He says: the process still has not gone far enough, we are still only children ("The emancipation of European man is the great irreversible process of the present day; and the tendency should even be accelerated.") In his own writing and thought Nietzsche assists in the attempt at decodification—not in the relative sense, by deciphering former, present, or future codes, but in an absolute sense, by expressing something that can not be codified, confounding all codes. But to confound all codes is not easy, even on the simplest level of writing and thought. The only parallel I can find here is with Kafka, in what he does to German, working within the language of Prague Jewry: he constructs a battering ram out of German and turns it against itself. By dint of a certain indeterminacy and sobriety, he expresses something within the codified limits of the German language that had never before been conveyed. Similarly, Nietzsche maintained or supposed himself to be Polish in his use of German. His masterful siege of the language permits him to transmit something uncodifiable: the notion of style as politics.

In more general terms, what is the purpose of such thought that pretends to express its dynamism within the compass of laws (while rejecting them), of contractual relations (while denying them), and of institutions (while ridiculing them)? Let us go back briefly to the example of psychoanalysis and ask why such an original thinker as Melanie Klein remains within the psychoanalvtic system. She explains it clearly enough herself: the part-objects she discusses, with their outbursts, their flow, are fantasies: the patients bring in their lived, intense experiences, and Melanie Klein translates them into fantasies. Thus, a contract, a specific contract is established: give me your states of experience and I'll give you back fantasies. The contract implies an exchange, of money and of words. Now, a psychoanalyst like Winnicott works at the limits of psychoanalysis because he feels at a certain point this contractual procedure is no longer appropriate. There comes a time when translating fantasies, interpreting signifier or signified, is no longer to the point. There comes a moment that has to be shared: you must put yourself in the patient's situation, you must enter into it. Is this sharing a kind of sympathy, or empathy, or identification? Surely it is more complicated than this. What we sense is the implied necessity for a relationship that is neither legal, nor contractual, nor institutional—and it is the same with Nietzsche.

We read an aphorism or a poem by Zarathustra, but materially and formally texts like these cannot be understood in terms of the creation or application of a law, or the offer of a contractual relation, or the establishment of an institution. The only conceivable key, perhaps, would be in the concept of "embarkation." Here, there is something Pascalian that contraverts Pascal. We embark, then, in a kind of raft of "the Medusa;" bombs fall all around the raft as it drifts toward icy subterranean streams—or toward torrid rivers, the Orinoco, the Amazon; the passengers row together, they are not supposed to like one another, they fight with one another, they eat one another. To row together is to share, to share something beyond law, contract, or institution. It is a period of drifting, of "deterritorialization." I say this in a very loose and confused way, since it is a hypothesis, a vague impression concerning the originality of Nietzsche's texts, a new kind of book.

What are the characteristics of Nietzsche's aphorisms, then, that give this impression? Maurice Blanchot has illuminated one in his work *L'Entretien infini:* the relation with the outside, the exterior. Opening one of Nietzsche's books at random, you have the almost novel experience of *not* continuing on by way of an interiority, whether this be called the inner soul of consciousness, or the inner essence or concept—that is, what has always served as the guiding principle of philosophy. It is characteristic of philosophical writing that relations with an exterior are always mediated and dissolved by an interior, and this process always takes place within some given interiority. Nietzsche, on the contrary, grounds his thought, his writing, on an immediate relation with the outside, the exterior. Like any handsome painting or drawing, an aphorism is framed—but at what point does it become handsome? From the moment one knows and feels that the movement, the framed line, comes from without, that it does not begin within the limits of the frame. It began beneath or beside the frame, and traverses the frame. As in Godard's film, one paints the painting *with* the wall. Far from being the delimitation of a pictorial surface, the frame immediately relates this surface to an outside. Now, to hang thought on the outside is what philosophers have literally never done, even when they spoke about, for example, politics; even when they treated such subjects as walking or fresh air. It is not sufficient to talk about fresh air or the outdoors in order to suspend thought directly and immediately upon the outside. "They come like fate, without reason, consideration, or pretext; they appear as lightning appears, too terrible, too sudden, too convincing, too *different* even to be hated." So runs Nietzsche's celebrated text on the founders of the state, "those artists with the look of bronze."

One is irresistibly reminded of Kafka's *Great Wall of China:* "It is impossible to understand how they have gotten through, all the way to the capital, which is so far from the border. However, they are here, and each morning their number seems to grow . . . To talk with them, impossible. They don't know our language . . . Even their horses are carnivorous." In any case, we can say that such texts are traversed by a movement that comes from without, that does not begin on the page (nor on the preceding pages), that is not bounded by the frame of the book; it is entirely different from the imaginary movement of representation or the abstract movement of concepts that habitually takes place among words and within the mind of the reader. Something leaps up from the book and enters a region completely exterior to it. And this, I believe, is the warrant for legitimately misunderstanding the whole of Nietzsche's work. An aphorism is an amalgam of forces that are always held apart from one another.

An aphorism means nothing, signifies nothing, and is no more a signifier than a signified: were it not so, the interiority of the text would remain undisturbed. An aphorism is a play of forces, the most recent of which—the latest, the newest, and provisionally the final force—is always *the most exterior*. Nietzsche puts this very clearly: if you want to know what I mean, then find the force that gives a new sense to what I say, and hang the text upon it. Following this approach, there is no problem of interpreting Nietzsche; there are only mechanical problems of plotting out his text, of trying to establish which exterior force actually enables the text to *transmit*, say, a current of energy.

At this point, we encounter the problems posed by those texts of Nietzsche that have a fascist or anti-Semitic resonance. We should first recognize here that Nietzsche nourished and still nourishes a great many young fascists. There was a time when it was important to show that Nietzsche had been misappropriated and completely deformed by the fascists. Jean Wahl, Bataille, and Klossowski did this in the review *Acéphale*. But today, this is no longer necessary. We need not argue Nietzsche at the level of textual analysis—not because we cannot dispute at that level, but because the dispute is no longer worthwhile. Instead, the problem takes the shape of finding, assessing, and assembling the exterior forces that give a sense of liberation, a sense of exteriority to each various phrase.

The revolutionary character of Nietzsche's thought becomes apparent at the level of method: it is his method that makes Nietzsche's text into something not to be characterized in itself as "fascist," "bourgeois," or "revolutionary," but to be regarded as an exterior field where fascist, bourgeois, and revolutionary forces meet head on. If we pose the problem this way, the response conforming to Nietzsche's method would be: find the revolutionary force. The problem is always to detect the new forces that come from without, that traverse and cut across the Nietzschean text within the framework of the aphorism. The legitimate misunderstanding here, then, would be to treat the aphorism as a phenomenon, one that waits for new forces to come and "subdue" it, or to make it work, or even to make it explode.

In addition to its relation to the exterior, the aphorism has an intensive relation. Yet, as Klossowski and Lyotard have shown, the two characteristics are identical. Let us return for a moment to those *states of experience* that, at a certain point, must not be translated into representations or fantasies, must not be transmitted by legal, contractual, or institutional codes, must not be exchanged or bartered away, but, on the contrary, must be seen as a dynamic flux that carries us away even further outside. This is precisely a process of intensity, of intensities. The state of experience is not subjective in origin, at least not inevitably so. Moreover, it is not individual. It is a continuous flux and the disruption of flux, and each pulsional intensity necessarily bears a relation to another intensity, a point of contact and transmission. *This* is what underlies all codes, what escapes all codes, and it is what the codes themselves seek to translate, convert, and mint anew. In his own pulsional form of writing, Nietzsche tells us not to barter away intensity for mere representations. Intensity refers neither to the signifier (the represented word) nor to the signified (the represented thing). Finally, then, how can we even conceive of it if it serves both as the agent and object of decodification? This is perhaps the most impenetrable mystery posed in Nietzsche's thought.

Proper names also play a role here, but they are not intended to be representations of things (or persons) or words. Presocratics, Romans, Jews, Christ, Antichrist, Julius Caesar, Borgia, Zarathustra—collective or individual, these proper names that come and go in Nietzsche's texts are neither signifiers nor signified. Rather, they are designations of intensity inscribed upon a body that could be the earth or a book, but could also be the suffering body of Nietzsche himself: *I am all the names of history* . . . There is a kind of nomadism, a perpetual displacement in the intensities designated by proper names, intensities that interpenetrate one another at the same time that they are lived, experienced, by a single body. Intensity can be experienced, then, only in connection with its mobile inscription in a body and under the shifting exterior of a proper name, and therefore the proper name is always a mask, a mask that masks its agent.

The aphorism has yet a third significant relation—in this case, to humor and irony. Those who read Nietzsche without laughing—without laughing often, richly, even hilariously—have, in a sense, not read Nietzsche at all. This is not only true for Nietzsche but for all the other authors who belong to the same horizon of our counterculture. One of the things that reflect our decadence, our degeneration, is the manner in which people feel the need to express their anguish, solitude, guilt, to dramatize encounters—in short, the whole tragedy of interiority. Max Brod recounts how the audience went wild with laughter when Kafka read *The Trial*. In fact, it is hard to read even Beckett without laughing, without going from one moment of delight to the next. Laughter—and not meaning. Schizophrenic laughter or revolutionary joy, this is what emerged from the great books; not the anguish of petty narcissism, the dread of guilt. We could call it a superhuman comedy, a divine jest. An indescribable delight always springs forth from the great books, even when they present things that are ugly, desperate, or terrifying. As it is, all great books bring about a transmutation; they give tomorrow's health. One cannot help but laugh when the codes are confounded.

If you put thought into contact with the exterior, it assumes an air of freedom, it gives birth to Dionysian laughter. When, as often happens, Nietzsche finds himself confronted with something he feels is nauseating, ignoble, wretched, he laughs—and he wants to intensify it, if at all possible. He says: a bit more effort, it's not disgusting enough; or, on the other hand: it's astounding because it is disgusting, it's a marvel, a masterpiece, a poisonous flower; finally, "man begins to become interesting." This is how Nietzsche considers—how he deals with—what he calls bad conscience, for example. But the Hegelian commentators, the ever-present commentators of interiority, who don't even have the wit to laugh, tell us: you *see*, Nietzsche takes bad conscience seriously, he makes it a moment in the evolution of spirit. Of course they quickly pass over what Nietzsche makes out of this spirituality because they sense the danger.

If Nietzsche does admit of a legitimate misinterpretation, there are also completely illegitimate misinterpretations—all those that spring from the spirit of seriousness, the spirit of gravity, Zarathustra's ape—that is, the cult of interiority. For Nietzsche, laughter always refers to an exterior movement of irony and humor, a movement of intensities, of intensive qualities, as Klossowski and Lyotard have pointed out. There is free play between the low and high intensities; a low intensity can undermine the highest, even become as high as the highest. Not only does this play on scales of intensity affect the ebb and flow of irony and humor in Nietzsche, but it also constitutes or qualifies experience from without. An aphorism is a matter of laughter and joy. If we have not discovered what it is in the aphorism that makes us laugh, what the distribution of humor and irony is, what the division of intensities is, then we have not found anything.

One final point remains to be made. Let us go back to that grand passage in *The Genealogy of Morals* about the founders of empires. There we encounter men of Asiatic production, so to speak. On a base of primitive rural communities, these despots construct their imperial machines that codify everything to excess. With an administrative bureaucracy that organizes huge projects, they feed off an overabundance of labor ("Wherever they appear something new soon arises, a ruling structure that *lives,* in which parts and functions are delimited and coordinated, in which nothing whatever finds a place that has not first been assigned and coordinated, in which nothing whatever finds a place that has not first been assigned a 'meaning' in relation to the whole"). It is questionable, however, whether this text does not tie together two forces that in other respects would be held apart—two forces that Kafka distinguished, even opposed, in *The Great Wall of China.* For, when one tries to discover how primitive segmented communities give rise to other forms of sovereignty—a question Nietzsche raises in the second part of *The Genealogy*—one sees that two entirely different yet strictly related phenomena occur. It is true that, at the center, the rural communities are absorbed by the despot's bureaucratic machine, which includes its scribes, its priests, its functionaries. But on the periphery, these communities commence a sort of adventure. They enter into another kind of unit, this time a nomadic association, a nomadic war machine, and they begin to decodify instead of allowing themselves to become overcodified. Whole groups depart; they become nomads. Archaeologists have led us to conceive of this nomadism not as a primary state, but as an adventure suddenly embarked upon by sedentary groups impelled by the attraction of movement, of what lies outside. The nomad and his war machine oppose the despot with his administrative machine: an extrinsic nomadic unit as opposed to an intrinsic despotic unit. And yet the societies are correlative, interrelated; the despot's purpose will be to integrate, to internalize the nomadic war machine, while that of the nomad will be to invent an administration for the newly conquered empire. They ceaselessly oppose one another—to the point where they become confused with one another.

Philosophic discourse is born out of the imperial state, and it passes through innumerable metamorphoses, the same metamorphoses that lead us from the foundations of empire to the Greek city. Even within the Greek city-state, philosophic discourse remained in a strict relation with the despot (or at least within the shadow of despotism), with imperialism, with the administration of things and people (Leo Strauss and Kojève give a variety of proofs of this in their work *On Tyranny*). Philosophic discourse has always been essentially related to law, institutions, and contracts—which, taken together, constitute the subject matter of sovereignty and have been part of the history of sedentary peoples from the earliest despotic states to modern democracies. The "signifier" is really the last philosophical metamorphosis of the despot. But if Nietzsche does not belong to philosophy, it is perhaps because he was the first to conceive of another kind of discourse as counter-philosophy. This discourse is above all nomadic; its statements can be conceived as the products of a mobile war machine and not the utterances of a rational, administrative machinery, whose philosophers would be bureaucrats of pure reason. It is perhaps in this sense that Nietzsche announces the advent of a new politics that begins with him (which Klossowski calls a plot against his own class).

It is common knowledge that nomads fare miserably under our kinds of regime: we will go to any lengths in order to settle them, and they barely have enough to subsist on. Nietzsche lived like such a nomad, reduced to a shadow, moving from furnished room to furnished room. But the nomad is not necessarily one who moves: some voyages take place *in situ,* are trips in intensity. Even historically, nomads are not necessarily those who move about like migrants. On the contrary, they do not move; nomads, they nevertheless stay in the same place and continually evade the codes of settled people. We also know that the problem for revolutionaries today is to unite within the purpose of the particular struggle without falling into the despotic and bureaucratic organization of the party or state apparatus. We seek a kind of war machine that will not re-create a state apparatus, a nomadic unit related to the outside that will not revive an internal despotic unity. Perhaps this is what is most profound in Nietzsche's thought and marks the extent of his break with philosophy, at least so far as it is manifested in the aphorism: he made thought into a machine of war—a battering ram—into a nomadic force. And even if the journey is a motionless one, even if it occurs on the spot, imperceptible, unexpected, and subterranean, we must ask ourselves, "Who are our nomads today, our real Nietzscheans?"

Eric Blondel

NIETZSCHE: LIFE AS METAPHOR

It is generally agreed that Nietzsche's language is nothing less than "Konigsbergian." As he himself proclaimed, "After Luther and after Goethe, there was a third step to be taken." But has anyone yet drawn all the *methodological* consequences of such a step, of such a peculiar use of language, one so rare among philosophers? Until now, most critics have insisted on considering Nietzsche's "poetic" and metaphorical style of writing as either the simple and often tasteless ornamentation of philosophical prose produced by a good-natured poet, or as the kind of decoration that is favored by "men of letters," but that philosophers try desperately to forget. Because of his deliberate use of polysemantic metaphors rather than neutral concepts, it would seem more judicious, or perhaps even more philosophic, to ask if Nietzsche's "style" does not necessarily embody a philosophical choice—if it is not analogous to what is found in the writings of the Presocratics, since, so far as Nietzsche is concerned, "for a genuine poet, metaphor is not a rhetorical figure but a vicarious image that he actually beholds in place of a concept."[1]

"We have been able to create forms long before knowing how to create concepts": why not apply this kind of remark to Nietzsche and his philosophy *from the start,* just as has so often been done (in the usual biographical and philosophical way) with other, much less fundamental observations? For until now, either too much or too little attention has been given to metaphors, to images, and, in general, to the forms of Nietzsche's discourse. Too much, because his stylistic eccentricities have often been considered either as poetical affectation, or as pure literature, designed to seduce philosophers or to arouse adolescents (hence the origin of the highly misplaced attention accorded to *Thus Spoke Zarathustra* by hurried readers). Too much also because, given the circumstances, his readers have tended to abstract his style of expression from the content of his thought; the philosopher has found himself "overwhelmed by the image" of the poet. Yet too little attention has been given as well: under the pretext of a philosophic or scientific rigor, Nietzsche's metaphors never seem to have been considered in their own right, except as rhetorical garb to be stripped away—and this in order to get at concepts that, of themselves, are admittedly vague.

We would like, instead, to show that Nietzsche's use of metaphor is demanded by a specifically philosophic necessity, and that his discourse is intrinsically metaphorical, precisely because his thought is *meta-phorical*. Here, we should understand the original sense of this term as transport or transposition. By returning a sense of coherency to these images or metaphors, and by examining several of his own examples, we hope to show how Nietzsche uses metaphor to designate the separation between body and thought, a kind of displacement that has structured the development of culture since its very inception. For our present analysis, it will be the central image of this *metaphorical thought* about *meta-phor*—namely, the *vita femina*—that will guide the order of our investigation.

Essentially, Nietzsche is concerned with the question of culture,[2] with its birth, its development, its sickness and decline—that is, nihilism, which, perhaps, coincides with the rebirth of culture. For Nietzsche, culture is originally established by and as a certain kind of separation (meta-phor) between the instincts (the "body") and thought or expression. Insofar as he is a cultural being, man is (normally) sick: "Man is, relatively speaking, the most unsuccessful animal, the sickliest, the one most dangerously strayed from its instincts." In fact, one's own body is not immediately present to man, but must, within the cultural economy, express itself (i.e., speak to itself) through the medium of a symptomatic language: consciousness or "spirit."

> "Spirit" is to us precisely a symptom of a relative imperfection of the organism, as an attempting, fumbling, blundering, as a toiling in which an unnecessarily large amount of nervous energy is expended—we deny that anything can be made perfect so long as it is still made conscious.[3]

The (cultural) "nature" of man is thus established as nonnatural, since it is based on distance and scission: language and thought thus appear as epidermal surfaces that like our skin, both conceal and exhibit the vicissitudes our bodies undergo. If culture is the original sickness of man, man as a cultural being is like the skin on a body or the surface of the earth: "The earth . . . has a skin, and this skin has diseases. One of these diseases, for example, is called 'man.' " And, "if morbidity is the regular state among members of the human race," we can ask, with Nietzsche, "the great question as to whether we can really dispense with illness." More strongly still—can we do without the constitutive and constitutional sickness that is bad conscience? "There can be no doubt that bad conscience is a sickness, but so, in a sense, is pregnancy. . . . This is the womb of all ideal and imaginative phenomena."[4] It is because of bad conscience that life is "pregnant" with culture. As a sickness of culture, man is born in and by bad conscience—which, itself, ushers in this meta-phorical, quasi-*hysterical*, and displaced language: it is the body's symptomatic *conversion* into language.

As a necessarily cultural being, man is thus born in the pain of a primal rupture, of a scission, which in these circumstances could quite properly be called maternal or matrical, since it constitutes the "reason" or the structural condition necessary for all those who follow and repeat this rupture. Nietzsche in fact speaks of "an abrupt break" or "a leap" of man's "violent severance from his animal past," and a "sudden leap and fall" into new conditions of existence.

If one follows Nietzsche's imagery, one perceives that the "work" of bad conscience is described as being a *primal repression (internalization)* of the body and of the "freedom" of its instincts. The turning back on itself of one's own "animality" also implies a split: it breaks the instinctive unity of the body, it shatters the immediate "guidance of unconscious drives." The fallibility of consciousness is therefore brought into the world by the paradoxical movement of repression: "They were forced to think, deduce, calculate, weigh cause and effect—unhappy people, reduced to their weakest, most fallible organ, their consciousness." The birth of consciousness was indeed the outcome of repressing the instincts and banishing them to the unconscious: "All instincts that do not discharge themselves outwardly turn inward—this is what I call the *internalization* of man; it alone provides the soil for the growth of what is later called man's *soul*."[5] As a result of this blockage, brought about by internalization, man's reflection becomes exaggerated and he becomes repressed, diverted: consciousness (or "mind")—this universe of symptoms—is thus the new field opened up by this translation. And we can, along with Nietzsche, designate it as *the* primal *meta-phor,* that which founds culture itself:

> It was not that these old instincts had abruptly ceased making their demands; but now their satisfaction was rare and difficult. For the most part they had to depend on new, convert satisfactions . . . Man's interior world, originally meager and tenuous, was expanding in every dimension, in proportion as the outward discharge of his feelings was curtailed.[6]

But this break with the instincts brought about by the first appearance of bad conscience, this scission or division that opens the shift between conscious and unconscious, is clearly viewed by Nietzsche as *primal*, as structural; which is to say that it is constitutive of man's humanity (or culture), of "his sickness with himself." Indeed, this split, this displacement, conditions all subsequent ones: it is their source, their promise, their rationale, "as though in man something were heralded, as though he were not a goal, but, in a way, only a stage, an interlude, a bridge, a great promise . . . ." And if, in fact, the separation brought about by bad conscience introduces "culture" as man's nonnatural nature, as the promise of a future, as "the greatest and most disastrous of maladies, of which humanity has not to this day been cured," then, on the contrary, *The Genealogy of Morals* announces the model of the *Overman*—i.e., a being who is beyond man, who is cured of the "sickness of man," and who is thus, strictly speaking, no longer a man.

But, with regard to this passage, one might ask whether Nietzsche in fact anticipated what Freud referred to as "primal repression," a theoretical hypothesis intended to account for the successive repressions of ontogenetic development. Furthermore, Freud's notion of a mental topography could well correspond to the primal meta-phor described by Nietzsche—i.e., to the transference resulting from the conscious-unconscious separation; it could also correspond to the splitting up of mental life—the occurrence of the latter most often being correlated, as with Nietzsche, to the pressure of reality: "the one [transformation] . . . that made him once and for all a sociable and pacific creature." In fact, repression "appears when the satisfaction of one drive, which in itself would be pleasurable, threatens to create discordance as regards other demands."[7] This is a defense mechanism of the same kind as conversion. Properly speaking, then, this ultimate or primal repression is the rationale for all subsequent repressions.

Now, this "sickness which is like pregnancy" insofar as it is primal and maternal makes life "rich with promise for the future" and makes life the "mother" of culture. In a corollary way, it makes man both sick and productive at the same time. Indeed, it creates what Nietzsche calls the man who is a "mother": "Consider a continually creative person, a 'mother' type in the grand sense, one who knows and hears nothing any more except about the pregnancies and deliveries of his spirit."[8] Thus, through conversion (through sublimation, regression, and so forth), these displaced instincts, which are both promising and fruitful, have a curious correspondence with what in Freudian terminology are called secondary or derived repressions (*Abkömmlingen*). Nietzsche gives several examples of this in his work entitled *The Will to Power:*

> Man's growing inwardness. Inwardness grows as powerful drives that have been denied outward release by the establishment of peace and society seeks compensation by turning inward in concert with the imagination. The thirst for enmity, cruelty, revenge, violence turns back, is repressed; in the desire for knowledge there is avarice and conquest; in the artist there reappears the repressed power to dissimulate and lie.[9]

It can thus be affirmed that bad conscience is the mother, or the primal condition of sublimation, in the same way that, for Freud, primal repression (as well as regression or fixation) first makes sublimation possible. Now, if we recall that Freud most often describes artistic activity and intellectual research as acts of sublimation, we find a confirmation of the preceding comparisons in another of Nietzsche's works:

> When an instinct becomes *intellectualized,* it takes on a new name, a new charm, a new price. We often oppose it to an instinct of prime importance as if it were its contrary (cruelty, for example). Many instincts—e.g., the sexual instinct—are susceptible of being greatly refined by the intelligence (the love of humanity, the cult of Mary and the saints, artistic enthusiasm; Plato thinks that the love of knowledge and philosophy is a sublimated sexual instinct). But its former direct action subsists, *alongside.*[10]

Unlocking the space of culture by means of its implied meta-phorical scission, bad conscience thus promises a fable—i.e., a mediate course, a wandering of thought away from the instincts—like the promise of secondary repressions, themselves derived from repressed instincts. To speak symbolically, bad conscience appears as the "mother" of man, insofar as it is the sickness peculiar to man. More profoundly, perhaps, bad conscience is indeed a sickness—it is the sickness of man as such—but it is also the sickness of life in general: and it is life that is pregnant in this respect. Using the privileged metaphor of the *vita femina,* then, life will denote the Will to Power as fertility, productivity, creativity, and self-overcoming.

Now, it is clear that when he discusses life as a state of pregnancy, a state that gives birth to the "mother" type and thus to (artificial) man as a cultural being, Nietzsche is not concerned with revealing a father. Should we take this as an inconsistency in the metaphorical sequence, or, rather, as an unconsciously deliberate coherence? Is it enough to acknowledge a Nietzschean phantasm, a sort of Oedipus? On the other hand, we also know—and this explanation is compatible with the preceding—that bad conscience "makes the mind maternal, exclusively maternal," and gives birth to "that terrible artists' egoism that has the look of bronze and knows itself justified to all eternity in its 'work,' like a mother in her child."[11] But isn't it precisely this *question of the father* that constitutes the originality of what Nietzsche specifically calls the *genealogical* analysis? Who, then, is the father of the mind, of consciousness? The philosophers of metaphysical idealism "act as if pure intellectuality presented them with the problems of knowledge and metaphysics . . . Against the former I direct my *psychology of philosophers:* their most alienated calculations and their 'intellectuality' are still only the last pallid impression of a physiological fact; the voluntary is absolutely lacking, everything is instinct."[12] Metaphysical idealism, "the philosophy of concealment," is indeed eager to provide its thought with a legitimate father (for example, consciousness or reason): this conscious and rational subject allows the preservation of a moral façade. But

Nietzsche, in his genealogical research, is *suspicious* of, and proceeds to interrogate, the *natural* character of this legitimate father. The Nietzschean genealogy thus literally understands itself to be a search for the father, an investigation into the paternity of thought. When Nietzsche finally reveals the natural father in hiding, the father who makes life problematic for the philosopher (indeed, the philosopher sees it as a dubious woman), the father turns out to be *the body*—precisely what the "born organizers" of bad conscience forced into a state of latency.

Here, then, is the legitimate father, the body: repressed, thwarted, and left for dead. This repression, this concealment or death of the father, does not immediately signify decadence, however: in art, for example, the body is allowed to speak, albeit in an indirect, displaced, and metaphorical manner. Nonetheless, there is the structural possibility of it: the body makes decadence possible without necessarily implying it, in the same way that repression does not always lead to neurosis. But insofar as this meta-phorical concealment of the father at least promises the possibility of decadence, we should not be surprised by the passage in *Ecce Homo* in which Nietzsche prides himself on having a particularly acute understanding of this phenomenon:

> The good fortune of my existence, its uniqueness perhaps, lies in its fatality: I am, to express it in the form of a riddle, already dead as my father, while as my mother I am still living and becoming old. This dual descent, as it were, both from the highest and the lowest rung on the ladder of life, at the same time a *decadent* and a *beginning*—this, if anything, explains that neutrality, that freedom from all partiality in relation to the total problem of life, that perhaps distinguishes me. I have a subtler sense of smell for the signs of ascent and decline than any other human being before me; I am the teacher *par excellence* for this—I know both, I am both. [13]

In making man into a meta-phorically cultured being, bad conscience thus gives birth to a man who is somewhat "Oedipal." Whether healthy or morbid, culture in fact conceals and suppresses its "father" the body, in order to devote itself exclusively to its children, its thoughts. As a consequence, man in turn—here, Nietzsche himself, the psychologist of decadence—identifies himself with his "mother," and, no longer caring for the body, becomes the "mother type" of man. He is man without a father, "forgetful" about his body, but bountiful in all the vicissitudes of culture. What takes place, then, in this original Oedipus, who is created by the primal repression of the body and the splitting up of his life into *instincts* (the unconscious) and the *thinking ego* (the conscious)? The father of thought, the body, is repressed for the sake of the secondary or derived repressions of consciousness. Initially undivided, life finds itself split into instincts and ego, or into body and thought. Ultimately, this split promises to structure the development of decadence as the repression of the body, the parthenogenesis of thought by reason, as well as the divinization of consciousness ("The abdomen is the reason why man does not easily take himself for a god"). On the other hand, this split will foresee the subsequent development of mind as the self-overcoming, self-surpassing, and self-suppression of morality.

If life is thus represented as split, as belabored by bad conscience, then it is on the basis of this "Oedipus" that the *vita femina* is held forth: like the sphinx, it conceals the paternity, the origin of man and his thoughts. She appears—body and soul, from without and within, an unfathomable reality and disguise—across a series of oppositions whose structural basis is this original split.

Now, we must attempt to investigate the coherency of the *vita femina* metaphor in connection with what we have designated as the primal metaphor, the transfer or displacement (brought about by bad conscience) of the body toward thought, toward the conscious surface. "Yes, life is a woman!"[14] This metaphorical statement of the *vita femina* can lead us to a far clearer conception of Nietzsche's "ontology" of the metaphor: i.e., as the scission, as the equivocal play of being, that underlies his theory of culture as meta-phor. And it is here, indeed, that one encounters what must be called Nietzsche's "ontological" discourse—a non-ontological discourse cast in the figurative or metaphorical terms of woman. One could indeed characterize Nietzsche's "ontology" as feminine, or even as gynecological, for this ontology speaks of being as a woman who has no being, as appearance and disguise, as the illusion and mystery of a woman who has no nature, who is pure spectacle—a woman who, "when she gives herself, gives herself as a spectacle." Also, if it is true that "Woman, the Eternal Feminine, is an imaginary notion, which man is alone in believing," then the metaphysical idealist, who congeals the *vita femina* into an imaginary essence, will be alone in believing in the identity, eternity, and permanence of being.

As the privileged metaphor of life, woman is thus enigma and appearance. The culture she gives birth to begins with the initial lie, which is the repression of the body, the dissimulation of the father. She dwells in a zone of ambiguity, and obscures her own fundamental duplicity by means of a profusion of deceptive appearances, of secondary or derived repressions (thought, reason, morality, religion, art, etc.). But the following question arises: is this naïveté, modesty, or hypocrisy? By taking refuge in the appearance she presents, and only presenting herself as appearance, as pure appearance at that, does the *vita femina* veil a reality that she wants to hide or *must* hide? Whereas the classic problematic of appearance always involves some reality behind or beyond the appearance (for want of which this concept would be inconceivable), this opposition disappears for Nietzsche.

For him, appearance and reality are not opposed to one another, nor do they mutually entail one another; rather, they coincide. Appearance and appearing are the only reality of the *vita femina* when this is taken as the metaphor of meta-phor. If one were to look for an opposition, it would be found more easily between the fragmentary truth of appearing and the fiction of a "real" being, an essentially false entity. In this way, the notion of a truth *beyond* appearance, underneath or behind the veil, is rendered null and void. It is certainly true that life deceives us with her ambiguous apparitions: but she deceives us not because she conceals an essence or a reality beneath appearances, but because she has *no* essence and would only like to make us think that she does. Her "essence" is to appear.

Let us call this modesty: not to reveal everything, not to show everything all at once. Correlatively, we must find out whether the philosopher, when confronting life, is a *clairvoyant* (who sees behind what is immediately visible to what appears in turn from behind the trappings) or a *voyeur* (who imagines without seeing, who "realizes" the invisible by supposing the reality of that which has none). But all modesty is potentially erotic, since to conceal is often to suggest:

> Woman, conscious of man's feelings concerning women, assists his efforts at idealization by adorning herself, walking beautifully, dancing, expressing delicate thoughts: in the same way, she *practices modesty,* reserve, distance—realizing instinctively that in this way the idealizing capacity of the man will grow. (Given the tremendous subtlety of woman's instinct, modesty remains by no means conscious hypocrisy: she divines that it is precisely an actual naïve modesty that most seduces a man and impels him to overestimate her. Therefore woman is naïve from the subtlety of her instinct, which advises her of the utility of innocence. A deliberate *closing of one's eyes to oneself*—wherever dissembling produces a stronger effect when it is unconscious, it *becomes* unconscious.[15]

Being modest in fact means being able to show something in order to conceal it, to forget and to make someone else forget what is hidden, and it would take an almost impossible naïveté to believe that there is no hidden motive, ground, or world. It would be to believe exclusively in the reality of what is seen, and to believe oneself completely visible. But this modest naïveté encounters the imagination of the idealist philosopher, who invents or reinstates a hidden reality, who turns naïveté into a hypocritical eroticism— i.e., who conceals only in order to suggest and exhibit. Thus everything depends on the philosopher's attitude. And when it is a question of "systematic" philosophers, Nietzsche suspects that they have never understood anything about women. Love of life is like "the love for a woman who raises doubts in us." In order to overcome this doubt, the metaphysician works out a contrived, an occult, essence for the *vita femina*. And it is of little importance to him that this be imposture and illusion, for "whatever their detractors say about them, a beautiful woman, all the same, has something in common with truth: both give more happiness when one desires them than when one possesses them." Nonetheless, the innocence of life, forgetful of all "reality," mindful only of these appearances as pure becoming—this, as the metaphorical image for the "innocence of becoming," is fraught with hypocrisy:

> There are realities that one may never admit to oneself; after all, one is a woman; after all, one has a woman's *modesties*—those young creatures dancing over there are obviously beyond all reality: they are dancing with nothing but palpable ideals . . . They look incomparably better when they are a little tipsy like that, these pretty creatures—oh, how well they know that, too. They actually become amiable *because* they know it. —Finally, they are also inspired by their finery; their finery is their *third* intoxication [after love and the dance]: they believe in their tailors as they believe in their God—and who would dissuade them from this faith? This faith makes blessed! And self-admiration is healthy! Self-admiration protects against colds. Has a pretty woman who knew herself to be well dressed ever caught cold? Never! I am even assuming that she was barely dressed.[16]

Faced with the *vita femina*, a spectacle wholly naïve and therefore enigmatic, we find the perplexed philosopher. He (whom we have called "Oedipal") is Oedipus in front of the sphinx woman, who, in turn, poses all these riddles. The philosopher's "truth," we have seen, is Oedipal, since it is brought about by the murder of the father (the body). The philosopher searches for truth as if it were (in both senses of the term) obscene; i.e., both hidden and indecent. But, as Nietzsche suggests, "*why not rather* untruth? and uncertainty? even ignorance? The problem of the value of truth came before us—or was it we who came before the problem? Who of us is Oedipus here? Who the Sphinx?"[17] Confronted with this female spectacle, the philosopher must learn to protect appearances and to consider truth indecent:

> But perhaps this is the most powerful magic of life: it is covered by a veil interwoven with gold, a veil of beautiful possibilities, sparkling with promise, resistance, bashfulness, mockery, pity, and seduction. Yes, life is a woman![18]

What follows is that

> . . . one cannot think too well of women—which is no reason to be deceived by them . . . It is improbable that women can enlighten men

about "the eternal feminine;" they don't have the necessary distance—and, to top it off, the act of enlightenment has always properly been the natural prerogative of man. As for all that women write about their own sex, there is room for a good dose of suspicion; when she writes, doesn't she apply what has always been the "eternal feminine": cosmetics? Has one ever granted depth to a woman's brain? or justice to a woman's heart? And with neither depth nor justice, what use is served by women writing about woman?[19]

Thus, when confronted by the *theoretical* man—i.e., the voyeur (*theoria* means vision or sight)—who appeals to visual if not voyeuristic theories of contemplation, clarity, "divine insight," intuition, and so forth, the *vita femina* learns to close her eyes to herself, to take refuge in the superficiality of her dress, her appearance. From *modesty* she passes to *naïveté* (unconsciousness becomes involuntary)—but this does not prohibit the metaphysician from thinking of her as *seductive*—i.e., from supposing that there is something "behind" the appearance. On the other hand, the philosopher-physician that Nietzsche invokes would voluntarily keep to appearances, and would return to life her innocence by regarding her with an equal naïveté, without concealing any motives or having any motives about what is concealed. As far as the philosopher-physician is concerned, the *vita femina* conceals no secret charms, but she offers herself just as she is, across the unfolding train of her appearances, as the pure spectacle of becoming. Strictly speaking, then, the philosopher-physician will return life to the innocence of becoming, without imputing any unacknowledged designs or ends to her appearance—finality always being of an erotic nature, insofar as life implies a hidden intention.

"Man created woman—but what out of? Out of a rib of his God, of his 'ideal.' " Thus, depending on the attitude of the philosophical man who considers it, the female chastity of life takes on several different meanings: modesty, naïveté, eroticism, innocence—and the development of life can be *interpreted*—for all that one can say about the *vita femina* is nothing more than interpretation—in several different ways, depending upon the predispositions of the philosopher: timidity or shame, repression, dissimulation, erotic intentions, or feminine concern with one's appearance. But, just

. . . supposing truth is a woman—what then? Are there not grounds for the suspicion that all philosophers, insofar as they were dogmatists, have been very inexpert about women? That the gruesome seriousness, the clumsy obtrusiveness with which they have usually approached truth so far have been awkward and very improper methods for winning a woman's heart? What is certain is that she has not allowed herself to be won.[20]

What has not been understood by the philosopher is the question, "What is truth to woman? From the beginning, nothing has been more alien, repugnant, and hostile to woman than truth—her great art is the lie, her highest concern is mere appearance and beauty."[21] Nietzsche's anti-feminism is thus not misogyny: on the contrary, it is the metaphysician who collaborates with the feminists, believers in the "eternal feminine," in the "eternally boring in women," in the "general uglification of Europe." The statement that "women should be silent about women" invites a similar warning to philosophers. In this regard, one might point out that the philosopher's aversion to marriage, noted by Nietzsche, is in the same vein as the metaphor under consideration:

> Thus the philosopher abhors marriage and all that would persuade him to marriage, for he sees the married state as an obstacle to fulfillment. What great philosopher has ever been married? Heraclitus, Plato, Descartes, Spinoza, Leibniz, Kant, Schopenhauer—not one of them was married; moreover, it is impossible to imagine any of them married. I maintain that a married philosopher belongs in comedy, and as for that great exception, Socrates, it would almost seem that the malicious Socrates got married in a spirit of irony, precisely in order to prove that contention.[22]

The text is undoubtedly ironic; yet it seems less so if one is familiar with Nietzsche's further deliberations about Socrates. In any case, for the problem that concerns us, we can conclude that Nietzsche wants to pose the alternative between a biological conception of culture, meta-phor, and fertility, and a philosophical kind of metaphor, culture, and fertility. Elsewhere, he will say: "Either children or freedom."

The philosopher's misogyny (a result of his doubtful feminism) is answered by the misology of the *vita femina*. Women like neither philosophy nor truth: "Among women. —'Truth? Oh, you don't know the truth, do you! Is it not an outrage on all our modesties?' " Indeed, in the same way that vision or voyeurism objectifies the essence of the "eternal feminine," knowledge pretends to be hidden behind the appearances of life; it, too, takes on the meaning of a diabolically erotic intent:

> The attraction of knowledge would be small if one did not have to overcome so much shame on the way. . . . Science offends the modesty of all real women. It makes them feel as if one wanted to peep under their skin—worse yet, under their dress and finery.[23]

What, then, will the philosopher-physician's attitude be when he confronts life? He must admit that the *vita femina* plays and composes herself with an innocent duplicity; that she naïvely creates the illusion of letting one believe that at every moment she *is* (and is *only*) *this* particular appearance—even when in fact she is a multiplicity of appearances, growing ever more ambiguous. Hence the necessity for this Dionysian philosopher to have a strong Will to Power, one capable of dealing with the ambiguities and contradictions of life—as opposed to the metaphysician's powerless voyeurism, which cannot withstand life except at the cost of his "visions," which congeal it into a quasi-cadaverous, impossible essence: the Ideal. Ideas, Nietzsche says,

> . . . have always lived on the "blood" of the philosopher, they always consumed his senses and even, if you will believe us, his "heart." These old philosophers were heartless; philosophizing was always a kind of vampirism. Looking at these figures, even Spinoza, don't you have a sense of something profoundly enigmatic and uncanny? Don't you notice the spectacle that unrolls before you, how they *become ever paler*—how desensualization is interpreted more and more ideally? Don't you sense a long-concealed vampire in the background who begins with the senses and in the end is left with, and leaves, mere bones, mere clatter? I mean categories, formulas, *words* (for, forgive me, what was left of Spinoza, *amor intellectualis dei,* is mere clatter and no more than that: what is *amor,* what *deus,* if there is not a drop of blood in them?).[24]

The process of idealization—originally intended to suppress the doubts that life inspired in them—thus awakened an attitude of necrophilia on the part of philosophers: *"messieurs* the metaphysicians, the conceptual albinos" kill life by making her into an ideal.

To be wise in a Dionysian way would be to stay near the surface, to "adore the epidermis" of the *vita femina.* Zarathustra, himself having failed to take this precaution, is saddened after his conversation with Life, wherein it is said to him:

> "Thus runs the speech of all fish," you said; "what *they* do not fathom is unfathomable. But I am merely changeable and wild and a woman in every way, and not virtuous—even if you men call me profound, faithful, eternal, and mysterious. But you men always present us with your own virtues, O you virtuous men!"[25]

A text from the preface to *The Gay Science* (taken up again in *Nietzsche Contra Wagner*) sums up the entire preceding analysis of the feminine metaphor in order to define the attitude required by the philosopher-physician, who here reveals himself to be an artist:

No, this bad taste, this will to truth, to "truth at any price," this youthful madness in the love of truth, have lost their charm for us: for that we are too experienced, too serious, too merry, too burned, too *profound*. We no longer believe that truth remains truth when the veils are withdrawn; we have lived too much to believe this. Today we consider it a matter of decency not to wish to see everything naked, or to be present at everything, or to understand and "know" everything. To understand all is to despise all.

"Is it true that God is present everywhere?" a little girl asked her mother; "I think that's indecent"—a hint for philosophers! One should have more respect for the bashfulness with which nature has hidden behind riddles and iridescent uncertainties. Perhaps truth is a woman who has reasons for not letting us see her reasons? Perhaps her name is—to speak Greek—Baubo?

Oh, those Greeks! They knew how to live. What is required for that is to stop courageously at the surface, the fold, the skin, to adore appearance, to believe in forms, tones, words, in the whole Olympus of appearance. Those Greeks were superficial—*out of profundity*.[26]

Thus, the *vita femina plays* like a child; she offers herself only as spectacle and gives of herself only in error and illusion. In discussing this, Nietzsche in fact recovers the profound superficiality of the Greeks, and, more particularly, that of the Ephesian, Heraclitus ("the Obscure"), who speaks about "the child playing . . .", already having claimed that "being loves to hide itself." Being reveals itself by means of the *vita femina* metaphor as a developing plurality: it offers itself as displaced, as equivocal, in appearance and in illusion, for "all of life is based on semblance, art, deception, points of view, and the necessity of perspective and error." Like an explosion of becoming, Dionysus adopts Apollo's veil and his enigmatic visage: a necessary shift from one divinity to another that could, strictly, be called metaphor, especially since Nietzsche expresses this in a language that is above all Apollonian—the metaphorical discourse, poetic and imagist: "Dionysus speaks the language of Apollo; and Apollo, finally, the language of Dionysus; and so the highest goal of tragedy and of all art is attained."

We know that Dionysian exuberance has to borrow Apollo's veil, but also that Dionysus without Apollo would lead to nothingness, to the deadly abyss of truth, and would once again become Oedipus—i.e., as Nietzsche sees him in Greek tragedy:

Oedipus, the murderer of his father, the husband of his mother, the solver of the riddle of the Sphinx! . . . The myth seems to wish to whisper to us that wisdom, and particularly Dionysian wisdom, is an unnatural abomination; that he who by means of his knowledge plunges

nature into the abyss of destruction must also suffer the dissolution of
nature in his own person.[27]

Oedipus' deciphering of the sphinx's riddle, the image of life, amounts to
the discovery that life is not possible unless one *forgets* having murdered the
father (the body, the instincts). In other words, life, like culture, is based on
the murder of the father; as we have tried to show, therefore, life and culture
are possible only as meta-phor—i.e., as dissimulation, lies, and the displacement of instincts or drives. Conscious through and through, is life
anything other than madness, absolute tragedy, and death? As shift or
divergence, as transposition and censure, meta-phor is in fact what separates
neurosis from psychosis—if, with Freud, we define psychosis as the immediate and complete fulfillment of drives, without diverting their expression away from the exclusive sphere of the primary process. "Material that
is ordinarily unconscious can transform itself into preconscious material and
then becomes conscious—a thing that happens to a large extent in psychotic
states."[28] Reciprocally, dreams temporarily and partially abolish the metaphor, the separation or split between the conscious and unconscious: "the
dream is a psychosis." Psychosis is thus "the absence of the
unconscious"—the absolute "consciousness" of instinctual drives—and
life is made possible only by means of the metaphor of the unconscious.
Therefore, one's own state must be "spiritualized," one must have "a
certain contempt for the body," an "art of transfiguration"—and Nietzsche
concludes: "Those are well who have forgotten." Perhaps Nietzsche's most
comprehensive formulation is from *Ecce Homo:* "Is Hamlet understood?
Not doubt, *certainty* is what drives one insane." Now Hamlet—that other
famous "Oedipan," as we know from Freud—understood that "we cannot
live with the truth" and that "there are more things in heaven and earth than
are dreamt of in your philosophy." If Oedipus gouges out his eyes so he can
no longer see the terrible truth to which his drives have destined him, then
Hamlet plays with appearances, he reproduces them on stage; he avoids the
truth that would make him completely mad by theatrically feigning insanity
itself. "We hide ourselves in life, in its appearance, its falsity, its superficiality, in its radiant deception"—to escape the tragic truth communicated
by our instincts and drives, and to resolve the tragic opposition between truth
and life.

Depicted in this way, truth is mortal and illusion is the condition of life.
But one could also say, inversely: death is true and life is "false" (as could
be said of a woman, that she is "false"). Life *is* illusion, it deceives us *about*
death—or, more accurately, it is the deceitful form *of* death. "Let us beware
of saying that death is opposed to life. The living is merely a type of what is
dead and a very rare type." What governs this duplicity is the Will to Power,
manifested as Dionysian creativity and Apollonian illusion, or as the duality

life-death, illusion-truth. Thus there appears a tragic conflict, an irreducible conflict, between truth and illusion, between death and life—inasmuch as life is an illusion against death, or that life is death's ultimate illusion, its last trick:

> The tragic conflict. Everything that is good and beautiful depends on illusion: truth kills—and she even kills herself insofar as she realizes that she is founded on error.[29]

On the other hand, "life needs illusions, that is to say, untruths which are taken for truths." After the philosopher-physician, who unravels the "mistakes of the body," comes the "philosopher of tragic knowledge," also named the philosopher-artist: *"The philosopher of tragic knowledge.* He controls the unbridled instinct for knowledge, but not by a new metaphysics . . . For the tragic philosopher fills in the image of existence according to which everything that is the result of knowledge appears as nothing more than anthropomorphic. What is tragic is that one must *desire* even the *illusion.*" Now, this last philosopher "demonstrates the necessity of illusion, of art and the necessity of art dominating life. It is not possible for us ever again to produce a race of philosophers such as there was in Greece at the time of tragedy. It is art alone which can henceforth accomplish their task."[30] Thus, "we have art in order not to die of truth."

It requires a powerful man to confront life; the impotent voyeurism of the metaphysician is not enough. This "powerful man" will most certainly be the artist, and his derivative "repressions" (which are beyond the metaphorical split) shall glorify the body and remain faithful to the earth:

> What pleases all pious women, old or young? Answer: A saint with beautiful legs, still young, still an idiot . . . Artists, if they are any good, are (physically as well) strong, full of surplus energy, powerful animals, sensual; without a certain overheating of the sexual system a Raphael is unthinkable—making music is another way of making children; chastity is merely the economy of an artist—and in any event, even with artists, fruitfulness ceases when potency ceases.[31]

Nietzsche then invokes the Dionysian mysteries, where

> . . . the *fundamental fact* of the Hellenic instinct expresses itself. . . . *What* did the Hellene guarantee to himself with these mysteries? Eternal life, the eternal recurrence of life; the future promised and consecrated in the past; the triumphant Yes to life beyond death and change; *true* life as collective continuation of life through procreation, through the mysteries of sexuality. It was for this reason that the *sexual* symbol

was to the Greeks the symbol venerable as such, the intrinsic profound meaning of all antique piety. Every individual detail in the act of procreation, pregnancy, birth, awoke the most exalted and solemn feelings. In the teachings of the mysteries, *pain* is sanctified: the "pains of childbirth" sanctify pain in general—all becoming and growing, all that guarantees the future, *postulates* pain . . . For the eternal joy in creating to exist, for the will to life eternally to affirm itself, the "torment of childbirth" *must* also exist eternally . . . All this is contained in the word Dionysus: I know of no more exalted symbolism than this *Greek* symbolism, the symbolism of the Dionysian . . . It was only Christianity, with *ressentiment against* life in its foundations, which made of sexuality something impure: it threw *filth* on the beginning, on the prerequisite of our life.[32]

This text, together with the preceding ones, allows us to grasp the connection that Nietzsche establishes—on the level of metaphor—between art and the affirmation of life through the mysteries of sexuality. The sexual symbol, "symbol" of life, thus appears to us as the privileged metaphor: i.e., as the image of life at the level of art this symbol augments itself, since in its own right it is the very image of art's fertility. In fact, it is across the sexual metaphor that life is presented both as fertility and as artistic fertility: *the meta-phoric creativity of life is expressed on the metaphorical level of procreation*. In this regard, the Dionysian character of Peeperkorn in Thomas Mann's *Magic Mountain* constitutes the most convincing artistic incarnation of the Nietzschean problematic of life.

The philosopher-artist, however, is not unaware (to the extent he is also the philosopher-physician) that this beautiful illusion of life as a fertile woman also signifies the flourishing ambiguity of death: that life is fundamentally a sickness, that it is split between instincts and thoughts, and, consequently, that it claims an ambiguous mortality. Indeed, life's creativity implies that "there are no eternally enduring substances." Life had already told Zarathustra: "Where there is perishing and a falling of leaves, behold, there life sacrifices itself—for power." As a cultural meta-phor of the body, based on what we called the primal rift or scission, life promises the death of the body: both, therefore, shall be cut off, broken. And we know that mind "is the life that cuts into life" so far as repression of the body goes—a repression that bears the ever present threat of its totally anemic decline into decadence. As the metaphor of the repressed body and as Dionysus dismembered, culture is nothing other than the obverse of morality—i.e., if we take this word in the general sense as the conditions for existence, as the assemblage "of the steps which an organism takes in order to *adapt itself*"—in this sense, metaphysical morality is only one particular case of morality. Now, in choosing life or woman, one also chooses death, a particular form of death. Since culture indicates a meta-phorical wandering away from the instincts—namely, ''morality''—cultural choices will be given within a necessarily ambiguous zone. The choices will always be uncertain, for, in ''choosing'' this or that fate, this or that kind of culture or morality, one correspondingly chooses this or that kind of sickness, this or that sort of bodily death in the space opened up by the meta-phor. To choose one's life is thus to opt for this or that form of death. We can clarify this by making a comparison with Freud. While Nietzsche interprets the death of the body as a cultural meta-phor, the Freudian Eros, fated by the instincts, is always at the service of the death instinct. Inversely, to interpret culture— and for Nietzsche this is to do a genealogy of morals—amounts to ''asking what is its force, what does it act upon, what becomes of humanity (or Europe) under its spell, does it render man healthier, more sickly, more subtle, more desirous of art, etc.''[33] This would be to examine culture as if it were a symptom—i.e., a compromise between life and death thrown over the split between body and culture, instituted by meta-phor (or, in Freudian terms, by primal repression).

We could add here that what Nietzsche presents as the ambiguity established by bad conscience corresponds to what Freud called ''the plasticity of the libido,'' which function allows for the possible satisfaction of different instinctual aims, and is a consequence of primal repression. On the basis of this structure, it can be easily understood that so far as death (the death instinct or the Dionysian abyss) is a cleavage, a split, it always strikes us as a sickness, as neurosis, as culture or morality. Such is the final ambiguity of the *vita femina,* the ultimate meta-phor of death. The coincidence of this with Freud's analysis is too striking not to mention one of Freud's most explicit texts about this particular problem of metaphorical ambiguity: his essay on ''The Theme of the Three Caskets.'' In *The Merchant of Venice* and *King Lear,* Freud in fact says, the third woman to be chosen would have to be Death. But, by an act of *substitution* (or, as Nietzsche would have it, meta-phor), which is usually performed by the dream, it is the most beautiful that is chosen. Interpretation of the dream allows us to conclude that ''whenever our theme occurs, the choice between the women is free, and yet it falls on Death. For after all, no one chooses death, and it is only by fatality that one falls victim to it.'' Thanks to this substitution, ''the third of the sisters is no longer Death; she was the fairest, best, most desirable, and most lovable of women,'' the Goddess of Love. In the case of *King Lear:*

> We might argue that what is represented here are the three inevitable relations a man has with a woman—the woman who bears him, the woman who is his mate, and the woman who destroys him; or that they are the three forms taken by the figure of the mother in the case of a man's life—the mother herself, the beloved who is chosen after her

pattern, and, lastly, the Mother Earth who receives him once more. But it is in vain that an old man yearns for the love of woman as he had it first from his mother; the third of the Fates alone, the silent Goddess of Death, will take him into her arms.[34]

In order to exhibit the metaphorical sequence of the *vita femina,* we have invoked the concept of metaphor (written as ''meta-phor'') in a seemingly pragmatic way: it now remains to establish and clarify this concept within Nietzsche's discourse as a whole. We can presently claim that, for Nietzsche, it constitutes the link that joins the theory of instincts to the problematic of culture, and is based on what has been called the primal schism or split of bad conscience. Indeed, ''life is not possible without the help of this *falsifying apparatus*'' that is consciousness. Let us understand this to mean ''that one must have in consciousness a (certain) instinct which *excludes, sets aside,* chooses, and allows only certain facts to exhibit themselves.'' Thus, due to the primal split, ''the sequence of phenomena that really are connected takes place on a *subconscious* level; the apparent series and successions are *symptoms* of the real sequences.'' Or, even more precisely, ''thought is not itself the internal phenomenon, but another coded language, which expresses a compromise between the powers of the different affects,'' for ''thought, sensation, and will consist in falsifying by transformation; everywhere, the faculty of assimilation is at work, and it supposes a will on our part to have external things resemble one another.''[35]

Now, it is in precisely these terms that Nietzsche explains his theory of metaphor in his early writings. These early writings allow us to grasp the modes of ''falsification'' that result from the primal metaphorical split, and they again confirm that the problem of metaphor cannot be dissociated from the general problem of culture—which Nietzsche begins with from the viewpoint of tragic Greek culture.

Culture is neither questioned nor revealed as such except when it is transposed and altered. *''Metaphora,''* which means transport or displacement, transfer or transposition, points to the fact that culture—as a ''sickness,'' resulting from the original split or diremption—is never really exposed to us except as being already changed with regard to itself. For culture:

> What, then, is truth? A mobile army of metaphors, metonyms, and anthropomorphisms—in short, a sum of human relations, which have been enhanced, transposed, and embellished poetically and rhetorically, and which after long use seem firm, canonical, and obligatory to a people: truths are illusions about which one has forgotten that this is what they are; metaphors which are worn out and without sensuous power.[36]

In meta-phorical culture, man can do no more than guess or interpret. I cannot grasp myself directly, once my space is filled by the manifestations of culture. This is why Nietzsche, who denies the fantastical notion of a direct insight (be it "intuitive" or "voyeuristic") into our drives, our desires, our "interiority," goes so far as to say that "there is nothing inside." This brutal formulation by no means implies that these symptoms, these metaphors, displacements, or transpositions by which culture is expressed are only pure and simple epiphenomena without any basis; it implies, rather, that desire (or, the *vita femina*'s will to power) cannot be hypostasized, reified, or realized into an immediately visible or intelligible essence, since it is not itself given openly, but only as something interpreted, and this within the symptomatic and displaced metaphorical manifestations of culture. It should be said, then, that culture is always interpreted: to understand a culture is to interpret an interpretation. And, consequently, it's understandable that Nietzsche's discourse about culture as metaphor cannot itself be anything but metaphorical.

> For between two utterly different spheres, as between subject and object, there is no causality, no accuracy, no expression, but at the utmost an *aesthetic* relation, I mean a suggestive transposition, a stammering translation into quite a distinct foreign language, for which purpose however there is needed at any rate an intermediate sphere, an intermediate force, freely composing and freely inventing.[37]

Why so? Because as a cultural being, man's relation to the world and to things is originally—or even "structurally"—metaphorical: "A nerve stimulus, first transposed into an image—first metaphor. The image, in turn, imitated by a sound—second metaphor. And each time there is a leap, completely out of one sphere right into the midst of an entirely different one." To be truthful, then, "means using the customary metaphors . . . the obligation to lie according to a fixed convention."[38]

If culture (as our primitive connection with "things") is, from the start, displacement, transposition, and translation, then we could strictly call it a meta-phor. But Nietzsche describes this meta-phor only in metaphorical terms—this time, in the rhetorical sense of the term: for what concerns the *vita femina*, his description is in feminine terms, and as regards the theory of instincts, his description is cast in terms of gastric digestion. This reciprocal implication is explained by the fact that metaphor is *originally* an *artistic transposition*: "We organized the world—into forms and shapes—long before we had concepts." As the young Nietzsche says, this is because "the concept . . . is nothing other than the *residue of a metaphor*—and the illusion of an artistic transposition of a nerve-stimulus into images is, if not the mother, then the grandmother of every concept." Even when it attempts to set forth its own origin, the language of culture is metaphorical—since meta-phor is an aesthetic phenomenon. Nietzsche's entire reflection on the Presocratics is oriented in this manner. This way of thinking, as exhibited in *Philosophy in the Tragic Age of the Greeks* and *The Philosopher's Book,* can be considered as a commentary on Heraclitus' famous remark: "It neither hides nor speaks, but it signifies." All vision or comprehension of the world, or of being, is here presented by Nietzsche as metaphorical—as a prerational language full of images. However far back one goes in the history of culture, one finds that it speaks metaphorically of its correspondence with the world—i.e., of its correspondence with itself: "Thus Thales had seen the unity of all that is, but when he went to communicate it, he found himself talking about water." It is better understood, then, why art occupies such a privileged position for Nietzsche; also better understood is the essential and primary necessity he felt to announce a new type of culture by means of the metaphorical figures and mythologies of Dionysus, Apollo, and Ariadne, and to analyze its birth with the help of the images of woman, of Oedipus, and of "neikos" and "philia"—indeed, with the images of physiology:

> The concept of being! As though it did not show its low empirical origin in its very etymology! For *esse* basically means "to breathe." And if man uses it of all things other than himself as well, he projects his conviction that he himself breathes and lives by means of a metaphor, i.e., a non-logical process, upon all other things.[39]

But Nietzsche's reflections on primitive meta-phor as an artistic phenomenon later give rise to a theory of instincts and signification that conditions the earlier analysis. That meta-phor is an artistic phenomenon, and that Nietzsche values art as the cultural paradigm of meta-phor is what proves the fact that this theory of the instincts is governed by the term "fiction" or "fable" (*Erdichten*). In aphorism 119 of *The Dawn,* within the framework of the metaphor of gastric digestion, Nietzsche explains what he elsewhere calls his "belief in the truth of dreams." He explains that these "fictions" (*Erdichtungen*), belonging both to conscious life and to dreams, "are interpretations of our nerve stimuli during sleep, very free and arbitrary interpretations of the movements of our blood and intestines." In fact,

> . . .the laws of [the instincts'] nutrition remain entirely unknown. This nutrition, therefore, is the work of chance: the daily experiences of our lives throw their prey now to this instinct and now to that, and the instinct greedily seizes upon it; but the ebb and flow of these experiences does not stand in any rational relationship to the nutritive needs of the total number of the instincts.[40]

Nietzsche thus explains that our conscious life and our dreams are the consequent interpretations of these instinctual states of surfeit and starvation: thus, even if

> . . . waking life is not as free as dream life, is less fictional, less unrestrained . . . our instincts, when we are awake, likewise merely interpret our nerve stimuli and determine their "causes" in accordance with their requirements. There is no really essential difference between waking and dreaming . . . Our moral judgments and valuations are only the images and fantasies of a physiological process unknown to us, a kind of convenient language to describe certain nerve stimuli. All our so-called consciousness is only a more or less fantastic commentary upon an unconscious text, one which is perhaps unknowable but yet felt . . . What are our experiences, then? Much *more* what we attribute to them than what they really are. Or should we go so far as to say that nothing is contained in them? To experience is to fictionalize. [41]

To live is thus to assimilate: to reduce the different to the identical and to transform the instincts' "food"—but it is also to interpret, to transform the identical into a manifold. In the dream, "which does not differ essentially from the waking state," there is a condensation (assimilation), but also a *displacement* (interpretation). In fact, according to Freud, "as a result of condensation, one element in the manifest dream may correspond to numerous elements in the latent dream-thoughts; but conversely, too, one element in the dream-thought may be represented by several images in the dream." [42]

Now, "condensation" is the precise translation for the German word *"Verdichtung."* The synonymy between fiction and condensation (*Erdichten-Verdichten*), as well as Nietzsche's formulations about dreams, permit us to consider the "dream-work" as a paradigm of metaphorical activity. To read the artist's dream of culture, one must reverse the transformations, diversions, or perversions of his instincts. And the metaphor of hearing that Nietzsche often uses to describe this task of interpretation (e.g., in *Zarathustra; Twilight of the Idols,* Prologue, §9; *Ecce Homo*, Preface and "Why I Am So Wise," §8, etc.) confirms that the shift from the manifest sign to its latent meaning is a dissimulation of a particular type: a removal not so much of the hidden from the manifest as of the simple from the multiple—and the multiple from the simple. Once interpreted, the metaphorical illusion does not fall away to reveal any truth or entity. Indeed, for this cryptogram of culture, everything happens as if other meta-phorical forms appeared simultaneously: genealogy does not set upon a "false" text that hides a "true" one—rather, it sets upon a metaphorical rebus, and it is in this way that "when they say 'I am just,' it always sounds like 'I am just—revenged.' " Thus, from justice to revenge, one does not pass from the false to the true, but from one unequivocal metaphor to the revelation of another *Leitmotiv,* which can only be heard within the same phonic range: one passes without any transition from plainsong to polyphony. This is the same as in the famous example of the Dionysian "JA," which is also and *simultaneously* understood by the reader-hearer of the metaphor as the "I-A" (hee-haw) of the ass. One needs the "fine ear" that Freud speaks about, as well as Zarathustra's acute hearing; for example, when the latter hears the scholars speak, he declares that "their wisdom often has an odor as if it came from the swamps: and verily, I have also heard frogs croak out of it." Interpreting cultural meta-phors, consequently, amounts to reading, or rereading, the meta-phor of a different instinct into a particular manifestation. It amounts to hearing several voices where, before, only one was heard. But we must also have an ear capable of perceiving the polyphonic or polysemantic aspects of the metaphor, since the latter serves as its own meta-phor.

Furthermore, Nietzsche claims that man's relation to existence is fictional or poetic, inasmuch as it is a condensation, a kind of poetry about poetry:

> All forms of culture begin with the fact that a multitude of things are veiled . . . A superior physiology will assuredly understand the artistic forces in our development—not only in man's development, but also in that of animals: a superior physiology will say that the *artistic* also begins with the *organic*. The chemical transformations of inorganic nature are perhaps also artistic processes.[43]

Thus, from the start, knowledge has no privileged position: on the contrary, "there is no intrinsic knowledge without metaphor." Also, "all knowing is mirrored in forms which are completely determined, yet which do not exist *a priori.*" Nietzsche does not understand by this that everything is tantamount to the illusions of fantasy: rather, the real manipulation of appearances— lying appearances at that—has been performed by science, morality, and religion—precisely what had formerly passed themselves off as "the truth." Only art, by virtue of its acknowledged metaphorical character, is true: "Art treats *appearance as appearance,* therefore it does *not* seek to deceive; it *is true.*"

The criterion of "truth" will thus be paradoxical: art is truthful because it enhances and increases metaphor—hence the illusion: precisely what, for science, morality, and religion, is blocked. What is false—indeed, morbid—is thus designated as the repetitive blockage of metaphor. A comparison with Freud on this point is once again illuminating. What Nietzsche describes as the movement of meta-phor (sometimes as the "capacity to forget") corresponds to Freud's "plasticity of the libido"—

that is, "the capacity of the libido to more or less easily alter both the object and the mode of its satisfaction."[44] Both "plasticity" and "metaphor" equally suggest the image of transportation and displacement. The child, for example, as a polymorphously perverse being, is the extreme image of this metaphorical mobility; this is opposed to the fixations that result from the libido's "viscosity" or "inertia" in the case of neurotic individuals or cultures, a blocking of the metaphorical movement (by religion, morality, etc.). Here, decadence is measured according to the greater or lesser degree of plasticity or viscosity—according to the metaphorical capacity to connect the instinctual forces in the secondary process. And, in fact, Freud writes in *Civilization and Its Discontents:*

> We have treated the difficulty of cultural development as a general difficulty of development by tracing it to the inertia of the libido—to its disinclination to give up an old position for a new one.[45]

If metaphor is a manifestation of forgetting, what proves to be morbid and false will result from a lack of abreaction (i.e., of catharsis) and metaphorical fictionalizing, and would render man *reactive.* Man is a "naturally forgetful animal," since he is an animal that interprets by means of metaphor: inversely, the reactive man, the resentful man, is incapable of metaphor.

> It will be immediately obvious how there could be no happiness, no pride, no *present,* without forgetfulness. The man in whom this apparatus of repression is damaged and ceases to function properly may be compared (and more than merely compared) with a dyspeptic—he cannot "have done" with anything.[46]

Yet in art, on the other hand, man forgets that he forgets, that he lies, that he invents metaphors, whereas the reactive man forgets to forget. Thus Nietzsche writes, in *On Truth and Lie in an Extra-Moral Sense:*

> Only by forgetting that metaphorically primitive world . . . only by the fact that man forgets himself as a subject, and what is more, as an *artistically creating* subject, does he live with some security and consequence.[47]

Indeed, if man were aware of living in an originally and fundamentally metaphorical world, he would succumb to Dionysian madness. And Dionysian truth is mortal.

Thus, Apollo—god of the veil—hyperbolically obscures the metaphorical element in art, the metaphorical appearance of the *vita femina.* By metaphor and its excess, man forgets that he is originally a metaphoric being—and the height of metaphor is to forget that it is such. Apollo is thus the metaphor of Dionysus. In the Apollonian metaphor of art, what is forgotten is Dionysian death: the demented flowering of metaphor, the infinite efflorescence of appearances, polymorphous perversion to the point of fatality.[48] The artistic metaphor thus appears as a game governed by the Same and the Other: primal meta-phor opens up the space of the Other as the realm of Dionysian metaphor, and thus, at its *height,* is lethal madness. But for Apollo, metaphor of metaphors, the Other of the Other, the metaphor is itself forgotten out of childish innocence, artistic illusion: "And man's maturity—consists in having found again the seriousness one had as a child, at play.'' From this perspective, " 'will to truth'—that might be a concealed will to death." Moreover, "In this sense science would be a prolonged process of caution," ever deceiving itself in refusing to let itself be deceived: it wills death in willing the truth. If, behind Apollo in his artistic forgetfulness, the voyeur—the Other of the Same—were to be surreptitiously sketched in as he who congeals the vital metaphor of the *vita femina* into a deadly essence, then it would be the scholar—the Same as the Other—who hides himself behind Dionysus, the destroyer of appearances. But both of them "are deceived" by "not wanting to be deceived," in going from the similar to the Same, in accordance with a literally primary process, where the metaphorical movement of life is blocked, and by which process Apollo, as the Other of the Other, seconds Dionysus—for "Dionysus speaks the language of Apollo; and Apollo, finally, the language of Dionysus."

Here, these two divinities hold forth the promise of the Overman as the metaphor of meta-phor, the meta-phor of Man.

NOTES

1. *The Birth of Tragedy,* §8.
2. Here, we take the word in its wider sense (*Kultur:* culture, civilization), in the way that Freud defines it in *Civilization and Its Discontents,* III: "The word '*Kultur*' describes the whole sum of the achievements and the regulations that distinguish our lives from those of our animal ancestors and serve two purposes—namely, to protect men against nature, and to adjust their mutual relations."
3. *The Antichrist,* §14.
4. *The Genealogy of Morals;* II, §§18, 19.
5. *GM;* II, §16.
6. *Ibid.*
7. Laplanche and Pontalis, *Vocabulaire de la psychanalyse* (Paris: Presses Universitaires de France, 1971), p. 392.
8. *The Gay Science,* §369.
9. *The Will to Power,* §376.

10. Kröner; XII; I, §298.
11. *GM;* II, §17.
12. *WP,* §458.
13. *Ecce Homo;* "Why I Am So Wise," §1.
14. *GS,* §339.
15. *WP,* §806.
16. *WP,* §807.
17. *Beyond Good and Evil,* §1.
18. *GS,* §339.
19. *Oeuvres Posthumes,* §389 (p. 154, Fr. ed.).
20. *BGE,* Preface.
21. *BGE,* §232.
22. *GM;* III, §7.
23. *Twilight of the Idols;* "Maxims and Arrows," §16; *BGE,* §65.
24. *GS,* §372.
25. *Thus Spoke Zarathustra;* II, "The Dancing Song."
26. *GS;* Preface, §4; *Nietzsche Contra Wagner;* Epilogue, §2.
27. *BT,* §9.
28. Freud, *An Outline of Psychoanalysis,* in *The Complete Psychological Works of Sigmund Freud,* standard edition (London: The Hogarth Press, 1964), vol. XXIII, p. 161.
29. Note following *On Truth and Lie in an Extra-Moral Sense;* dated summer 1873.
30. *The Last Philosopher,* §§47, 77–78, 37, 38.
31. *WP,* §800.
32. *TI,* "What I Owe to the Ancients," §4.
33. K; XIII, §261.
34. Freud, "The Theme of the Three Caskets," in *Comp. Psych. Works,* vol. XII, pp. 298–301.
35. K; XIII, §§163, 172; XIV, pt. 1, §§69, 85.
36. *OTL,* pt. 1.
37. *Ibid.*
38. *Ibid.*
39. *Philosophy in the Tragic Age of the Greeks,* §11.
40. *The Dawn,* §119.
41. *Ibid.*
42. Freud, *New Lectures on Psychoanalysis I,* in *Comp. Psych. Works,* vol. XXII, p. 22
43. *LP,* §52.
44. Laplanche and Pontalis, *op. cit.,* p. 315.
45. Freud, *Civilization and Its Discontents,* chap. V.
46. *GM;* II, §I.
47. *OTL,* pt. 1.

48. "We know that the pleasure principle is proper to a *primary* method of working on the part of the mental apparatus, but that, from the point of view of the self-preservation of the organism among the difficulties of the external world, it is from the very outset inefficient and even highly dangerous." Freud, *Beyond the Pleasure Principle,* chap. I.

Jacques Derrida

THE QUESTION OF STYLE

The title for this discussion will be the question of style. But my subject shall be woman.

The question of style—it is always the question of a pointed object. Sometimes only a pen, but just as well a stylet, or even a dagger. With their help, to be sure, we can resolutely attack all that philosophy calls forth under the name of matter or matrix, so as to stave a mark in it, leave an impression or form; but these implements also help us to repel a threatening force, to keep it at bay, to repress and guard against it—all the while bending back or doubling up, in flight, keeping us hidden, veiled. And as for veils—which we all are—Nietzsche will have used all kinds.

Style will jut out, then, like a *spur,* like the spur on an old sailing vessel: like the *rostrum,* the prong that goes out in front to break the attack and cleave open the opposing surface. Or, again, always in a nautical sense, like the point of rock that is also called a spur and that "breaks up the waves at the entrance to a harbor."

With its spur, style can also protect against whatever terrifying, blinding, or mortal threat might present itself or be obstinately encountered: i.e., the presence, and, hence, the content, of things themselves, of meaning, of truth—unless this is *already* the deflowered abyss that goes along with the unveiling of difference. *Already,* the name of what is effaced, of what eludes us in advance, yet which nonetheless leaves a mark, a suspended signature, in the very thing into which it withdraws—the here and now—is something we should and will take into account, although this operation can neither be simple, nor can it be done in one stroke.

What in French is *éperon* is in High German *sporo;* in Gaelic it is *spor,* and in English one says "*spur.*" In *Les Mots Anglais,* Mallarmé relates it to *spurn*—to despise, repel, reject with contempt. This is not simply a fascinating homonomy; rather, it is the operation of a historical and semantic necessity that extends from one tongue to another. The English *spur,* the French *éperon,* is the "same word" as the German *Spur:* trace, wake, index, mark.

The spurring style is the long, the oblong, object that serves to parry as well as to perforate; the point is oblong-foliated, with an apotropaic power of cloth, fabric, veils, and sails that stretch, fold, and unfold themselves around it.

To insist on what it is that impresses the mark of the styled spur upon the question of woman (I do not say the appearance of woman, as is often done, because here it will be a matter of seeing her appearance stripped away, the question of appearance being both opened *and closed* by what is termed woman); to announce what it is that, from here on, governs the play of sails (as on a ship) over an apotropaic anguish; finally, to let some sort of exchange arise between style and woman in Nietzsche—for all this, we must turn to *The Gay Science* (§60): *"Women, and their action at a distance. Do I still have ears? Am I all ears and nothing else?"* All of Nietzsche's questions, those on woman in particular, are coiled up in the labyrinth of an ear; and just a bit further on in *The Gay Science* (*"Women who master the masters,"* §70), a drapery or hanging, a *curtain,* is raised ("upon possibilities in which we usually do not believe") when the deep and powerful alto voice soars. This voice seems, as the best of man in woman, to surmount the difference between the sexes and to incarnate the ideal.

But as with the voices of eunuchs, those "that are supposed to represent the ideal, virile lover, Romeo, for instance," Nietzsche expresses his reserve: *"Such* lovers are unconvincing; such voices always retain some motherly and housewifely coloration—most of all when they make one think of love."

Am I all ears and nothing else? Here I stand in the flaming surf [*Hier stehe ich inmitten des Brandes der Brandung. Brandung* is tied to the embrace of *Brand,* meaning the red mark of fire, the return of the waves over themselves when they meet the chains of rock or when they break against the reefs, the cliffs, the spurs, etc.] whose white tongues are licking at my feet [hence, I too am the spur]; from all sides I hear howling, threats, screaming, roaring coming at me, while the old earth-shaker sings his aria in the lowest depths, deep as a bellowing bull, while pounding such an earth-shaking beat that the hearts of even these weather-beaten rocky monsters are trembling in their bodies. Then, suddenly, as if born out of nothing, there appears before the gate of this hellish labyrinth, only a few fathoms away—a large sailboat, gliding along as silently as a ghost. Oh, what ghostly beauty! How magically it touches me! Has all the calm and taciturnity of the world embarked on it? Does my happiness itself sit in this quiet place—my happier ego, my second, immortalized self? Not to be dead and yet no longer alive? A spiritlike intermediate being: quietly observing, gliding, floating? As the boat that with its white sails moves like an immense butterfly over the dark sea. Yes! To move *over* existence! That's it! That would be something! —It seems as if the noise here had led me into fantasies. All great noise leads us to move happiness into some quiet distance. When a man stands in the midst of his own noise, in the midst of his own surf of plans and projects, then he is apt also to see quiet, magical beings gliding past him and to long for their happiness and seclusion: *women*. He almost thinks that his better self dwells there among the women, and that in these quiet regions even the loudest surf turns into deathly quiet, the life itself into a dream about life.[1]

The preceding section of *The Gay Science* ("We Artists," §59), which begins with "When we love a woman," describes the movement that *simultaneously* marks the sonambulistic risk of death, the dream of death, and the sublimation and dissimulation of nature. And throughout, the value of dissimulation is not dissociated from the relation between art and woman:

And right away the spirit and power of the dream overcomes us, and with our eyes open, coldly contemptuous of all danger, we climb up on the most hazardous paths to scale the roofs and spires of fantasy—without any sense of dizziness, as if we had been born to climb, we sonambulists of the day! We artists! We dissimulators of nature! We moonstruck and God-struck ones! We wander, still as death, unwearied, on heights that we do not see as heights but as our plains, as our safety.[2]

Yet! Yet! Noble enthusiast, even on the most beautiful sailboat there is a lot of noise, and unfortunately much small and petty noise. The magic and the most powerful effect of women is, in philosophical language, action at a distance, *actio in distans;* but this requires first of all and above all—*distance*.[3]

What move opens up this *distance?* Nietzsche's writing already mimics it with an effect of style that is borne *between* the Latin citation (*actio in distans,* parodying the language of philosophers) *and* the exclamation, the dash that suspends the word *distance:* through a piroutte or a play of silhouettes, it invites us to keep our distance from the multiple veils that make us dream of death.

Woman's seductiveness operates at a distance, and distance is the element of her power. But one must stay aloof from this chant, this charm, one must keep one's distance from distance itself—not only, as one might expect, to guard against this fascination, but equally as well to experience it. There *must* be (we *need*) distance; we must keep our distance from that which we lack, from that which we fail to do—and this resembles the advice given from one man to another: to seduce, and not to allow oneself to be seduced.

If we have to keep our distance from the feminine operation (of *actio in distans*)—which doesn't amount to simply not approaching it, except at the risk of death *itself*—it is perhaps because "woman" is *not* just any thing, *not* just an identifiably determinate appearance that is imported at a distance from somewhere else, an appearance to draw back from or to approach. Perhaps, as non-identity, non-appearance, simulacrum, she is the *abyss* of distance, the distancing of distance, the thrust of spacing, distance itself—distance *as such,* if one could still say that, which is no longer possible.

Here, we must turn to the Heideggerian usage of the word *Entfernung* (distancing): it means separation, removal, and removal of the removal, removal of the far, re-moval, the constituting destruction (*Ent-*) of the far as such, the veiled enigma of proximation.

The opening, separation or spread brought about by distancing gives rise to truth—from which woman separates herself in turn.

There is no essence of woman because woman separates, and separates herself off from herself. From the endless, bottomless depths, she submerges all essentiality, all identity, all propriety, and every property. Blinded in such a way, philosophical discourse founders, and is left to dash headlong to its ruin. There is no truth about woman, just because this abysmal separation from truth, this nontruth, is *the* "truth." Woman is one name for this nontruth of truth.

Thus, distance is operative when it conceals the proper identity of woman and unsaddles the cavalier philosopher—unless he receives from her two spurs, two thrusts of style, or the slash of a dagger, an exchange that quickly scrambles sexual identity:

> If someone cannot defend himself and therefore does not want to, we do not consider this a disgrace; but we have little respect for anyone who lacks both the capacity and the good will for revenge—regardless of whether it is a man or a woman. Would a woman be able to hold us (or, as they say, "enthrall" us) if we did not consider it quite possible that under certain circumstances she could wield a dagger (any kind of dagger) *against* us? Or against herself—which in certain cases would be a crueler revenge (Chinese revenge).[4]

We know the opening words from the preface to *Beyond Good and Evil!* "Supposing truth is a woman . . ." But at this point Nietzsche makes the truth of woman, or the truth of truth, veer:

> What is certain is that she has not allowed herself to be won—and today every kind of dogmatism is left standing dispirited and discouraged. *If it is left standing at all!*[5]

Woman (truth) does not allow herself to be possessed.
The truth about woman does not allow itself to be possessed.
That which truthfully does not allow itself to be possessed is *feminine*. One must not hasten to translate this as femininity, as the femininity of

woman, the feminine sexuality, or other essentializing fetishes: this is precisely what is assumed when one remains at the vacuous level of dogmatic philosophers, impotent artists, or inexperienced seducers.

This deviation of truth, its stripping away and rising up to quotation marks (machination, cry, theft, the grip of an easy woman), all that which, for Nietzsche's writing, will produce the quotation marks of "truth," and in rapid succession, all the rest, all that will *inscribe* truth, inscription in general—all this is, let us not say, feminine: it is the feminine "operation."

She writes. It is to her that style resorts. Even more: if style were man (as for Freud, the penis would be "the normal prototype of the fetish"), writing would be woman.

If all these weapons circulate from one hand to another, if they go from one contrary to another, the question still remains as to what I am doing now.

Shouldn't these *apparently* feminist propositions be reconciled with the enormous corpus of inveterate anti-feminism in Nietzsche?

The congruence—a word I shall here oppose to coherence—of feminist and anti-feminist propositions is quite enigmatic, and at the same time strictly necessary—that, at least, would be the thesis of the present discussion.

The woman, truth, is skepticism or veiling dissimulation; and this is what we have to think through. Consider the *skepsis* of "truth" in woman's old age:

> I am afraid that aged women are more skeptical in the most secret recesses of their hearts than men: they consider the superficiality of existence as its essence, and all virtue and profundity is to them merely a veil over this "truth," a very welcome veil over a *pudendum*—in other words, a matter of modesty and shame, and no more than that![6]

"Truth" would be but a surface; it would only become a profound, raw, and desirable truth by the effect of a veil falling over it. It would not be suspended by quotation marks, but would recover the surface in a movement of modesty. It is enough to suspend the veil or to let it fall in some other manner for there to be no more truth, or only "truth"—so written.

Why, then, the fright, the fear, the "modesty"?

Feminine distance abstracts truth from itself by *suspending* the relation to castration—to suspend as one can raise or extend a cloth, a relation, etc., that at the same time can be—suspended—in indecision.

A suspended relation to castration: not, indeed, to the truth of castration, which woman does not believe in, nor to truth as castration, nor to truth-castration. Truth-castration—that is precisely the affair of man, the masculine business that is never old enough, or skeptical or dissimulated enough, and that, in its credulity, its foolishness (which is always sexual, and is sometimes represented as expert mastery), castrates itself in order to produce the lure of truth-castration. It is at this juncture, for example, that the deployment of the veil, of truth that speaks, of castration and phallocentrism, could perhaps be interrogated or unpacked within the work of Lacan.

"Woman"—the word now marks an epoch—no longer believes in the honest inverse of castration, anti-castration. She is too sly for that, and she knows—about it, about its operation, at least—what we (but which we?) should learn: that such a reversal would take away from her all possibility of simulacra, that in truth it would amount to the same thing, and would install her more surely than ever back in the same old machine, in phallogocentrism, helped by its accomplice, the inverted image of the rowdy student—i.e., the disciplined disciple of the master.

Now, "woman" needs the effect of castration, for without it she would neither know how to seduce nor to stir desire—but evidently she does not believe in it. "Woman" is this; she does not believe in it, but she plays with it. Plays with: with a new concept or a new structure of belief that points to laughter. She knows about man—and with a knowing that no dogmatic or credulous philosopher could attain to—that castration *has not taken place*.

We should be cautious in altering any part of this formula. To begin with, it points out that the place of castration is not determinable, that it is an undecidable mark or nonmark, and that a discreet margin should be allowed for incalculable consequences. One of these, as I have elsewhere observed, amounts to the strict equivalence between the affirmation and the negation of castration, as well as between the assumption or the denial of anti-castration. All this, perhaps, will be developed later, under the heading *argument of the belt*, borrowed from Freud's text on fetishism.

If it had taken place, castration would have been the syntax of the undecidable that would fix (by annulment and equalization) all discourse in a *pro et contra*. It is the throw for nothing—which, nonetheless, is never attempted without some interest.

Whence the extreme "skepticism of women." From the moment she tears open the veil of modesty or truth—in which she had been enveloped and kept "in the greatest possible ignorance *in eroticis*"—her skepticism has no limits. Let someone merely read "On Feminine Chastity" (*GS*, §71): in the "contradiction between love and modesty," in the "proximity of god and beast," between "the enigma of the solution" and "the solution of the enigma," how "the ultimate philosophy and skepticism of woman casts anchor at this point." It is in this void that she throws her anchor.

"Woman," then, is not so interested in truth; she believes in it so little that even the truth of her own subject does not concern her. It is "man" who believes that his discourse on woman or on truth *concerns* woman—who in turn circumvents it. Such is the topographic question I sketched out as to the undecidable circuit of castration, and it now, as always, proves to be elusive. It is "man" who believes in the truth of woman, in woman-truth. And in point of fact, the feminist women against whom Nietzsche pours out all his sarcasm—are men. Feminism, indeed, is the operation by which woman wants to come to resemble man, the philosophical dogmatist who insists on truth, science, objectivity—together with the whole virile illusion, the whole castration effect that goes with it. Feminism wants castration, even that of woman. It wants to lose its style. Nietzsche strongly denounces this want of style in feminism:

> Is it not in the worst of taste when woman sets about becoming scientific that way? So far, enlightenment of this sort was fortunately man's affair, man's lot. We remained "among ourselves" in this.[7]

The whole process of the feminine operation is spread out along this apparent contradiction. Two times woman is the model: the two being contradictory, she is both praised and condemned. As writing does, regularly and not by accident, so does woman ply the accuser's argument into the *logic of the kettle*. Model of truth, she enjoys a power of seduction that governs dogmatism, bewilders men, and sends them fleeing—the credulous ones, the philosophers. But insofar as she does not believe in truth, yet nonetheless finds herself attracted by this truth that does not interest her, she is again the model—this time the good model; or, rather, the bad model insofar as it is a good model. She plays at dissimulation, adornment, lying, art, at artistic philosophy; she is a power of affirmation. If she were still to be condemned, it would be to the extent that she denies this affirmative power—but from man's perspective. All of which amounts to lying while still believing in the truth; hence, she is a specular reflection of the foolish dogmatism she provokes.

The question of art, style, and truth do not allow disassociation from the question of woman. But the simple formation of this common problematic suspends the question "what is woman?" It is no longer possible to go looking for woman, or for the femininity of woman, or for feminine sexuality. At least, they cannot be found by any familiar mode of thought, or knowledge—even if one cannot stop looking for them.

Enter woman. In the section of *Twilight of the Idols* entitled "The History of an Error," Nietzsche gives a brief account of six sequences, six epochs. In the second epoch, the only words underlined by Nietzsche are *"it [the Idea] becomes female"*:

> The true world—unattainable for now, but promised for the sage, the pious, the virtuous man ("for the sinner who repents").
> (Progress of the idea: it becomes more subtle, more insidious, incomprehensible—*it becomes female . . .*).

Let us try to decipher this *inscription* of, and about, *woman:* surely it is neither a metaphorical or allegorical illustration free of all conceptual content, nor is it simply a pure concept with no imaginative import. The context illustrates it clearly: what becomes female is the idea. Becoming female is a "progress of the idea." The idea is one form of self-presentation of the truth. Hence, truth has not always been female. Woman is not always truth. The one and the other have a history, they form a history—perhaps history itself, if history in the strict sense has always been presented this way, in a movement of truth—something philosophy alone could not decipher, since it is itself included within that history.

Before this progress in the history of the "true world" occurred, the idea was Platonic. And the transcription, the periphrase or paraphrase for the Platonic statement of truth in that inaugural moment of the idea was "I, Plato, *am* the truth."

The second age—the becoming-female of the idea, as presence or as the staging of truth—is the moment when Plato can no longer say "I am the truth," when the philosopher is no longer the truth, when he detaches himself from it as well as from himself and only pursues its trace—at which point either he becomes exiled or he lets the idea go into exile. Then it is that history commences, that histories commence. Now, distance—woman—puts aside truth—the philosopher—and yields the idea. And the idea becomes distant, it becomes transcendent, inaccessible, seductive; the idea takes over and shows the way *in the distance*. Its sails billow out from afar, the dream of death commences: it is woman.

All the attributes, all the traits, all the attractions that Nietzsche saw in woman—the seductive distance, captivating yet inaccessible; the infinitely veiled promise; the transcendence producing desire; the *distancing*—all belong as fittingly to the history of truth as to the history of error.

Now, as if in apposition, as if to clarify and analyze the "it becomes female," Nietzsche adds ". . . it becomes Christian"—and closes the parenthesis.

It is within the epoch set off by this parenthesis that one can attempt to direct this somewhat fabulous account toward the motif of castration that is found *within* Nietzsche's own text—i.e., toward the enigma of truth as nonpresence.

I shall try to show that what appears in big red letters in "*it becomes female*, it becomes Christian" is, "it castrates (itself)": the idea castrates because it is castrated, it plays out its castration for the epoch of a parenthesis, it feigns castration—suffered and inflicted—in order to master the master from afar, to produce desire, and, by the same stroke—which here amounts to "the same thing"—to kill it. This is a necessary phase (and a necessary kind of periphrase) in the history of woman-truth; of woman as truth, of verification, and feminization.

Let's turn the page, and go on, in the *Twilight of the Idols,* to the section that follows "The History of an Error"—i.e., "Morality as Anti-Nature." Christianity is interpreted there as *castratism (Kastratismus)*. The extraction of the tooth, the plucking-out of the eye, Nietzsche says, are both Christian operations. They are the violence of the Christian idea, of the idea become female.

> All the old moral monsters are agreed in this: *il faut tuer les passions* [the passions must be killed]. The most famous formula for this is to be found in the New Testament, in that Sermon on the Mount where, incidentally, things are by no means regarded from a *lofty* standpoint. There it is said, for example, with particular reference to sexuality: "If the eye offend thee, pluck it out." Fortunately, no Christian follows this prescription. To *exterminate* the passions and desires, merely as a preventive measure against their folly and against the unpleasant consequences of that folly—today, this itself strikes us as merely another acute form of folly. We no longer admire dentists who *pluck out* the teeth so that they will not hurt any more.

As opposed to the Christian extirpation or castration, at least that of the "first church" (but nobody has left the church), Nietzsche recommends the spiritualization of passion. He seems to imply by this that castration is not at work in such a spiritualization—which is by no means obvious. I leave this problem open.

Hence, the first church, the truth of the female-idea, proceeds by ablation, by extirpation, by excision:

> The church fights passion with excision in every sense [*Ausschneidung;* clipping, castration]: its practice, its "cure," is *castratism*. It never asks: "How can we spiritualize, beautify, deify a desire?" It has at all times laid the stress of discipline on extirpation (of sensuality, pride, of the lust to rule, of avarice, of vengefulness). But an attack on the roots of passion means an attack on the roots of life: the practice of the church is *hostile to life*.

Hence, hostile to woman who is life (*femina vita*): castration is an operation of woman against woman, no less than of each sex against itself and against the other.

> The same means in the fight against a craving—castration, extirpation—is instinctively chosen by those who are too weak-willed, too degenerate, to be able to impose moderation on themselves . . . One should survey the whole history of the priests and philosophers, including the artists: the most poisonous things against the senses have been said *not* by the impotent, not by ascetics, but by the impossible ascetics, by those who really were in dire need of being ascetics. The spiritualization of sensuality is called *love:* it represents a great

triumph over Christianity. Another triumph is our spiritualization of *hostility*. It consists in a profound appreciation of the value of having enemies: in short, it means acting and thinking in the opposite way from that which has been the rule. The church always wanted the destruction of its enemies; we, we immoralists and Antichristians, find our advantage in this, that the church exists . . . The saint in whom God delights is the ideal eunuch.[8]

The heterogeneity of the text shows it well: Nietzsche did not delude himself and claim to know what the effects of woman, truth, and castration were, or what the *ontological* effects of presence and absence were. Rather, he analyzed this very delusion. He guarded himself carefully against the sort of precipitous denial that would consist in erecting a simple discourse against castration and its entailed system. Without a kind of discreet parody, without a writing strategy, without a difference or divergence of pens, without style— "the grand style"—the reversal would simply amount to a noisy declaration of the antithesis.

Whence the heterogeneity of the text.

Passing over an inordinately large number of statements about woman, I shall nonetheless attempt to formalize their rule and reduce them to a finite number of typical and matrical propositions. Then I shall mark out the essential limits of such a codification and the problems it entails for a subsequent reading.

Three types of statements, then, three fundamental propositions—each of which has a different value position, each stemming from a different place. Perhaps these value positions could also, according to a kind of work I could only point out here, take on the sense that psychoanalysis (for example) gives to the word "position."

1. Woman is condemned, humiliated, and scorned as a figure or power of lying. The category of accusation is now set forth under the name of truth, of dogmatic metaphysics, of the credulous man who advances truth and the phallus as his own attributes. The phallogocentric texts written in the light of this reactive and negative appeal are numerous indeed.

2. Woman is condemned, humiliated, and scorned as a figure or power of truth, as a philosophical and Christian being, whether she identifies herself with truth, or, at a distance, whether she still plays with it as a fetish—to her advantage, and without in the least believing in it. Yet by ruse and naïveté (and ruse is always contaminated by naïveté), she remains within the system and economy of truth, within the space of phallogocentrism. The whole affair, then, is conducted from the point of view of the masked artist. Yet this personage still believes in the castration of woman, and thus he remains within the inversion of the reactive and negative case.

3. Beyond this double negation, woman is recognized, affirmed, as an affirmative, dissimulating, artistic, and Dionysian power. She is not af-

firmed by man; rather, she affirms herself both in herself and in man (in the sense in which, a short while ago, I said that castration had not taken place). Anti-feminism is thus reversed in turn, for it did not condemn woman except insofar as she was identified with, or responded to, the man of the two reactive positions.

To form an exhaustive code out of these three types of statement, to try to reconstitute them into a systematic unity, one would have to master parody and a heterogeneous style, or styles, and reduce them to the content of a thesis. On the other hand, it would be necessary (and these two conditions are indissociable) for each value implied in the three schemas to be *decidable* within a set of coupled oppositions, as if for each term there were a contrary; e.g., for woman, for truth, or for castration.

But the graphics of *hymen* or *pharmakon*, [9] which registers the effect of castration without being reduced to it—and which is everywhere operative, particularly in Nietzsche's texts—limits the pertinence of these hermeneutical or systematic questions and grants no appeal. This graphics always withdraws a margin of control from the meaning, from the code.

Not that we should passively side with heterogeneity or parody (which would still be to reduce them). Nor should it be concluded from all this that the unobtainability of the unique and ungraftable master meaning is actually due to Nietzsche's infinite mastery, to his impregnable power, to his impeccable manipulation of some trap, or to a sort of infinite calculus, like that of Leibniz' God—but rather, this time, to an infinite calculus of the undecidable, so as to foil the grasp of hermeneutics. To escape the latter with any surety, however, would be just as surely to fall back into the trap. It would turn parody or simulacrum into an instrument of mastery in the service of truth or castration—and in doing so, it would reconstitute religion (the cult of Nietzsche, for example) and find its own interest there, as a priesthood for interpreters and parodists.

No, parody always presupposes some sort of naïveté, backed up by the unconscious and the vertigo of noncontrol, a loss of consciousness. The absolutely calculated parody would either be a confession or a table of law.

It must be said, stupidly, that if the aphorisms on woman cannot be assimilated—to each other, first of all, and to the rest—it is also because Nietzsche did not see too clearly into these matters, with a single wink of the eye, in an instant; and that such a regular, rhythmical blindness, never to be done with, takes place within the text. Nietzsche is a bit lost there. Loss occurs, and this can be asserted, as soon as there is hymen.

Nietzsche is a bit lost in the web of the text, like a spider, unequal to what he has produced—like a spider, I say, or like many spiders, those of Nietzsche, those of Lautréamont, of Mallarmé, of Freud and Abraham.

He was, and he dreaded, such a castrated woman.

He was, and he dreaded, such a castrating woman.

He was, and he loved, such an affirmative woman.

All this at once; simultaneously or successively, according to the place of his body and the position of his history. He had so much to do, in himself, outside himself, with so many women.

There is no one woman, no one truth as such about woman as such. He has told us that, at least, as well as of a quite varied typology of women—the crowd of mothers, sisters, old maids, spouses, governesses, prostitutes, virgins, grandmothers—the grand and small daughters of his work.

For this same reason, there is no one truth to Nietzsche or to Nietzsche's texts. When one reads "these are *my* truths" in *Beyond Good and Evil*— when Nietzsche underlines *my,* it is precisely in a paragraph about women. *My* truths; that undoubtedly implies that they are not truths, since they are multiple, varicolored, contradictory. There is therefore no one truth as such, and besides, even for me, even about me, truth is plural.

There is thus no truth as such about the sexual difference as such, about man or woman as such; on the contrary, the whole of ontology itself results from a kind of inspection and boarding, an appropriation, identification, and verification of identity—even though it presupposes or harbors this indecidability.

Beyond the mythology of the signature, beyond the theology of the author, one's biographical desire gets inscribed in the text, and it leaves an irreducible mark, a mark that is also irreducibly plural. Everyone's own "granite of spiritual *fatum*" gives and receives these marks, thus forming its matter. The erection falls. The biographical text is fixed and stabilized for an uncertain duration, and for a long time it constitutes an immovable stele, with all the dangers of a *"monumental history"*—already forseen by the *Untimely Meditations*. This granite is a system of

> . . . predetermined decisions and answers to predetermined selected questions. Whenever a cardinal problem is at stake, there speaks an unchangeable "this is *I;*" about man and woman, for example, a thinker cannot relearn but only finish learning—only discover ultimately how this is "settled in him" . . . After this abundant civility that I have just evidenced in relation to myself [after defining spiritual *fatum* as our stupidity] I shall perhaps be permitted more readily to state a few truths about "woman as such"—assuming that it is now known from the outset how very much these are after all only—*my* truths.[10]

And in *Ecce Homo* ("Why I Write Such Good Books"), two paragraphs follow one another (IV and V) in which Nietzsche successively proposes that there are "a great number of possible styles," or that there is no "style in itself," because—as he says—he "knows women well" (or rather, females: *Weiblein*):

That is part of my Dionysian dowry. Who knows? Perhaps I am the first psychologist of the eternally feminine. They all love me—an old story—not counting *abortive* females, the "emancipated" who lack the stuff for children. —Fortunately, I am not willing to be torn to pieces: the perfect woman tears to pieces when she loves.

From the moment the question of woman suspends the decidable opposition between the true and nontrue, from the moment it installs the epochal regime of quotation marks for all the concepts that belong to the system of philosophical decidability, when it disqualifies the hermeneutical project of postulating a true sense for the text and liberates reading from the horizon of the meaning or the truth of being, of the values of production and produced, of the presence and the present—from that moment on, it becomes the question of style as the question of writing, the question of a spurring operation, more powerful than any content, any thesis, any meaning. The styled spur traverses the veil: not only does it tear it in order to see or produce the thing itself, but it actually undoes the opposition to itself, the opposition plied over upon itself, of veiled/unveiled, of truth as production, of the unveiling/dissimulation—of what is brought to presence. The question no more lifts the veil than lets it fall: it delimits it in suspense—the epoch. To delimit, to undo, or to be done away with: when it is a question of the veil, doesn't this once again amount to unveiling? Indeed, to destroying a fetish? This question, *considered as a question* (between *logos* and *theoria*, saying and seeing), remains, interminably.

NOTES

1. *The Gay Science*, §60.
2. *GS*, §59.
3. *GS*, §60.
4. *GS*, §69.
5. *Beyond Good and Evil*, Preface.
6. *GS*, §64.
7. *BGE*, §232; see also §233.
8. *Twilight of the Idols;* "Morality as Anti-Nature," §§2–4.
9. *"Hymen"* and *"pharmakon."* Derrida proposes these two "concepts" in the course of interpreting certain texts of Mallarmé and Plato, respectively—the terms gather their strategic significance and power from the reading that they, as key concepts, incorporate. See J. Derrida, *La Dissémination* (Ed. du Seuil, 1972); "La Pharmacie de Platon," pp. 71–197, for the concept of "pharmakon" as both poison and remedy—a logic that goes beyond that of Aristotle (like Freud's unconscious). See also pp. 201–318 (and particularly pp. 237–245) for "hymen" in Mallarmé's text.

Among many other passages, we quote the following from *La Dissémination:* "Hymen signifies first of all the fusion, or consummation, of marriage, the identification or confusion between two. *Between* two, there is no longer any difference; rather, an identity. In that fusion, there is no longer any distance between desire . . . and the fulfillment of presence, between distance and nondistance; no more difference between desire and its satisfaction. Not only is the difference abolished . . . but the difference between difference and nondifference equally . . . The hymen, confusion between the present and nonpresent . . . "has taken place" in the *between*; it is the spacing between wish and fulfillment, between perpetration and memory . . . Hymen—consummation of differents, continuity and confusion of coitus, marriage—becomes confused with what seems to be its place of derivation: hymen as protective screen, casket of virginity, vaginal partition, thin and invisible veil that, for the hysteric, maintains itself *between* the inside and the outside of woman—hence between the wish and its fulfillment. It is neither the desire nor the pleasure but between the two. It is the hymen that the desire dreams of piercing, of bursting, with a violence that is (either both or between) love and murder. If the one or the other had taken place, there would be no hymen—but even if they had not occurred, there would still be no hymen. Hymen, with its completely undecidable meaning, hasn't happened except when it has not happened, when nothing *really* happens, when there is consummation without violence or violence without thrust, or thrust without mark, mark without mark (margin), etc., when the veil is torn *without being* torn; for example, when someone is made to die of laughter or happiness." (pp. 237–241)—Ed.

10. *BGE,* §231.

Jean Granier

PERSPECTIVISM AND INTERPRETATION

For Nietzsche, thought is never external to Being: "Our highest and most daring thoughts are characteristic fragments of 'reality.' Our thought is made of the same substance as everything else."[1] This statement is not a profession of idealism, however, because, for Nietzsche, thought participates in Being: it is integrated with reality, but it is neither the cause, principle, nor measure of reality. Thus, it cannot be identified with the whole of Being: "They say: the world is only thought, or will, or war, or love, or hate . . . separately, all this is false: added up, it is *true*."[2] We must go even further and take exception to the idea that there is a unity of Being, because the whole is a metaphysical chimera:

> It seems to me important that one should get rid of the all, the unity, some force, something unconditioned; otherwise one will never cease regarding it as the highest court of appeal and baptizing it "God." One must shatter the all; unlearn respect for the all.[3]

The idea of the fundamental perspectivism of knowledge has as its precise function the uprooting of the metaphysical conviction that subjectivity is capable of dominating the totality of Being. From the start, this notion excludes the possibility that thought can grasp the essence of Being by an immediate intuition, or that it can constitute a world spread out before the eyes of the spectator-subject. The epistemological subject is necessarily situated, his field of knowledge is finite; thus, no one perspective can exhaust the richness of reality. What he discerns is a certain number of "aspects" of this reality, and one can say that understanding itself essentially has the form of perceptive knowledge, since it only apprehends visual "profiles," which in turn refer to an infinitude of possible series. Nevertheless, these aspects are not simple appearances that hide an in-itself of things: the dualism between the appearance and the thing in itself is definitively resolved. Each appearance is an *apparition*—that is, a *real manifestation*—and there is nothing to look for beyond these manifestations. To be is to appear—not in the sense that appearing is the equivalent of Being, but in that every apparition is a revelation of Being. Nietzschean perspectivism is thus by no means a conventional phenomenalism: "The task: to see things as they are. The means: to contemplate them through hundreds of eyes, across many people." By affirming the perspectivism of knowledge, Nietzsche in fact defends an ontological *pluralism:* the essence of Being is to show itself, and to show itself according to an *infinity of viewpoints*. Our experience reveals a Being that, in the mask of Dionysus, is "torn to pieces in the infinite dispersion of the universe."

The Nietzschean notion of perspectivism overlaps that of interpretation, and Nietzsche often regards them as synonymous. Not only does the latter clarify and complete the former, however, but it imparts a new orientation to the problem of knowledge. Perspectivism, in effect, evokes images that are tied to the perceptual sphere—and therefore to man's situation in space. Interpretation is connected to another category of images. The person who translates one language into another is called an "interpreter;" even when his task demands a personal effort to discover adequate equivalences between the two, his translation itself can never be absolutely faithful to the "text." Similarly, we say that a painter has "interpreted" his subject, thereby implying that the artist was not content simply to copy a landscape, a figure, or a still life; rather, following his own temperament and technique, he accentuated certain traits and eliminated others in order to bring out what to his mind best expressed the truth of his theme. Art introduces a coefficient of subjectivity—that is, a coefficient of invention and originality—into the representation of the world. Now, far from constituting some simple addition to reality, this coefficient makes reality appear even more true than when directly perceived. When we say that a virtuoso or conductor interprets a musical score, we mean that his approach is a way of re-creating the work itself, not that it is the mechanical and anonymous reconstitution of sound groups that the author has symbolically marked down on the score. The virtuoso impresses his own style upon the work—that is, his inimitable manner of understanding and execution. The historian, faced with a group of documents, must also "interpret" these raw data—which themselves already suggest a certain number of hypotheses. Nonetheless, these data must be organized and shaped in order to obtain an image of the past that has some rational coherence, and in such a way that this image will never be entirely separable from the personal vision of the particular historian. From these examples, it becomes clear that interpretation supposes some *creative initiative* on the part of the interpreter, one that does not signal any absent-mindedness, offhandedness, or dilettantism, but, rather, one that is required by the very nature of the "text."

> For between two absolutely different spheres, as between subject and object, there is no causality, no exact correlation, and no expression, but, at best, an *aesthetic* relation; I mean an allusive transposition, a

halting translation into an entirely foreign language: but, in any case, there must be an intermediary sphere and a mediating force, freely composing and freely inventing.[4]

By introducing the notion of interpretation, Nietzsche imposes a definition of Being as "text." Being is similar to a text that requires our exegesis, a task complicated by the fact that the text is obscure, often full of gaps, by the fact that several "readings" are possible and that certain fragments even remain undeciphered. Let us add that previous textual interpretations, accumulated during the course of human history, are mixed together with the "original" and constitute a whole set of glosses that we must learn to recognize as such in order to extract the primitive text. What we view as Being is already a *cultural* product, a monument of human civilization. While the idea of perspectivism tended to emphasize the plurality of ways by which Being is disclosed, the idea of interpretation accentuates its equivocal character. Being, Nietzsche explains, is not a translucent *logos* because, if it were, there would be no room for hesitation about what sense to give it. Doubt and error would be excluded, and man would spontaneously possess knowledge. The organization of our ideas would be in conformity with the order of things, which would be fixed *a priori* and for eternity. On the contrary, viewed as "text," Being cannot consist of a system of clear and distinct ideas, cannot be an omnipresent rationality, but rather must be a *confused or clouded intelligibility*. It is, in Kafka's words, the strange message whose meaning is modified and altered as it is shouted out from house to house by the different messengers charged with transmitting it across the kingdom of the earth. For Nietzsche, Being is not the full light of sense but rather a tremor of sense, a series of cautious allusions, an expressive phenomenon.

By the same token, the traditional concept of knowledge appears as a pseudo-concept. According to this definition, knowledge is the act by which a subject conforms to a truth-substance, an absolute "in-itself." Nietzsche argues that an absolute must naturally escape all knowledge since knowledge is a relation, and since an absolute would cease to be absolute if it sustained a relation to an *other* being outside itself. Thus, either Being renounces its quality of a substantial "in-itself" and internalizes the mediation, or else knowledge is a groundless play—that is to say, knowledge of nothing.

The biggest fable of all is the fable of knowledge. One would like to know what things-in-themselves are; but behold, there are no things-in-themselves! But even supposing there were an in-itself, an unconditioned thing, it would for that very reason be unknowable! Something unconditioned cannot be known; otherwise it would not be unconditioned! Coming to know, however, is always "placing oneself in a

conditional relation to something" . . . it is therefore under all circumstances establishing, denoting, and making-conscious of conditions (not forthcoming entities, things, what is "in-itself").[5]

Knowledge is immanent to Being, and subjectivity (the existence of multiple
"viewpoints") is not an accident that befalls Being, impairing its truth;
rather, it is an essential moment of the life of Being:

> That things possess a constitution in themselves quite apart from
> interpretation and subjectivity, is a quite idle hypothesis: it presupposes
> that interpretation and subjectivity are not essential, that a thing freed
> from all relationships would still be a thing.[6]

The Nietzschean idea of interpretation, however, does not incorporate the
rational dynamism of Hegelian mediation: for Nietzsche, Being is not a
subject that passes through various phenomenal stages toward absolute
knowledge, and interpretation is not a dialectical mediation of the whole.
Interpretation is the expression of a basic ontological dispersion, and therefore the possibility of gathering up different particular viewpoints into a
superior synthesis is necessarily excluded: " 'To grasp everything' would
be to do away with all perspectivist relations, it would mean to grasp
nothing, to misapprehend the nature of knowledge." Thus, for Nietzsche,
the word "interpretation" can only be used in the plural.

But this notion of interpretation draws us along still further. By asserting
that all existence is essentially "interpretation," Nietzsche indicates that the
existing subject is never simply presented with a text to be investigated.[7]
Rather, the subject himself constitutes the sense of the text by an operation
that engages him in a radical way. "Ultimately, the individual derives the
values of his acts from himself; because he has to *interpret in a quite
individual way* even the words he has inherited. His *interpretation* of a
formula at least is personal, even if he does not create a formula: as an
interpreter he is still creative."[8]

To interpret is to run a risk, to risk a wager. The interpreting subject is not
like the conscientious philologist who labors over deciphering a manuscript;
he throws himself into interpretation with the same energy that fires his
appetite for living, for growth, for conquest. The *act* of interpreting is the
surge of life. Interpretation is not an operation added onto the will to live; it is
not an accessory operation that the subject resigns himself to after having
acquitted himself of his immediate and mundane tasks; for him *to be* and *to
interpret* are one and the same. But then, what we call the original "text"
must *provoke* this initiative, it must contain a kind of fundamental *indetermination* that leaves open a free field for the individual's *creative* activity.
The subject adapts himself at the same time that he interprets, his will to
knowledge is already Will to Power: it involves the domination of nature,

ordering the environment, creating the conditions under which a kind of life can prosper by extending its control to the utmost over reality. The relation between interpretation and text is not contemplative; it belongs to the realm of combat and conquest. It implies the activity of formation, of selection, of set purpose. Perspectivist knowledge, then, is partial in both senses: one-sided and incomplete. "The *interpretive* character of all phenomena. There is no fact *per se*. What occurs is a group of phenomena selected and united by an interpreting being." This is why Nietzsche allows himself to use, or to reuse, the term "appearance"—but now in a radically anti-metaphysical way. To the extent that interpretation represents a certain way of arranging reality according to the needs and demands of a particular kind of life, it creates a system of appearances whose *truth* becomes identified with the *value* that this kind of life attributes to it: "Appearance is an arranged and simplified world, at which our practical instincts have been at work; it is perfectly true for us; that is to say, we live, we are able to live in it: proof of its truth for us."[9]

The idea of interpretation thus leads to what Nietzsche calls a new kind of "phenomenalism": according to this conception of knowledge, what is "known" represents a group of "phenomena" or appearances that are tried together and ordered in terms of a particular "perspective" and reflect the vital demands of a center of Will to Power. This Will to Power, in turn, struggles to annex reality while it "translates" the text of Being according to its own norms. The term "appearance"—like "phenomenon"—is intended to stress the partial, artificial, and fabricated aspects that belong to all relations with reality. "This is the essence of phenomenalism and perspectivism as I understand them: Owing to the nature of *animal consciousness,* the world of which we can become conscious is only a surface and sign-world, a world that is made common and meaner."[10] What we term "the real" is what we are referred to by the images of our desires, our fears, our hopes, and our fundamental choices. It is the correlate of all the projective acts that emanate from the flowing centers of Will to Power.

But now, what becomes of the "text"? Must it be admitted that interpretation itself invents sense and projects it onto what in the end is only an absurd *chaos*? This is the solution that Nietzsche seems to adopt when he writes: "Our values are interpreted *into* things." Values are projected onto things by the operation of our interpretation, and it is thanks to this projection that the world is disclosed to us as significant. Likewise, we read in §556 of *Will to Power:* "There are no 'facts-in-themselves,' for a sense must always be projected into them before there can be 'facts.' " In this case, there is nothing for the interpreting subject to "read" in the text of reality; he is entirely free to decide on the sense that suits him best and to build a universe according to his idiosyncratic options. He need not rely on vigilant attention to the text since, by sovereign *fiat*, he decrees what the essence of things must be. "Ultimately, man finds in things nothing but what he himself has imported into them: the finding is called science, the importing—art, religion, love, pride." [11] But one may ask, "What sort of text can tolerate the most divergent kinds of interpretation?" Would such a text not be entirely empty, a simple blank, an "in-itself"—something on which we could leisurely scrawl whatever we wanted? Are we dealing with a text here, or a pretext?

Having chosen this somewhat extreme position, how can we legitimate the complementary notions of "value," "need," and "vital interest"? In order for values to play their regulatory role in the disposition of a world, reality must already offer objective guidelines; there must exist some "geography of Being," and man must discover himself situated in a world whose structures offer a base of support for his initiatives. A strictly neutral reality would be comparable to the vertical wall that utterly discourages one's slightest desire to climb. Nietzsche grasps all this clearly, defining religious interpretation, for example, as the *assignment of value* of a set of characteristics that have already existed in a historical community; in short, as the establishment of an order that was prefigured, for instance, in a certain economic and social field; here there is a selective operation, but no absolute "imposition" of sense.

> The distinctive invention of the founders of religions is, first: to posit a particular kind of life and everyday customs that have the effect of disciplining the will and at the same time of abolishing boredom—and then: to bestow on this life style an *interpretation* that makes it appear to be illuminated by the highest value so that this life style becomes something for which one fights and under certain circumstances sacrifices one's life. Actually, the second of these two inventions is more essential. The first, the way of life, was usually there before, but alongside other ways of life and without any sense of its special value. The significance and originality of the founder of a religion usually consists of his *seeing* it, *selecting* it, and *guessing* for the first time to what use it can be put, how it can be interpreted. [12]

Nonetheless, so little does Nietzsche find the "text" dissolved in the swirl of different interpretations that he wants to teach philosophers "the inestimable art of *reading* well," to instruct them in the principles of *rigorous philology*. He calls for a return to the book of nature, he seeks to reveal "natural man."

> To translate man back into nature; to become master over the many vain and overly enthusiastic interpretations and connotations that have so far been scrawled and painted over that eternal basic text of *homo natura;*

to see to it that man henceforth stands before man as even today, hardened in the discipline of science, he stands before the *rest* of nature, with intrepid Oedipus eyes and sealed Odysseus ears, deaf to the siren songs of old metaphysical bird catchers.[13]

But now Nietzsche demands that the real "facts" be disentangled from "beliefs," that the text be separated from the interpretations that obscure its original meaning.

Here, philology should be understood, in a very general sense, as the art of reading well—being able to pluck out the facts *without* falsifying them by interpretation, *without* losing caution, patience, subtlety in the search for understanding.[14]

Here, value ceases to be the criterion of truth, and it is not enough that an interpretation favor the growth of a certain type of Will to Power for it to be legitimate. In cases like this, the moral and metaphysical interpretation of Being stems from a defective philology; it is the product of ignorance, duplicity, and lack of culture. Metaphysics "introduced interpretation into the text and into the facts, as an error." "Seriousness for *true* things"— which rests on the integrity of what Nietzsche calls "the instinct for reality"—is completely lacking in Christianity:

A religion like Christianity, which is at no point in contact with actuality, which crumbles away as soon as actuality comes into its own at any point whatever, must naturally be a mortal enemy of the "wisdom of the world," that is to say of *science* . . . Paul *wants* to confound the "wisdom of the world": his enemies are the *good* philologists of the Alexandrian school—upon them he makes war. In fact, one is not philologist and physician without also being at the same time *anti-Christian*.[15]

Nietzsche addresses this reproach—respecting the absence of philological probity—to the Christian religion in *The Dawn:*

How little Christianity educates the sense of honesty and justice can be seen pretty well from the writings of its scholars: they advance their conjectures as blandly as dogmas . . . and the interpretation that follows is of such impudent arbitrariness that a philologist is stopped in his tracks, torn between anger and laughter, and keeps asking himself: Is it possible? Is this honest? Is it even decent?[16]

By comparing these remarks with the earlier ones that concerned the "introduction" of sense by a creative act of human interpretation, we

quickly sense that an underlying antinomy disturbs Nietzsche's whole reflection. He seems to oscillate between a wholly *perspectivist
phenomenalism*—which results in identifying truth with value, and, ultimately, abolishes the very notion of "text"—and a definition of authentic
knowledge as strict "philology," which, taken literally, risks issuing into
dogmatism. Sometimes the text becomes exhausted by a multitude of interpretations, each claiming to justify itself according to some criterion of
"vital utility" (i.e., "value"). Sometimes the text seems to recover complete independence from its interpretations and to attain a univocal sense; the
task of the good philologist, then, would be to restore this sense to its
original truth. In a curious fragment from *Will to Power* Nietzsche ventures a
brief outline of knowledge quite striking in its dogmatically naïve character:
supposing that the individual's different instincts each project an image onto
reality that would correspond to his own ideal, he concludes that truth would
consist in the chance agreement to be established between one of the many
projections and reality itself.

> With the aid of these numerous phantasms, they almost necessarily
> finish by guessing reality and truth; they construct so many images that
> one of them turns out to be *correct*. With a multitude of weapons they
> shoot a single quarry; it is a huge game of dice—not for the individual
> alone, but for the many—that lasts for several generations.[17]

But this last example is a matter of extreme conjecture on Nietzsche's part.
In fact, Nietzsche *overcomes the antinomy between relativism and dogmatism on the basis of his intuition of Being as interpreted Being:* on the one
hand, he indeed sidesteps the threat of dogmatism by insisting on the
impossibility of a definitive interpretation that would exhaust the richness of
reality: Being is equivocal and there is no absolute truth for man to possess as
an inalienable right; Being remains essentially "open."

> The basic presupposition that there is a correct interpretation at all—or
> rather *one* single correct one—seems to me to be empirically false . . .
> What is incorrect can be ascertained in innumerable cases; what is
> correct is *almost always unascertainable. . .* In a word, the old
> philologist says: There is no single beatific interpretation.[18]

As the art of reading well, philology only helps us to eliminate errors; it
does not confide the ultimate secret of Being. Nothing can free us from the
task that has befallen us; namely, to question Being and to risk our own
interpretations. But, on the other hand, and as a corollary, we do not have the
right to spirit away the text and substitute the idea of a fundamental chaos—
if we take chaos to mean some absolute nonsense that, like Platonic matter,
could be imprinted with any form. The text *is,* it has its own subsistence, and

all perspectives on it are not equally legitimate. When Nietzsche talks about "chaos," then, he means that Being is not reducible to a human ideal, whatever that may be. It is mobility itself, it is the flux of interpretations that constitute the "world" that is, according to a happy formula of Heidegger, "the inexhaustible, overflowing, and uncontrolled abundance of the self-creating and self-destroying."

Thus, to Nietzsche, "chaos" designates the fluid and unbounded power of life—insofar as the latter includes an element of the *inhuman*, the *terrible*, the *indomitable*. By defining Being as chaos, he liberates nature from the realm of human idealization; he dehumanizes nature while, at the same time, he naturalizes man. "When will we complete our de-deification of nature? When may we begin to 'naturalize' humanity in terms of a pure, newly discovered, newly redeemed nature?"[19] Thus, precisely when we substitute the chaos of Dionysian life for the *logos* of metaphysical idealism, we see that "the total character of the world . . . is in all eternity chaos—in the sense not of a lack of necessity but a lack of order, arrangement, form, beauty, wisdom, and whatever other names there are for our aesthetic anthropomorphisms."[20] The antinomy we encountered before reflected our inability to view the limits of Nietzsche's thought with enough flexibility; instead, we tended to congeal them into independent poles. As Jaspers notes,

> . . . Nietzsche's contradictions show us what he is driving at. Existence both provides and is a product of exegesis. It is regarded as a circle that renews itself constantly while seeming to annul itself. It is now objectivity and now subjectivity; it appears first as substance and then as constantly annulled substance; though unquestionably there, it is constantly questioning and questionable; it is both being and not-being, the real and the apparent.[21]

These "limits" nevertheless are constantly in evidence, and they mark the double gradient of Nietzsche's meditations. On the one hand, by accentuating the creative, dominating, and Caesarian aspects in the notion of interpretation, one is led to the doctrine of *perspectivist pragmatism*, according to which "to know" means "to introduce sense into the world"—thus bending the latter to one's own vital interests. *Here, knowledge is annexation, effort of appropriation, will to dominate reality.* Consequently, insofar as it renders as much violence to reality as does every center of Will to Power, a perspectivist pragmatist interpretation is necessarily a "falsification." On the other hand, if one is concerned with the objective side of interpretation—that is, with the text that bears each of the interpretations—one is led to contest the ultimate validity of the criterion itself (vital utility) and to deny that any interpretation is admissible as soon as it favors the expansion of one type or another of Will to Power. The rules of true philology require that we sacrifice interest and utility for the demands of a textual understanding, one that would restore, to the extent to which it is possible, the original meaning of the text. The text is not a plaything of human subjectivity; "basically there is within us, way 'down below,' something unteachable—a granite of spiritual fate." Here we must set out to discover this primordial ground, upon which every interpretation grows. For the noblest and most courageous spirits, one voice speaks louder than that of their own vital interests, commanding us to *do justice* to nature, to reveal things as they are in their own being. Philological probity cannot accommodate itself to the falsifications of a biased biology; rather, it animates an authentic "passion to know," attached to reality itself, preferring dispiriting truths to fallacious ideals.

Our examination of the Nietzschean idea of interpretation has prepared us for a reflection that can be further developed on two distinct levels: the level of a perspectivist pragmatism, and that of an ontological problem. It has given us the key to what constitutes the paradox of Nietzschean philosophy; that is, the dual and contradictory assertion that truth is measured by the value it has for life and that—nevertheless—truth demands the kind of strict reading that sacrifices utility for truth.

NOTES

1. Kröner; XII, Part I, §2.
2. K, XII; part II, §7.
3. *The Will to Power*, §331.
4. *On Truth and Lie in an Extra-Moral Sense*, §1.
5. *WP*, §555.
6. *WP*, §560.
7. "How far the perspective character of existence extends or whether existence has any other character than this; whether existence without interpretation, without 'sense,' does not become 'nonsense;' whether, on the other hand, all existence is not essentially actively engaged in *interpretation*." *The Gay Science*, §374.
8. *WP*, §767.
9. *WP*, §568.
10. *GS*, §354.
11. *WP*, §606.
12. *GS*, §353.
13. *Beyond Good and Evil*, §230.
14. *The Dawn*, §52.
15. *The Antichrist*, §47.

16. *Dawn*, §84.

17. K, XII; part I, §12.

18. Letter to Fuchs, 26 August 1888.

19. *GS*, §109.

20. *Ibid*.

21. Karl Jaspers, *Nietzsche* (Chicago: Henry Regnery Company, 1969), p. 290.

Sarah Kofman

METAPHOR, SYMBOL, METAMORPHOSIS

In the Dionysian dithyramb man is incited to the greatest exaltation of all his symbolic faculties; something never before experienced struggles for utterance—the annihilation of the veil of *māyā,* oneness as the soul of the race and of nature itself. The essence of nature is now to be expressed symbolically; we need a new world of symbols; and the entire symbolism of the body is called into play, not the mere symbolism of the lips, face, and speech but the whole pantomine of dancing, forcing every member into rhythmic movement. Then the other symbolic powers suddenly press forward, particularly those of music, in rhythmics, dynamics, and harmony. To grasp this collective release of all the symbolic powers, man must have already attained that height of self-abnegation which seeks to express itself symbolically through all these powers—and so the dithyrambic votary of Dionysus is understood only by his peers. With what astonishment must the Apollonian Greek have beheld him! With an astonishment that was all the greater the more it was mingled with the shuddering suspicion that all this was actually not so very alien to him after all, in fact, that it was only his Apollonian consciousness which, like a veil, hid this Dionysian world from his vision.[1]

MUSIC, THE PRIVILEGED ART

As early as *The Birth of Tragedy,* Nietzsche judges the language of philosophical concepts to be the most inadequate way of expressing any "truth" about the world: thrice removed from reality, concepts are only metaphors of metaphors. In fact, the essence of things is only represented to us. We and the universe with us are only images of their hidden and undecipherable nature. Nonetheless, we can distinguish two categories of representations together with their corresponding symbolic spheres. Those representations that appear in the form of pleasure and pain are the most important: not only do they accompany all *other* representations (what Nietzsche calls "will"), but they are the basis for understanding all these other representations—i.e., for understanding the whole of the natural world. Similarly, the symbolic sphere that corresponds to pleasure and pain is as "fundamental for language as the appearance of pleasure and pain is for all the other representations": degrees of pleasure and pain are symbolized by the tone of speech, while all other representations are expressed by symbolic gestures. Moreover, because pleasure and pain manifest a "unique" substratum—one that is the same for everyone—the language of sounds is a universal language; i.e., it extends beyond the diversity of particular languages. The plurality of languages should be envisaged as the "strophic text of this primordial melody of pleasure and pain." The vowels and consonants of language belong to the symbolic order of gestures because they are deprived of a fundamental tone; they are only position-stops of bodily organs—i.e., gestures. What seems to ground symbolic gestures, then, is tonality, the echo of pleasure and pain. Written language is even more limited in its expressive powers than oral or sonorous language, where "interval, rhythm, speed, and accentuation symbolize the emotional content of expression." If words ("the most deficient kind of sign") are in any way meant to express feeling, therefore, they must necessarily be supplemented by music.

Thus *The Birth of Tragedy* establishes a hierarchy between the different symbolic languages—i.e., the different metaphorical transpositions of "worldly music." And because music is itself the best language, the one that best and most universally expresses the general phenomenal form of will, Nietzsche will metaphorically call it music or melody of the world. (By the same token, in saying that music is best suited to express the hidden nature of things, Nietzsche still remains tributary to an entire metaphysical tradition.)

Melody is thus the "first and foremost fact" to emerge (in so many different ways) from these early texts, which are themselves all so many metaphors. Furthermore, Nietzsche sees melody so impregnated with rhythm that, for him, real music not only incites or invites the dance, but is inseparable from it. The Dionysian dithyramb is a "total dance that excites all one's members by its rhythm." In this sense, lyric poetry is an Apollonian metaphor of Dionysian music. The lyric poet tends to imitate music by using images that are colored by rapid variation and spun in a mad whirl. To express music in images this way, he needs to grasp every impassioned movement—for each serves as a metaphor for music. And because the lyric poet only gains self-awareness through the prism of music, all he can express is its miraculous effects upon himself. Thus, through visions and sentiments adorned with images, lyric poetry becomes the metaphorical expression of Dionysian music. The metaphor must not be understood here as a figure of rhetoric, but as "an image that the poet really perceives in place of the idea," a living spectacle. By way of images, the lyrical genius expresses what the Dionysian musician sounds out, what he performs, when he identifies himself with the primitive echo of the world.

Nonetheless, if lyrical emotion can symbolize music, it can in no way replace it. The world of sound and the world of images are two languages that have no necessary interrelations. Every image, every sentiment analogically suggested by music, is only a rude expression of the evanescent sound, which must vanish in the face of such images, even in the face of Dionysus himself and his most authentic symbols. Moreover, when the lyric poem is set to music, it inspires neither images nor representations, nor any content of feeling. Musical emotion, which comes from quite another direction, can only be metaphorically expressed in a text that is itself "just a symbol, and stands to music in the same relation as the hieroglyph of bravery does to the brave warrior . . . In the presence of the supreme God and his authentic revelation, the symbol is no longer meaningful; it appears as an offensive trapping."[2]

Far from rendering music "intelligible," images only obscure it. For the servant of Dionysus, music is intelligible by itself: also, it is "an essential feature of Dionysian art not to take an audience into account." Likewise, it is not for the listener but for himself that the poet interprets his music with the help of symbolic imagery and emotions. Alternatively, however, sound can never be used as a metaphor for images without reversing the legitimate hierarchical order: the different symbolic spheres (all of which are improper transpositions of things) are never equivalent to one another. To pretend to illustrate a poem musically by subordinating the music to the text is to grant an improper place to a rude metaphor, to put a metaphor in place of what is really appropriate: it is the same desire as to substitute the son for the father, man for God—it is to want the impossible, since the Apollonian world cannot produce the sound that symbolizes the Dionysian realm, a world that was itself defeated and excluded by the Apollonian vision:

We shall be compelled to assert that the relationship between the lyric poem and its musical composition must in any case be a different one from that between a father and his child. . . . What a perverted world! A task that appears to my mind like that of a son wanting to create his father! Music can create metaphors out of itself, which will always however be but schemata, instances as it were of her intrinsic general contents. But how should the metaphor, the conception, create music out of itself! Much less could the idea, or, as one has said, the "poetical idea" do this. As certainly as a bridge leads out of the mysterious castle of the musical into the free land of the metaphors—and the lyric poet steps across it—as certainly is it impossible to go the contrary way, although some are said to exist who fancy they have done so.[3]

To reverse this hierarchy between the different symbolic spheres by making sound a metaphor of the image is, as in opera, to make bad music. Musical symbolism, then, is purely conventional, and music is thereby transformed into rhetoric, into a "system of mnemonic signs," as if it were destined to do nothing but stimulate limp or deadened nerves. This is what Nietzsche later denounces in Wagner: as a musician he practiced rhetoric, he placed music at the service of the text and sought above all else to be "expressive," to expound an idea across a thousand symbols, to stimulate the senses like a veritable Circe. This is how "good" music, the Dionysian music that makes one dance—Wagner's own early music that broke all unity of force and time—begins to decline. Rhetorical music is no more than a caricature of Dionysianism; it is a counterfeit, a comedy.

Operatic culture now becomes synonymous with "Socratic culture." The need that gave birth to modern opera was not aesthetic in nature, but moral and theoretical—witness the narrative representational style. The subjugation of music to the recitative answers to the nostalgia for an idyllic life, for the faith "in the primordial existence of the artistic and good man." Opera in this sense is a remedy for pessimism. While Dionysian music takes no account of the listener, here the audience usurps control by demanding the subordination of music to the text:

> It was the demand of thoroughly unmusical hearers that before everything else the words must be understood, so that according to them a rebirth of music is to be expected only when some mode of singing has been discovered in which text word lords it over counterpoint like master over servant. For the words, it is argued, are as much nobler than the accompanying harmonic system as the soul is nobler than the body.
>
> According to the most exact accounts, opera begins with the pretension that the listener understand the words. What? The listener would have pretentions? The words must be understood?[4]

Thus, deciphered by what could already be called a genealogical reading, opera marks the triumph of Socrates or Christ over Dionysus, of Nihilism over the affirmation of life, of the slave over his master.

Music is the most suitable symbolic sphere only because it is able to affirm the multifarious diversity of life. In fact it is the mother of all the arts, for it gives birth to a thousand metaphors; it is a language "capable of infinite interpretations." And while Apollonian drunkenness merely produces a visual irritation, in the Dionysian state the whole emotional system is excited and intensified:

> So that it discharges all its powers of representation, imitation, transfiguration, transmutation, every kind of mimicry and play-acting . . . The Dionysian man enters into every skin, into every emotion; he is continually transforming himself.[5]

As a particular art, music is a late specialization of hearing, and it develops to the detriment of the other senses, particularly to the muscular senses; it is the kind of specialization that puts an end to the corporeal symbolism of the real Dionysian state. All the arts are related: they form a whole whose parts have become more and more specialized. Specialization indicates a poverty of taste, an inability to enjoy something with all one's senses, and this is a characteristic of modern aesthetics:

> It is generally admitted as an axiom in aesthetics that the union of two or more arts, far from reinforcing aesthetic enjoyment, is a barbarous aberration of taste. But, at best, this axiom reveals the unpleasant modern practice which prevents us from enjoying something with the whole of our human faculties. We find ourselves torn in some sense between the particular arts and we no longer know how to enjoy except through bits and pieces of ourselves; sometimes by way of our ears, other times our eyes, etc. Let us now confront the image of antique drama, of total art.[6]

It is only when the various arts are taken in their respective hierarchies, subordinated to music, and seen as a totality, that we say that art symbolizes Dionysus: the god Dionysus, torn into a thousand pieces, who every year is brought back to life. Bacchic masquerades depict the god's metamorphosis, and mythic metaphors indirectly bespeak his nature across a multitude of languages.

For the artist to symbolize Dionysus, however, he must himself be metamorphosed, be stripped of his individuality. He must be identified in kind with the very being of nature. In this state the artist can express his unity with the whole: his "self" symbolizes totality. The artist becomes a metaphor of the world, and, as such, he is a medium that reflects eternal being. All truly authentic art implies a kind of drunkenness and, with it, a loss of oneself, a transporting beyond oneself, that is the sole power of symbolization. To express oneself metaphorically and to become metamorphosed are thus comparable. It is this ecstasis outside of oneself that is at the origin of Greek musical drama, that total art *par excellence:* the author of the ancient musical drama is thus like the athlete of the pentathlon, gifted in five kinds of game. The drama itself can be symbolized by the flowing curtains introduced by Aeschylus: it triumphs over everything that forced constraint, over everything that was isolated in the different arts; it reconciles discipline and grace, unity and diversity, Apollo and Dionysus. In the drama, moreover, each art can serve as the metaphorical expression of another: the revolutions of the chorus as they sketch out an arabesque, rendering the music visible, so to speak, while the music reinforces the poem's bold metaphors and leaps of thought. But just as it is only the totality of the arts that expresses Dionysus, so it is only music that has given birth to the tragic myth—the symbolic expression of all the Dionysian truths.

THE STRATEGIC STATUS OF METAPHOR

Now we understand why Nietzsche should have sung rather than spoken or, even, expressed himself poetically when he wrote *The Birth of Tragedy:* philosophic language is the most imperfect of all because it petrifies the "music of the world" into concepts. Dialectics and scientific reflection play the same role for the philosopher as the poet's verse, yet they are just as inadequate to express philosophic intuition as verse is to translate the poet's metamorphosis:

> And just as for the dramatist words and verse are but the stammering of an alien tongue, needed to tell what he has seen and lived, what he could utter directly only through music or gesture, just so every profound philosophic intuition expressed through dialectic and through scientific reflection is the only means for the philosopher to communicate what he has seen. But it is a sad means; basically a metaphoric and entirely unfaithful translation into a totally different sphere and speech. Thus Thales had seen the unity of all that is, but when he went to communicate it, he found himself talking about water.[7]

Beginning with *The Birth of Tragedy,* then, Nietzsche's generalized theory of metaphor rests on the loss of the self, and this in two senses: on the one hand, there is no metaphor without the stripping away of individuality, without masquerade, without metamorphosis. To transpose, one must be able to transpose oneself, to have conquered the limits of individuality; the same must partake of the other, it must become the other. At this level the metaphor is founded on the ontological unity of life, symbolized by Dionysus. And it is because this unity is always and already parceled out, and can only be reconstituted through the symbolic transposition of art, that there can be any metaphor at all. Beyond the individual separation symbolized by Dionysus' dismemberment, the metaphor enables one to reconstitute the primordial unity of all beings—as symbolized by the god's resurrection.

On the other hand, the metaphor is tied to the loss of what properly belongs to the "nature" of the world; but since this is undecipherable in any case, the subject can only have "unnatural" representations of it. And while more or less appropriate symbolic spheres correspond to these representations, neither the representations nor the symbolic languages are equivalent to one another. Since the language of music is the best metaphor, all other forms of expression are in turn more or less rude metaphors of it: in relation to all others, the most suitable metaphor is the most natural, it claims the greatest "propriety." Conceptual language is the poorest; its symbolic sense is the weakest, and any force it gains is only thanks to music or poetic images.

Beginning with this early work, which is still indebted to Schopenhauer, Nietzsche reverses the relation between metaphor and concept in a way that will prove to be extremely symptomatic of his later thought. In contrast with the Aristotelian tradition, the metaphor is no longer referred to the concept, but, rather, the concept is referred to the metaphor. For Aristotle, the concept is prior in relation to the metaphor, with the metaphor defined as the transfer of one concept to another, or as the passage from one logical place to another, from a "proper" to a figurative place. [8] The Aristotelian definition of metaphor as such cannot be retained by Nietzsche, for it rests on a division of the world into clearly defined genera and species, which correspond to concrete essences. For Nietzsche, the essence or nature of things is itself enigmatic; genera and species, then, are only human, all too human, metaphors. Here "transfer" must not be conceived as a passage from one place to another. Rather, as defined in *The Birth of Tragedy,* it must itself be taken as a metaphorical condensation of several senses: transfiguration, transformation, ecstasy, self-dispossession, metamorphosis (which is only possible if one eliminates the distinctions between sharply defined genera and species), and, finally, the transposition of truth into symbolic languages. The traditional relation between "proper" and figurative use now emerges somewhat differently in the case of transposition, since these languages are symbolic only insofar as they refer to the nature of the world or to the most suitable symbolic sphere.

When Nietzsche discusses metaphor, he makes a rather revealing remark about the relation between his own early text and the metaphysical tradition. The remark itself is metaphorical, and it borrows heavily from the Aristotelian definition: what is "proper" is like the father and what is "figurative" or metaphorical is like the son or grandson. Secondary metaphorical languages would in turn derive from the most nearly suitable or appropriate symbolic language. The process could not be reversed, just as the son cannot generate the father, nor grandsons the original sons. And in relation to the father or God—essence or nature itself—what is the son after all but a useless accessory, something to be suppressed?

This metaphorical remark implies a devaluation of metaphor. It seems to consider metaphor as being inferior, if not to the concept (which is itself metaphorical), then at least to essence or nature, to what is properly authentic, to Dionysus. The hierarchical distinction between a "good" rhetoric (naturally symbolic) and a "bad" rhetoric (purely conventional) should not make us forget that "good rhetoric" itself is only a last resort, that it too is an improper way of speaking about what is proper, what is natural, etc. To think of the essence of language as rhetoric (even if we have to wait until *The*

Philosopher's Book for all the consequences of this) is to refer it from the start to a "just" language to subordinate it to the latter. From what we gather in *The Birth of Tragedy*, then, Nietzsche's generalization of metaphor really remains bound up in the "closure of metaphysics." Is it at all possible to escape this state of affairs so long as one continues to refer the metaphor to what is proper or natural? But, at the same time, how can one conclude a generalized theory of metaphor by eliminating all reference to a proper or natural term? As Nietzsche has taught us, two opposing terms belong to the same system, and if we deconstruct the one only by generalizing the other, the deconstruction remains bounded by the field it originally sought to escape. It is also remarkable that Nietzsche turns the "metaphor" into a basic operational notion in his early works (*The Birth of Tragedy, Philosophy in the Tragic Age of the Greeks, The Philosopher's Book,* and fragments from the same period)—in precisely those works he still seems to admit that there is a hidden nature to things, one quite independent of any symbolizing metaphors. In the later texts the metaphor loses its strategic importance— i.e., after already having served to deconstruct what is "proper" or "natural" through the process of generalization. Nietzsche then substitutes the notions of "text" and "interpretation," and even though they still have a metaphysical aura about them, they at least have the advantage of no longer being directly opposed to what is "proper." In the later works, where metaphor is eliminated as a strategic notion, what is "proper" or "natural" thus becomes a simple interpretation. And in light of its new operational notion, metaphor will now symbolize the artistic force that constitutes the very interpretation of what is "proper"—and of the concept, and metaphysics itself. This artistic force will be termed, metaphorically, "will to power." The notion of metaphor now becomes entirely "improper" because it is no longer referred to a proper or natural term, but to an interpretation. To continue to use metaphor as a key notion after this point would have been dangerous because of its metaphysical implications, and we understand why, after having made strategic use of it, Nietzsche abandoned it.

REHABILITATION OF METAPHOR

Despite all their traditional elements, Nietzsche's early works reveal an original conception both of philosophy and philosophical "style"— especially with regard to the treatment of metaphor—an originality that introduces new relations between philosophy, art, and science. Until Nietzsche, philosophy and science had relegated metaphor to a poetic sphere because they sought to speak "properly." They sought to demonstrate, and not to convince by way of images or comparisons. Philosophers formerly appealed to metaphor only for didactic reasons or as the last resort, and even then with great prudence. But by granting such precise limits to the metaphor, they concealed the fact that concepts, too, are metaphorical. So when Nietzsche eliminates the opposition between metaphor and concept, only to replace it with a difference of degree, he inaugurates a kind of philosophy that deliberately makes use of metaphors, even if it risks being confused with poetry. This is a confusion, however, that Nietzsche does not find regrettable: the opposition between philosophy and poetry reinstates metaphysical thought; it rests on the fictional separation between the real and the imaginary, and on the no less fictional separation of different "faculties." To speak in metaphor, then, is to have language regain its most natural expression, its "most accurate, most simple, most direct" style.

The form in question, then, is simply poetry, because the new kind of philosopher does not use metaphor rhetorically; rather, he subordinates it to the aims of linguistic accuracy or to a strategic goal: he uses nonstereotyped metaphors to dramatize the fact that metaphors constitute all concepts. The philosopher does not only "play" with metaphors; his game is "terribly serious"—to destroy the very opposition between game and gravity, dream and reality, to show that

> . . . the mathematical account does not belong to the essence of philosophy . . . We want to transpose the world into such images as to make you shudder from them . . . If you block your ears, your eyes will see our myth. Our maledictions await you.[9]

"The imagination" plays as important a role in philosophy as in poetry. "The philosopher knows while he invents and invents while he knows." Imagination permits us to grasp analogies; only afterwards does reflection intervene to replace analogies with equivalences. suggestions with causal relations, and to impose any standardization of concepts. Philosophy, then, for Nietzsche, remains "a prolongation of the mythic instinct."

THE PRESOCRATIC MODEL

If Nietzsche can venture a new kind of philosophy in this way, it is because it has always and already existed; such a philosophy is possible because it had already been alive for the Presocratics. We must recall this earliest Greek philosophy; we must draw it out of the forgotten past where the triumph of nihilistic forces brought it to ruin and reclaim it by taking it as our model. When Nietzsche undertakes his genealogical reading of the Greek philosophers in *Philosophy in the Tragic Age of the Greeks,* he uses the philosophers' "style" as his touchstone. "What does a philosopher who writes metaphorically *need?* What does one who writes abstractly *need?* To shift from one kind of writing to another, what is this symptomatic of?"

Such are the implicit questions of this work, questions that are substituted for the more conventional ones about the truth or falsity of a given system. [10] But Nietzsche's aim is neither to prove nor to disprove them, because in any case, one cannot refute the conditions for existence: each system is like a plant, and in the same way that one can go from the plant back to the ground that produced it, so can one trace a system back to its author and see it as his image. The system must be evaluated not in terms of its truth, but in terms of its force and beauty. We should know whether it was made possible by superabundance or by a poverty of life, and if, through its means, the philosopher affirmed or denied life. The metaphorical style indicates the fullness of life, just as the "demonstrative" style indicates its poverty. To deliberately use metaphor is to affirm life, in the same way that favoring concepts reveals a will to nothingness, an adherence to the ascetic ideal.

The opposition between these two "styles" is expressed by that between two types of philosopher, the one following Heraclitus, the other Aristotle: Dionysus and Socrates. The passage from one to the other is marked by the death of tragedy—Euripides following Aeschylus, the word replacing the chant. The affirmation of life in its multifarious diversity gives way, then, to the triumph of the individual; consciousness outweighs the unconscious, self-awareness and reflection take precedence over naïveté. Thus, Anaxagoras and Euripides emerge as "the first sober thinkers among a race transported."

> The fact that an *indemonstrable* philosophy still has value—most often, even more so than a scientific proposition—stems from the *aesthetic* value of such a philosophizing, that is, from its beauty and sublimity. Philosophizing still remains as a *work of art,* even if it cannot be demonstrated as a philosophic construct . . . Heraclitus' hardly demonstrable philosophy has an artistic worth superior to all the propositions of Aristotle.
>
> It is rare for the Greeks to translate the depths of their wisdom and knowledge verbally. Between the great man of concepts, Aristotle, and the manners and art of the Hellenes, there stands an immense *abyss.* [11]

The metaphor of the *abyss* does not merely indicate a historical separation between two epochs. It is also the metaphor for "the pathos of distance" that separates two kinds of life that have always been with us: one is flourishing, superabundant, and projects its own excesses onto things and embellishes them with it. The other is degenerative, and it can only impoverish the world by reducing it to the narrow and ugly bounds of the concept—it does this out of spite against itself and out of resentment toward life. The abyss separates but also engulfs; it is thus a metaphor for talking about forgetfulness: about

the forgotten import of Presocratic philosophy, of metaphor, and of the
totality of instincts as opposed to a single one (i.e., knowledge).

The forgetfulness was made possible not "because of the times," but by
the triumph of the ascetic ideal, which deliberately kept the abyss empty.
After the Presocratic Greeks, philosophers were no more than "gaping
figures, pale and depressed, counterfeiters of theology": logic and reason,
then, prevailed over intuition, and Aristotle over Heraclitus and the artistic
instinct.

It is also not astonishing that Aristotle accuses Heraclitus of disobeying
the principle of noncontradiction by his enigmatic formulation that "every
thing at every time reunites all contraries in itself." But even when Heraclitus uses conceptual language, when intuition necessarily has to fail, he still
falls subject to the charge of inconsistency. Braving all logical contradiction, nonetheless, he uses the most incredible of all cosmic metaphors—the
world as the divine game of Zeus—to propose what is rationally inconceivable: the one is at the same time many. Zeus' game is that of the artist and
child who innocently create and destroy. The artistic instinct in life
ceaselessly gives birth to new worlds with as much freedom and necessity as
the game admits.

The fact that Aristotle charges the Presocratics with a "crime against
reason" reveals his own reductionist tendencies in reading previous
thinkers. Aristotle would then have had the privilege of realizing certain
truths that were only implicit in earlier philosophers—implicit meaning
potential, confused, obscure or unrecognized. Mythic philosophy contains a
hidden *logos* for Aristotle, one not yet articulated; it is the childhood of
philosophy. For Aristotle, metaphorical writing is no indication of an
affirmative and flourishing life; rather it signifies a lack of maturity, it is an
incomplete state. By reading the Presocratics in this way, Aristotle takes
away their originality, their personality, their resolute uniqueness, and
submits them to his own authority. The kind of reading by which Aristotle
absorbs the individuality of each philosopher into the identity of philosophy
as such—into Aristotle's own starting point—is the antinomy of that practiced by Nietzsche. After having been so long suspended in metaphysical
deafness (for the benefit of the clamoring "dwarfs," he says), Nietzsche
once again resumes the dialogue with the Presocratic "giants."

Nietzsche leaps the empty abyss: he goes beyond the Western philosophical tradition of Aristotle back to Heraclitus, where he takes up the
metaphor of world as game or play. He is the disciple who personally
re-enacts Presocratic philosophy by reversing the opposition between
metaphor and concept, by reinstating metaphor itself, after its eradication by
the concept and within the concept.[12] And since each philosopher is an
expression of the soil that gave him birth, the person who retraces his life's
thought must not do so by way of abstract and general concepts. Such a life

must not be abridged as in a handbook, for this would simply transform the philosopher into a phantom. On the contrary, one must bring the most typical aspects of his personality to life again with the aid of his own expressive and animated metaphors.

> A complete enumeration of all the transmitted doctrines, as it is the custom of the ordinary handbooks to give, has but one sure result: the complete silencing of personality. That is why those reports are so dull.
>
> I am going to emphasize only that point of each of their systems which constitutes a slice of *personality* and hence belongs to that incontrovertible, nondebatable evidence which it is the task of history to preserve. It is meant to be a beginning, by means of a comparative approach, toward the recovery and re-creation of certain ancient names, so that the polyphony of Greek nature at long last may resound once more.[13]

Instead of considering Presocratic philosophy to be a simple and im- pedimented speech that was gradually smoothed out by later Greek thought—as Aristotle does—Nietzsche finds a veritable break between the dawn of philosophy and its later development: the Presocratics belong to a rare type; they are irreducible to any other. To reconstitute their image, it is best "to paper the walls with them a thousand times." So it is in this sense that—instead of giving an "evolutionary" history of philosophy— Nietzsche proposes a typological reading.

We should portray or depict the Presocratics, then, but not by caricaturing them, not by "reducing" them in stature. The alternative of a simple résumé eradicates their personality, just as the concept does to the metaphor. Moreover, the relation between these two "eradications" is not a simple, analogical one: the forgetting of metaphor is the eradication of personality.

NOTES

1. *The Birth of Tragedy,* §3.
2. *On Music and Words* (fragment, 1871).
3. *Ibid.*
4. *BT,* §19. Nietzsche's aim of freeing music from the text could be related to that of Artaud, for whom the theater as total art—integrating music and dance—can escape the tyranny of the text. The theater of cruelty is also a theater without spectators, without players. On this, see J. Derrida, "La Parole soufflée," in *L'Écriture et la différence.*
5. *Twilight of the Idols;* "Skirmishes . . . ," §10.
6. *The Greek Musical Drama,* Lecture of 18 January 1870.
7. *Philosophy in the Tragic Age of the Greeks,* §3.

8. Aristotle, in *Poetics* 1457b, defined metaphor in the following way: "Metaphor is the application of an alien name by transference, either from genus to species or from species to genus, or from species to species, or by analogy."

9. *The Philosopher's Book;* "The Last Philosopher," §§53, 56.

10. Another genealogical test—ask yourself whether the author of a book knows how to dance, and if he can make his readers dance: "We do not belong to those who have ideas only among books, when stimulated by books. It is our habit to think outdoors—walking, leaping, climbing, dancing, preferably on lonely mountains or near the sea where even the trails become thoughtful. Our first questions about the value of a book, of a human being, or a musical composition are: Can they walk? Even more, can they dance?

"We read rarely, but not worse on that account. How quickly we guess how someone has come by his ideas; whether it was while sitting in front of his inkwell, with a pinched belly, his head bowed low over the paper—in which case we are quickly finished with his book, too! Cramped intestines betray themselves—you can bet on that—no less than closed air, closet ceilings, closet narrowness." *The Gay Science,* §366.

11. *PB;* "The Last Philosopher," §61. See also introduction to *La Naissance de la philosophie,* p. 17.

12. This is to say that the concept, which is itself produced by a metaphorical activity, plays a privileged role in the forgetting of metaphor—i.e., so far as it covers up the metaphorical character of the generalizing process by founding it on a general essence: the concept is responsible for metaphorical "falsehood" and "dishonesty." It stabilizes these processes by forgetting their very genesis, by forgetting all genesis. In Freudian terms, one could say that the concept plays the role of counter-cathexis, the force that maintains repression. Along with primary "forgetting," it brings about a secondary repression. Concepts permit the edification of a system of secondary and subsequent rationalizations, rationalizations that efface the founding character of metaphorical activity—namely, of what is found at the origin of all knowledge and activity. Thus, it is at the conceptual level that metaphorical activity becomes the most dissimulated and, hence, the most dangerous activity. In fact, the concept is neither an *a priori* idea nor the model we pretend it to be. It is a durable impression that becomes "fixed and hardened in the memory and is suited to a broad variety of phenomena; for this very reason it is quite inappropriate and inadequate to deal with any one phenomenon in particular."

Fixation and generalization are brought about by a series of metaphors. The point of departure, the "impression," is itself a metaphor, a transposition of nervous excitations (which vary according to the individual) that produces individual sensation-images in the symbolic language of one of the five senses. Next, and by an "unconscious reasoning from analogy," every new and foreign impression is metaphorically tied to previous ones by an "imitative" transfer. Imitation is the repetition of the perceived image by a thousand metaphors, all of which serve as so many analogues to it. Imitation discovers and restores resemblances while adapting to what is foreign and different. It makes all related images abound.

The third stage, marked by the imposition of words, is the passage to concepts as such. This is the passage from the analogous to the identical, from similarity to unity, and it implies the intervention of language and society as well as an "unjust" application of the principle of reason and of substance.

13. *PTAG*, Preface.

PART III
Transfiguration

When Nietzsche discusses the consequences of God's death, he describes the impending age as one of "breakdown, destruction, ruin, and cataclysm." But, at first sight, Nietzsche's benign attitude toward this nihilistic age of "gloom and eclipse" hardly seems warranted: "as regards ourselves," the prospects are "not at all sad and depressing, but rather like a new and indescribable variety of light, happiness, relief, enlivenment, encouragement, and dawning day . . . our heart overflows with gratitude, astonishment, presentiment and expectation." The old Sun wanes. It is a period of twilight—but also of a new dawn. "We are waiting," he says, "posted between today and tomorrow, and engirt by their contradiction." What would appear to be the joyous new light (sun, dawn, day) is certainly not any "divine" illumination—which even St. Augustine said, we rarely, if ever, see anyway. Perhaps it is not even a "natural" light. Indeed, the very dimness and pall of this "horizon" confronted Nietzsche with the idea of a new kind of optics. For Nietzsche, this was the effulgent light, the efflorescent vision, of a newly transformed self—and its source was the clairvoyance of a transfigured attitude.

Henri Birault addresses this issue of a transfigured human attitude in his essay "Beatitude in Nietzsche." He begins by raising the question whether an idea such as "beatitude" is really consistent with Nietzsche's main themes at all, since it would seem to be more of a conventionally "religious" issue. And, when beatitude is taken to mean a sort of spiritual "peace," it appears to seriously contradict the very foundations of Nietzsche's thought—e.g., the dynamic character of Will to Power, the continual process of self-overcoming wrought by the Overman, not to mention the "terrible burden" required by the doctrine of Eternal Recurrence. Even worse, the desire for anything such as "beatitude" seems motivated by the most extreme case of poverty, weakness, and wretched suffering. In short, the very idea of beatitude strikes of escapism: the morbid bliss of perpetual "sabbath," of stasis, of nihilism. Surely. Yet, by focusing on a brief passage from Nietzsche's posthumous work, Birault shows that there *is* a strictly Nietzschean idea of beatitude. But in this case, beatitude becomes the highest expression of a noble will, of an artistic creativity and superabundance—it suffers no constraints, and must no longer be conceived on the basis of indigence, lack, servility, and unhappiness. Rather, Nietzschean beatitude is a kind of "gratitude" for the plentitude and excess of existence itself. It is a joyous affirmation of chance and creativity *within* the "superior fatalism" of eternity. For Birault, beatitude becomes "the high point" of Nietzsche's meditation. Active and creative, it wills the eternalization of existence "in the moment," and at each moment.

Thomas Altizer sees Zarathustra as the prophet of a new historical destiny, one of Dionysian innocence and affirmation that follows the death of God. This would be a baptism of the instincts, a reversal of bad conscience; in short, a "resurrection of the body" and of all things. Together, this is Nietzsche's account of a "new creation," one meant to replace the Creator's creation—of a world apprehended in guilt, terror, and cruelty. Altizer finds Nietzsche's antipathy directed against ecclesiastical Christianity, and rightly so, but not against Christian *praxis* as such. Indeed, he sees the latter—the "evangelical" Jesus—forcefully expressed through Zarathustra's own "glad tidings." But Zarathustra no longer speaks about something promised or transcendent. Rather, he affirms the Dionysian life *within* the human subject. Thus, if the New Testament's "Kingdom of God"—the symbol of eternal life—was a contradiction to life, this can now be reversed. With Zarathustra's pronouncement of the Eternal Return, eternity is no longer conceived apart from time (as its transcendent antidote), but is identified with the human and historical passage of time itself. For Altizer, then, it is precisely by emptying the heavens that the Kingdom of God can appear once again, as immanent, as humanity's "second innocence."

By stressing the opposition between the Dionysian ideal and that of Pauline Christianity ("Dionysus *Versus* the Crucified"—the phrase is Nietzsche's), Paul Valadier argues that both positions share, at least implicitly, a common "religious" dimension. He sees this reflected in the attitude of their respective practitioners as well as in the fact that they address themselves to the same "totality" of existence. But unlike the Crucified, who doesn't want to die, Dionysus wills death—as the very condition for affirming life—the death that supposes the eternal recurrence of all existence. This is the tragic conception of life, wherein suffering is intrinsic to the very sanctity of life. It does not point to a realm of painless bliss beyond life, but rather opens up existence itself to the excess of chaos, to the image of the labyrinth. To enter this labyrinth is to lose oneself in a multitude of galaxies, in the endless play of metamorphosis. For Valadier, the Eternal Return is ultimately a reflection on the most profound nature of reality at the same time that it dispels the Christian form of nihilism, its "center of gravity." It is neither a return of resentment nor of nihilism's "once and for all," but of reaffirmation—of one time that wills a second time and an eternity of times.

Henri Birault

BEATITUDE IN NIETZSCHE

There is something paradoxical in choosing the idea of beatitude as an introduction to Nietzsche's thought. On the one hand, beatitude never presents itself as an introduction, but as a conclusion; it is not initial or initiating, but terminal or concluding. It is always at the end of a certain itinerary of the soul that we find it—as the recompense, the fine flower or beautiful mirage of a great labor achieved, a slow maturation, an old nostalgia. Logically, then, we should not begin with it; at most we might end with it.

But on the other hand, and especially because we are now concerned with the very legitimacy of the notion, we may justifiably ask what beatitude really has to do with Nietzsche's thought.

What are the fundamental concepts of his philosophy? Tradition distinguishes three: the Overman, the Eternal Return, and the Will to Power. The proper meaning and the logical (and even simply chronological) order of these three notions remain, even today, rather obscure. But at least one thing is clear: none of these three essential themes seems to have a direct relationship with beatitude. In connection with his thought, then, the idea that all the philosophies and religions of the world bring us of beatitude cannot fail to arouse immediate and perhaps invincible resistances in the informed Nietzschean.

The relatively well-informed Nietzschean easily forgets the Eternal Return and immediately wonders how one could ever reconcile the inevitable peace of beatitude with the idea of unlimited overcoming evoked by the theme of the Overman ("a bridge and not a goal," an arrow and not a target) and by that of the Will to Power—which, likewise, is always a will to *more* power.

The well-informed Nietzschean, however, remembers the religious or "evangelical" character of the doctrine of the Eternal Return.[1] And he distrusts beatitude, for he recalls that Nietzsche does not want to pour new wine into old vessels; he knows that the religion in this religion is formally different from that in all other religions—as essentially, substantially different as the joyous knowledge of tragic wisdom in its form and content is different from all the other kinds of wisdom, as different as the fifth gospel, that of Zarathustra, is from the other four. He knows that the Will to Power does not open upon, does not sink into the *amor fati* or the thought of the Eternal Return, finding in it something like the rest of the Seventh Day. For the Eternal Return is as much the *terminus a quo* as the *terminus ad quem* of the Will to Power—the Eternal Return is the "heaviest burden" that only the strongest of men can endure. In this sense, the Will to Power is the condition for the Eternal Return. But on the other hand, with this thought is produced "the greatest elevation of the consciousness of strength in man, as he creates the Overman."[2] In this sense it is the thought of the Eternal Return that is now the condition for the Will to Power, conferring upon it that increase of force through which it can create the Overman. In the end, Heidegger is right when he writes: "The Will to Power is, in its essence and according to its internal possibility, the eternal return of the same."[3]

Thus, the commentator who endeavors to think not *like* Nietzsche (foolish project, impossible imitation!) but to think *with* Nietzsche what Nietzsche wished to conceive—this commentator comes to disengage little by little the underlying, still enigmatic unity of the three themes. But everything that brings him closer to this unity seems to take him further from beatitude, for is it not true that at the very moment and in the very place that Nietzsche announces this sublime religion, he also asks us to have "tested all the degrees of skepticism" and to have "bathed with pleasure in icy torrents"? Otherwise, he says, "you will have no right to this thought. . . . I will be *on my guard,"* Nietzsche continues, "against credulous and exalted minds."[4] And where is there more credulousness and greater exaltation, or at least greater *risk* of credulousness and exaltation, than in beatitude? If, as Nietzsche repeats several times, the doctrine of the Eternal Return is to be considered "as a hammer in the hands of the most powerful man"—how can there be contained in this most hammering and hammered-out doctrine anything that is still in any way close to what we call beatitude? How can the philosopher who philosophizes with a hammer ever be blissful, *agapé,* or *beatus?*

"I am bitterly opposed," Nietzsche writes, "to all teachings that look to an end, a peace, a 'Sabbath of Sabbaths.' Such modes of thought indicate fermenting, suffering, often even morbid breeds. . . ."[5]

Why this animosity toward beatitude? Perhaps because Nietzsche perceives the abyss that separates true happiness from beatitude. Happiness (but not the happiness of the "last man," that bastard form of beatitude) arises out of chance, hazard, accident, events, fortune, the fortuitous. Beatitude is not the height of, but the opposite of, this free and gratuitous happiness. The concern for beatitude expresses the will to conjure away that part of contingency that is the very essence of happiness. The man of beatitude no longer wishes to be exposed to the thousand blows of fortune, to the stupor and the rending that happiness as well as unhappiness provoke, both of them always unwonted and rather monstrous. He wishes to have his feet on the ground once and for all. It is not enough for him to be happy; he wishes to be blissful, he wishes to rest in the certainty of the *unum necessarium*. He wishes to die, to sleep, and this eternal rest and sleep he calls eternal life and eternal bliss! Thus beatitude saves us—it works our salvation, we save ourselves, we flee from ourselves, we are no longer here below. A phenomenon of withdrawal, flight, and resentment, beatitude always wants the unconditioned, the absolute, the eternal; it refuses, it impugns the tender, innocent, puerile cruelty of chance; it casts an evil eye on all the favors and disfavors of existence. It says *no* to life.

The man who seeks beatitude is the man with an *idée fixe,* a solid block with one sole love, one sole god, one sole faith—a barbarian, in fact. "Love of *one* is a barbarism: for it is exercised at the expense of all else. The love of God, too."[6] To this monoideism, this monotheism, this "monotono-theism" (Nietzsche's expression), incapable for two thousand years of inventing a single new god,[7] Nietzsche constantly opposed a spirit of aristocratic tolerance, the virile and military (but not "militant") skepticism of those in whom the creative instinct for new gods awakens. The man seeking beatitude has finally entered the temple *(fanum)*, the unique temple of virtue, truth, and felicity—curiously enough identified. How can such a man not be a fanatic? But fanaticism, always the symptom of a weak and servile will, is precisely what prevents us from becoming creators; he alone, Nietzsche says, is capable of creating who no longer believes in anything. "I no longer believe in anything—such is the right way of thinking of the creative man."[8]

Thus, against "sabbatical" beatitude, and in the shadow of perfect nihilism, Nietzsche inaugurates a new alliance: that of heroic sentiments and warlike skepticism, of military discipline and scientific discipline, of the true creator and the noble traitor to knowledge. To everything that gapes in beatitude Nietzsche opposes the openness of an ever openended creation: to the Buddha's smile, Dionysus' demented laughter; to the man in search of beatitude, priest of his ideal, the Overman who is its master; to priesthood, mastery; to the spirit of faith, which is the subsiding or downward inclination of creation, the strange conjunction of love and scorn; to intuitive, infused, diffused, confused science, the perception, the sentiment, the "pathos of distance," and the clear gaze of him who no longer wishes to know other abysses than the "abysses of light;" to the ancient will to find the true, the young will to create it. At the same time the form, the very essence of this will is modified. It no longer has any moorings, any anchorage, anything more to lose, anything more to ask; it is finally left only for this will to be generous, imperial, legislating, ordaining, sense-giving. Precisely because there is no longer any being, any truth in things, everything must be given to this will; it does not give itself or lose itself in its gifts. It gives meaning because essences are dead; it creates values because there are no longer any existing values: it gives birth to new gods because there is no longer any God. And thus, Nietzsche writes, Nihilism as the negation of a true world, of a being, might indeed be a divine way of thinking. [9] It *might* be, Nietzsche says—but it is not yet so. . . .

For the image of solid earth Nietzsche substitutes that of the sea, a sea that he says was never full enough; to homesickness—a sickness that is indeed philosophy itself (philosophy is a true homesickness, Novalis said)—he opposes "the longing for a land without homeland." Since, in the end, the instinct for beatitude is only a death instinct, how can we still speak of beatitude in Nietzsche?

Now, then, we will attempt the impossible: we will try to find a certain idea of beatitude in Nietzsche. What path shall we take? The narrowest path. We will not compile all the passages in which Nietzsche speaks in positive terms of beatitude and, for example, of the happiness of forgetfulness, of the "blessed isles," of involuntary beatitude, etc. No, we will choose but three lines from the posthumous writings to try to acquire a necessarily narrow, not necessarily superficial, view of Nietzschean beatitude. These few lines are: "What must I do to be happy? That I know not, but I say to you: Be happy, and then do what you please." [10]

According to the chronology set up by Nietzsche's editors, this fragment dates from 1882–84. Let us accept this hypothesis and consider the text in itself—first the aphoristic form of the text.

There is a question and an answer. The question is presumably that of a disciple, who presumably questions a master; the answer is that of a man who does not know given to a man who is presumed to know. The answer itself is composed essentially of two propositions: an admission of ignorance, this time a very explicit admission on the part of the master, and the declaration of a new maxim. Between the two, there is the transitional formula, "But I say to you."

The interplay of question and answer, and, in the answer, the mixture of ignorance and knowledge, modesty and prophecy, cannot fail to evoke in a rather troubling way the two hitherto most venerable forms of dialogue: the Socratic and the evangelical.

What is Socratic is, of course, first the apparent ignorance of the master, and then the apparent irony of an answer that does not answer the question raised, and finally the stupor and silence of the disciple before this paradoxical way to answer, which cannot satisfy him and to which he can still find nothing to say.

What is more evangelical than Socratic is that the initiative of the question comes from the disciple and not from the master; the question is put to a master who is not interrogating, but is first taciturn and then dogmatic enough. And what is frankly evangelical is the "But I say to you," which obviously echoes the distinctive *"sed dico vobis."*

The form of this passage is already instructive, for it has the twofold character, both metaphysical and evangelical, of Nietzsche's teaching. We must therefore consider it a little more closely before examining the content or the basis of the text.

Nietzsche presents himself often, on the one hand, as a philosopher of a new kind (''misosopher'' as much as philosopher) and even as a metaphysician (a metaphysician, however, who is an enemy of all the worlds behind the scenes), and, on the other hand, as the messenger, the spokesman, the evangelist of news that could at last be the *good* news. His thought is thus, for example, said to be a *"Künstler Metaphysik"* and an *"Artisten Evangelium"* (an artist-metaphysics and an artist-gospel). This metaphysico-evangelical ambiguity of Nietzschean thought raises problems, for what *is* metaphysics? It is the ontological science of immutable being, of the eternal essence of all that is; it is the onto-theological science of the first principles and the first causes; it is the catholic and radical science of the *omnitudo realitatis.* And what is a gospel? It is the announcement of a blessed event, of good news, of something fundamentally historical—deeds and gestures of the man or the man-God that concern the destiny of men. But this announcement, the news of this deed, this knowledge by hearsay—all this does not have much to do with metaphysical speculation. Will we then have to choose between a ''metaphysical'' interpretation and an ''evangelical'' interpretation of Nietzsche's doctrine? Will we have to try to elaborate some patchwork compromise between these two possible readings? No; we should rather remember that Nietzsche wishes to rework both the form of metaphysics and the form of religion, and that this reworking is to be so profound that it will end by destroying even the possibility of such a compromise.

Nietzsche can say, for example, that the Will to Power is the essence of the world and present at the same time, and infinitely more modestly, this same Will to Power as a new fixation—a holding down, an arresting—of the concept of life.[11] It is ''the last fact back to which we can come.'' Here the word ''fact'' represents nothing else than the last instance, the final jurisdiction to which we can address ourselves to judge what life is about—or, rather, what it *could* be about.

No essence, as we see, is then lodged in the heart of things; ''essence'' is not something eidetic or ontological. On the contrary, it is the result of a certain subsumption, a certain schematization, a certain imposition—the imposition of a meaning, the assessment of a price; in the end, a fundamentally human appreciation, an estimation. This is why, far from being the in-itself or the true, ''essence'' is a view, a perspective, a position taken with regard to the thing on the basis of something other than itself: ''The question 'what is that?' is an imposition of meaning from some other viewpoint. 'Essence,' the 'essential nature,' is something perspective.''[12]

This is also true for a *fact,* which at bottom is nothing else than the little in-itself with which the positivist physicists are ready to content them-

selves.[13] It too is not simply self-made; it too *is not:* on the contrary, it is
always the result of a certain setting up, the montage of a certain experience.
A fact is never a mere fact, "stupid like a calf," Nietzsche says. It can only
interest us; more, it only begins to be "produced" when it speaks. But in fact
the facts never speak all by themselves, they always have to be made to
speak a language that can only be *our* language; in short, we have to
intervene to interpret them.

To conceive an essence as a meaning, a substance as an instance, and a
fact as always "made" is to move toward bringing about a certain *rapprochement* between metaphysics and the gospel. What the essence has lost,
the word—a certain word that at bottom is a will—will recuperate. The
gospel is the announcement of a deed or exploit: this news, this announcement of itself, gives configuration to a certain history, a certain truth, always
without foundation, but not necessarily always without value. Here the most
"prosaic" saying is essentially "poetic," because it is fundamentally action
and creation: it gives form to what is formless, meaning to what is meaningless, and being to what has no being; it is a veritable creation *ex nihilo*—that
is, here, out of nihilism. In Nietzsche, to name things is always the privilege
of the dominant classes, the creators, the legislators—in short, the masters,
who teach and command by virtue of their word alone. The true master is
both lord and teacher, despot and pedagogue: he states the elementary things
and institutes them by stating them, and asks us to repeat them in order to
instruct ourselves.

Zarathustra says: "I teach you the Overman! The Overman is the meaning
of the earth. Your will says: the Overman is the meaning of the earth." The
Overman is the meaning of the earth, and yet it is necessary that the will *state*
this meaning in order that the being of meaning become the meaning of
being.

What is meaning? It is the last residue of essences in a nihilistic philosophy. What is meaning? Meaning is a certain "wishing to say" that we
ascribe to things—a desire to say that *is,* and yet must be stated in order that it
be. What is meaning? It is also the direction, the goal, the end, that which
things are on their way to, where they wish to come to, the last word of their
history, this becoming that is their being, this being that is their becoming.

The saying that Zarathustra gives and commends to his disciples is always
the saying of a will that orders, the saying of those genuine philosophers
who, Nietzsche assures us, command and legislate: "They say, 'thus it *shall*
be!' "[14] Here what must be is what will be in any case, and yet what
nonetheless can be *only* through the force of this will that states: a strange
situation, in which meaning is and nonetheless is *only* if it is uttered. Thus,
the word that states the meaning is here clearly ascribed to the will, and not to
the understanding or to reason. This word is still *logos,* but in this imperious
and ordaining *logos* there is now something that is akin to the *deka logoi* of

the Decalogue. In Nietzsche, as in the Bible, the word is the scepter of power. And meaning, in turn, is a function of power

But on the other hand, this will that states and dictates the form and the truth is in no way arbitrary. It is fully a will and a Will to Power only when it wills what is, when it loves the necessary: then it conceives itself as a destiny or a fatality, a storm or lightning bolt of truth. *Ego fatum,* Nietzsche often says, always conscious of the profound identity of the will (here the *ego*) and of necessity (here the *fatum*). The perfect will is delivered from the caprices of desire, and destiny, for its part, is no longer (as Leibniz put it) a "Turkish fate" *(fatum mahumetanum)*. Meaning is only for the will, and the will is only for meaning. Thus the authentic master of the philosopher is indeed the evangelical metaphysician, Nietzsche says: Caesar with the soul of Christ. It is such a master who speaks in the aphorism we have chosen. It is time to hear his words.

What does the master say—or rather, what does the disciple ask? He asks: "What must I do in order to become happy or blissful?" If the master does not answer this question, he nevertheless understands it. His silence is not that of distraction, but that of meditation and voluntary abstention. The proof of this is that in time he admits that he does not know what to answer, and this admission itself shows, on the one hand, the attention given the question, and, on the other hand, the distance that Nietzsche means to put between this demand and his own teaching.

Let us then first try to perceive the stress of the question, and, through the stress, the type of man who speaks. Nietzsche is and wishes to be a psychologist; let us then work out the psychology of the questioner, a psychology or psychoanalysis that in his eyes constitutes the sole genuine analysis of the question. There is no mistaking it: the stress of this question is the stress of distress, and the man who speaks here is an unhappy man who asks what he must do in order to be unhappy no longer. What, then, is the question? It is at bottom the oldest question in the world, the question that has fed all the religions and all the philosophies we know—all of them daughters of a poverty that seeks to evade its situation, to save itself from its poverty—daughters of a suffering that can no longer suffer its suffering. Philosophies of poverty, poverty of philosophy! Religions *of* suffering— they are always anxious to relieve the suffering from which they proceed, and that at the highest cost, the cost of death and sacrifice, the cost of a sublime and subtle cruelty, and hence at the price of an excess of suffering, a suffering "more profound, more inward, more poisonous, more deadly— but calming, reassuring, redemptive in spite of everything, because through it the primal pain of life is finally interpreted, justified, systematized, ordered, put into perspective: into the perspective of fault. Man suffered still and could suffer even more: he suffered because of . . . , through the fault of. . . . The pain henceforth had a cause, a reason, an end, a why, and this *meaning* allowed the *essential* to be saved—that is, the will, at least a certain will, that which wills the meaning of suffering because first it considers suffering an accident, a stumbling block, something that is but should not be and that elsewhere, in another world, another life, another nature, would *not* be. This will, avid for meaning, we see, is at bottom a will for annihilation, a will that begins by saying "no" to existence, to our meaningless, immoral, unreasonable existence. Revolt or resignation—what difference?—it is always first resentment, and also always first aversion to suffering. And yet this will to annihilation, this will to nothingness that generates the ascetic ideal, is something quite different from a nothingness of will: "It is and remains a *will,*" and, as Nietzsche says, in conclusion "man would rather will *nothingness* than *not* will."[15]

Given this, why does the master not answer the question? Why does he remain deaf to the disciple's anxiety—not the anxiety of suffering (for man is the animal who calls for the most suffering, and in the end the animal that suffers most because he is the most courageous, and not the most courageous because he suffers the most), but, much more prosaically, the anxiety of this man *tired* of suffering, this candidate for beatitude, a rather insipid beatitude? "What must I do to become happy? That I know not!" Why this nonknowing, and this assurance and placidity in not knowing? Perhaps first, quite simply, because there is in the end never anything to say to the man who, being unhappy, asks what he has to do to become happy. Perhaps no action can ever make us pass imperceptibly from unhappiness to happiness, from the present reality of this unhappiness that *is* to the becoming of happiness that *is not yet*. Vanity of all those discourses! Vanity of all those practices, of all those becomings! Perhaps there is, strictly speaking, nothing to do to become happy when one is not already happy; perhaps there is no transition possible, but rather indeed an abrupt mutation, a qualitative leap, an instantaneous conversion—or, again, and to speak a more precisely Nietzschean language (one more in accord with that "intellectuality of suffering" Nietzsche continually insists on), a sudden change of outlook, of evaluation, of interpretation, of perspective?

Yet there is something else in this admission of ignorance on the part of the master. There is the will to establish distance from all the traditional philosophies, and, at the same time, the still unspoken elaboration of a new philosophy, or rather of a new manner of philosophizing: the joyous knowing—no longer the ascending knowing, but the declining knowing; no longer the knowing that rises from unhappiness toward happiness, but the knowing that descends, that overflows, that pours out of the over-full cup, the over-ripe cluster, the over-rich star: a primal abundance and superabundance, joyous and painful, of a Dionysian wisdom and beatitude! This joyous knowing, this tragic wisdom, has no connection with the question that has been put. The absence of a "response" is here the absence of a "correspondence." To respond to a question is always in the end to answer *for* the question—that is, to assume it, to take charge of it, to take "responsibility" for it. Nietzsche refuses this community of thought, its poverty and hope. That is why he keeps silence; that is also why he declares (and this time not without some pride) his resolute ignorance, his *will* to not know.

The beatitude that the unhappy man wishes to attain is that vesperal beatitude that Nietzsche calls an ideal state of laziness.[16] To those sabbatical, hedonist, or Buddhist philosophers, those philosophers of the setting sun, those essentially reclining philosophers, Nietzsche opposes the philosophy of the morning and the midday, the standing philosophers, the men of the great north, "We Hyperboreans."

The Hyperboreans mock happiness and virtue, all the promised lands, the paths and the threads capable of taking us to this beatitude that has lost its first "terrorist" breath and today is nothing but the happiness of the last man.

> But I ask you, gentlemen, what have we to do with happiness? What matters to us your virtue (the new way to happiness)? Why do we hold ourselves back? To become philosophers, rhinoceroses, cave bears, phantoms? Is it not to *rid ourselves* of virtue and happiness? We are by nature much too happy, much too virtuous not to experience a little temptation, to become immoralists and adventurers. We are especially curious to explore the labyrinth, we try to make acquaintance with Mr. Minotaur, about whom they tell such terrible things; but what matters to us your way that *ascends,* your thread that leads out, that leads to happiness and to virtue, that leads *to you,* I fear . . . You wish to save us with the aid of this thread? And we—we pray you earnestly, lose this thread![17]

There is always, in the same sense of this solar and glacial, divine and infernal wisdom,

> . . . preoccupation with itself and with its "eternal salvation" [that] is not the expression of a rich and self-confident type; for that type does not give a damn about its salvation—it has no such interest in happiness of any kind; it is force, deed, desire—it imposes itself on things, it lays violent hands on things. Christianity is romantic hypochondria of those whose legs are shaky. Wherever the hedonist perspective comes into the foreground one may infer suffering and a type that represents a failure,[18]

The man who persists in saying, *"But I say to you . . ."* is a philosopher of a new kind. His doctrine is hyperborean: it is no longer a question of knowing what one must do to avoid unhappiness; it is now a question of letting everything that can issue forth from happiness do so. The "but" is the sign of this conversion.

What does the master say? He says: "Be happy or blissful and do what you please." The response is cavalier; it supposes the problem solved: in fact, the terms have been reversed. In the old perspective—that of Plato and of Hegel—desire, will, love, action, labor all proceeded from unhappiness, indigence, lack, need, hunger, appetite—in short, from negativity. Correlatively, happiness presented itself as the fulfillment, the contentment of this void, the release of this tension, the solution or the dissolution of what first presented itself as insoluble. In short, to will was fundamentally to will to will no more. Happiness was always at the end of the road—for tomorrow, for the day after tomorrow, for our children, our grandchildren, in another world, in another life. . . . Of course, this happiness could begin even now, but it never made anything but a timid beginning. Of course, we might find a certain happiness in preparing our happiness, but this transitional happiness was not yet the true happiness, beatitude.

In saying "be happy," Nietzsche shows himself a thousand times more impatient: what he wants is the whole of happiness and not only its premises, and this whole he wants at once. All happiness and at once—or else never! "Midday of life, second youth! Summer garden." Impatient happiness, under arrest, on the alert, looking forward.

We can now measure the abyss that separates these two apparently similar maxims: to make one's happiness, and to be happy. (But does not Nietzsche himself say that the narrowest abysses are the most difficult to cross?) Nietzsche implicitly opposes the baseness of the man who wishes to make his happiness, to prepare his beatitude, and to operate his salvation to the nobility of the man who has understood the grandeur of this new commandment: Be happy, blissful, eternally happy at the very heart of happiness, of one sole instant of happiness; at the very heart of unhappiness, of an abyss of unhappiness.

Happiness of adventure, happiness of the adventurer, to be sure—chance remains king, the contingency of happiness is intact. But it is also happiness in rest, perfect happiness, accomplished happiness—though still and always open—dazzling affirmation that no desire will ever more tarnish, and yet chaotic and creative affirmation. The identification of happiness and beatitude with that height, that depth of thought can be well understood only on the basis of another identification, that which this simple sentence of Nietzsche expresses: "Supreme fatalism, nonetheless identical with chance and creative activity (no repetition in things, but one has to first create it)."[19]

The master goes on: "Be happy, and then do what you please." This means that, on the basis of beatitude, all desires are sanctified. He who would interpret in terms of facility this last proposition would be very mistaken. The precept is as strict as, even more strict than, those of all the old moralities; it does not open the way to all our desires—on the contrary, it closes the door to almost everything that up to now has been called love, desire, or will. All desires that proceed from unhappiness, from lack, indigence, envy, hatred are condemned. If Nietzsche's philosophy is not a new philosophy but a new way to philosophize, it is just because of this revolution worked in the very form or essence of desire. While the *sophia* changes its content, the *philein* changes its form. It is not a question of desiring other things or of desiring the same things by other means; it is a question of desiring all things in another way—the material and the spiritual, the good and the bad, for ourselves and for others.

What will this new desire be? And what will this new doing be? What can we will to desire and to do when we are blissful? Nothing. Such is the response that the disciple might make in his turn to the master's answer. And this reponse would be a new misunderstanding. The master's command is neither hedonist nor quietist. The master does not say to the disciple, "Do anything whatever," and he also does not tell him, "Do nothing." He rather tells him that it is only out of the over-fullness of his beatitude that all the desires and all the actions that please him can flow. Thus desire now has as its father (or rather its mother) wealth, and no longer poverty; action is the child of happiness and no longer of unhappiness; beatitude is initial and no longer terminal.

What will this desire be? Nietzsche tells us in *Zarathustra* that it will be the "great desire," that which wishes to give and no longer to take, to thank and no longer ask, to bless and no longer supplicate. Of this desire Nietzsche says, "All desire wills eternity—wills deep, deep eternity."

This desire wills eternity, but *what* eternity? Not an eternity that is beyond or above becoming, an eternity that casts an evil eye on the instant that passes, but, on the contrary, the eternity, the eternalization of what is and what is *at this very instant*. The blissful man has made his peace with reality. He is happy from what is and with what is, with the very brevity of the instant that passes. He does not demand the prolongation or the nonlimitation of this instant in time. To tell the truth, he does not demand anything at all; he orders, he wills that this instant return as it is, in its very fleetingness, an eternity of times. It is then not a mere coincidence that the fragment upon which we are commenting is contemporary with the time when Nietzsche conceived the doctrine of the Eternal Return of the same.

We can also understand that the "doing" issuing out of this beatitude is, in turn, totally foreign to the most traditionally admitted forms of action and praxis. The blissful man is more concerned with creating than with acting; or, rather, the sole action that seems to him to be at the height of his beatitude is precisely creation, that labor of creation which is that of child-bearing. A surprising word, one that seems to contradict what we have just said, affirming that the happy man rejoices over being, and, finally, over the becoming of things. This surprise rests, however, in the failure to recognize an essential difference between action and creation—or, more precisely, between action conceived in terms of Platonic, Hegelian, Marxist, or Sartrean (as one prefers) negativity, and creation as Nietzsche conceives it—that is, in essentially affirmative and playful terms, and this at the very moment when he associates it with destruction (but always under the aegis of love, of love that rejoices over what is).

Let us observe first, in general, that a philosophy of action is not necessarily a philosophy of creation, just as, conversely, a philosophy of creation (such as that of Bergson, for example) is not necessarily a philosophy of action. In reality, action is something quite different from a nascent creation, and creation for its part is something quite different from a fully developed action. It would perhaps not force Nietzsche's thought too much if we said that, for him, the principal source of all that we call action today is hatred for or discontent with what is, while every veritable creation proceeds from love and love only, from an immense gratitude for what is, a gratitude that seeks to impress the seal of eternity on what is and what, for Nietzsche, is always only in becoming. This is why the desire that wills eternity is an essentially creative desire, the extreme, playful, and artistic form of the Will to Power. It is then that the will becomes love, without ceasing to be will and Will to Power. It is then that this love becomes the love of the necessary, *"amor fati,"* without ceasing to be love and will for the contingency of the most contingent things. It is then that beatitude is beatitude in the heaven of chance, innocence and a fully positive indetermination. In this Dionysian beatitude, necessity is reconciled with chance, eternity with the instant, being with becoming—but all that outside of time, its lengths, its progress, its moments, its mediations. Speaking of this "recapitulation," in which the world of becoming comes extremely close to that of being—a "recapitulation that the doctrine of the Eternal Return alone can accomplish—we see that it is not for nothing that Nietzsche calls it the "high point of the meditation."[20]

NOTES

1. "This thought contains more than all religions that teach us to regard this life as evanescent and directed to an indefinite *other* life." It will be, Nietzsche says further, "the religion of the freest, happiest, most composed souls—a lovely place between gilded iron and pure heaven." Kröner; XII; part I, §132.

2. *The Will to Power,* §1060.

3. Martin Heidegger, *Nietzsche* (Pfullingen: Verlag Günther Neske, 1961), I, p. 467.

4. K, XII; part I, §132.

5. *The Innocence of Becoming;* Kröner ed., II, p. 342.

6. *Beyond Good and Evil,* §67.

7. "Almost two thousand years—and not a single new god." *The Antichrist*, §19.

8. K, XII: part II, §68.

9. "To this extent, nihilism, as the denial of a truthful world, of being, might be *a divine way of thinking*." *WP*, §15.

10. K, XII; part II, §274.

11. *WP*, §617.

12. *WP*, §556.

13. *WP*, §481: "Against positivism, which halts at phenomena—'there are only *facts*'—I would say: No, facts are precisely what there is not, only interpretations."

14. *BGE*, §211.

15. *The Genealogy of Morals;* III, §28.

16. *WP*, §335.

17. K, XVI; pp. 439–40.

18. *WP*, §781.

19. *IB;* II, p. 492.

20. *WP*, §617.

Thomas J. J. Altizer

ETERNAL RECURRENCE
AND KINGDOM OF GOD

Nietzsche's Zarathustra is a product of the Second Innocence of atheism, the new historical destiny created by the death of God. Man has been surpassed in Zarathustra, for Zarathustra has negated all previous history, and this negation is but the obverse of the deepest affirmation. As Nietzsche declares in *Ecce Homo:*

> The psychological problem in the type of Zarathustra is how he that says No and *does* No to an unheard-of degree, to everything to which one has so far said Yes, can nevertheless be the opposite of a No-saying spirit; how the spirit who bears the heaviest fate, a fatality of a task, can nevertheless be the lightest and most transcendent—Zarathustra is a dancer—how he that has the hardest, most terrible insight into reality, that has thought the "most abysmal idea," nevertheless does not consider it an objection to existence, not even to its eternal recurrence—but rather one reason more for being himself the eternal Yes to all things, "the tremendous, unbounded . . . Yes and Amen"—"Into all abysses I still carry the blessings of . . . saying Yes"—*But this is the concept of Dionysus once again.*[1]

Zarathustra calls his hearers to a new Dionysian existence, an existence of total yes-saying to the sheer horror of a naked reality that is first revealed by Zarathustra and that can only be understood by a reversal of no-saying: Nietzsche's most profound symbol of the meaning of history. If, as Nietzsche taught, bad conscience came into existence with the advent of history and originated with the interiorization or internalization *(Verinnerlichung)* of the instincts, with the birth of a "soul" opposed to the "body," then Dionysian existence demands a baptism of the instincts, a new innocence created by the sanctification of the forbidden. In short, Zarathustra calls for the resurrection of the body.

Nietzsche confessed that he chose the name of Zarathustra for his prophet of Eternal Recurrence because he believed that the Persian prophet Zarathustra created the first moral vision of the world: "the transposition of morality into the metaphysical realm, as a force, cause, and end in itself, is *his* work."[2] Now Nietzsche, the first "immoralist," has created the exact opposite of the historical Zarathustra: "The self-overcoming of morality, out of truthfulness; the self-overcoming of the moralist into his opposite—into me—that is what the name of Zarathustra means in my mouth."[3] Eternal Recurrence as the self-overcoming of morality? The self-overcoming not of self-righteousness or goodness itself? Through Zarathustra's self-overcoming, morality undergoes a metamorphosis and appears as the spirit of revenge: "the will's ill will against time and its 'it was.' "[4] The life that Zarathustra promises is a life that will bring "it was" to an end:

> To redeem those who lived in the past and to re-create all "it was" into a "thus I willed it"—that alone should I call redemption. Will—that is the name of the liberator and joy-bringer; thus I taught you, my friends. But now learn this too: the will itself is still a prisoner. Willing liberates; but what is it that puts even the liberator himself in fetters? "It was"—that is the name of the will's gnashing of teeth and most secret melancholy. Powerless against what has been done, he is an angry spectator of all that is past. The will cannot will backwards; and that he cannot break time and time's covetousness, that is the will's loneliest melancholy.[5]

Can there be any doubt as to the Biblical identity of this "it was"? We have only to listen once again to the opening words of the Bible to be assured of this.

> In the beginning God created the heaven and the earth. And the earth was without form, and void; and darkness *was* upon the face of the deep. And the Spirit of God moved upon the face of the waters. And God said, Let there be light: and there was light. And God saw the light, that it *was* good: and God divided the light from the darkness. And God called the light Day, and the darkness he called Night. And the evening and the morning were the first day.

The "first day" of creation was the day when God divided the light from the darkness, a division following His perception of the goodness of the light that He had created. But darkness existed before the creation; hence, it was not created by God, and the reader can only conclude that in some sense it is an "other" of God. In the primeval chaos or void, darkness *was* upon the face of the deep, and it was upon that face that God moved when He created light. God saw that the light was good, and clearly this light is the opposite of darkness. Even though for two millennia Christian theologians have declared that these words deny all ultimate forms of dualism, it would be idle to pretend that a dichotomy does not lie at the center of this myth. Can it be that it is "Zarathustra" and not "Moses" who is the first of our prophets?

Of course, *Isaiah II* and *Job* and not *Genesis* are the real ground and source of the Biblical understanding of God the Creator. *Isaiah II* comforts his people by speaking of the glory of the Lord:

> Have ye not known? have ye not heard?
> Have ye not understood from the foundations of the earth?
> It is he that sitteth upon the circle of the earth,
> And the inhabitants thereof are as grasshoppers;
> That stretcheth out the heavens as a curtain,
> And spreadeth them out as a tent to dwell in:
> That bringeth the princes to nothing;
> He maketh the judges of the earth as vanity . . .
> He calleth them all by names
> By the greatness of his might,
> For that *he is* strong in power;
> Not one faileth.

To speak of God the Creator is to speak of the absolute sovereignty of God that can appear only as an infinitely distant transcendence, which reduces the earth to insignificance. Moreover, to know that God is the Creator is to know the ultimate impotence of man, as *Job* makes clear.

> Then the Lord answered Job out of the whirlwind, and said . . .
> Where was thou when I laid the foundations of the earth?
> Declare, if thou hast understanding.
> Who hath laid the measures thereof, if thou knowest?
> Or who hath stretched the line upon it?
> Whereupon are the foundations thereof fastened?
> Or who laid the corner stone thereof;
> When the morning stars sang together,
> And all the sons of God shouted for Job?

Christianity knows God as the Creator, as the absolutely sovereign and transcendent Lord—what Nietzsche called the maximum god attained so far. But this maximum god, for Nietzsche, was accompanied by a maximum feeling of guilt, and was, indeed, the product of a madness of the will, the will of man to find himself totally and finally guilty. Of man's ultimate act of projection, Nietzsche says,

> . . . he ejects from himself all his denial of himself, of his nature, naturalness, and actuality, in the form of an affirmation, as something existent, corporeal, real, as God, as the holiness of God, as God the Judge, as God the Hangman, as the beyond, as eternity, as torment without end, as hell, as the immeasurability of punishment and guilt.[6]

While beyond any doubt Nietzsche judged this projection to be sickness, it is not an illusory sickness, as an earlier passage in *The Genealogy of Morals* makes manifest:

> At this point I can no longer avoid giving a first, provisional statement of my own hypothesis concerning the origin of the "bad conscience": it may sound rather strange and needs to be pondered, lived with, and slept on for a long time. I regard the bad conscience as the serious illness that man was bound to contract under the stress of the most fundamental change he ever experienced—that change which occurred when he found himself finally enclosed within the walls of society and of peace. The situation that faced sea animals when they were compelled to become land animals or perish was the same as that which faced these semi-animals, well adapted to the wilderness, to war, to prowling, to adventure: suddenly all their instincts were disvalued and "suspended." From now on they had to walk on their feet and "bear themselves" whereas hitherto they had been borne by the water: a dreadful heaviness lay upon them. They felt unable to cope with the simplest undertakings; in this new world they no longer possessed their former guides, their regulating, unconscious, and infallible drives: they were reduced to thinking, inferring, reckoning, coordinating cause and effect, these unfortunate creatures; they were reduced to their "consciousness," their weakest and most fallible organ! I believe there has never been such a feeling of misery on earth, such a leaden discomfort.[7]

Now, these words may well be as close as Nietzsche ever came to rewriting the opening page of the Bible. Certainly they give a new and decisive meaning to the "first day" of creation, and likewise they give an "innocent" meaning to the primordial division between light and darkness.

But is this meaning truly innocent? If the advent of man—of pure consciousness—is identical with the *internalization* of man, of the birth of a "soul" that is other than the body—then, in Nietzschean language, one may truly speak of creation as "fall." Here, the original fall would mean a primordial division between light and darkness, between "soul" and body that establishes a dichotomy at the center of life and existence. With the birth of consciousness, what Nietzsche calls our unconscious and infallible drives become reduced to thought or consciousness, and hence are no longer describable in terms of their original identity. Or, rather, they are describable only in the negative language of "bad conscience":

> The entire inner world, originally as thin as if it were stretched between two membranes, expanded and extended itself, acquired depth,

breadth, and height, in the same measure as outward discharge was *inhibited*. Those fearful bulwarks with which the political organization protected itself against the old instincts of freedom—punishments belong among these bulwarks—brought it about that all those instincts of wild, free, prowling man turned backward *against man himself*. Hostility, cruelty, joy in persecuting, in attacking, in change, in destruction—all this turned against the possessors of such instincts: *that* is the origin of the "bad conscience."[8]

Nor did bad conscience come into existence by way of a gradual and organic adaption to new conditions. On the contrary, it was the consequence of a fall, a sudden fall. Thus Nietzsche declares that the origin of the bad conscience was "a break, a leap, a compulsion, an ineluctable disaster which precluded all struggle and even all *ressentiment*."[9]

Consciousness as light? And our unconscious and infallible drives as darkness? Then the division of light from darkness becomes manifestly the primal originating event, and bad conscience appears as the origin of "man." If bad conscience is the serious illness that man was *bound* to contract under the stress of the most fundamental change he ever experienced, then it can neither be a simple illusion nor an accidental stumbling. It must rather be a necessary fate, an inescapable destiny, and hence a tragic fall. Furthermore, if the Christian God is identified as the projection of bad conscience, then that god is neither illusory nor accidental. The Christian God, the almighty and transcendent Creator, is the source and the ground of our tragic destiny, of the evolutionary movement of man. The utter holiness of the Christian God may well be a reverse image of the utter guilt of man. But that guilt is real, as real as the terror and cruelty of history; consequently, the Christian God is real, at least within the horizon of history, of "man." Or should we rather say that the Christian God is real so long as He is unnameable, is mysterious and beyond? And He must perish and disappear to the extent that His mystery is humanly spoken. Yet His mystery must remain mystery so long as it is apprehended in guilt, for it is guilt that evokes the mystery, just as it is the advent of bad conscience that establishes the infinite distance between the creature and the Creator.

Of course, morality is also a consequence of the advent of bad conscience. Morality is bound to that primal dichotomy between light and darkness or "soul" and body. Thereby it is sealed in a dual form, its every "yes" being inseparable from a parallel "no," and its every "no" a compulsive "no" that continually evokes an echoing "yes." This is the moral universe that Nietzsche called a madhouse, but it is identical with history itself and thereby inseparable from "man." The madness has an origin, a beginning, and thus it has a mythical meaning. *Genesis* is one expression of such a meaning, and *The Genealogy of Morals* is another. Both agree that morality is a consequence of an original and catastrophic fall. Paul anticipated

Nietzsche in understanding morality, or the law, as a no-saying that makes guilt inescapable and final. Within this framework of understanding, Paul created a new dichotomy between "old" and "new," bringing a new and eschatological meaning to "it was." "It was" lies within the domain of "old aeon" or "old creation," and is therefore inextricably bound up with morality and law. This is precisely the domain that will come to an end with the Resurrection, for the realm of "it was" is the opposite of resurrection, if only because it is entirely subject to the judgment of guilt and death. From the standpoint of "new aeon" or "new creation," morality is the law of judgment and death, and as such it is not only the spirit but also the embodiment of revenge.

Paul, who may justly be regarded as the creator of Christian theology—indeed, of theology itself—offers us a means of understanding guilt and judgment as the contrary or reverse images of life and resurrection. Guilt only appears as total and irrevocable in the presence of its negation and transcendence. Here, guilt and death assume their full meaning only in an eschatological form, only when they are seen as even now coming to an end. Zarathustra, too, can realize the meaning of no-saying and *ressentiment* only by undergoing a self-overcoming of morality. Death and guilt become truly manifest only when they no longer sting, only when they no longer bind and enslave. Only then do they become all-comprehending images, for only the negation of their power can make their meaning manifest, can make it speakable. Just as hell, damnation, and final judgment are not found in the Old Testament, so the full meaning of guilt did not dawn until the modern age (beginning with Luther and culminating in Nietzsche). Even Augustine was unaware of the full meaning of guilt; his pagan roots protected him, for he was not aware of a guilt so complete that it ravages and inverts all expressions of consciousness and experience. The meaning of guilt can occur only when it comes to an end, only when its dark and negative ground becomes fully speakable.

Zarathustra is a prophet, that much is clear, at least to those who can hear his voice. Is not a prophet one who speaks what is unsayable to others, but which, once spoken, immediately carries its own authority? Prophetic speech is unmediated, unargued, and unadorned, but it nevertheless commands a hearing that cannot be denied so long as its voice is heard. The simple test of prophecy is whether or not its voice can be stilled or denied by those who hear it, and by that test Zarathustra is manifestly a prophet. One does not ask of prophecy whether or not it is true, for it lies far deeper than "truth," far deeper than logic, science, or knowledge. Even to inquire whether a prophecy is "good" is to evade its prophetic voice. Genuine prophecy invariably challenges what is established as goodness or truth—to the extent that one can even measure the degree to which prophecy is present by the shock that its utterance evokes. What is most shocking to us? Is it not quite simply the proclamation of the death of God? Nietzsche's madman, an earlier voice of Zarathustra, not only declares that God is dead, but that we have killed him—you and I. "How could we drink up the sea?" This is perhaps the most overwhelming question that Zarathustra asks us. Like all prophetic questions, it answers itself to the extent that we can speak it. To say that God is dead, and actually to say it, is to will the death of God. The prophet is the speaker, and his word is not his alone, it demands to be spoken by all who hear it. Here, listening is speaking. To hear the voice of prophecy is to speak it. Hence, to hear the prophetic announcement that God is dead is to proclaim the death of God oneself. How is such speech possible? How is such hearing possible? Is it not possible because we have finally been given the power both to hear and to speak the name of God? Zarathustra is the one who goes under, because he realizes the meaning of no-saying and *ressentiment,* that total guilt that is our "other," both our history and ourselves. That is the "other" that Zarathustra addresses when he pronounces the death of God. For to see that ultimate "other" and to name it is to proclaim the death of God.

Nietzsche concludes *Ecce Homo* by asking: "Have I been understood? —*Dionysus versus the Crucified.*" The new Dionysus, who is not simply to be identified with the Greek Dionysus, is the symbol of Eternal Recurrence. Nietzsche's Dionysus is fully born through the death of God, the most important event in history: "There has never been a greater deed; and whoever will be born after us—for the sake of this deed he will be part of a higher history than all history hitherto."[10] Yet Nietzsche's opposition to Christ is directed against religion itself, rather than against the actual figure of Jesus. In the same year that he wrote *Ecce Homo* (1888), he said in *The Antichrist:*

> Using the expression somewhat tolerantly, one could call Jesus a "free spirit"—he does not care for anything solid: the word kills, all that is solid kills. The concept, the *experience* of "life" in the only way he knows it, resists any kind of word, formula, law, faith, dogma. He speaks only of the innermost—all the rest, the whole of reality, the whole of nature, language itself, has for him only the value of a sign, a simile.[11]

Viewed in this light, Jesus stands outside of Christianity, and Nietzsche's portrait of him bears a strong resemblance to the new Zarathustra:

> Make no mistake at this point, however seductive the Christian, in other words, the *ecclesiastical,* prejudice may be: such a symbolist *par excellence* stands outside all religion, all cult concepts, all history, all natural science, all experience of the world, all knowledge, all politics, all psychology, all books, all art—his "knowledge" is pure *foolishness* precisely concerning the fact that such things exist. *Culture* is not

known to him even by hearsay, he does not need to fight it—he does not negate it. The same applies to the state, to the whole civic order and society, to work, to war—he never had any reason to negate "the world;" the ecclesiastical concept of "world" never occurred to him. To negate is the very thing that is impossible for him. [12]

Again and again in *The Antichrist,* Nietzsche portrays Jesus as a kind of innocent forerunner of Zarathustra; he is incapable of *ressentiment,* is free of history, and is himself exactly opposed to Christianity.

> If one were to look for signs that an ironical divinity has its fingers in the great play of the world, one would find no small support in the *tremendous question mark* called Christianity. Mankind lies on its knees before the opposite of that which was the origin, the meaning, the *right* of the evangel; in the concept of "church" it has pronounced holy precisely what the "bringer of the glad tidings" felt to be *beneath* and *behind* himself—one would look in vain for a greater example of *world-historical irony.* [13]

The very word "Christianity" is a misunderstanding; there was only one Christian, and he and his gospel died on the cross. "What has been called 'evangel' from that moment was actually the opposite of that which *he* lived: *'ill* tidings,' a dysangel." [14] True Christianity is not "faith" in redemption through Christ, nor is it repentance or prayer; only Christian *praxis* is Christian: "True life, eternal life, has been found—it is not promised, it is here, it is *in you:* as a living in love, in love without subtraction and exclusion, without regard for station." [15]

In the whole psychology of the "evangel" the concept of guilt and punishment is absent—as is also the concept of reward. "Sin"—any distance separating God and man—is abolished: *this is precisely the "glad tidings."* Blessedness is not promised, it is not tied to conditions: it is the only reality—the rest is a sign with which to speak of it. [16] Only the practice, the immediate living, of the "glad tidings" leads to God. Indeed, Nietzsche proclaims that "it *is* God." [17]

What god? Surely not the Christian God, the absolutely sovereign and transcendent God, the God of eternity. The God of Jesus? The God of the crucified? Less than a year after writing *The Antichrist,* when insanity was bursting upon him, Nietzsche alternately signed his notes "Dionysus" and "The Crucified." Of course, Dionysus *is* the crucified. At least, the Greek Dionysus is a god who dies and is resurrected. Zarathustra, too, is Dionysus, and Zarathustra suffers as a god. [18] Again, what god? Is this the god or God who becomes manifest in the death of God? Could we say that the "glad tidings," both of Jesus and of Zarathustra, are the announcement of the death of God? Surely the death of God abolishes any distance separating God and man, and with that abolition, sin and guilt disappear. Does blessedness *then* become the only reality? All promise, all future hope and expectation, come to an end in the death of God. If the "glad tidings" are the announcement of the death of God, then living the "glad tidings" does lead to God. But it leads to that God who appears when all distance separating God and man disappears and is no more. True life is then found not in the life of God but in the death of God. Thereby life is not promised, it is here, it is *in you,* in you and me. For you and I have killed God, and we kill God when we pronounce His name, when we say life, and eternal life, and say it here and now. That life, that yes-saying, is not promised, it is found; and it is found in Christian *praxis,* in the immediate and total living of the "glad tidings" of the death of God.

The symbol of eternal life predominant in the New Testament is the Kingdom of God, but it eroded and virtually disappeared even before the completion of the New Testament itself. Yet it did not simply disappear—it reversed itself, becoming its own "other" in the Christian doctrine of God. This is the most fundamental insight of modern theology, and we owe it to Nietzsche. True, Hegel had fully realized it conceptually, but only conceptually, not humanly and immediately. The theme is also imaginatively worked out in Blake's apocalyptic epics, but, like the whole body of modern literature and art, they remain a theological cipher. *The Antichrist* is not a cipher, or not wholly so; in large measure it is luminously clear, and it is clearest in its portrait of the Christian God:

> The Christian conception of God—God as god of the sick, God as a spider, God as spirit—is one of the most corrupt conceptions of the divine ever held. It may even represent the low-water mark in the descending development of divine types. God degenerated into the *contradiction* of life, instead of being its transfiguration and eternal "yes!" God became a declaration of war against life, against nature, against the will to live; the formula for every slander against "this world," for every lie about the "beyond;" the deification of nothingness, the will to nothingness pronounced holy.[19]

The Christian, at least, can recognize this as a true portrait of the God whom he knows in faith—albeit in bad faith, which is both a refusal of and a flight from the "glad tidings." Again and again the modern Christian has learned that his faith in God is a flight from the Gospel. But if it is a flight from the Gospel, a full and total flight, then the Christian God is opposed to the Kingdom of God.

Like Jesus, Zarathustra is a prophet of glad tidings, and his are of the "great noon" of Eternal Recurrence. Nietzsche regarded his discovery of Eternal Recurrence as his greatest creation, his triumphant hymn in praise of the earth, of life and immediate existence. Yet it was created out of the deepest pain, for Nietzsche himself looked upon the idea of Eternal Recurrence as the nightmare of nightmares. As early as *The Gay Science,* he expressed his conception in its most terrible form.

> *The greatest weight.* —What if some day or night a demon were to steal after you into your loneliest loneliness and say to you: "This life as you now live it and have lived it, you will have to live once more and innumerable times more; and there will be nothing new in it, but every pain and every joy and every thought and sigh and everything unutterably small or great in your life will have to return to you, all in the same succession and sequence—even this spider and this moonlight between the trees, and even this moment and I myself. The eternal hourglass of existence is turned upside down again and again, and you with it, speck of dust!" Would you not throw yourself down and gnash your teeth and curse the demon who spoke thus? Or have you once experienced a tremendous moment when you would have answered him: "You are a god and never have I heard anything more divine." If this thought gained possession of you, it would change you as you are or perhaps crush you. The question in each and everything, "Do you desire this once more and innumerable times more?" would lie upon your actions as the greatest weight. Or how well disposed would you have to become to yourself and to life *to crave nothing more fervently* than this ultimate eternal confirmation and seal?[20]

The idea of Eternal Recurrence is the supreme challenge we can face, the ultimate test of courage, of life, for it poses the question whether we can affirm life, *our* life, here and now. Here is Nietzsche's categorical imperative—the most awful and awesome that man has ever faced, for it calls for an act of total affirmation.

Nietzsche· knew that this conception was not new; found in ancient Stoicism, it parallels, if it does not exactly coincide with, the archaic myths of Eternal Return. What is new, radically new, is that Eternal Recurrence is here freed from the image of eternity. Eternity becomes identical with time itself. Zarathustra says:

> "Behold," I continued, "this moment! From this gateway, Moment, a long, eternal lane leads *backward:* behind us lies an eternity. Must not whatever *can* walk have walked on this lane before? Must not whatever *can* happen have happened, have been done, have passed by before? And if everything has been there before—what do you think, dwarf, of this moment? Must not this gateway too have been there before? And are not all things knotted together so firmly that this moment draws after it *all* that is to come? Therefore—itself too? For whatever *can* walk—in this long lane out *there* too, it *must* walk once more.[21]

Eternity lies both behind and ahead of every actual and present moment; it is a circle that cannot admit any eternal "other" beyond the present moment. Consequently, the Eternal Recurrence proclaimed by Zarathustra is an eternity, an actual and present eternity, embodying the death of God.

The "great noon" of Eternal Recurrence is created by the death of God, with which the beyond is abolished and disappears: eternal life is this life, the earth, the present moment.

> "O Zarathustra," the animals said, "to those who think as we do, all things themselves are dancing: they come and offer their hands and laugh and flee—and come back. Everything goes, everything comes back; eternally rolls the wheel of being. Everything dies, everything blossoms again; eternally runs the year of being. Everything breaks, everything is joined anew; eternally the same house is being built. Everything parts, everything greets every other thing again; eternally the ring of being remains faithful to itself. In every Now, being begins; round every Here rolls the sphere There. The center is everywhere. Bent is the path of eternity.[22]

Nowhere did Nietzsche more triumphantly reach his goal of speaking volumes in a few words than in this passage of *Zarathustra*. The meaning of Eternal Recurrence shatters and reverses every sacred meaning of eternity. The "wheel of being" is an archaic symbol in both East and West of an eternal round of existence without meaning, purpose, or direction, except insofar as mere existence in such a "wheel" brings atonement from a primal guilt. At a moment when Zarathustra himself cannot yet affirm the Eternal Recurrence of all things, his animals celebrate the wheel of being, not as a horrible cycle of perpetual pain, but as an eternal dance. Now pain becomes joy, meaninglessness becomes order, guilt becomes grace. As opposed to the Hindu symbol of the world as the divine but meaningless play *(lila)* of an ultimately inactive and unmoving One, the Dionysian symbol of Eternal Recurrence reflects the ultimate reality of things themselves as they here and now become manifest as sheer delight. Only the Second Innocence created by the death of God is wholly devoid of guilt, and it is precisely through such innocence that the most abysmal depths of a now naked reality become manifest as a cosmic dance.

Note the order of the images establishing this new meaning of reality or being: *Rad* ("wheel," "cycle"), *Jahr* ("year"). *Haus* ("house," "home," "family," "race"), and *Ring* ("ring," "circle," "cycle"). The imagery itself is cyclical, moving to and from the image and idea of the circle, and comprehending first a cyclical image of time *(Jahr),* and then what can only have been intended as a cyclical image of space *(gleich Haus)*. Furthermore, all of these images are created by affirmation, by yes-saying, as is revealed by the first sentence of the passage ("to those who think as we do, all things themselves are dancing''), and then by the association of the word *treu* (''faithful,'' ''loyal,'' ''true'') with the eternal cycle of being. When manifest and known in total affirmation, the abyss of the eternal round of suffering and pain is transformed into the highest order of perfection, as symbolized by the circle.

The culmination of the passage is in the last three sentences, which are perhaps the most important lines that Nietzsche ever wrote: ''Being begins in every Now.'' When Heidegger declared that Nietzsche's proclamation of the death of God was the nihilistic fulfillment of our historical destiny, he meant that with Nietzsche philosophy or primal thinking is completed; it has gone through the sphere of its prefigured possibilities. Yet this ending is an eschatological ending, which is to say that it is a radical new beginning. The death of God, which brings to an end the transcendence of being, the beyondness of eternity, makes Being manifest in every Now. Being assumes a totally new meaning and identity: no longer is it eternal; rather, it begins or dawns in every actual moment. Here, the verb *begins* is all-important, for it defines or establishes both the subject and the predicate. We might even say that in this affirmation the subject ceases to be, with the result that it is no longer possible to say that being *is,* or that anything whatsoever is, as everything *begins* in every Now. Thereby it is revealed that the proposition ''Being *is*'' is a product of the detachment of the speaker from the immediate moment: to be totally immersed in the Now is to be free of a permanent existence of any kind.

When life or existence is most deeply affirmed, Being becomes identical with the Now: the actual moment of existence becomes *Being*. The act, the affirmation, the willing of the moment is the eternal creation and re-creation of everything. Totally to will the moment is to will that it eternally recur, and eternally recur as the same, as this moment, this life, this existence. It is the death of God or the reversal of a transcendent eternity that makes possible the resurrection of the Now, of time, of the body. This transvaluation of the whole traditional identity of Being is carried forward in the next phrase: ''the world of There revolves about every Here.'' If every moment is Being itself, then all moments of being are equivalent, because every moment must coincide with every other. So, likewise, every point of space must be equivalent to every other point, for there is no transcendent order to define either the meaning or the value of point or direction. Any point in space— any fragment of world or self—can be said to have neither direction nor meaning; therefore, the given or established distinction between ''here'' and ''there'' collapses. To exist ''here'' is to exist ''there,'' to will ''here'' is to will ''there.'' All things are firmly bound together; or, rather, all things flow into one another, with the result that it is no longer possible to say here or there, I or Thou, he or it. The veil of Being crumbles and dissolves in the yes-saying of Eternal Recurrence, a yes-saying negating and bringing to an end those worlds and eternities created by our primal flight or fall from the "body." "Man" has thereby been surpassed, has been negated and transcended, and with him has been surpassed every meaning, every order, every value created by our "soul." Yet what the soul had known as chaos, the body now knows as bliss: yes-saying delights in the resurrection of the brute reality of things.

"The Center is everywhere." The new Dionysian life wants *all* things, wants all things now, and wants them eternally the same. Truly to accept, to know, the sameness of the same, is to know that the Center is everywhere. By dissolving the "here" and "there" of things, every unique and singular center disappears, and with that disappearance, all hierarchical judgment and comprehension become impossible. The traditional symbol of the Center is meaningful only when a chasm between it and the void is assumed. That chasm disappears when God is dead, and with it disappears every chasm or real or ultimate distance whatsoever. Now all transcendent centers pass into total immanence, and "center" as such ceases to be either singular or distinct. Therefore, real distinction becomes impossible; no longer is it possible to apprehend boundaries between things, to know a "this" which is "other" than a "that." When all things are firmly bound together, no lines or limits are possible, and all things spontaneously or immediately flow into each other. Now everything is a center, is *the* center, because the center is everywhere. God as the Center that is everywhere? Yes, but only when God is dead, only when the negation of his sovereignty and transcendence invests every point and moment with the totality of Being.

"The path of eternity is curved [*krumm:* also, "bent" or "crooked"]." Once again we find a circular image, although this time an ironic one, to symbolize eternity. The way of eternity is not only curved or bowed, it is also artfully crooked and circuitous. An image of a maze is evoked by this line—a circular maze, to be sure, and a maze that is never-ending, or eternal. What can Eternal Recurrence mean here? Being begins in every Now; the world of There revolves about every Here; and the Center is everywhere. Clearly, the very possibility of metaphysical or cosmological understanding has been denied by these affirmations: yes-saying can know no *logos* of things. There is no *logos* of eternity when its path is both curved and crooked, both circular and circuitous. Nietzsche's eternity is the very antithesis of the eternity of the philosophers and theologians, and he intends it to bring about a deep revulsion in the man of "faith." In his drunken midnight song, Zarathustra sings: "Woe says: Go! But all joy [*Lust*] wants Eternity—wants deep, deep Eternity." As Zarathustra himself interprets these words: "Joy, however, does not want heirs, or children—joy wants itself, wants eternity, wants recurrence, wants everything eternally the same."

Have you ever said Yes to a single joy? O my friends, then you said Yes too to *all* woe. All things are entangled, ensnared, enamored; if you ever wanted one thing twice, if you said, ''You please me, happiness! Abide, moment!'' then you wanted *all* back. All anew, all eternally, all entangled, ensnared, enamored—oh, then you *loved* the world. Eternal ones, love it eternally and evermore; and to woe too, you say: go, but return! *For all joy wants*—eternity.[23]

Finally, yes-saying and Eternal Recurrence are identical: the deepest affirmation of existence can only mean the willing of the Eternal Recurrence of all things, the willing of *this* life, of *this* moment, of this pain, and in such a manner as to will that it recur eternally, and recur eternally the same. No metaphysical cosmology lies here at hand, nor even an ''idea'' of Eternal Recurrence, but rather a total existence in the present Now, a now that is here and there, a center that is everywhere.

At bottom, Eternal Recurrence is a way of totally loving the world, and not only a way of loving the world but also a way of speaking of love itself in a time and world in which God is dead. Zarathustra's symbol of Eternal Recurrence is radically distinguished from its classical and archaic counterparts, but so, likewise, is it distinguished from the historical language of Christianity. A decisive consequence of Christianity's loss of its original eschatological symbol of the Kingdom of God was that it was thereby led into an apprehension of a gulf or chasm between God and the world and a consequent apprehension of pure or total love as being ''other'' than the world. With the significant exceptions of its great mystics and its radical apocalyptic seers and groups, historical Christianity was more distantly removed from the proclamation of Jesus, for his ''glad tidings'' were a proclamation of the advent here and now of the Kingdom of God. Nietzsche knew this better than any theologian of his time or ours. Did he know it because of his very knowledge that God is dead? Does the death of the Christian God make manifest the Kingdom of God that Jesus proclaimed? Is the language of Eternal Recurrence a new eschatological language reflecting the presence of the Kingdom of God? A Kingdom of God that is totally present must necessarily empty the heavens of the absolutely sovereign and transcendent God, and consequently the ancient and sacred heavens are no more. With the disappearance of the Creator, creation ceases to be creation; or, rather, ''old creation'' becomes ''new creation;'' ''it was'' becomes affirmation and grace. Now, ''old aeon'' becomes identical with guilt and revenge, and ''new aeon'' becomes manifest as a radically new and total innocence. Is the new Zarathustra a new or renewed Jesus?

NOTES

1. *Ecce Homo;* "Thus Spoke Zarathustra," §6.
2. *EH;* "Why I Am a Destiny,"§3.
3. *Ibid.*
4. *Thus Spoke Zarathustra;* II, "On Redemption."
5. *Ibid.*
6. *The Genealogy of Morals;* II, §22.
7. *GM;* II, §16.
8. *Ibid.*
9. *GM;* II, §17.
10. *The Gay Science,* §125.
11. *The Antichrist,* §32.
12. *Ibid.*
13. *Antichrist,* §36.
14. *Antichrist,* §39.
15. *Antichrist,* §33.
16. *Ibid.*
17. *Ibid.*
18. *EH;* "Thus Spoke Zarathustra," §8.
19. *Antichrist,* §18.
20. *GS,* §341.
21. *Zarathustra;* III, "On the Vision and the Riddle," §2.
22. *Zarathustra;* III, "The Convalescent," §2.
23. *Zarathustra;* IV, "The Drunken Song," §10.

Paul Valadier

DIONYSUS VERSUS
THE CRUCIFIED

TRANSFIGURED EXISTENCE: THE DIONYSIAN

Without going into all the consequences that affirmation holds for the psychological depths of the individual or for human history, we shall point out the kind of contrast that places Dionysian affirmation on the same plane as what can be called reactive religion.[1] Nietzsche himself has elsewhere expressed this opposition in an unpublished text of 1888, "The Two Types: Dionysus and the Crucified."[2] He introduced this thought by a series of questions that concern the religious man, not religion itself. The whole fragment thus balances between the two attitudes he describes, and both are closer to the aspect of the act that grasps the reality than to the positive truth of the act itself (i.e., religion *as such*). If one pretends that the typical *religious* man is decadent, one would seem to be left with another kind of religious man, the pagan. If one reads the religious phenomenon as the manifestation of a moral sickness—itself rooted in the morbid denial of an overwhelmingly abundant existence—one would seem to submit the religious man to a single type of interpretation and exclude certain others. For example, there are those for whom the religious act, far from being an act of asceticism or self-torture, is a form of "appreciation and affirmation of life." Wouldn't they be spirits who seek salvation not elsewhere or in an other, but, rather, by accepting "the oppositions and the problematic character of existence"? Their response to these questions leaves no ambiguity. The Greek affirmation of life, which Nietzsche synthesized in the term Dionysus, is a religious attitude that escapes the critic's verdict of decadence. Thus the Dionysian type can be brought into conjunction with the crucified. If we take up the analyses that conclude the first essay of *The Genealogy of Morals*,[3] we can say that the conflict between paganism and Judeaism (which punctutates all of Western history) not only is symbolized in Christian literature but finds its symbol in Dionysus. The conflict places two religious types *within* the oppositions precipitated by this essay: affirmation and negation are forcefully opposed to one another, and they are not opposed only as empty alternatives. Rather, the basis of their opposition stems from the positions taken with respect to that reality which Nietzsche equivocally calls the Whole—life, existence, or, indeed, things themselves.

This would signify a flexibility of will on Nietzsche's part that would not reduce the unnameable reality either to a concept or to a totality of being. Here, it is a question of letting it speak for itself, fleetingly, transiently, in the way of the tempting god, Dionysus.

How is this fundamental opposition manifested? The ascetic ideal—which for Judeao-Christian thought (not to mention Buddhism) predominates over religion as such—keeps a certain distance from life due to its fear of life. Thus, it is an illusory ideal based on a will to illusion, although not recognized as such. The Dionysian ideal, on the contrary, aims at an identification with life—a temporary identification, moreover, that does not claim the right of definitive fusion, but nonetheless does not refuse the principle of adhesion to life. Distrusting life and desiccating the individual, the ascetic ideal seeks a reason, a meaning, an end for life that can serve as the individual's ordering principle: an arbitrary creation that professes to dictate life's purpose, yet one that in fact perverts the problematic meaning of existence. The Dionysian ideal, on the contrary, seeks no other justification for life than that which it can itself give. Its world is beyond finality; it is a chaotic world that resembles a sea, agitated by eternally changing yet always self-identical forces. [4] Turning bad conscience back upon itself, the ascetic ideal provokes the individual to self-mutilation as he desperately tries to escape life and self-affirmation; and by denying self-affirmation, he only manages to affirm it once more. The Dionysian ideal, on the other hand, aims at a *real* overcoming of the individual by way of a metamorphosis, a self-transformation by steadfast affirmation (i.e., of Will to Power). "The word 'Dionysian' means . . . a reaching out beyond personality, the everyday, society, reality, across the abyss of transitoriness." [5] This overcoming, for Nietzsche, has nothing to do either with bacchic intoxication, as the intellectual tradition describes it in reference to the cult of Dionysus, or with personality alteration brought about by the delirium of self-annihilation. [6] The first text to use the term "Dionysian pessimism" (*The Gay Science*, §370) strictly distinguishes the desire for hateful destruction (a kind of devastating impotence) from the desire for destruction motivated by a creative will, one that freely submits to a new superabundance. Dionysian desire has nothing at all to do with the former. Here, we must go right to the texts that express this overcoming, as well as look at the passages from *Zarathustra* that describe how one acquires "the virtue that gives," the gratitude that reserves nothing for itself (for it leaves the self behind). The insistent use in these texts of the term "clarification" evokes the Dionysian reconciliation between the sense faculties and the mind. While the ascetic ideal denies the senses by arbitrarily choosing one part of man and elevating it to the status of a thing in itself, the Dionysian ideal aims for "a mind as peaceful and at home in the senses as the senses are at home and peaceful in it." This illuminating transformation warrants our speaking about "a sort of divinization of the body." Because of the body/soul dualism that it postulates, the ascetic ideal results in an obsession with the body.[7] The Dionysian ideal, however, is to strive for the mastery of the accomplished dancer who can forget his own body—not out of lack or insufficiency, but by supreme mastery. Divinization, then, must be understood as supreme liberty, since the only recognized attribute of divinity is to have light feet. Sexuality, therefore, is neither denied nor disparaged, nor is it any longer exalted as a privileged and exclusive kind of affirmation: rather, it arouses "profound, secret veneration."[8]

Certainly it is here that one should bring in the mysterious image of Ariadne, whose secret Nietzsche thought himself alone in possessing—a human figure encountering the divine figure of Dionysus.[9] Every text dedicated to him arises out of the purest lyricism, not out of orgiastic delirium. "Ariadne's lament" is a call for the transfiguring advent of the god, but it bears the traces of a most spiritualized love, in the sense just discussed. Here is a human figure whose discreet presence removes the distance between man and the god Dionysus (but this is not to identify them), whose presence also indicates that man must assume an authentically "feminine" attitude in welcoming Dionysus. Far from affirming Dionysus on the basis of a powerful pride, he is called forth in an amorous feminine lament. Ariadne's relation to Dionysus is a remarkable complement to the relation between man and He who is. Part III of *Zarathustra* (closing with the song to eternity) describes a virile relation between man and eternity— the latter symbolized as woman and mother, the former as male and father. It is with *Beyond Good and Evil*, §295 (subsequent to *Zarathustra*), that the character Ariadne appears. She often points back allusively; for example, as when "Ariadne's lament" takes up the song of the Magician from the fourth part of *Zarathustra,* save for some few subtle differences.[10] Everything occurs as if this figure symbolized an inverted relation with eternity, so far as the Amen Song has it: after the virile appeal to eternity, our expectation must be removed and the relation reversed, changed from that of a virile affirmation to that of a feminine lament. And yet, the lament does not exclude the ambiguous remarks of the Magician. In describing a double relation—virile, then feminine—this play of symbols points out the contrasting nature of man's relation with eternity (or with the gods).

SUFFERING AND DEATH

The transmutation demanded by Dionysian affirmation, if it is inspired by an overabundance and not by a destructive weakness, must not be sweetened or adulterated, for it comes about by suffering and even death. The difference, then, between Dionysus and the Crucified is not that the latter focuses on passion and death while the former points to an overflowing exaltation of life. The supporting posthumous text is unambiguous: between Dionysus and the Crucified, "it is not martyrdom which constitutes the difference: it just has two different meanings."[11] Thus, one wouldn't say that the Nietzschean affirmation of life is made in a terrible ignorance of death: the god Dionysus is himself torn to pieces and knows death. He too dies, but, like the real gods that *Zarathustra* speaks of, he is reborn from his ashes. The death of this god is no argument against life. It doesn't foster guilt as the Pauline vision does—overburdened by an interpretation that sees in guilt the means to salvation and eternity—a vision that amounts to replacing, and thus denaturing, life. Dionysus' death is not the unforeseen and unwanted death of Jesus. As the anti-type of the Crucified, Dionysus is opposed to the Pauline invention of the Savior on the cross, and thus to the obsession with a redeeming death, a redeeming of self. But, by the same token, Dionysus is close to the non-Pauline Jesus. Jesus said yes, he affirmed, but he did not want death. This is the decisive difference between Dionysus and Jesus. Dionysus, the more lucid and vigorous, *wants* to be a martyr: not for himself, but as an inner condition for the affirmation of life. In contrast to the Pauline crucified Jesus, who exalts death over life—who is close, but not identical, to the Jesus who wanted life without facing death—Dionysus confronts death, certain of the over-fullness of life and his own re-creative power. "The desire for destruction, change, becoming, *can* be the expression of an over-full power pregnant with the future (my term for this, as is known, is the word 'Dionysian')."[12] Death, then, is a consent that presupposes one's affirming the Eternal Recurrence of the same throughout its own process of internal differentiation. As undergone by the disciples of this god, suffering and death are not the last word about things. Indeed, according to the beautiful text of *Nietzsche Contra Wagner,* they are not the last letter of the alphabet: "Only great pain is the ultimate liberator of the spirit, as the teacher of great suspicion which turns every Y into an X, a real genuine X, that is, the letter before the penultimate one."[13] Even suffering keeps a respectful distance from the ultimate reality: it only gives access, it conditions affirmation in being implied by it. It is always present in all human experience,[14] but its meaning changes: the tragic sense is opposed to the prevailing Christian notion. For the former, suffering is intrinsic to the sanctity of life, just as the "no" is interior to all unlimited "affirmation."[15]

The tragedy of Dionysian suffering originates in the faithful and active affirmation of existence; it is tied to the chaotic and labyrinthine aspect of a universe that *makes* no sense (but which, for all that, is not absurd).

> Whoever looks into himself as into a vast space and carries galaxies in himself, also knows how irregular all galaxies are: they lead into the chaos and labyrinth of existence.[16]

The symbol of the galaxy, which already illuminates the relation to the other as friendship,[17] suggests the unfathomable "relation" of the star to the vast reaches of celestial space: however "illuminating" the relation is, here is a light that does not disregard the immensity of this space. In commenting on this text, G. Morel writes, "Galaxies can only be discerned on the background of immense—of a profoundly immense space. On the other hand, the space itself cannot be disregarded; galaxies illuminate it with a dark and rapidly diffused light. It is luminous enough, however, that the temptation to travel to other worlds seems wonderfully grotesque."[18] Such an endless voyage is analogous to the path in a labyrinth: another symbol joining Dionysus and Ariadne. Instead of adhering to a planned route, the explorer of the labyrinth knows that, although there is an end, there is no direct way to it. "Labyrinth"—this is a symbol for *chaos;* it signifies not nothingness, but the absence of predetermined organization. The world is characterized more by an excess than by an absence of forms (i.e., there are too many paths in the labyrinth, just as there is a multitude of galaxies, of Milky Ways, in the sky: each star follows a "law above itself"[19]). Only out of chaos, with great pain and difficulty, can each open his own creative way: "One must still have chaos in oneself to be able to give birth to a dancing star."[20] The image of the Dionysian man, then, is a star that follows its own way to a determined place in the heart of a limitless space. As a posthumous publication (written at the time of *Zarathustra*) expresses it: "A labyrinthian man does not look for truth, he forever seeks only his Ariadne."[21] He does not stupidly try to attain to celestial profundity; however, he does seek "the golden equilibrium of all things," whose name is Ariadne. Such images must not be interpreted in an absolute sense. Much like "labyrinth," the term "chaos" should neither be defined in an overly romantic or nihilistic way, nor should it escape all connotation of danger or frenzy. The affirmation of chaos does not entail the attitude of disinterested observation: chaos is within everyone, just as everyone is lost within the labyrinth. Affirmation thus belongs to a move that lessens the value of the self (to know how to throw the dice, and to do it over again); it is an invitation to enter into the game where someone plays with us. But the person undergoing such a metamorphosis pays the price of his own blood. Following Dionysus, he suffers self-dismemberment and unremitting death. Redemption is not assured by one's faith in salvation through bloodshed by another (Saint Paul); rather, it involves shedding one's own blood.

With this perspective, we can assess Nietzsche's identification with Dionysus in light of certain texts. Just prior to going insane, Nietzsche often signed his letters "Dionysus," oftentimes "The Crucified." Does this gesture mean that Nietzsche took himself to be Dionysus? Or, even more seriously, that in his final moments of lucidity, he tended to blur the opposition between Dionysus and the crucified, an opposition he still maintained elsewhere? First, we should note that the last letters speak of an identification with many historical characters, not only with Dionysus. This identification is developed as the term for self-metamorphosis, a process pursued explicitly and painfully by Nietzsche himself. Here, we could follow G. Morel's plausible interpretation:

> How are we to understand that Nietzsche is essentially all the names of history? In its positive aspect this proposal asserts that an individual really becomes a self only by losing his given identity, by passing through ever-changing alterations. Only in this way can eternity be life: the metamorphosis of one countenance out of several completely different ones. This is the movement of a real identity—passing from the criminal to Dionysus. Nietzsche tends to partake of precisely what belonged to these disfigured characters: he is Jesus and Prado, in the aforementioned sense.[22]

But also, and consistent with this first remark, it is normal that the disciple of the god should live out the martyrdom of Dionysus in his own way. This identification is neither an identity nor a confusion of beings, but is the natural result of a disciple's fidelity; i.e., once he understands that Dionysus wanted to affirm all things, once he himself enters into the crucifying moment of affirmation.[23] Finally, let us not underestimate the facetiousness and the "light jesting" character of these final letters: at the boundary of conscious and unconscious, Nietzsche still played at putting on masks that would hide, even from his closest friends, the reality of his disappearance. (He assumed the garb of the student before Burckhardt, "our greatest master," and even compared his relationship with his work to that of God toward his creation.) Isn't this the very point at which Dionysian frenzy irrevocably took the upper hand, the will to conceal this reality under an Apollonian fantasy?

Nietzsche's theory can be distinguished from its origin and involvement in lived experience. Dionysian self-sacrifice, announced in *Beyond Good and Evil,* is hardly a mere stylistic phrase. Rather, it alone allows Nietzsche's madness to be interpreted as the assent to unfathomable reality: an assent at first dreaded to the point of anguish, and then accepted ever more seriously. Morel's unanswerable question still remains: "To what extent was Nietzsche's chaos transformable, and to what extent was it transformed? It is not important that we cannot answer this. It is extraordinary, though, how despite the delirium and rantings of encroaching madness, Nietzsche tried to give a desperate indication of his ordeal—and his doctrine. It is a doctrine stained with blood, because it is only the negative side of his own ordeal."[24]

DIONYSUS AND ETERNAL RECURRENCE

With this perspective on the tragic sense of suffering (the will to self-annihilation), we can now situate the relationship between Dionysus and the

Eternal Recurrence—for it is through Dionysus' own death that life can be affirmed: "Life itself, its eternal fruitfulness and recurrence, involves agony, destruction, the will to annihilation."[25] As a god, Dionysus submits to the Eternal Recurrence: he wills the unremitting return of his own suffering and death precisely in order to affirm life. Likewise, his disciple must not try to immortalize the present moment, but, rather, he should try to fracture it, so that eternity may surge forth from him.[26] This is an eternity that is present and not promised, as with Saint Paul. Redemption is not sought by relying on another's death or by bowing to a faith in this other. On the contrary, it is achieved through the affirmation of a life that denies, that annihilates, all reserve. Unlike the teaching of Jesus, the kingdom is not only within: now, illuminated by the flash of eternity, it transfigures the entire cosmos.

The thought of Eternal Recurrence, itself so difficult to clarify, now makes sense if we see it as replacing the Christian center of gravity. Then we can understand it as a reflection on the most profound nature of reality (and, thus, as a kind of "religious" thought) and not as a cosmology or scientific pretension.[27] Likewise, it is not primarily a "selective thought,"[28] one to "elevate" or educate, for then it would serve only secondarily as a principle of choice and discernment. This is why the content of this idea should not be compared with Greek philosophies or be analyzed for its implied conception of time; nor should its form of expression be the source of diverse analyses. To describe the course of its powerful presentation to Nietzsche and of Zarathustra's painful affirmation demands an attitude that reflects the direction this course has taken. Its opposition to Christian nihilism suggests that this thought is the great yet innocent affirmation of life—an affirmation that would once again be betrayed if it were restricted to one substitute form of expression. This thought is also akin to the Will to Power, since the latter qualifies the will that wills Eternal Recurrence: here is a will that keenly and purely (i.e., without nostalgia or resentment) wills an eternity of the same. Nonetheless, the affirmation of Eternal recurrence is not *identical* to that of the Will to Power. As the organization of *Zarathustra* suggests, part II (focusing on the Will to Power) introduces the great thought that dominates part III: even if Eternal Recurrence can only be affirmed by a will that wills the Will to Power, the affirmation of Will to Power is not yet the thought of Eternal Recurrence. To conceive such a thought, or to will an eternity of the same (which presupposes the will to power), is to express a pure affirmation *not* of a particular thing, but of the eternal redemption of *all* things. It is to wish for eternal fertility: "Never yet have I found the woman from whom I wanted children, unless it be this woman whom I love: for I love you, O eternity!"[29] The Will to Power, far from being primarily brought about by the technical conquest of the universe, is really only affirmed when it wills eternity: its essence is to will the existence of eternity,[30] for it is not primarily a will to existence.[31] It is the will to lose oneself in order to assent to what of itself saves all becoming and reality.

But the Amen to eternity does not lead the yea-sayer to any fusion or communion with eternity: he is neither engulfed by it, nor is its unfathomable reality suddenly revealed to him. The yes must be repeated, not only because his own self-becoming is a never-ending process of affirming joy and suffering, good and evil, but also because eternity evermore reveals its own feminine, mysterious identity. Recurrence of the same, therefore, is not the monotonous repetition of the identical moment: such a version appears only where the doctrine is still seen as a nightmare announced by a demon,[32] or as a dream confused with reality that fades as the mist upon awakening.[33] Its aspect and meaning have already changed by the time the animals appear in *Zarathustra*. (For *Zarathustra*, the animals are the real interlocutors; they are neither the disciples of part II, who have surrendered to their fate, nor the so-called superior men, deathlike figures of decadence.) By means of this doctrine, they do not see some monotonous permanence to all things, but rather a movement by which they come before and give themselves over to man, as in a dance: "Everything goes, everything comes back; eternally rolls the wheel of being. Everything dies, everything blossoms again; eternally runs the year of being. Everything breaks, everything is joined anew; eternally the same house of being is built."[34] Here is a still unstable movement, yet one whose insight penetrates far beyond the eternally fixed and static, since it enters into the very movement of being, understood now both as absence *and* presence. According to Zarathustra, however, the animals repeat a doctrine without affirming it (they offer an exact, but empty and abstract, expression of it). Thus, their *ritornello* is opposed to Zarathustra's song in "The Seven Seals" or to "The Drunken Song" of part IV: to affirm the smallest joy is also to say yes to all suffering—life is inseparable from death in that the affirmation of joy entails the return of suffering. The return to the same is thus a return to the same affirmation. Yet this affirmation is neither a sacramental adhesion to being, which would come at the expense of difference, nor is it an arrest of movement. To make an affirmation is to entail its own return; but there is a radical alteration in the move from one to the other. The return of the same affirmation cannot be a return to the same affirmation, since we must once again affirm the inseparable joy and pain in a new act of beginning—a recommencement whose three metamorphoses already proclaimed it to be childhood itself.

Eternal Recurrence is that affirmation which always entails another yes; it entails a return, but a return that is no longer the insistent and stultified past of the resentful man. Also, it considers the particular situation and the temporal situation of him who affirms, him who (not himself, eternity) must once again will eternity at the heart of time. Thus, we can now discern the relationship between the affirmation of Eternal Recurrence and Dionysus. The tempting god sometimes comes to visit him who awaits him, him who expects the god and is prepared to affirm him. Part IV of *Zarathustra* culminates in the expectation of a sign (which is the title of the last song).

Reaffirmation—reiteration of the yes—anticipates what may come, and the mere possibility of its coming is sufficient to "justify" all reality (as Nietzsche audaciously uses this term once again). But since the visitor passes by without wreaking violence upon his followers, without piercing them with his look, as did the old God, each vigil requires a new preparation and a reassertion of the yes as the very core of its condition. Here, any illusions that the sign can be *grasped* must die: Dionysus is what he is, a passage, a trace. He who is "devoted" to this god is not uprooted from his condition, but is enriched and deepened by the announcement of his possible visit. Yea-saying entails its return, the "one time" wills the "second time," and an eternity of times, and thus a renunciation of any will to end it, of any aspiration for Nihilism's "once and for all."

This is why transfigured existence is an ever renewed act of transfiguration: it is neither a giving in to resentment, nor is it a deliverance from the necessity of having to will oneself. Rather, it is the ever new return of affirmation, an affirmation of reality that is itself always other.

Can the relationship between Dionysus and the Eternal Recurrence be specified more clearly? The absence of explicit references to Dionysus in *Thus Spoke Zarathustra* should caution against making hypothetical comparisons that, however insightful, lack textual support. On the other hand, if we compare *The Birth of Tragedy* with *Zarathustra,* the relationship is clear. *The Attempt at Self-Criticism* (1886) notes that the entire *Birth of Tragedy* "knows only an artistic meaning and crypto-meaning behind all events—a 'god,' if you please."[35] Now, such a god (Dionysus) is presented in this work as the one who "opens the way to the Mothers of Being, to the innermost heart of things":[36] his cult requires detachment from appearances and leads the way to a bacchic delirium that involves excess and madness. But this excess "revealed itself as truth. Contradiction, the bliss born of suffering, spoke out from the very heart of nature."[37] Excess thus introduces a relation to things that enables one to hear their primordial secret. The Dionysian cult has neither itself nor excess as an end: it seeks a tragic knowledge of the reality playing in and behind appearances. The chorus has an equivalent meaning: its songs clarify what current, civilized life tends to obfuscate, and it "represents existence more truthfully, really, and completely."[38] A metamorphosis is brought about by the action represented on the stage: the metamorphosis of one self into another—and the effective realization of this passage is *seen*. Here, transmutation unites suffering and wisdom: "In its vision this chorus beholds its lord and master Dionysus and is therefore eternally the serving chorus . . . sharing his suffering it also shares something of his wisdom and proclaims the truth from the heart of the world."[39]

Although only briefly noted, these elements indicate a profound structural identity between what is described as the Dionysian movement (in *The Birth of Tragedy*) and the wisdom Zarathustra seeks to attain. However, with the absence of explicit references to Dionysus in *Thus Spoke Zarathustra*, we must be cautious. And, although Nietzsche's silence on the matter is problematic, this silence itself constitutes part of the data to be interpreted. First of all, even if Dionysus does recede, he doesn't entirely disappear; his presence becomes more subtle and concealed. The apparent withdrawal of the "god" with light feet only makes his discreet visits more significant. Thus, *Human, All Too Human* speaks of the appearance of an enigmatic visage, "so pure, so imbued with a transfiguring light of serene lucidity."[40] And later, it refers again to the voyager's difficult passage to hell, a voyage in the course of which he sacrifices not only lambs but his own blood.[41] That these references conclude, respectively, the first and second volumes of *Human, All Too Human* is significant: it indicates a presence who insists on discretion, exactly as does the last aphorism of *The Dawn,* which develops the intersecting themes of the bird-voyager and the sea. Finally, in the "Genealogy of Morals" section of *Ecce Homo,* Nietzsche again suggests the veiled presence of Dionysus, especially considered as the "god of darkness." The passage suggests that even when man descended to "moral ideal" making, Dionysus never ceased to inspire the process: this is affirmed, however discreetly, even at the stage where the genealogist unravels the complex of annihilating forces. Or, we could just as well say that the discreet presence of Dionysus after *The Birth of Tragedy* is tantamount to a sort of purification or "de-mythification." Nietzsche, as is well known, rejected the conceptual framework of his day—in which his own exciting insights are nevertheless concealed. Yet he did not repudiate Dionysianism. Perhaps the silence that surrounds this theme in his later work indicates a gradual purification and refinement of this major insight. In any event, both for his *Attempt at a Self-Criticism* (1886) and *Ecce Homo* (1888), Nietzsche places his incontrovertible opposition to Christianity on the same plane as his Dionysianism.

It is not surprising, then, that Dionysus reappears in *Thus Spoke Zarathustra;* but now he is transfigured. Stripped of his mythical garb, he is still the god who announced the vision and the doctrine of Eternal Recurrence. Despite their strikingly different literary characters, a structural analogy quickly arises between these two texts. Both works stand beyond good and evil, and thus both aspire to overcome morality for the sake of affirming existence. Also, both see the place of this affirmation to lie in suffering and self-overcoming. Again, just as Zarathustra begins to dream of Eternal Recurrence in part III, so does the expedient of a dream introduce Dionysus in part IV of *The Birth of Tragedy*. And if the chorus disappears in *Zarathustra*, the dithyramb plays exactly the same role (of course, the important difference here is its individual incantation). Moreover, Nietzsche claims to be the inventor of the language that "such a spirit will speak" (i.e., Dionysus).[42] In short, the dithyramb is to the affirmation of eternity as the ancient chorus was to Dionysianism. It is not incidental, then, that the

Attempt at a Self-Criticism ends with a song of Zarathustra (§7). In both cases, the laugh, the dance (i.e., levity and serenity), are evoked as constitutive traits. Finally, and perhaps most importantly, there are analogous aspirations for eternity: that the role of the chorus was to lead to a contemplation of the moment's eternal nature is just like Zarathustra's dithyramb, which exalts the present eternity. The difference in expression can't conceal the identity of attitude that is operative here. Thus, *Ecce Homo* can equate "the concept of Dionysus"[43] with Zarathustra, who affirms the overabundance of life.

In both cases, then, the god Dionysus leads his disciples to the doctrine of Eternal Recurrence. He does so not in the manner of an abstract god, but as a tragic god, because he leads to a reality to which *he* is the first to submit. Far from disguising eternity, he somehow effaces himself before it. Thus, again, he is opposed to the Pauline god (who confines all to the faith that substitutes another's death) as well as to the god of Jesus (whose diaphanous and immediate being enfeebles everything). Moreover, if Dionysus did not have these characteristics, it would be hard to understand why Nietzsche insists that we see him as the Antichrist or as the doctrine that stands opposed to Christianity.[44] While the Christian God let his own son die, without dying himself, the god Dionysus passes through death: as a sign of authenticity he must will his own self-effacement and disappearance. His presence must become absence for affirmation to occur once again. Both he and man are a kind of passage: not content merely to indicate the way without going through it himself, he does go through it and dies.

It has often been noted that "in texts published by Nietzsche, the Eternal Recurrence is not formally or 'definitively' revealed. It is only announced or anticipated with horror or ecstasy."[45] Is this accidental? Is it due to lack of time? Does it indicate an inability to thematize the most abysmal thought? But Nietzsche realized that in this respect *Thus Spoke Zarathustra* can't be surpassed; if the presuppositions of this thought must still be justified and its critical implications shown, we must turn to *Zarathustra* to find its most complete expression.[46] Consequently, an interpretation that does not consider the form in which this thought is given—and we know that for Nietzsche the authentic artist adopts as form what others take for content—would profoundly betray its very nature. If *Thus Spoke Zarathustra* only introduces this thought by leading up to it, if its disciples must go through a sort of initiation, if it reveals its meaning only beyond good and evil, beyond the true and the false (i.e., beyond intellectual abstractions, beyond the abusive simplifications of a morbid sensibility), then it is clear that a discreet approach to this doctrine is not only part of a prior preparation, but that a reserve and veneration based on the pathos of distance constitute its very core. Nietzsche too often stressed the disgusting aspects of the Christian God, shorn of his mystery and full of scheming mendaciousness. This was perhaps more effective than keeping a careful vigil over his own most abysmal thought, so that it too would not be emptied of all mystery by the wearisome scientists of philosophy, or so that it would not be transformed once again and coined into a herd faith by new apostles. To preserve such an abyss is not to reject this final thought as an addendum to the work, nor to renounce understanding, nor to reduce it to an empty formalism about the return of difference. Rather, if we have now been led toward a new center,[47] the presentation of this abyss indicates that its meaning is beyond *all* human meaning, that it is a matter of consenting to this "contemplation" through which we can "impress the character of being upon becoming."[48]

It is consistent with Nietzsche's entire critique of moral and Christian language that, at this final point, language itself shows its immutable otherness by denying its own efficacy. In wanting to be transparent to all things, Christian and moral language imprisons man, while the song of benediction (the supreme form of speech) welcomes the god or whatever else may come. To leave open what is to come, to leave the bidding yet unanswered, is not a sign of fatigue, but of respect and active expectation. Leaving the thought of Eternal Recurrence open to scientific interpretation is to affirm what *is* (which is consistent with Jesus' insight, even though it is quite different and more forceful) and to deny whatever opposes that which is yet to come. Only a child, therefore, can understand what it is all about, and not the scholar of the immaculate perception or the Magician who repeats Ariadne's words to Dionysus: while the words may be materially the same, they have a totally different intention, for the Magician doesn't believe a single word of his own incantation! Such words are only meant for those who find the most complete innocence and readiness in the face of the world—a readiness brought about in oneself by an act of labor. Zarathustra expresses this to a young man, in the section entitled "On the Tree on the Mountainside": "But the wind, which we do not see, tortures and bends this tree in whatever direction it pleases. It is by *invisible hands* that we are bent and tortured worse."[49] Nonetheless, this is a labor ordained to welcome: "What do we have in common with the rosebud, which trembles because a drop of dew lies on it?" Zarathustra asks nostalgically.[50] "For the voice of beauty speaks gently: it creeps only into the most awakened souls."[51]

NOTES

1. We know Nietzsche's reluctance to speak of "religion," although, by way of Dionysus, he introduces the term "common faith," and in many texts he asserts that believers are not necessarily religious. Therefore, we would like to discuss this general "area" of religion that he himself evokes—an area which, once entered into, should offer unexpected riches. In its radicalism, is the Nietzschean experience carried to a level other than

that of religion in general? Or, at least, other than that of those religions for which moral and religious acts are not completely identical?

2. *The Will to Power,* §1052.

3. *The Genealogy of Morals;* I, §16.

4. *WP,* §1067.

5. *WP,* §1050.

6. As seems to be the case with Rimbaud, who has aims *apparently* very close to those of Nietzsche, together with an analogous admiration for the Far Eastern mystical tradition, emphasized by a scathing criticism of modernity. Rimbaud aspires "to arrive at the unknown by the disorder of *all the senses.*"

7. *Thus Spoke Zarathustra;* I, "On the Afterworldly."

8. *WP,* §1052.

9. *Ecce Homo;* "Thus Spoke Zarathustra," §8: "Who besides me knows what Ariadne is?"

10. *Twilight of the Idols;* "Skirmishes . . . ," §19. See also *EH;* "Thus Spoke Zarathustra," §8.

11. *WP,* §1052.

12. *WP,* §846.

13. *Nietzsche Contra Wagner;* Epilogue, §1. Likewise, *The Gay Science;* Preface, §3—here philosophy is presented as an "art of transfiguration." This would serve as another verification of the essential identity between philosophy and (Dionysian) religion.

14. Against this, Nietzsche accuses the socialists of wanting to suppress suffering (and, thus, to deny life); paradoxically, this amounts to willing death (the will to nothingness).

15. *EH;* "Why I Am a Destiny," §2: ". . . my Dionysian nature which does not know how to separate doing No from saying Yes."

16. *GS,* §322.

17. *GS,* §279.

18. G. Morel, *Nietzsche;* III, p. 108.

19. *GS,* §279. See also the preface to *The Dawn,* §4.

20. *Zarathustra;* Prologue, §5.

21. Letter to J. Burckhardt, 4 January 1889. Signed "Dionysus."

22. Morel, *op. cit.,* pp. 327–28.

23. Nietzsche employs the term "crucifixion" in the second postscript of his last letter to Burckhardt, 6 January 1889.

24. Morel, *op. cit.,* p. 329.

25. *WP,* §1052.

26. Such is Zarathustra's nightmare in "On the Vision and the Riddle": that everything comes back the same, identically reproduced in a stubborn monotony, is the horrifying aspect of this most profound thought. But this is only an immediate and superficial understanding: it is the first aspect,

though, that Zarathustra is struck by (e.g., in *GS,* §341). Moreover, it is presented by a demon. But the essence of the thought makes possible the redemption of every thing and every moment when, at any moment, the presence of eternity is grasped. Then the development of the will to eternity is possible—a will that transfigures the moment (keeping only its eternalizable aspects). The doctrine makes sense only if one considers *how* it is introduced at the end of part III of *Zarathustra.* It is developed on the basis of "The Convalescent" and is opposed to the way the animals theorized about the doctrine—they immediately congealed it. It is now prescribed in the solitude of Zarathustra's soliloquy: leaving the animals to their futile chatter *about* the Eternal Recurrence, Zarathustra, beginning from "On the Great Longing," makes an invocation to *his* soul; he rejoices in a song directed to life ("The Other Dancing Song")—which answers him, moreover—until the meditation culminates in the Amen to eternity ("The Seven Seals"). The coincidence of midday with eternity "saves" the universe from its shadows. Only there does Zarathustra consent to follow an itinerary out to its end, where there is no longer any need to look for *the* reason to things. The end is given in the splendor of an eternity that justifies every moment. Such an eternity is given as an overflowing and sufficient experience, beyond which there is nothing else. It is heard in the lyricism of the final pages, where Zarathustra talks to eternity as if to a person. The doctrine is unintelligible if one does not consider its various (i.e., its non-identical) versions; or if one does not see that to follow these versions is already to enter into the doctrine (which is in no way "outside" the text).

27. Despite Nietzsche's attempts to do so. We think that such attempts are explained by the fact that the intuition "revealed" to him in Sils-Maria was not adequately expressed right away. Thus, Nietzsche tried to provide an equivalent scientific formulation for what he thought gave value to all reality. He was unsure that "Eternal Recurrence of the Same" was really adequate to express the experience it was supposed to indicate. The very image of a *da capo* present in *Beyond Good and Evil,* §61—which, borrowed from musical notation, suggests a re-beginning of the same melody—still falls short of the evocation in the song to eternity in *Zarathustra;* III, "The Seven Seals."

28. G. Deleuze characterized the Eternal Recurrence as a selective thought. In his *Nietzsche* (pp. 85 f.), he relies on a text from *The Will to Power* that presents this thought as a Kantian moral imperative: "Can you will an infinity of times what you will once?" There is no mention here or anywhere else of the word or the idea of *selection*. J. Granier rightly criticizes such an interpretation, which makes the Eternal Recurrence (at least in part) a criterion for a universalizable practical maxim. See J. Granier, *Le Problème de la vérité dans la philosophie de Nietzsche,* pp. 567 f. It implies, whether one wills it or not, a recurrence on *this side* of good and evil. We could construct a typology that would situate the commentators

according to the function of their interpretation of the Eternal Recurrence: as we see it, this thought is as radical and fundamental in scope as religion traditionally has been. Those for whom the religious experience is meaningless also have difficulty in making sense of the Eternal Recurrence. Deleuze makes it a repetition devoid of difference, as well as a new ethical principle. For Klossowski, it indicates an explosion of the subject following the death of God. K. Löwith feels it can be superimposed on the earliest Greek thought. For Heidegger, it marks man's forgetting of Being and determines the existence of beings. J. Trotignon, on the contrary, shows that "the relation of Dionysus to eternal recurrence indicates a theory of 'God's Being.'" See *Revue Philosophique,* 1971; No. 1022, p. 306: *"Circulus vitiosus: deus-circulus: vitiosus deus."*

29. *Zarathustra;* III, "The Seven Seals."
30. A Heideggerian, rather than Nietzschean, expression.
31. *Zarathustra;* II, "On Self-Overcoming."
32. *GS,* §341.
33. *Zarathustra;* III, "On the Vision and the Riddle," §2.
34. *Zarathustra;* III, "The Convalescent," §2.
35. *Attempt at a Self-Criticism,* §5.
36. *The Birth of Tragedy,* §16.
37. *BT,* §4.
38. *BT,* §8.
39. *Ibid.*
40. *Human, All Too Human;* I, §638; "The Voyager."
41. *HAH;* II, §408.
42. *EH;* "Thus Spoke Zarathustra," §7.
43. *EH;* "Thus Spoke Zarathustra," §6.
44. *ASC,* §5.
45. For example, G. Deleuze in the conclusion to the *Colloque de Royaumont, Cahier VI,* p. 283.
46. Thus, the importance of the critical work following Zarathustra; in particular, *Beyond Good and Evil* and *The Genealogy of Morals,* as well as the fifth book of *The Gay Science.* See *EH;* "Beyond Good and Evil," §1 on this relation.
47. *WP,* §417.
48. *WP,* §617.
49. *Zarathustra;* I, "On the Tree on the Mountainside." My emphasis.
50. *Zarathustra;* I, "Reading and Writing."
51. *Zarathustra;* II, "On the Virtuous."

NIETZSCHE: SELECT BIBLIOGRAPHY

Alderman, Harold G. *Nietzsche's Gift*. Columbus: Ohio University Press, 1977.

Andler, Charles. *Nietzsche, sa vie et sa pensée*. 3 vols. Paris: Gallimard, 1958.

Andreas-Salome, Lou. *Nietzsche*. New York: Gordon & Breach, 1970.

Bataille, Georges. *Sur Nietzsche, volonté de chance*. Paris: Gallimard, 1945.

Beaufret, Jean. *Dialogue avec Heidegger, philosophie moderne*, vol. 2. Paris: Ed. de Minuit, 1973.

Birault, Henri. "Sur un texte de Nietzsche: 'En quoi nous aussi, nous sommes encore pieux' (*GS*, §344)," in *Revue de Métaphysique et de Morale*. January–March, 1962, pp. 25–64.

———. "Nietzsche et le pari de Pascal," in *Archivo de Filosofia*. Padua: Castelli, 1962.

———. "La critique nietzschéene de la théologie," in *Atti del Convegno indetto dal Centro Internazionale de Studi humanistic e dall'Istituto de Studi Filosofici, Roma 16–21 January 1961, a cura di Entico Castelli, "Il problema della Demitizzazione."* Rome: Istituto di Studi Filosofici, 1961.

Bueb, Bernard. *Nietzsches Kritik der praktischen Vernunft*. Stuttgart: Ernst Klett, 1972.

Cahiers du Royaumont: Nietzsche. Philosophie no. VI. Paris: Ed. de Minuit, 1967.

Danto, Arthur. *Nietzsche as Philosopher*. New York: Macmillan, 1965.

Deleuze, Gilles. *Nietzsche and Philosophy*. Tr. Hugh Tomlinson. New York: Columbia University Press, 1983.

———. *Nietzsche et la philosophie*. Paris: Presses Universitaires de France, 1970.

———. *Nietzsche*. Paris: Presses Universitaires de France, 1965.

de Man, Paul. *Allegories of Reading: Figural Language in Rousseau, Nietzsche, Rilke, and Proust*. New Haven: Yale University Press, 1979.

Dionne, James. *Pascal et Nietzsche*. New York: Burt Franklin, 1974.

Fink, Eugen. *Nietzsches Philosophie*. Stuttgart: Kohlhammer, 1960.

Fischer-Dieskau, Dietrich. *Wagner and Nietzsche*. New York: Seabury, 1976.

Foucault, Michel. *Language, Counter-Memory, Practice*. Tr. Donald F. Bouchard. Ithaca: Cornell University Press, 1977.

Fuss, Peter, and Shapiro, Henry, eds. *Nietzsche: A Self-Portrait from His Letters*. Cambridge, Mass.: Harvard University Press, 1971.

Goicoechea, David, ed. *The Great Year of Zarathustra (1881–1981)*. Lanham: University Press of America, 1983.

Granier, Jean. *Le problème de la vérité dans la philosophie de Nietzsche*. Paris: Ed. du Seuil, 1966.

Grimm, Ruediger H. *Nietzsche's Theory of Knowledge*. Berlin: de Gruyter, 1977.

Guerin, Michel. *Nietzsche, Socrate héroique*. Paris: Gasset, 1975.

Hayman, Ronald. *Nietzsche, a Critical Life*. New York: Oxford University Press, 1980.

Heidegger, Martin. *Nietzsche*. Vol. I: *The Will to Power as Art*. Tr. David F. Krell. New York: Harper & Row, 1979. Vol. IV: *Nihilism*. Tr. Frank Capuzzi. New York: Harper & Row, 1982.

———. *Nietzsche*. 2 vols. Pfullingen: Neske, 1961.

———. "Nietzsches Wort 'Got ist tot,' " in *Holzwege*. Frankfort: Klosterman, 1950.

Hollingdale, R. J. *Nietzsche*. London: Routledge & Kegan Paul, 1973.

———. *Nietzsche: The Man and His Philosophy*. Baton Rouge: Louisiana State University Press, 1965.

Irigary, Luce. *Amante marine de Friedrich Nietzsche*. Paris: Ed. de Minuit, 1980.

Jaspers, Karl, *Nietzsche: An Introduction to the Understanding of His Philosophical Activity*. Tucson: University of Arizona Press, 1965.

———. *Nietzsche and Christianity*. Chicago: Regnery-Gateway, 1961.

Kaufmann, Walter. *Nietzsche: Philosopher, Psychologist, Antichrist*. Princeton: Princeton University Press, 1950.

Klossowski, Pierre. *Nietzsche et le cercle vicieux*. Paris: Mercure, 1969.

———. *Un si funeste désir*. Paris: Gallimard, 1963.

Kofman, Sarah. *Nietzsche et la scène philosophique*. Paris: Union Générale d'Éditions, 1979.

———. *Nietzsche et la métaphor*. Paris: Payot, 1972.

———. "Nietzsche et la métaphor," in *Poetique*. Vol. 2, no. 5, 1971.

Kremer-Marietti, Angèle. *L'homme et ses labyrinthes*. Paris: Union Générale d'Éditions, 1972.

———. *Thèmes et structures dans l'oeuvre de Nietzsche*. Paris: Lettres Modernes, 1957.

Kröner, ed., *Werke, Grossoktavausgabe*, 2nd ed., 20 vols. (Leipzig: Kröner, 1901–13 and 1926).

Laruelle, François. *Nietzsche contre Heidegger*. Paris: Payot, 1977.

Larvin, Janko. *Nietzsche, a Biographical Introduction.* New York: Scribner's, 1971.

Laurent-Assoun, Paul. *Freud et Nietzsche.* Paris: Presses Universitaires de France, 1980.

Lea. F. A. *The Tragic Philosopher: A Study of Friedrich Nietzsche.* New York: Philosophical Library, 1957.

Leigh, James, and McKeon, Roger, eds. *Nietzsche's Return* (special issue of *Semiotexte*, vol. III, no. 1, 1978).

Löwith, Karl. *From Hegel to Nietzsche.* New York: Doubleday, 1967.

Magnus, Bernd. *Nietzsche's Existential Imperative.* Bloomington: Indiana University Press, 1978.

Montinari, Mazzino. *Nietzsche lesen.* Berlin: de Gruyter, 1982.

Morel, Georges. *Nietzsche.* 3 vols. Paris: Aubier-Montaigne, 1970.

Nietzsche aujourd'hui? 2 vols. Paris: Union Générale d'Éditions, 1973.

O'Hara, Daniel, ed. *Why Nietzsche Now? A Boundary 2 Symposium* (special issue of *Boundary 2*, vols. IX, no. 3, and X, no. 1, spring/fall, 1981).

Pautrat, Bernard. *Versions du soleil.* Paris: Ed. du Seuil, 1971.

Reboul, Olivier. *Nietzsche, Critique de Kant.* Paris: Presses Universitaires de France, 1974.

Reichert, H. W., and Schlecta, K., eds. *International Nietzsche Bibliography.* Chapel Hill: University of North Carolina Press, 1960.

Rey, Jean-Michel. *L'enjeu des signes.* Paris: Ed. du Seuil, 1971.

Schacht, Richard. *Nietzsche.* London: Routledge & Kegan Paul, 1983.

Silk, M. S. and Stern, J. P. *Nietzsche on Tragedy.* Cambridge: Cambridge University Press, 1981.

Solomon, Robert, ed. *Nietzsche, a Collection of Critical Essays.* New York: Doubleday-Anchor, 1973.

Stambaugh, Joan. *Nietzsche's Thought of the Eternal Return.* Baltimore: The Johns Hopkins University Press, 1972.

Strong, Tracy. *Friedrich Nietzsche and the Politics of Transfiguration.* Berkeley: University of California Press, 1975.

Valadier, Paul. *Nietzsche: l'Athée de rigeur.* Paris: Desclée de Brower, 1975.

———. *Nietzsche et la critique du christianisme.* Paris: Ed. du Cerf, 1974.

Wilcox, John T. *Truth and Value in Nietzsche.* Ann Arbor: University of Michigan Press, 1974.

NOTES ON CONTRIBUTORS

THOMAS J. J. ALTIZER is a Christian atheistic theologian, deeply influenced by the work of Nietzsche. His work includes *The Gospel of Christian Atheism*, *The Self-Embodiment of God*, *Total Presence*, and *History as Apocalypse*. He is a professor of English and religious studies at S.U.N.Y., Stony Brook.

HENRI BIRAULT occupies the chair of contemporary philosophy at the University of Paris (IV–Sorbonne). His work has focused on the thought of Heidegger, Nietzsche, and Pascal. He has most recently published the long-awaited *Heidegger et l'expérience de la pensée*.

MAURICE BLANCHOT is one of France's most original and important writers. His work includes essays, literary and philosophical criticism, studies on aesthetics, and several novels. He is perhaps best known for his *La Part du feu*, *L'Espace littéraire*, *Lautréamont et Sade*, and *L'Entretien infini*.

ERIC BLONDEL is a professor of philosophy at the University of Nancy (II). He has written several important articles on Nietzsche, contemporary thought, and the theory of criticism.

GILLES DELEUZE has written several influential texts on modern philosophy and contemporary thought—particularly *Différence et répétition*, *Logique du sens*, *Nietzsche and Philosophy*, and, together with Felix Guattari, *Capitalism and Schizophrenia: Anti-Oedipus* and *Mille plateaux*. He presently teaches philosophy at the University of Paris (VIII–St. Denis).

JACQUES DERRIDA is the author of *Speech and Phenomena*, *Of Grammatology*, *Writing and Difference*, *Margins of Philosophy*, and *Dissemination*, works which have already enjoyed a seminal importance in contemporary French thought. Professor Derrida is currently codirector of the Collège International de Philosophie and teaches at the Ecole des Hautes Etudes.

JEAN GRANIER has written extensively on the subject of Nietzsche and modern thought. A professor of arts and humanities at the University of Rouen, his major text to date is *Le Problème de la vérité dans la philosophie de Nietzsche*.

MICHEL HAAR teaches philosophy at the University of Paris (IV–Sorbonne). In addition to his translations of Nietzsche for the French Colli-Montinari edition of the complete philosophical works, he has written extensively on Heidegger, Freud, and Marcuse.

MARTIN HEIDEGGER (1889–1976) was perhaps the most original and influential philosopher of the twentieth century. Together with Edmund Husserl, he was the founder of modern phenomenology and existentialism. He wrote extensively on Greek and modern philosophy, metaphysics, and aesthetics. Among his major works are *Being and Time*, *An Introduction to Metaphysics*, *Vorträge und Aufsätze*, and *On the Way to Language*. Heidegger's two-volume *Nietzsche* interpretation is perhaps most responsible for the recent interest in Nietzsche.

PIERRE KLOSSOWSKI has written numerous essays on Claudel, Gide, and Sade, among others; and several novels, including *Roberte ce Soir* and *The Revocation of the Edict of Nantes*. He has also translated Virgil, Suetonius, St. Augustine, Nietzsche, and Heidegger into French. His most recent work is *La Monnaie vivante*, which follows his brilliant *Nietzsche et le cercle vicieux*.

SARAH KOFMAN has published several important articles on contemporary interpretation, as well as *Nietzsche et la métaphor*, *L'Enfance de l'art*, and *Nietzsche et la scène philosophique*. She currently teaches philosophy in the University of Paris (I–Sorbonne).

ALPHONSO LINGIS has written extensively on the work of Husserl, Heidegger, and Merleau-Ponty. He has translated numerous texts by Merleau-Ponty and Emmanuel Levinas and has recently completed *Excesses* and *Libido: The French Existentialist Theories*. Professor Lingis teaches at the Pennsylvania State University.

PAUL VALADIER is a Jesuit philosopher who teaches at the Centre d'Etudes et de Recherches Philosophiques in Paris. His work on Nietzsche includes *Nietzsche et la critique du christianisme*, *Essais sur la modernité*, *Nietzsche et Marx*, and *Nietzsche, l'athée de rigueur*.

INDEX